C. L. R. JAMES IN
IMPERIAL BRITAIN

| | | | |

THE C. L. R. JAMES ARCHIVES
recovers and reproduces for a contemporary
audience the work of one of the great intellectual figures of the twentieth century, in
all their rich texture, and will present, over
and above historical works, new and current
scholarly explorations of James's oeuvre.

Robert A. Hill, Series Editor

C. L. R. JAMES IN
IMPERIAL BRITAIN

| | | | |

CHRISTIAN HØGSBJERG

DUKE UNIVERSITY PRESS   DURHAM AND LONDON   2014

Library of Congress Cataloging-in-Publication Data
Høgsbjerg, Christian.
C. L. R. James in imperial Britain / Christian Høgsbjerg.
pages cm—(C. L. R. James Archives)
Includes bibliographical references and index.
ISBN 978-0-8223-5612-7 (cloth : alk. paper)
ISBN 978-0-8223-5618-9 (pbk. : alk. paper)
1. James, C. L. R. (Cyril Lionel Robert), 1901–1989—Homes and
haunts—England—London. 2. James, C. L. R. (Cyril Lionel
Robert), 1901–1989—Political and social views. I. Title. II. Series:
C. L. R. James Archives (Series)
PR9272.9.J35Z69 2014
818'.5209—dc23   2013026379

FOR MY PARENTS

All who are alive today who remember him are old men. Some of them never spoke to him at all. Some saw him once. Some never saw him. Yet his personality still lives vividly with them. Those must be indeed great men, says Hazlitt, whose shadows lengthen out to posterity.

—C. L. R. JAMES,
"Michel Maxwell Philip" (1931)

CONTENTS

ACKNOWLEDGMENTS

The many intellectual debts I accumulated during the research and writing of this work over the course of about a decade are far too numerous to allow me to personally thank everyone who has ever offered me advice or assisted me at some point. The generosity and kindness I often encountered when I mentioned my research project are of course in large part testament to the intellectual respect for C. L. R. James himself, and I can only give my sincere apologies in advance to those many scholars, activists, friends, and comrades who provided either feedback on my ideas or support at some point but are not named here. Nonetheless, while I naturally take full responsibility for any errors of judgment or fact that remain, some cannot escape so easily acknowledgment for what follows. First and foremost here is David Howell, a model of partisan historical scholarship, who supervised the doctoral thesis from which this work originates ("C. L. R. James in Imperial Britain, 1932–38," Department of History, University of York, 2009). Howell is a model of partisan historical scholarship, and without his tireless and careful attention to detail, combined with a rare breadth and depth of knowledge and understanding, my work on James would be immeasurably poorer. Among the inspiring community of scholars who guided my doctoral research at the University of York, I also owe particular debts of gratitude to Allison Drew, Henrice Altink, and Alan Forrest, while I am also grateful to Stephen Howe for his rigorous and constructive criticism of my thesis in his role as external examiner.

Many other historians went above and beyond the call of duty by kindly and generously assisting my research through providing relevant source material and general counsel, including Ian Birchall, Paul Blackledge, Gidon Cohen, Charles Forsdick, Leslie James, David Renton, and Daniel Whittall. Two others in this category deserve special mention. First, David

Goodway, who has supported this project ever since possibly helping inspire it back in 2001, when he kindly gave me an original copy of the Independent Labour Party (ILP) discussion journal *Controversy* dated October 1937, helpfully pointing out an article on "Trotskyism" by James. Second, Marika Sherwood, who incredibly kindly and generously shared with me not only her collection of extremely rare and valuable material relating to James and the Pan-African movement in Britain during the 1930s, but also her warm memories of "Nello." I have been privileged to have had the kind support of Robert A. Hill, whose profound understanding of his former mentor and comrade's life and work so inspired me and fired my imagination when I first set out on this project, while I should also like to acknowledge my appreciation here for the enthusiastic encouragement of Bill Schwarz and Kent Worcester for my research, both also inspiring models of "James scholarship" in their own right and from whom I have learned much.

I would also like to thank the following institutions and their staff for access to various collections and their general resourcefulness and support: the British Library, particularly the Newspaper Library at Colindale; the BBC Written Archives Centre; the Bodleian Library of Commonwealth and African Studies at Rhodes House, Oxford University; Glasgow Caledonian University Archive of the Trotskyist Tradition; Hull History Centre; the Institute of Commonwealth Studies Library; the Labour History Archive and Study Centre, Manchester; Leeds Metropolitan University; the London School of Economics and Political Science; the Moorland-Spingarn Research Center, Howard University, Washington; the National Archives at Kew; Nelson Library; the University of Hull; the University of Leeds; Victoria and Albert Museum, London; Wayne State University; the Working Class Movement Library, Salford; and University of York.

Some of the most insightful moments of my research took place outside the libraries and archives. One early inspiration who shaped the writing of this work was the outstanding revolutionary socialist journalist Paul Foot (1937–2004), whom I had the privilege of seeing and hearing speak at various meetings and rallies. Foot's passionately held enthusiasm for the Haitian Revolution and his great admiration for James was for me infectious. I have also had the great honor and privilege of meeting with some of those who, like Robert Hill, knew or were close to James. Selma James deserves a special mention here, but I am also indebted here to many others, including Prisca Allen, Margaret Busby, Raymond Challinor (1929–2011),

Mike Dibb, Stuart Hall, Paul Harber, Chris Harman (1942–2009), Darcus Howe, Linton Kwesi Johnson, John La Rose (1927–2006), Stan Newens, Chris Searle, and Sam Weinstein for sharing some of their memories of James with me. I have also had the honor of corresponding with Grace Lee Boggs. My first piece of scholarly work on James in 2002 had been dedicated to the memory of Audrey Farrell (1936–2001), an inspiring socialist in Leeds. In 2006, I was fortunate enough to spend a day with her brother Eric E. Robinson (1927–2011), who had attended school in Nelson with Learie Constantine's daughter Gloria during the 1930s and very kindly took me on an extensive guided tour of the town. As well as sharing his memories and some of his private collection of material from the period with me, his subsequent generous correspondence with me about Nelson's rich history was invaluable. Marika Sherwood kindly put me in touch with Gloria Valère (Learie Constantine's daughter), with whom it has been a privilege to correspond. I have also had the honor of corresponding with two veteran labor movement activists who saw James speak during the 1930s while ILP members, Sidney Robinson (1914–2012) and Len Edmondson (1912–2006). I remain grateful to Mildred Gordon, a former Trotskyist and later Labour MP, who had known James since the 1940s, for granting me an interview in 2005, which was kindly facilitated by Sheila Leslie (daughter of Charlie Lahr).

I have also greatly benefited from conversations and correspondence with a number of other archivists, scholars, writers, and activists, including Hakim Adi, Kevin B. Anderson, David Austin, Colin Barker, Weyman Bennett, David Berry, Robin Blackburn, Stephen Bourne, Sebastian Budgen, Paul Buhle, Andrew Burgin, Jodi Burkett, Barbara Bush, Alex Callinicos, Matthew Caygill, Colin Chambers, John Charlton, Joseph Choonara, Ted Crawford, Selwyn R. Cudjoe, Rachel Douglas, Joanna de Groot, Laurent Dubois, Andy Durgan, Max Farrar, David Featherstone, Carolyn Fick, Peter Fraser, Jeremy Glick, Richard Greeman, Anna Grimshaw, Catherine Hall, Christopher Hall, Julian Harber, Helen Harrison, Paget Henry, Peter Hudis, Aaron Kamugisha, Victor Kiernan (1913–2009), Nicole King, Rick Kuhn, David Lambert, William LeFevre, Staffan Lindhé, Hassan Mahamdallie, Minkah Makalani, Ravi Malhotra, John McIlroy, Scott McLemee, Bart Miller, Kevin Morgan, Michael Morris, Aldon Lynn Nielsen, Susan Pennybacker, Christer Petley, Caryl Phillips, Matthew Quest, Marcus Rediker, Amalia Ribi, Emily Robins Sharpe, Frank Rosengarten, David Scott, Andrew Smith, Fionnghuala Sweeney, Paul Trewhela, James Walvin, Barry

Winter, James D. Young (1931–2012), and Jacob Zumoff. Others—including many dear friends and comrades—who were also of great help and support include Talat Ahmed, Anne Alexander, Charlotte Argyle, Gaverne Bennett, Graham Campbell, Alex Davidson, Andrea Enisuoh, Keith Flett, Nicholas Godwin, Phil Goodfield, Gráinne Goodwin, John Gregson, Lea Haro, James Harvey, Robert Holman, Sally Kincaid, James McGrath, Andrew Murphy, Marven Scott, Gajendra Singh, Liz Stainforth, Oliver Tooth, and Osama Zumam.

I am grateful to the editors of *International Socialism* and *Socialist History* for publishing some of my work on James in this period, while much of my first chapter appeared in an earlier form in "'We Lived According to the Tenets of Matthew Arnold': Reflections on the 'Colonial Victorianism' of the Young C. L. R. James," *Twentieth Century British History*, 24, no. 2 (2013). For permission to use and other help with images, I would like to thank Ted Crawford and Socialist Platform, Anna Grimshaw, and the family of Chris Braithwaite. With respect to other permissions, I am indebted to the C. L. R. James Estate, while the lines from the poem "How Beastly the Bourgeois Is," by D. H. Lawrence, are reproduced by permission of Pollinger Limited and the Estate of Frieda Lawrence Ravagli.

Finally, I would like to thank the team at Duke University Press, particularly Gisela Fosado, Valerie Millholland, and Danielle Szulczewski, for their patience, kind support, and editorial expertise, as well as the two anonymous readers for their generous and perceptive reports. Last but very far from least, I would like to take the opportunity to sincerely thank my family, above all my parents, Sue and John.

ABBREVIATIONS

ARPS	Aborigines' Rights Protection Society (Gold Coast)
BUF	British Union of Fascists
BWIR	British West Indies Regiment
CGT	General Confederation of Labour (France)
CPGB	Communist Party of Great Britain
CSA	Colonial Seamen's Association
IAFA	International African Friends of Abyssinia
IASB	International African Service Bureau
ICS	Institute of Commonwealth Studies
ILD	International Labour Defence
ILP	Independent Labour Party
ITUC-NW	International Trade Union Committee of Negro Workers
LAI	League against Imperialism
LCP	League of Coloured Peoples
LHA	Labour History Archive and Study Centre (Manchester)
NAACP	National Association for the Advancement of Colored People (America)
NWA	Negro Welfare Association
QRC	Queen's Royal College
TNA	The National Archives (Kew, London)
TWA	Trinidad Workingmen's Association
UNIA	Universal Negro Improvement Association
WASU	West African Students' Union

"Revolutionaries, Artists
and Wicket-Keepers"

C. L. R. James's Place in History

What is now happening to Marx's doctrine has occurred time after time in history to the doctrine of revolutionary thinkers and leaders of oppressed classes struggling for liberation. . . . Attempts are made after their death to convert them into harmless icons, to canonize them, so to speak, and to confer a certain prestige on their names so as to "console" the oppressed classes by emasculating the essence of the revolutionary teaching, blunting its revolutionary edge and vulgarizing it.
—Vladimir I. Lenin, *The State and Revolution* (1918)

Idiots and bourgeois scoundrels always emphasise Trotsky's personal brilliance whereby they seek to disparage Trotsky's method. The two are inseparable. His natural gifts were trained and developed by Marxism and he could probe these depths of understanding and ascend to these peaks of foresight because he based himself on the Marxian theory of the class struggle and the revolutionary and predominant role of the proletariat in the crisis of bourgeois society.
—C. L. R. James, "Trotsky's Place in History" (1940)

"One of the abiding ironies of Cyril Lionel Robert James's intellectual career," Grant Farred noted in 1996, is that "since his death in London in 1989, and for perhaps half a decade before that, the Caribbean thinker has already been able to secure a status denied to him during most of his life."[1] One might wonder just how much of an "abiding irony" it is for a revolutionary socialist, who felt toward the end of his life that one of his "greatest contributions" had been "to clarify and extend the heritage of Marx and Lenin," not to have secured more of a status in late capitalist society.[2] Nevertheless, the belated "discovery" of C. L. R. James since the 1980s has been quite remarkable. Every year it seems a new biography or collection of his writings or speeches adds to what we already know, and as Farred noted, "With the emergence of fields such as cultural studies, popular culture, and postcolonial studies, James is now an object of research."[3]

All this attention is welcome, and that the Trinidadian historian, theorist, and activist has posthumously become a fashionable "object of research" has not been without value for anyone attempting to understand the life and work of this generally long-overlooked political thinker. What, then, could be the possible justification for adding another work—and on a biographical theme—to the now voluminous secondary literature on James? Surely we know more than enough after multiple biographies on top of nearly thirty years of relatively sustained "James scholarship." A crucial part of the answer lies in the fact that the recent surge of writing about James has markedly reflected its time and place. The prevailing contemporary, intellectual fashion in modern—or perhaps "postmodern"—academia remains set against any attempt to see James's life's work as a coherent totality with any unity to it beyond a slightly abstract sense in which he "rethought race, politics, and poetics" through "a critique of modernity" and engaged in a "struggle for a new society."[4] The tone was set with the very first biography, *C. L. R. James: The Artist as Revolutionary* (1989), in which Paul Buhle argued that a poststructuralist "de-centering may bring a reconciliation of the myriad varieties of particular genius, not merely of a few powerful cultures in our own age but of every cultural expression from the past which is still, in any meaningful sense, recuperable."[5]

This Foucauldian focus on the "fragment" might seem at first a far more appropriate approach than any attempt to directly make a claim for James as simply, say, a Marxist, or a Pan-Africanist, as his concerns and means of expressing them were extremely broad. As Martin Glaberman once observed, "It is the very richness of his life that makes an assessment of James more difficult" as we "have not and could not share the range of what James has done."[6] Peter Fryer once described how James's "stature simply bursts any category a writer tries to squeeze him into. . . . One can no more catch and label the essence of C. L. R. James than one can cage a cloud."[7] However, a number of problems have since emerged with the "decentered" perspective. Rather than seeing a "reconciliation" of the "myriad varieties" of James's genius, as a number of scholars collectively worked toward building up a single portrait, Glaberman noted that what he saw instead emerging in the literature was "a fragmented James: James as cultural critic, James as Marxist theoretician, James as Third World guru, James as expert on sports, etc." That scholars would produce "their own James" was not inevitable, but it was always going to be a danger, given the highly specialized nature of modern academia and contemporary pressures to publish, and consequently Glaberman described how many writers have simply "taken from him what they found useful and imputed to him what they felt necessary."[8]

More critically, a general lack of concern for the fine complexities of his life has not been overcome by what Farred celebrates as "the centrality of cultural studies within James scholarship."[9] This has steadily led to one "James" in particular coming to the fore, and some of the consequences of being "claimed" by cultural and postcolonial studies can be usefully seen through a comparison with Frantz Fanon, another towering West Indian revolutionary figure. David Macey, Fanon's biographer, once described postcolonial studies as "a continuation of English literature by other means" and warned that "the danger is that Fanon will be absorbed into accounts of 'the colonial experience' that are so generalized as to obscure both the specific features of his work and the trajectory of his life." Many studies of Fanon, Macey continued, focused "almost exclusively" on his psychoanalysis and his work *Black Skin, White Masks*: "The 'post-colonial' Fanon worries about identity politics, and often about his own sexual identity, but he is no longer angry. And yet, if there is a truly Fanonian emotion it is anger." Indeed, postcolonial readings of Fanon "studiously avoid the question of violence," his commitment to the Algerian Revolution, and even his classic *The Wretched of the Earth*.[10]

James's posthumous canonization as a "pioneering icon" of "cultural studies" and "postcolonial studies" has not perhaps come at such a price as that paid by Fanon, but this is not to say that it has not come without its price.[11] In his insightful study published in 1997, Aldon Lynn Nielsen suggested that while "James is patently not a 'deconstructionist,' ... it is equally clear that James's analyses ... are part of an international theoretical development that brings us to the threshold of poststructuralist, post-Marxist, and postcolonial critiques."[12] Since then, a recent study by the sociologist Brett St. Louis, written from a standpoint of unconditional but critical support for what he calls the "irresistible march of identity politics and postmodernism," has insisted that, given the apparent "epistemological erosion of the 'old' certainties of (organised) class struggle and framework of historical materialism signals the death of unitary subjectivity and its explanatory 'grand narratives,'" James's significance lies in the way that he "grapples with a proto-post-marxist problematic."[13] The extent to which such views have become "common sense" in contemporary academia, even among many James scholars, is apparent from Farred's edited collection, *Rethinking C. L. R. James* (1995). Disparaging "earlier modes of James studies" and the "debates that occupied sectarian James scholars" about such matters as class struggle and revolutionary theory, Farred salutes James's seminal semiautobiographical cultural history of cricket, *Beyond a Boundary* (1963), a work "eminently suited to the burgeoning field of cultural studies[,] . . . a testament to subtle, heavily coded anti-colonial resistance, a work which maps the problematic trajectory of the postcolonial through the colonial[,] . . . a work we can return to again and again."[14] *Beyond a Boundary* indeed deserves such acclamation, but Farred then goes on to declare the work not simply "the major achievement of [James's] cultural activism" but "undoubtedly James's definitive work" and a "salient" alternative to James's "texts on 'real' politics." What, a student might in that case justifiably ask, is the point of studying *The Black Jacobins*, James's "grand narrative" of the Haitian Revolution (or, heaven forbid, reading his other more directly "sectarian" political writings), if it is the case that, as Farred tells us, any "insight and brilliance" in such works is "matched" by the way *Beyond a Boundary* "was able to profile the radical potentialities of the Caribbean proletariat" open to it through playing cricket?[15]

In 1989 Buhle was optimistic about what he called the emerging "field" of "James scholarship." As Buhle put it, "My satisfaction lies chiefly in imagining the myriad creative possibilities to which James's contributions can be put."[16] Yet, more recently, Buhle has not sounded a particularly satisfied note, reflecting on almost twenty years of sustained James scholarship that "the very 'field' had barely emerged before it veered away from social history and outright political claims, tending toward literary criticism and cultural studies." Consequently, "interest in James the revolutionary thinker lagged badly. . . . Mostly, he seemed a prophet neglected if not scorned."[17]

This then is one important justification for beginning a reexamination of James's intellectual and political evolution in imperial Britain from 1932 to 1938, a period that has long been "neglected if not scorned" in the literature of James scholarship. Despite being a period of James's life and work that is as full of inherent "creative possibilities" as any other, these were the fateful years in which James made a shift away from primarily "cultural activism" to embrace "real" politics. Accordingly, the "possibilities" that most concerned James since the mid-1930s — socialist revolution and anti-imperialist revolt — are those no postmodern academic today would even dare admit to "imagining," let alone commit themselves to agitating for. Yet without a clear understanding of these years there is no possibility of ever fully understanding James, "the revolutionary thinker." When asked "what would you most like to be remembered for" in an interview in 1980, James was quite explicit and unequivocal:

> The contributions I have made to the Marxist movement are the things that matter most to me. And those contributions have been political, in various ways; they have been literary: the book [on] *Moby Dick* [*Mariners, Renegades, and Castaways*] is a study of the Marxist approach to literature. All of my studies on the Black question are [Marxist] in reality. . . . On the whole, I like to think of myself as a Marxist who has made serious contributions to Marxism in various fields. I want to be considered one of the important Marxists.[18]

Given this, one might have thought that James's years in 1930s Britain would be considered as critical as the years in which he developed into an important Marxist intellectual, among other things. Yet the comparative lack of attention in recent James scholarship to this period remains striking. As Buhle noted with regret in 2006, reflecting on his own early biography of James, "The subsequent biographies, up to the present, have not pushed appreciatively further in respect to his Caribbean background (and continuing connections) and his sojourn in the United Kingdom in the 1930s."[19] The situation here remains much as Buhle found it in the early 1990s, when he noted that "James's English years, his milieux, political activities, and influences" remained "the least studied" and "surely deserve a volume of their own."[20]

Without such studies, we are too often prisoners left trapped with the prevailing image of James as simply the urbane "Grand Old Man of Letters," perhaps slumbering in an armchair. Timothy Brennan has described how in later life James's characteristic "manner of working was to spend his days for the most part in disheveled bedrooms, under sheets, reading T. S. Eliot with the TV on."[21] It is this seemingly "harmless icon" who has too often been commemorated and whose praises have been sung by all and sundry, including shameless, hypocritical, careerist New Labour politicians in Britain.[22] Something of the paradox of the veteran socialist James was well captured by the dub poet Linton Kwesi Johnson in "Di Good Life," his eloquent tribute to the "wise ole shephad": "Some sey him is a sage but nobody really know him riteful age ar whe him come from."[23] This book aims to not just advance general understanding about the "wise ole shephad" but also help answer the question of "whe him come from."

C. L. R. James in 1930s Britain: Image and Reality

If, as art historian David Craven once noted of James, "few defining figures of the 20th century are as famous and as unknown," then there can be few areas of his life where he is both more famous and yet more unknown as the six years he spent in Britain, from 1932 to 1938.[24] In 1981, in an outstanding article on this period of James's life, Robert Hill wrote that "in order that the full stature of James's actual accomplishments may be settled and recognized from the outset, it would be best to simply itemize them." The following is a list of just the main achievements and activity, adapted and updated from that provided by Hill in 1981:

1. Author of *The Case for West Indian Self-Government* (1933), an abridgement of *The Life of Captain Cipriani: An Account of British Government in the West Indies* (1932)

2. Ghostwriter for Learie Constantine's *Cricket and I* (1933), cricket reporter for the *Manchester Guardian* (1933–35), and author of a weekly column on "English cricket" for the *Glasgow Herald* (1937–38)

3. Executive member of the League of Coloured Peoples, 1933–34, chair of the International African Friends of Abyssinia (Ethiopia), 1935–36, executive member of the International African Service Bureau (IASB), 1937–38, with primary responsibility as editorial director of *Africa and the World* (1937) and *International African Opinion* (1938)

4. Playwright, writing *Toussaint Louverture: The Story of the Only Successful Slave Revolt in History* (1934), a play about the leader of the Haitian Revolution, performed by the Stage Society in London's Westminster Theatre in 1936 and starring Paul Robeson in the title role

5. Author of *World Revolution, 1917–1936: The Rise and Fall of the Communist International* (1937)

6. Chair of the Finchley branch of the Independent Labour Party (ILP), 1935–36, chair of the Marxist Group and editor of *Fight* and *Workers' Fight* (1936–38), International Executive Committee member of the Fourth International, 1938

7. Author of *The Black Jacobins: Toussaint Louverture and the San Domingo Revolution* (1938)

8. Author of *A History of Negro Revolt* (1938)

9. English translator of Boris Souvarine's biography *Stalin* (1939).[25]

As Hill explains,

> All this was done between March 1932 and October 1938, when he sailed for the United States, a period of just over six and a half years. In method it meant prodigious effort and concentration; in measurement, the results were prolific and gave example of the man's tremendous diversity of interest and capacities; in consequence, it touched all corners of the world-wide revolutionary struggle. . . . By anyone's standards, it was a monumental achievement, which staggers the mind simply in the recounting of it.[26]

Yet while the significance of the monumental achievement itself can never be dismissed completely, one inevitable consequence of the paucity of serious historical research about this period of James's life is that the dominant image left by both recent popular biographies and some scholarly studies is that he was essentially a would-be bourgeois dilettante playing around with Marxist ideas while living the high life as a feted writer.[27] For St Louis, James "was unable to privilege the materiality of political praxis over the ideality of cultural and intellectual life."[28] Even Scott McLemee can write that before James came to America in 1938, he was not a "professional revolutionist" who saw Lenin and Trotsky as "chief influences" but a "man of letters (on the model of William Hazlitt or Arnold Bennett)." The move to America was thus more than "a 'turn' in James's career." It marked "a profound shift in the co-ordinates of his personal identity."[29]

One would have thought such arguments would rest on a considerable amount of evidence. In fact, they appear to rest almost entirely on one sentence in the testimony of one man, James's publisher from 1936 to 1938, Fredric Warburg. Warburg's testimony, written during the 1950s when a member of the CIA-funded British Society for Cultural Freedom, though well known, remains worth quoting nonetheless:

> James himself was one of the most delightful and easy-going personalities I have known, colourful in more senses than one. A dark-skinned West Indian Negro from Trinidad, he stood six feet three inches in his

socks and was noticeably good-looking. His memory was extraordinary. He could quote, not only passages from the Marxist classics but long extracts from Shakespeare, in a soft lilting English which was a delight to hear. Immensely amiable, he loved the flesh-pots of capitalism, fine cooking, fine clothes, fine furniture and beautiful women, without a trace of the guilty remorse to be expected from a seasoned warrior of the class war.[30]

The last, particularly evocative sentence about James's love for the flesh-pots of capitalism is the critical one, and the authority given to this assertion by even some of the most dedicated James scholars is quite remarkable. McLemee, for example, describes Warburg's testimony as "the most vivid portrait of James during the 1930s," showing him to be not simply "a revolutionary" but "a gentleman."[31] It should be noted that Warburg was not totally misrepresenting James, as he *did* of course love fine cooking, fine clothes, fine furniture, and beautiful women (including, it seems, Warburg's wife, Pamela de Bayou). After signing with publishers Secker and Warburg in 1936, James would spend odd weekends away at the Warburgs' cottage, near West Hoathly, in Sussex, where, as Warburg remembers, "politics were forgotten" and no doubt James did take advantage of the finer things in life. Yet what needs to be remembered is that beautiful women aside, and they should of course be separated from a depiction of the fleshpots of capitalism, James's access to such things during this period was rather limited.

As Warburg himself noted, James's work covering cricket meant "it was only between April and October that he was in funds."[32] As for "fine clothes," one comrade of James's in the early British Trotskyist movement, Louise Cripps—another beautiful (and also married) woman with whom he had a relationship during the 1930s—remembered his clothing was "unnoticeable," usually "a medium-priced, medium-coloured suit, white shirt, and darkish tie. . . . He never wore flamboyant colours. They were a dull sort of clothes. I had often thought that he must have deliberately changed from the lighter clothes of the tropics to ones reflecting the sober greys of England's rainy climate."[33] When James left for America, in 1938, he remembered that Learie Constantine took one look at his "literary-political grey flannels and sports jacket" and decided it was necessary to buy him a new suit. "You cannot go to the United States that way. . . . It wouldn't do."[34] As for fine furniture, Cripps has described the first time she visited

James's top-floor central London flat on 9 Heathcote Street, where he lived for several years beginning in 1934:

> We walked up a couple of flights of stairs, and when we went, we found a medium-sized room with a fairly large window looking out onto the street. The room was moderately large, about twenty feet by sixteen feet. The walls had once been a cream colour. Now with age there were tinges of green and brown, not exactly unpleasant, but not in any way a bright room. Short old curtains hung at the windows, curtains that had turned grey with age. . . . There was no fireplace, but a gas heater had been installed. It was operated by putting a shilling into a meter. . . . There was also a single plate heater on a small stool. It was also coin-operated and allowed James to make tea. There was a kettle settled permanently on it. The only other fixture in the room was a small cupboard in which James kept a can of Carnation milk, Lipton's tea, and tins of biscuits. . . . It was not an attractive room, and James had done nothing to brighten it. He seemed quite content with the way it looked. There were no pictures on the wall, framed reproductions, not any photographs at all. . . . On the floor was well-worn brown Linoleum. There was a good deal of dust in the room . . . [but] not much furniture. . . . The major piece was the large round table where everyone sat. There was also a divan in one corner and a small bookcase. But books were not confined to that small space. There were books everywhere: books up the walls, books on the floor, books and papers on the table.[35]

A multitude of books aside, James in this period was not first and foremost a literary or cultural man of letters, at least not on the traditional English model. This is not to say that James neglected cultural matters. Warburg's portrait of James omits any mention of not only his anti-imperialist play *Toussaint Louverture*, but also the importance for black, radical, anti-colonialist activists of developing their own alternative counterculture of resistance in the imperial metropolis alongside more directly political anti-colonial campaigning in Pan-Africanist organizations like the IASB. One of James's friends and comrades in this struggle was the Jamaican Pan-Africanist Amy Ashwood Garvey, the former wife of Marcus Garvey and cofounder of the Universal Negro Improvement Association. Amy Ashwood was also a playwright (and theater producer) who had taken her shows across America and the Caribbean in the 1920s, and since moving to London had, in 1934, investigated the possibility of taking a com-

FIGURE INTRO.I Amy Ashwood Garvey, 1940s.

pany of artists of African descent to the West Coast of Africa. When this plan fell through, she and her partner, the Trinidadian musician and actor Sam Manning, first opened the International Afro Restaurant in 1935, at 62 New Oxford Street, and then in 1936, with the Guyanese clarinetist Rudolph Dunbar, opened a nightclub nearby. The Florence Mills Social Parlour, on London's Carnaby Street, named in tribute to the black American actress, quickly became "a haunt of black intellectuals."[36] Delia Jarrett-Macauley gives a vivid sense of the importance of such centers in 1930s London, noting "a steady stream of black artists was trickling into Britain." "They brought jazz, they brought blues. . . . In the evenings artists, activists, students drank and supped and kept their spirits high at Amy Ashwood Garvey's West End restaurant." James himself recalled that Amy Ashwood was "a wonderful cook" and "if you were lucky, the 78s of Trinidadian calypsonian Sam Manning, Amy's partner, spun late into the night."[37] In London, Manning, who headed the West Indian Rhythm Boys band, put on black British musical and comic revues with "singers and actors from Liverpool, Cardiff and the West Indies."[38]

It was not that James was not offered the opportunity to become a writer full time. He later recalled how his "publisher's wife," Pamela de Bayou, "a wonderful woman . . . begged [him] almost with tears to settle down and write." James recounted his response: "I said NO. . . . A fine sight I would have been with two or three books or a play or two to my credit and hanging around the political world, as all these other writers do, treating as amateurs, what is the most serious business in the world today."[39]

Rather, as Warburg remembers of James, "politics was his religion and Marx his god," and not only could he recite "passages from the Marxist classics" from memory but as a tireless propagandist for Trotskyism "he was brave." Warburg recalls James's activism: "Night after night he would address meetings in London and the provinces, denouncing the crimes of the blood-thirsty Stalin. . . . If you told him of some new communist argument, he would listen with a smile of infinite tolerance on his dark face, wag the index finger of his right hand solemnly, and announce in an understanding tone—'we know them, we know them.'"[40] The theme running through the testimony from almost all of those who knew James during the 1930s—both in the British Trotskyist movement and outside it—only confirms just how seriously he took revolutionary politics. Charlie van Gelderen, a veteran of the British Trotskyist movement, for example, thought James "quickly grasped" the "essentials" of Marxism, and overall "enriched Marxist theory with original ideas."[41] For what it is worth, even the British government's Special Branch agents noted on January 18, 1937, that James was "a fluent speaker and [appeared] to be very well versed in the doctrines of Karl Marx and other revolutionary writers."[42] As Kent Worcester judged in his still unsurpassed biography of James, published in 1996, "There was nothing dilettantish about his commitment to Trotskyism."[43]

Perhaps one of the best-known incidents relating to James's time in Britain came when he was invited to take Sunday afternoon tea at the home of the young, socialist, feminist novelist Ethel Mannin, a "determined collector of 'interesting people.'"[44] Her husband, the anti-imperialist writer Reginald Reynolds, remembers Mannin "had long hoped to meet C. L. R. James, whose intellect and good looks were praised by all except the Stalinists."[45] Mannin unfortunately did not know that James found the English custom of taking Sunday afternoon tea tiresome. As James put it, "Fidgeting about with tea cups and bits of cake, and saying how many lumps I took, and all that sort of business bored me stiff."[46] Mannin's satirical novel written in 1945, *Comrade O Comrade*, describes how an "extremely hand-some young Negro" and "eminent Trotskyist" avoided making small talk when the character loosely modeled on Mannin herself asked if he took "sugar" or wanted "cake" or "more tea." Instead, James apparently arrived at her home near Wimbledon Common, Oak Cottage, engrossed in a deep political discussion with a fellow Trotskyist, a discussion the two never apparently abandoned during the hour they were there. While admitting that others present were "hypnotized" by James's "dark rich beautiful voice," which "flowed like music," Mannin subsequently found it easy enough to satirize "the non-stop Trotskyists who came to tea," using quotes from James's *World Revolution* to reconstruct their thoughts on matters ranging from the French Popular Front, Spain, and Ethiopia, to "the real nature of Imperialism," and their stress throughout about how "Permanent Revolution and International Socialism must form the basis of all revolutionary strategy."[47]

Probably the most common criticism from those outside the Trotskyist movement who knew James during this period was not at all that he was too involved with literary and cultural matters, to the detriment of his political understanding—rather, quite the reverse. As Reynolds put it in his memoir, *My Life and Crimes* (1956), while James was "a man of brilliant intellect and an excellent writer[;] . . . unfortunately he turned his back on the problems of his own people—and also on the much broader cultural interests for which his talents suited him so admirably—to follow the barren cult of Trotskyism."[48] Even this statement bears examination, for Reynolds would have known that in 1930s Britain James had not "turned his back on the problems of his own people" after becoming a Trotskyist but was a leading campaigner in solidarity with the Caribbean labor rebellions, and an important Pan-Africanist more generally, an aspect of his thought that both he and Mannin greatly admired. And while it seems unlikely that Reynolds saw Paul Robeson star in the title role of *Toussaint Louverture*, Mannin's interest in Robeson alone meant they would have known about it. It is partly because Reynolds knew of James's sterling anticolonial work and close connection to cultural life in Britain during the 1930s, epitomized by his professional work as a leading cricket correspondent, that he felt his subsequent career after leaving Britain for the world of American Trotskyism—about which we can presume he knew very little—had been a waste,

James having apparently neglected his "broader cultural interests" to follow a "barren cult."

One perhaps might also note the shift in Reynolds's politics that had taken place by the 1950s, which were a far cry from the 1930s, when he had cut a distinctive figure on the British far Left. In 1929, aged just twenty-four, as a young middle-class Quaker, Reynolds had traveled to India, met Gandhi, and returned to Britain a hardened anti-imperialist and champion of Indian nationalism who was to be one of Gandhi's leading English supporters. In 1932 Reynolds's militant Gandhism won him the position of general secretary of the No More War Movement before he also steadily radicalized politically, supporting the ILP and breaking from pacifism and Gandhism during the Spanish Civil War. He once noted, tongue in cheek, that he was so left-wing in the 1930s that he "could see Trotskyism at some distance to [his] right." His sense of humor meant that one friend thought he was rather like a character out of a P. G. Wodehouse novel, "a sort of Bertie Wooster, if you can imagine a Wooster who was a radical revolutionary." The high point of Reynolds's "revolutionary radicalism" came in 1937 with *The White Sahibs in India*, a superb historical indictment of British colonialism that carried an appreciative foreword from Nehru. Yet as Reynolds's biographer notes, "After the Second World War, Reg's disillusionment with politics was complete," and he drifted back to his early concern with Gandhi and Quakerism.[49] Yet there was never a chance that James would neglect his "broader cultural interests." In 1982 James sat for a portrait by the artist Paul Harber, son of Denzil Dean Harber, another veteran of the early British Trotskyist movement. During the sittings, James remarked, "Besides revolutionaries, there are two other lots of people I admire — artists and wicket-keepers."[50]

The Aim of This Work

In 1981, Robert Hill stressed the importance of the years James spent in 1930s Britain to James's overall intellectual development, describing the profound political transformation that took place as "a leap out of the world of Thackeray and nineteenth-century intellectual concerns into the world of international socialist revolution." But Hill also suggested that a "great deal of further research" on this period of James's life was necessary: "It would be trying to reach for the impossible if we sought after a complete description of James's evolution over this pivotal six-year stretch in England. Many separate histories are bound up together in each stage of the work, and each would separately necessitate a great deal of further research. In addition, it would alike be too much to attempt an exhaustive analysis of each work."[51]

Though Hill was writing in 1981, and in an article of only twenty pages, this book will not pretend to offer "a complete description of James's evolution over this pivotal six-year stretch" either. Though James was perhaps the critical intellectual driving force of early British Trotskyism, this study will not itself detail his relationship and activism in that movement or the full complexities and subtleties of his early Marxism. Nor will it "attempt an exhaustive analysis of each work" of James's written during this period, some of which, particularly *The Black Jacobins*, deserve and demand whole books devoted to them. While Hill's article was entitled "In England, 1932–1938," this study will also have as its main focus the work James did in England, and only touch in passing on his visits to France, Ireland, Scotland, and Wales.[52] That said, this book is based on a detailed examination of several of the "many separate histories bound up in each stage" of James's life during this "pivotal" period, using new sources that have recently come to light, including the Special Branch file kept on him. We will begin by examining James's early identification with imperial British culture while growing up in colonial Trinidad, and his creative use as a young, Caribbean, literary intellectual of the Victorian cultural critic Matthew Arnold in the cause of West Indian nationalism. We will then closely detail the critical ten months that the young Trinidadian writer spent in "Red Nelson," in Lancashire, soon after his move to Britain, and his first encounter with the English working-class movement. A lengthy chapter will follow, examining James's turn to revolutionary politics, and how his Marxism and militant Pan-Africanism manifested itself in anticolonial agitation and anticapitalist activism in the imperial metropolis. We will then turn to James's relationship with metropolitan imperial culture in Britain through a study of his professional work as a cricket reporter. The work will conclude with a discussion of what are perhaps James's finest works during this period, his inspiring invocations of the spirit of the Haitian Revolution through both drama and history, *Toussaint Louverture* and *The Black Jacobins*.

In all of this, the initial pioneering biographical work of scholars such as Paul Buhle and Kent Worcester on this period of James's life, together with the other advances that have been made over the past decades of

James scholarship, and on imperialism, race, and resistance more generally, again deserve recognition and acknowledgment. For example, in March 1932, after arriving in London, James had taken residence in the district of Bloomsbury, then "still the Mecca of suburban and provincial intellectuals," according to Reginald Reynolds.[53] While James only stayed for ten weeks, until May 1932, he sent his "first impressions" of London back home to be published (in five parts) in the *Port of Spain Gazette*. These essays allow scholars a unique and fascinating glimpse into James's "voyage in" and his mentality at the point of arrival in Britain, and in 2003 many of them were republished in a well-received collection entitled *Letters from London*, with an introduction by Kenneth Ramchand.[54]

Overall, this study might be seen as attempting to evoke a detailed and historical sense of the totality of critical aspects of James's life and work in Britain, explicitly rejecting the fragmented and decentered approach of much recent scholarship. Worcester has suggested that we can construct such a concrete totality of James's life if we accept that "no one problematic—Marxism, black nationalism, West Indian history and culture, and so on—can be used by itself."[55] However, only one "problematic" he lists has any intrinsic interest in explaining the totality of anyone's life and work, the Marxist method that James himself used to construct his great biographical portrait of the Haitian revolutionary Toussaint Louverture in *The Black Jacobins*. There is also perhaps one other way this study might be said to aspire to be "Jamesian." As Paul Le Blanc has noted, "An essential aspect of James's method is to make links between seemingly diverse realities, sometimes to take something that is commonly perceived as marginal and to demonstrate that it is central. This is done in a manner that profoundly alters (rather than displaces) the traditionally 'central' categories."[56] This book aims, through a careful historical examination of a particular past reality, one currently perceived as marginal and peripheral, to alter our traditional understanding of what is of central importance about the life and work of James.

C. L. R. James's sojourn in imperial Britain in the 1930s deserves a place in history, and not simply because as an outstanding black West Indian intellectual and anticolonial activist he made a tremendous contribution to helping forge the rise of modern multicultural, "postcolonial" Britain. To borrow a metaphor from his beloved world of cricket, James was also one of the great "opening batsmen" of the international Trotskyist movement. Yet in racking up the runs at the expense of racism, imperialism, fascism, and Stalinism, James was following in the footsteps of other great revolutionary figures who had courageously fought for liberty and equality in the face of overwhelming odds. Amid the Haitian Revolution, Toussaint famously chose to adopt the name "Louverture," "the opening," and Polverel, the French commissioner, "is said to have exclaimed at the news of another victory by Toussaint: 'This man makes an opening everywhere.'"[57] As a courageous, creative, revolutionary socialist thinker and activist, James also helped "make an opening" that—like Toussaint's—might still encourage and inspire those engaged in all manner of liberation struggles against exploitation and oppression everywhere today.

ONE | "We Lived According to the Tenets
of Matthew Arnold"

Colonial Victorianism and the Creative
Realism of the Young C. L. R. James

C. L. R. James, as his friend the Barbadian poet and novelist George Lamming would eloquently note, was "a spirit that came to life in the rich and humble soil of a British colony in the Caribbean."[1] In *Beyond a Boundary*, James recalled some of his hobbies and interests — aside from cricket and a fascination with indigenous popular cultural traditions such as calypso and Carnival — while growing to intellectual maturity as an aspiring writer in Trinidad during the 1920s and early 1930s: "I had a circle of friends (most of them white) with whom I exchanged ideas, books, records and manuscripts. We published local magazines and gave lectures or wrote articles on Wordsworth, the English Drama, and Poetry as a Criticism of Life. We lived according to the tenets of Matthew Arnold, spreading sweetness and light and the best that has been thought and said in the world."[2]

This statement by James, testifying to the profound, early intellectual inspiration provided by the Victorian cultural critic Matthew Arnold, stands as evidence for what Bill Schwarz calls "the unusually deep penetration of the institutions of Victorian civic life into the cultural organisation of the colonial Caribbean."[3] Harvey R. Neptune has drawn attention to how the "literary societies and debating clubs" of interwar Trinidad were "Arnoldian to the core" as "the local establishment took culture to be virtually synonymous with an idealized Victorian literariness."[4] Outside the white colonial elite, such a view of culture had a particularly powerful purchase among the emerging black middle class — the class into which James was born. As Anne Spry Rush has noted in *Bonds of Empire*, many black, middle-class West Indians "rested their status on an affinity for British culture and an understanding of British imperial identity as something that they could claim as their own." Crucially, however, Rush also recognizes that they "were not passive recipients of a British imperial culture," but "shaped it to fit their own (dark-skinned, colonial) circumstances and used it for their own purposes."[5]

James did not just then passively absorb and "live according to the tenets of Matthew Arnold" (as might almost be expected of a black, middle-class colonial subject with literary ambitions for reasons of "respectability" and "status"), but rather increasingly actively and creatively shaped Arnold's tenets so that they could serve his own purposes as he orientated toward West Indian nationalism during the 1920s. Though a matter to be understood generally as an aspect of James's early general identification with "imperial Britishness," Simon Gikandi has usefully drawn attention to the specificities and peculiarities of "colonial Victorianism," noting how James's early Arnoldianism is a fine example of how distinctly nonegalitarian Victorian cultural categories could be taken up, transformed, and used for progressive ends by generations of British colonial subjects across Africa, Asia, and the Caribbean. For Gikandi, what is particularly striking about the "productive contradictions" of Victorianism is "the unanticipated fact that forces, values, and cultures intended to consolidate colonial conquest could so easily be transformed into the foundational narratives of black self-determination and rights."[6]

Such a transformation was comparatively more difficult for black colonial subjects in the Caribbean than elsewhere, given what Paget Henry and Paul Buhle, in their important edited collection *C. L. R. James's Caribbean* (1992), have noted as the "extreme and extended" processes of imperial "cultural penetration and control . . . which resulted in comparatively high degrees of Westernization."[7] Writing on the "presence of blacks in the Caribbean and its impact on culture" in 1975, James stressed how "the African . . . had to adapt what he brought with him to the particular circumstances which he found. . . . His philosophy and religion proved to be a combination of what he brought with him and what his new masters sought to impose on him."[8] Paget Henry, in a recent discussion of African philosophical thought, "an original metaphysics that reflects the experiences of Africana peoples and the distinct knowledge-producing practices that were developed under the world-shattering conditions of racialization and colonization amidst slavery and colonial domination," has stressed the inherently "provisional and improvisational nature of the creative codes" that necessarily guided its formation. Henry calls this tradition "creative realism," as "what it assumes to be ultimately real is the creative act in its spontaneous movements rather than any of its specific creations."[9] To begin to understand how "the tenets of Matthew Arnold" were reimagined and re-invented by James in the context of colonial Trinidad, it is therefore critical to see more here than simply James's own outstanding originality and audacity as a thinker involved in what Gikandi calls "the appropriation, rehearsal, and reformulation of a belated Victorianism by colonial subjects."[10] Rather, James's engagement with Arnoldianism might be seen in its own right as an intellectual act that illuminates, and is representative of, a wider, deeper, and older improvisational tradition of "creative realism" that would come to be characteristic of much Caribbean cultural and philosophical thought.

The Making of an Afro-Victorianist

"Victorianism to me is not a thing to be amused at in books, but a very vivid and sometimes painful memory," James wrote in 1933.[11] James was born in 1901, while Queen Victoria was still on the throne, into the nascent, black middle class in colonial Trinidad.[12] Aged just nine, and trained up by his father, Robert Alexander, a schoolmaster, James became the youngest boy ever to win the necessary exhibition to the elite Queen's Royal College (QRC). This institution was modeled on the English public school, and as James noted later, "more suitable to Portsmouth than to Port of Spain."[13] Soon after enrolling, in 1911, James demonstrated he was more than capable of fulfilling the great expectations for him from family and friends, coming second in an island-wide school competition open to all (even those seven years older), when told to write about the "British Empire."[14] V. S. Naipaul, in his novel *A House for Mr. Biswas* (1961), set decades later, contains an ill-disguised spoof of the schoolboy James as an unnamed "negro boy" who had made the "biggest surprise" by winning first place among those competing for school exhibitions:

> He was a negro boy of astonishing size.... He had been loud in his denun-ciations of crammers; he had taken a leading part in discussions about films and sport; he had a phenomenal knowledge of English county cricket scores throughout the nineteen-thirties; and he had introduced the topic of sex.... He displayed a convincing knowledge of the female body and its functions; and the conception of his life away from school as one of indifference to books and notes and homework was reinforced

by his passionate devotion to the novels of P. G. Wodehouse, whose style he successfully imitated in his English compositions.[15]

Naipaul captures well the essential truth in the point made by Eric Williams, a historian and compatriot of James, that Trinidad by the twentieth century was "politically, economically, socially, educationally, culturally literally a British colony."[16] That said, as Stephen Howe notes, "there was nothing inevitable about the Englishness of James's education, or of Trinidad." As Howe puts it, "Given its Spanish and French inheritance, the island could have remained a minimally anglicized hybrid, one where the formerly dominant languages remained the preferred, and prized idioms of the elite. . . . It required conscious decisions, acts of will — on the part of both colonisers and colonised — for a British-model educational system and cultural ethos to take root there."[17]

Perhaps mindful of this heritage, Queen Victoria herself, apparently in 1897 at her Jubilee, asked Emmanuel Mzumbo Lazare, a black Trinidad-born solicitor, "Do you speak English in Trinidad?" only to be informed, "Madam in Trinidad we are all English."[18] By the twentieth century, in places such as the Anglophone Caribbean, as Schwarz has noted, Britishness had become "hegemonic" and "worked as a symbolic force-field though which the power of the metropolis operated."[19] James recalled, "Our masters, our curriculum, our code of morals [at QRC], *everything* began from the basis that Britain was the source of all light and leading, and our business was to admire, wonder, imitate, learn." Yet the young James himself, who had inherited a love of reading from his mother, Ida Elizabeth, certainly also willfully embraced the British educational and cultural ethos.[20]

James emerged from QRC then in some senses irrevocably shaped as a "Victorianist."[21] "I began to study Latin and French, then Greek, and much else. . . . I learnt and obeyed and taught a code, the English public-school code," he recalled in *Beyond a Boundary*.[22] After graduating with a classical education fit for the rulers of the world's most powerful empire, James spent much of the following decade teaching English and History back at QRC before moving on to teach at the Government Training College.[23] Yet if James was a "Victorianist" in his taste and manners, he was, as George Lamming put it, "a Victorian with the rebel seed."[24] This "rebel seed" was perhaps first sown through James's reading of English literature in general and Victorian writers critical of Victorianism in particular. In his study of James, *Urbane Revolutionary*, Frank Rosengarten draws particular attention to four English writers with the first name William "whom [James] especially enjoyed—Shakespeare, Wordsworth, Hazlitt, and Thackeray."[25] James's early love of Thackeray's *Vanity Fair* is well known, and it almost certainly provides the inspiration for Naipaul's jibe about the "passionate devotion to the novels of P. G. Wodehouse" by the "negro boy."[26]

Thackeray, for James, seems to have helped pave the way for a dangerously subversive critique of the strict hierarchy of colonial society.[27] James recalled of *Vanity Fair*—itself rich in colonial and imperial themes—that he had "no notion that it was a classical novel" but just "laughed without satiety at Thackeray's constant jokes and sneers and gibes at the aristocracy and at people in high places."[28] The prestige of the monarchy in particular, so important in a Crown Colony like Trinidad, lost any power it might have had over the young James. "I have been a republican since I was eight years old. An Englishman, William Makepeace Thackeray, taught it to me," James later recalled.[29] Further reading of the likes of Thackeray and Dickens ensured James would steadily become critical of what E. P. Thompson called "that shallow culture in which both sentimentality and hypocrisy flourished," "the characteristic 'Victorian' middle-class sensibility" that was so widespread among the black and colored middle class of Trinidad.[30]

Another critical reason why James quickly became "a Victorianist with the rebel seed" relates to the question of race. Though, as James put it in *Beyond a Boundary*, "when [he] left school . . . [he] had educated [himself] into a member of the British middle class with literary gifts," in reality he was still a member of the West Indian, black, lower-middle class, an "Afro-Victorianist."[31] Critically, James's blackness and his identification of himself as not just "British" but also as a "West Indian Negro," is vital with respect to understanding what the great black American historian W. E. B. Du Bois called the "double consciousness" of the oppressed in a racist climate.[32] For example, while James's public school education had trained him to lead men forward for "King and Country," when James tried to do just that by offering to enlist with the Merchants' Contingent in 1918, he was blocked on account of being black.[33] The importance of race should not be understated, even though James had been able to cultivate his passion for history and literature while at QRC and, as Stuart Hall points out, so turn the "double consciousness" into a positive thing, "a gift," and "his colonial education—which has unhinged so many—into a source of intellectual strength."[34]

Nonetheless, it is not surprising that James felt that on graduating from QRC, his education meant that "there was no world for which [he] was fitted, least of all the one [he] was now to enter," the materially impoverished small island of colonial Trinidad.[35] James had not made the academic grade necessary for an Island Scholarship and further study abroad, typically medicine or law at a college or university in Britain, and so he now found himself spending more time with others like him, those who had also not "made it" abroad, including his childhood friend Malcolm Nurse. James recalls, "I began to teach and do journalism [as a cricket reporter with the *Sporting Chronicle*]" and Nurse "got a job on the *Mirror* as a reporter with the result that we both became familiar with a lot of things."[36] Critically, James would now have the opportunity to mix with a wider cross-section of Trinidadian society and gain a deeper appreciation of its rich indigenous popular culture. As James later told Consuelo López Springfield, he might well have known "all the finest books of Western civilization" as a result of his formal education at QRC and his own private studies, but "exposure" to ordinary Trinidadians would give him a "special social education."[37]

The 1919 Mass Strike in Trinidad and Its Aftermath

After graduating in 1918, and before returning to the classroom to teach, James worked for about eight months on Brechin Castle sugar estate, in the chemist department mixing sugar.[38] In 1919, James remembered "a big strike" on the sugar estate, just one of many precursors of a rolling mass strike that would shake colonial Trinidad later that year.[39] Workers' resentment had steadily built up during the Great War, as the bloody conflict had dragged on without an apparent end in sight. In 1915, farmers demonstrated for a rise in the price of sugar, and in March 1917, oilfield, dock, and asphalt workers had taken strike action against the United British Oilfields company and the American-owned Trinidad Lake Asphalt Company.[40] In December 1918, the black troops of the British West Indies Regiment (BWIR) revolted in Italy against the war and the institutional racism of the British army, and their anger as they returned to price rises, poverty, and overcrowded housing in Trinidad was the spark that threw Trinidadian society into turmoil.[41] From mid-November 1919, a mass dockworker's strike rocked the Port of Spain waterfront for three weeks, and when, on December 1, the strikers took to the streets, council workers and coal carriers stopped work to join them in solidarity. The striking workers and their thousands of supporters proceeded to shut Port of Spain down.[42] James recalled how striking dockers "patrolled the town, made business close down, and were at one time in charge of the city."[43]

The mass dockworkers' strike of 1919 came to an end on December 3, when they accepted an offer of a 25 percent pay raise from the shipping companies, but their inspiring victory, won through the most militant forms of action, now triggered what O. Nigel Bolland notes was "virtually a general strike" that rolled across Trinidad and Tobago into early 1920, encompassing other groups of workers, from Indian estate workers to oilfield workers in the south.[44] The chief political beneficiary of this revolt was the small, social-democratic, nationalist Trinidad Workingmen's Association (TWA), which grew massively as a political organization by playing a leading role in the industrial turmoil of 1919. Members of the TWA boldly wore red shirts in solidarity with the October Revolution in Russia, yet while editorials in *The Weekly Guardian*, the *Argos* and *Port of Spain Gazette* sternly warned of the danger of "Bolshevism extending to Trinidad," it was Garveyism, not socialism, that captured the imagination of most leading strikers, even many leading figures in the TWA.[45] James himself knew a few of the strike-leaders through playing cricket, and later recalled he felt "positive that they were Garveyites."[46] There was widespread enthusiasm for Garvey's Universal Negro Improvement Association (UNIA), founded in 1914 with an aim of uniting black people internationally, under the slogan "One god! One aim! One destiny!" Garvey's militant rhetoric fit with the new mood of resistance, and he declared in 1920 that the colors of the UNIA flag "showed their sympathy with the 'Reds' of the world, and the Green their sympathy for the Irish in their fight for freedom." However, Garvey himself was no revolutionary, once reminding an audience that though the Bolsheviks deserved the praise of black people, they were "not very much concerned as partakers in [those] revolutions."[47] The arrival of British cruisers and the mere presence of armed troops in Port of Spain proved enough to maintain "law and order."[48]

The colonial government then clamped down on formal political dissent, with a barrage of repressive legislation and a refusal to consider the legalization of trade union activity (as had happened in Guyana and Jamaica), and so culture became a critical means of expression for social grievances. From a young age James had been fascinated by calypso singers at Carnival time, and he gravitated naturally toward what Sylvia Wynter called the "popular underground counter-culture of Trinidad, a culture derived from

Africa, yet toughened."[49] With its deep roots in plantation society, the authorities had often made attempts to ban calypso before the abolition of slavery in the 1830s, and it now represented part of the popular collective memory of the struggle against slavery and what Susan Campbell has called "a shadowy but persistent form of oppositional culture." One calypsonian, known as Lord Protector (Patrick Jones, also known as "Chinee Patrick" because of his Chinese heritage), was threatened with arrest and imprisonment under the new "Seditious Acts and Publications Ordinance" for his song "Class Legislation" (1920), a reflection on the response of the colonial state to the 1919 mass strike. The song's lyrics are explicitly political:

> Class legislation is the order of the land
> We are ruled with an iron hand
> Class legislation the order of the land
> We are ruled by an iron hand
> Britain boasts of democracy
> Brotherly love and fraternity
> But British colonies have been ruled in
> perpetual misery
> Sans humanité.[50]

In the early 1920s, James became secretary of the Maverick Club, a social and cultural club independent of the white colonial elite. He later recalled how "for the most part we were Black people and one brown . . . we would give concerts."[51] James remembers a few Maverick Club members were highly politically conscious and were "reading W. E. B. Du Bois, they read an American Negro magazine called *The Crisis*. They were familiar with the Negro Question in the United States. . . . They were not militant, but the intellectual atmosphere and the very existence of the club was a symbol of things to come."[52]

Though James recalled that during the 1920s, in general "politics seemed remote from [him]," he was engaged with radical discourses of black liberation, for even as a teenager he had read Garvey's weekly paper, *The Negro World*, buying it "every Saturday down St. Vincent Street in Port of Spain."[53] Despite the political repression, Garveyism—the most powerful form of black nationalism until the "Black Power" movement in the 1960s—became a central vehicle for black bitterness in Trinidad, and by the late 1920s there were thirty UNIA branches.[54] "I read Garvey and I read Du Bois," James recalled, but not "with the insistence and concern" of others, in particular Malcolm Nurse, who "was always talking to me about them when we used to meet."[55] Such discussions — including with Garvey himself when he visited Port of Spain in 1929 — certainly helped awaken James to the reality of racial oppression in America and to colonial domination across the African diaspora.[56]

It would be, however, the democratic struggle for Trinidadian and wider West Indian national liberation that made the most political impact on the young James. After the upheaval of 1919, there had been minor constitutional reform. Though only a tiny wealthy or propertied minority were allowed to vote, the first "general election" in Trinidad took place in 1925, as seven members out of the twenty-six-strong Legislative Council would now be elected. In Port of Spain, Captain Arthur Andrew Cipriani, the former Commanding Officer of the BWIR who had become leader of the TWA, won one of the seven elected council seats. More critically, the charismatic Cipriani, the self-declared champion of "the unwashed and unsoaped barefooted men," now rallied an effective extraparliamentary movement around him.[57] As James recalled, Cipriani "built a mass labour movement and as this grew so did his power in the Legislature." James remembered, "This was *real*. I was caught up in it like many others and began to take notice. . . . My hitherto vague ideas of freedom crystalized around a political conviction: we should be free to govern ourselves. I said nothing to anyone. . . . When I told my brother some of my ideas his only comment was: 'You will end up in gaol.'"[58]

Arnoldianism and the Beacon Group

Alongside his growing sympathy with the TWA, James now also orientated around an emerging group of young black and white intellectuals in Port of Spain who wrote "barrack-yard" stories about the lives of the poor by way of implicit critique of colonial society, often publishing them themselves. The literary movement around independent journals such as *Trinidad* (1929–30) and *The Beacon* (1931–34), founded by James and others including Alfred Mendes and Ralph de Boissière, represented what Reinhard Sander terms "the Trinidad Awakening," a cultural response triggered by the stirring nationalism and organized labor politics on the island.[59] As Stuart Hall notes, Trinidad had "always had a vigorous independent intellectual life" and in the late 1920s "an anti-colonial culture coalesced," with the "Beacon Group" of writers very much at its heart.[60] One of their central aims, according to Harvey Neptune, was to "banalize Britishness," to "disturb its air of invulnerability and, indeed, inevitability." Neptune characterizes the group's methods: "Race, of course, would rest almost ineluctably at the center of this move, for Britishness stood as an identity inextricable from the culture of white supremacy. Indeed, it was dependent on a contradistinctive blackness. The challenge for Trinidad's patriots, therefore, was not only to undermine the rhetoric of empire but, more complexly, to expose its complicity with tropes of whiteness."[61]

The racism that underpinned the British colonial project was never far from the surface, and James later recalled how in 1931 Dr. Sidney Harland, a "distinguished scientist" from England resident in Trinidad, "foolishly took it upon himself to write an article proving that Negroes were as a race inferior in intelligence to whites." James remembered, "I wasn't going to stand for that and in our little local magazine I tore him apart."[62] James's vindicatory response in *The Beacon*, "The Intelligence of the Negro," noted, "I do not make excessive claims for West Indian negroes. I know only too well the shortcomings of my own people. But in one thing they are not inferior. And that thing is intelligence."[63]

However, it is perhaps too one-sided to see the Beacon Group's defining project as simply "banalizing Britishness," as Raymond Ramcharitar, for example, in a provocative and thought-provoking recent essay, does when he insists the group "rejected the British Arnoldian ideal of culture and tried to establish wholly local standards, whose principal characteristic was that they 'resisted' Britishness."[64] While this characterization contains an important element of truth, matters were rather more complicated. Rather than rejecting "the British Arnoldian ideal of culture," many Arnoldian tenets were taken up and transplanted in Trinidad by this little group of literary-minded nationalists, while James himself transformed them in a creative manner that few in Britain—least of all a figure such as Matthew Arnold—could have ever envisaged possible.

Arnold's "tenets" were perhaps most clearly laid down in *Culture and Anarchy* (1869), wherein he stressed the humanizing role culture could and should play in society. Culture was about "the passion for sweetness and light," but also "the passion for making them *prevail*" everywhere, even among "the raw and unkindled masses of humanity. . . . We must have a broad basis, must have sweetness and light for as many as possible." But it must be "*real* sweetness and *real* light. Plenty of people will try to give the masses, as they call them, an intellectual food prepared and adapted in the way they think proper for the actual condition of the masses," and "plenty of people will try to indoctrinate the masses with the set of ideas and judgments constituting the creed of their own profession or party." But "culture works differently" from both "ordinary popular literature" and "religious and political organisations." Arnold continued,

> It [culture] does not try to teach down to the level of inferior classes; it does not try to win them for this or that sect of its own, with ready-made judgments and watchwords. It seeks to do away with classes; to make the best that has been thought and known in the world current everywhere; to make all men live in an atmosphere of sweetness and light, where they may use ideas, as it uses them itself, freely, — nourished, and not bound by them.
>
> This is the *social idea*; and the men of culture are the true apostles of equality. The great men of culture are those who have had a passion for diffusing, for making prevail, for carrying from one end of society to the other, the best knowledge, the best ideas of their time; who have laboured to divest knowledge of all that was harsh, uncouth, difficult, abstract, professional, exclusive; to humanise it, to make it efficient outside the clique of the cultivated and the learned, yet still remaining the best knowledge and thought of the time, and a true source, therefore of sweetness and light.[65]

James's extensive reading and encyclopedic memory enabled him to use ideas "freely, nourished and not bound by them," while his background as a member of the black middle class, coupled with his relatively privileged position as a schoolmaster, ensured he was able to carry his liberal humanist ideas "from one end of society to the other," from members of the white colonial elite to the materially impoverished black residents of the barrack yards in Port of Spain. As James later remarked of himself and his group of friends, "We spread sweetness and light, and we studied the best that there was in literature in order to transmit it to the people — as we thought, the poor, backward West Indian people."[66] As he once recalled, "In time, before long, when anyone in Trinidad wanted to know something about literature, they came to me. James was the man." Even other teachers "looked upon [him] as an exceptional person. . . . The person to whom they applied for knowledge of literature, history, local history and so forth."[67]

How many of Arnold's tenets the Beacon Group took to heart can be seen from an examination of *The Beacon* itself, which billed itself as "A Guiding Light for All Who Are in Intellectual Darkness and Who Seek Great Things."[68] The first issue carried the banner slogan "Lux et veritas" (Light and truth) and the editor, Albert Gomes, explicitly declared the journal was about diffusing culture, not political propaganda: "The customary 'editorials' have been purposely omitted. There is no desire to give any definitive 'personality' to *The Beacon*—to associate its name with any policies or ideals." In his autobiography, *Through a Maze of Colour*, Gomes remembered how within a few issues "*The Beacon* became much more than just a literary magazine and mouthpiece of a clique." Gomes recalled: "Indeed, it became the focus of a movement of enlightenment spearheaded by Trinidad's angry young men of the Thirties. It was the torpor, the smugness and the hypocrisy of the Trinidad of the period that provoked the response which produced both the magazine and the defiant bohemianism of the movement that was built around it."[69] James's own Arnoldianism comes out clearly in one short article for *The Beacon*, a portrait of Michel Maxwell Philip (1829–88), a former member of Trinidad's free-colored population who rose to become solicitor general during the nineteenth century and wrote a remarkable romantic historical novel, *Emmanuel Appadocca* (1854). As James wrote of Philip, "True he was a distinguished lawyer[,] . . . a man of conspicuous public service. But . . . his chief claim to remembrance is because in addition to all these things, he was a man of that varied intellectual power and breadth of culture which make him and such as he the fine flower of a civilized society." In other words, Philip was a "great man of culture," and James praised Philip's mastery of "the grand style," a phrase coined by Arnold.[70] James singled out an after-dinner speech Philip made in 1886, when in the company of the great and good of the West Indian legal establishment who, after a lifetime of service, had deprived him of his rightful position of attorney general because of his color. It was, James declared, "one of the finest speeches of his career," and he quoted the following extract, noting they were "words which it is difficult to read today without sharing the feelings of him who spoke them."

> I am not a Chief Justice. I am not a Puisne Judge. I do not aspire either to be one or the other. I am not even an Attorney-General. It will suffice me in the afternoon of my life (whether attended with good or evil fortune) when, broken with the conflicts of the Forum, I should seek ease

in retirement, I shall be able to express my contentment in the language of the Roman wanderer to Sextilius, "Tell him you have seen Caius Marius, though not a fugitive, sitting on the ruins of Carthage."

As James commented, "It is a passage to linger over." James discussed Philip's speech at length:

First the simple reiterations of all that he was not, driving home to his audience all that he was, for he knew and they too knew that even in that talented assembly there was not one his peer; then the great phrase, "broken with the conflicts of the Forum," leading to the classical allusion, instantly comprehensible to every intelligent member of his audience, as any oratorical allusion should be, and yet with the characteristic touch of scholarship in the precision of the reference; the tremendous words of Marius himself; and behind it all, the disappointment of a lifetime, charging the words with emotion and so lifting the passage from rhetoric into literature.[71]

As James continued, "The most serious criticism made against him is that he did little for his people. It is true that Mr. Philip was not a man possessed by that passionate desire for the welfare of the poorer classes which distinguishes the present tribune of the people, the member for Port-of-Spain," Captain Cipriani. Yet for James this was not crucial, as "it takes all sorts to make a world and it takes all sorts to make a Government, a thing which extremists on both sides cannot realise. Conservatism unprodded hardens into tyranny, radicalism unchecked degenerates into chaos." The fact that Philip stood between the "anarchy" of the masses and also the "tyranny" of the few meant that he fulfilled the Arnoldian ideal of how a great man of culture should act. James noted, "As a people we are young and rather raw so that we do not understand these things. . . . He set a standard to which young men might aspire and by which older men might be judged. Always in the minds of his contemporaries loomed the gigantic figure of Mr. Maxwell Philip, to keep pretentious small men in their places and—a far more necessary task—presumptuous big men too."[72]

James himself, in this article, was possibly drawing on his own experience of how "conservatism unprodded hardens into tyranny," when he found himself giving part-time English lessons to the French consul to Trinidad. The French consul was, James remembered, an "intimate friend" of Governor Sir Claud Hollis, a reactionary figure once described by the Communist *Negro Worker* as "the Mussolini of Trinidad." One day the French consul asked James point blank, "What do you think would happen if the Government arrested Cipriani?" James recalled, "Like a flash it hit me that this step was being discussed in the circles he frequented." James, who had been inspired by the growing nationalist fervor to begin a study of West Indian political history, conjured up the specter of a repeat of the Water Riots of 1903, which left sixteen shot dead by the government and the home of the legislative assembly destroyed. James responded, "Arrest Cipriani! Why, the people would burn down Government House. They did it before, you know."[73] James was obviously convincing enough in portraying to the French consul a picture of the anarchy and chaos that would unfold if "radicalism" was allowed to "degenerate unchecked" without Cipriani's leadership. Arnold himself, who had personally deplored the working-class riots in London's Hyde Park in 1866, would doubtless have been proud of James's "timely prod" of a "presumptuous big man."[74]

Colonialism

More critically, Arnold's method of understanding metropolitan British society was taken up by James and used to analyze colonial society in Trinidad. In *Culture and Anarchy*, Arnold had divided British society up by class, with the aristocratic "Barbarians," the middle-class "Philistines," and the working-class "Populace." Arnold reserved his particular energies for undermining the philistinism, pomposity, and parochialism of the newly enriched English middle class. Arnold described "the very people whom we call the Philistines" as those who "believe that [their] greatness and welfare [were] proved by [their] being so very rich and who most [gave] their lives and thoughts to becoming rich."[75] Arnold's judgment seemed confirmed by what James found from his observation of his fellow teachers at QRC, as he noted in his first book, *The Life of Captain Cipriani* (1932): "If anyone happens to meet fairly frequently any group of Englishmen, even of university education, he will find that as a rule they dislike civilised conversation and look with suspicion, if not positive dislike, upon anyone who introduces it into their continual reverberations over the football match, the cricket match, the hockey match or the tennis match."[76]

In a slightly regretful passage in *Beyond a Boundary*, James remembered that "Matthew Arnold still had possession" of him at the time. James recalled, "In the book on self-government, throwing every brick to hand at the arrogance of English colonialism, I had indicted the English as a whole of being an unintellectual people"; and this was before he had actually been able to meet a wider cross-section of them.[77] While James perhaps too uncritically accepted Arnold's judgment of British society, in *The Life of Captain Cipriani* he creatively and originally adapted Arnold's class categories of Barbarian aristocrats, a Philistine middle class, and an unenlightened populace to fit colonial Trinidad during the 1920s. "The white people are the richer people, and naturally form what for the sake of a better term may be called the local aristocracy. This society is on the whole of no particular value, containing as it does little of the element of real culture."[78] Any young middle-class Englishman who arrived from England to play a role in governing a colonial society soon underwent a transformation. James described the process:

> Bourgeois at home, he finds himself after a few weeks at sea suddenly exalted into the position of being a member of a ruling class. Empire to him and most of his class, formerly but a mere word, becomes on his advent to the colonies a phrase charged with responsibilities, it is true, but bearing in its train the most delightful privileges, beneficial to his material well-being and flattering to his pride. . . . He owes his place to a system, and the system thereby becomes sacred. . . . The Colonial Office official worships the system of Crown Colony Government. . . . How he leaps to attention at the first bars of "God Save the King!" Empire Day, King's Birthday, days not so much neglected in England as ignored, give to the colonial Englishman an opportunity to sing the praises of the British Empire and of England, his own country, as its centre. . . . This excessive and vocal patriotism in an Englishman is but the natural smoke of unnatural fires burning within. That snobbishness which is so marked a characteristic of the Englishman at home, in the colonies develops into a morbid desire for the respect and homage of those over whom he rules. Uneasily conscious of the moral insecurity of his position, he is further handicapped by finding himself an aristocrat without having been trained as one. His nose for what he considers derogatory to his dignity becomes keener than a bloodhound's, which leads him into the most frightful solecisms.[79]

In short, the necessities of imperial domination had turned the colonial Englishman from a sanctimonious Philistine into a reactionary Barbarian. A system where the power of the ruling elite was legitimated by ideas of white supremacy meant an otherwise rational and educated Englishman in the colonies now felt he had some automatic or God-given right to govern because of his breeding, rather like some blue-blooded aristocrat lording it over his serfs. As James wrote,

> It is not surprising that the famous English tolerance leaves him almost entirely. At home he was distinguished for the liberality and freedom of his views. Hampden, Chatham, Fox, who has so little to his credit on the Statute Book of England and yet whose memory is adored by so many Englishmen, Dunning and his famous motion: "The power of the Crown has increased, is increasing, and ought to be diminished," these are the persons and things which Englishmen undemonstrative as they are, write and speak of with a subdued, but conscious pride. . . . But in the colonies any man who speaks for his country, any man who dares to question the authority of those who rule over him, any man who tries to do for his own people what Englishmen are so proud that other Englishmen have done for theirs, immediately becomes in the eyes of the colonial Englishman a dangerous person, a wild revolutionary, a man with no respect for law and order, a person actuated by the lowest motives, a reptile to be crushed at the first opportunity. What at home is the greatest virtue becomes in the colonies the greatest crime.[80]

After exposing the inherent hypocrisy and brutality at the heart of British colonial rule, James then turned his attention to his fellow black West Indians:[81] "What sort of people are these who live in the West Indies and claim their place as citizens and not as subjects of the British Empire?"[82] James tore into the British government's line of "self-government when fit for it," citing the success and rapid growth during the 1920s of the TWA, which after 1925 even carried weight beyond Cipriani himself inside the legislative council, as proof, if proof were needed, that the people of Trinidad had always been manifestly "fit" to govern and protect themselves. James described the faith both Cipriani and the local, black, working-class population had in each other: "The mutual confidence which is so powerful a factor in our political life today, confidence in Captain Cipriani as an unselfish and fearless leader, confidence in the masses as a people worthy to be led."[83] In powerfully making the democratic argument for what he would later call "The Case for West Indian Self-Government," James was of course following in the footsteps of a long, rich tradition of Trinidadian nationalism. His homage to Philip was in many ways an acknowledgment of what he felt he owed to what Selwyn Cudjoe has termed "the intellectual tradition of Trinidad and Tobago," a tradition naturally shaped by the indigenous popular culture and African heritage of the Caribbean.[84]

That said, for James, despite this tradition, unfortunately his own class, the black middle class, were too often fundamentally Philistines. As he put it in *The Life of Captain Cipriani*,

> Between the brown-skinned middle class and the black there is continual rivalry, distrust and ill-feeling, which, skilfully played upon by the European people poisons the life of the community.... The people most affected by this are people of the middle class who, lacking the hard contact with realities of the masses and unable to attain to the freedoms of a leisured class, are more than all types of people given to trivial divisions and subdivisions of social rank and precedence.[85]

Hope, for James, therefore lay in breaking from his middle-class background, facing up to the reality of colonial rule, and crucially making "hard contact with [the] realities of the masses." As for the West Indian masses themselves, James followed Arnold in stressing that the "populace" were still in need of enlightenment and education, as it was in the interests of colonialism to ensure "there is much ignorance."[86] Kenneth Ramchand notes, "The mutually impoverishing alienation of the educated West Indian from the people" would be one of the concerns of the pioneering "barrack-yard" novel written by James in the summer of 1928, *Minty Alley*, with its main character a young intellectual named Haynes (a thinly disguised, younger James).[87]

While Matthew Arnold himself was not an anti-imperialist by any means, and he did not really think that ideas of liberty, democracy, and so on were fit for subject peoples of the empire, his tenets did perhaps constitute an implicit challenge to imperial ideology when taken up, transplanted to, and reinvented in colonial Trinidad by the Beacon Group. As Arnold put it in *Culture and Anarchy*, "The happy moments of humanity," the "marking epochs of a people's life," "the flowering times for literature and art and all the creative power of genius" come when "the whole of society is in the fullest measure permeated by thought, sensible to beauty, intelligent and alive" and you get "a *national* glow of life and thought."[88] A national glow of the life and thought of the people of Trinidad was not what the white colonial elite desired but James saw glimpses of it in calypso and Carnival, and the Beacon Group tried to foster it in the sphere of literature with their realist barrack-yard stories like James's classic "Triumph." As James cheerfully noted in *The Beacon*, "Trinidadians are, as I have good cause to know, and as the educated traveller can easily see from their bookshops, music-stores, newspapers, and conversations, a highly refined and cultured people."[89]

There was perhaps an Arnoldian dimension to the literature of the Beacon Group—as Ramcharitar has suggested, the writers themselves were predominantly middle-class "urbane Creoles," and in general their fiction was ideologically shaped by "the binary of decadent upper, and savage lower portions of society."[90] Yet while certainly detached in an important sense from the working classes of Trinidad, as Buhle notes, James himself "knew the characters of his stories well from strolling the slums near his own dwellings" in Port of Spain and "was known as 'a great man to listen' to all who chose to talk. . . . In return for their stories, he gave them sympathetic attention."[91] James would later explain why he was so "fascinated by the life of the barrack yard":

> They were living passionate independent lives, individual but all tangled up with one another. *Triumph* and my novel *Minty Alley* explored these lives. The characters in both understood one another. They had at the back some idea of God, some kind of philosophy that they believed to be African in origin (that is a mixture of folklore with Roman Catholic traditions). They formed a collective grouping. They lived their life independently of the kind of pretence or desire to imitate the British style which so preoccupied the middle classes. It was the vitality and collectivity of that life which fascinated me.[92]

As Caryl Phillips has noted of James's writing, it was "characterised by an unsentimental concern with the life of the working-class poor of Trinidad" and did not "resort to rhetorical flourishes in form or narrative technique." Moreover, while developing individual characters out of the collective struggles of the barrack yards he had observed, James embraced "the Trinidadian vernacular" as opposed to "the usual imitations of metropolitan English" and so his dialogue "provided his successors, most notably V.S. Naipaul, with a model."[93]

From Liberal Humanism to Parliamentary Socialism

C. L. R. James's aim of moving to Britain in 1932 was to try to find an audience as a novelist. The mass illiteracy and material poverty of colonial Trinidad meant there was no chance for him to make any kind of independent life for himself as a writer if he stayed. Yet while James was never primarily a political figure in this period, as all the contradictions of colonial rule slowly dawned on him, one might detect a slow radicalization from Arnold's liberal humanism toward the social democratic worldview of Captain Cipriani. The TWA had fraternal relations with the British Labour Party, and when Labour came to power in 1929 in Britain, James must have entertained at least some hopes that Labour would deliver on its declared commitment to self-government for the British West Indies. Though Labour betrayed such hopes—as James angrily noted at the end of *The Life of Captain Cipriani*—it seems that the ideas of reformist, parliamentary socialism and perhaps in particular Fabianism still made an impression. In 1929, one of the founders of Fabianism, Sidney Webb, Lord Passfield, had become colonial secretary, and in August 1929 the British government appointed a commission under the chairmanship of another Fabian, Lord Sydney Olivier, to investigate the crisis in the West Indian sugar industry.[94] Paul Breines has drawn attention to the intellectual attraction for independent socialist intellectuals of Fabianism, noting it offered "a non-dogmatic and vigorously practical approach to socialist reform centering around a program of public education and enlightenment." Indeed, one strand of Fabianism was its "activism and philosophically eclectic anti-determinism."[95] It would not have been much of a shift for an Arnoldian like James to embrace Fabianism, as both Arnold and the Webbs distrusted laissez-faire and believed in social reform and public enlightenment from above, through the state.[96]

Though the roots of James's later political radicalism lie in his experiences in Trinidad, the limitations of his thinking in this early period are all too apparent, as he later readily acknowledged: "My sentiments were in the right place, but I was enclosed within the mould of nineteenth-century intellectualism."[97] E. P. Thompson has noted the elitism and moralism of even the most powerful Victorian critics of Victorianism:

> In truth, Carlyle, Ruskin, Arnold—all were too ready to appeal to the working class to lead the nation forth in battles for objectives which they themselves had at heart, which were derived from their own special

discontent, but which had little relevance to the immediate grievances under which working people were suffering. They were too inclined to see the workers as the rank and file of an Army of Light, struggling valiantly for culture or for a new morality, under the generalship of themselves and a few enlightened leaders who had broken free from the philistine middle class.[98]

James himself would later come to describe Arnold's ideas as "philistine" in nature.[99] Yet we should not forget how his sincere attempt to live by the ideals of liberal humanism in which he aspired to be a "true apostle of equality" exposed the hypocrisy of British colonial rule. Moreover, in keeping with the tradition of "creative realism," James's "Arnoldianism" was both an act of improvisation (and so what resulted was different from anything imagined by Arnold himself) and also only provisional (as he began to politically radicalize and move from liberal humanism toward parliamentary socialism). Yet there is also an important sense in which it never entirely left him. "Culture," said Matthew Arnold, "is not a having but a being and becoming."[100] James's famous declaration, in *Beyond a Boundary*, that "it is not the quality of goods and utility which matter, but movement; not where you are or what you have, but where you have come from, where you are going and the rate at which you are getting there" has a clear echo of this.[101]

In 1967, E. P. Thompson paid tribute to "Comrade James" as "one of the first one thinks of" when one thinks of those "who were at the same time Marxist with a hard theoretical basis, and close students of society, humanists with a tremendous response to and understanding of human culture."[102] Yet long before his turn to Marxism, as "Comrade James" himself once noted, "the basic constituent of my political activity and outlook" had already been set out in "the 'human' aspect" of *Minty Alley*.[103] Unlike the young Haynes at the close of that novel, after his experience of the collectivity and creativity of the great mass of the "populace," the young James would not turn inward and retreat from his concern for the working poor to settle for the relative security and routine of a middle-class life. James was repeatedly presented with just such an opportunity, for by the late 1920s he was widely respected in Trinidad as an intellectual who had spent much of the last twenty years inside an elite educational establishment, both as a pupil and then as a part-time teacher. James recalled, "They wanted me to take a degree and teach [full-time] at the Queen's Royal College. What kind of garbage is that? What scope do you have in Trinidad as head of the college?"[104] Instead of making his peace with colonial oppression and following his father into a safe and conventional career, James turned outward once more, making his "voyage in" to imperial Britain, the "dark heart" of the British Empire. James's humanist spirit and instinctive identification with the great mass of working people would not be diminished after he left the barrack yards of Port of Spain. After all, colonial Trinidadian society, with its clear divisions of race, class, and power, which James had been able to view and analyze in its totality, from top to bottom, was in a sense only a microcosm of the world system, where white supremacy ruled under the flags of competing European empires.

The English Working Class and

the Making of C. L. R. James

"He feels himself one of the people. But it isn't that he likes workers. It is that he hates authority and respectability of any kind." So wrote C. L. R. James of Ishmael, the young writer who joins the crew of the *Pequod* in Herman Melville's classic novel *Moby Dick*. In his work of literary criticism *Mariners, Renegades, and Castaways: The Story of Herman Melville and the World We Live In* (1953), James argued that Ishmael was representative of "a completely modern intellectual," and there are similarities between Ishmael and James himself in 1932, when he boarded a ship, the HMS *Columbia*, heading across the Atlantic for Britain.[1] James later described how back then he felt "one of the people." He recalls, "I had been taught to look. I had an instinctive prejudice against what the establishment and authority was telling me."[2]

After James's arrival in London, in March 1932, his "first impressions" of the capital city had, if anything, reinforced those traces that still remained of his early Arnoldianism, with its elitist attitude toward the great mass of working people. As James wrote of the English in the *Port of Spain Gazette*, "Millions of these people are still mentally adolescent. They live on cheap films and cheap newspapers" and hold a "bizarre" deference to the "great" and good. James sometimes experienced racism when out and about with young, intelligent, white women, and he concluded, "There remains something in the average Englishman which can only be called sheer blind prejudice." He put it with a characteristically Arnoldian flourish, "The men are usually Philistines."[3] After only ten weeks, he left London for Nelson, in late May 1932, where he stayed with the legendary Trinidadian cricketer Learie Constantine until late March 1933, and those ten months in northeast Lancashire would be "ten months that shook the world" of C. L. R. James.

Learie Constantine was a year younger than James and had been part of the West Indies team that had toured Britain in 1923.[4] When Constantine returned to Britain, in 1929, this great all-rounder had been invited to stay and turn professional by Nelson Cricket Club, to play in the Lancashire League.[5] He would return to his native country most winters, and James, who by 1930 had set his sights on Britain, would listen avidly to his friend's descriptions of the highs and lows of adjusting to life there. As the first black player to make it in English league cricket, Constantine had been looking for someone to help him with an autobiography, and the literary-minded James was only too happy to write up his memories. In the winter of 1931, when Constantine heard James wanted to come to Britain, he was enthusiastic. "You come onto England. Don't put it off. Do your writing and if things get too rough I'll see you through."[6] Six months later, James turned up at the doorstep of the tiny four-room house on Meredith Street in Nelson that Learie shared with his wife, Norma, and their four-year-old daughter, Gloria.[7]

Nelson in 1932 was a small town of about 38,000 people, set among the Pennine hills and built around one industry, cotton.[8] The meteoric rise of that industry in Britain during the nineteenth century, in particular after the development of the power loom in the 1840s, led to small farming hamlets with easy access to coal, stone, and rail lines, as Nelson had, growing rapidly into small weaving towns. Rural laborers had flooded in to manufacture cotton cloth in the new mills mushrooming up in such areas. As Jill Liddington notes, "Immigrants made towns like Nelson and Brierfield. The textile communities stretching up the valley from Burnley to Colne all came to boast the same kind of pioneering roughness of far-flung frontier towns. The abrasive newness, coupled with the scarcity of large-scale paternalistic mill owners, became grafted onto existing democratic traditions that flourished locally."[9]

In Nelson, these existing democratic traditions were rooted in religious nonconformity, and Independent Methodism in particular, which stressed self-government and self-education. This, together with a large proportion of (increasingly independently minded and organized) women in the workplace as weavers, meant that political radicalism (ranging from Gladstonian Liberalism to the ethical and idealist socialism of the new Independent Labour Party, or ILP) had flourished.[10] Jeffrey Hill notes, "The status of women in Nelson was not structured in inferiority through the operations of the labour market," ensuring a relatively good "family wage," which "gave Nelson weavers in general, and women weavers in particular, a sense of importance and self-confidence," shaping the distinctive "cultural life of the town."[11]

Yet when James arrived in Nelson, in 1932, it must have seemed very far from the bustling little "frontier town" of perhaps fifty years before. Just as the rise of the Lancashire cotton industry had shaped the making of towns such as Nelson, the steady decline and fall of "King Cotton" since the Great War, as a result of rising foreign competition and a contraction in world trade, threatened to be the "breaking" of such weaving towns. With the onset of the Great Depression, in the 1930s, cotton exports halved in value and capacity in the industry fell. One in three cotton weavers in the region found themselves thrown onto the dole, not that the means-tested unemployment benefit added up to much when there was rent to be paid. Liddington notes that "the whole region was rapidly becoming derelict."[12] While Nelson, which specialized in high-quality cloth for the home and dominion markets, escaped the worst of it with a level of unemployment half the regional average, there were still no jobs to be had in those mills that had not already been shut down and boarded up.[13] In 1931, a quarter of Nelson's weavers were out of work, and by the time James arrived, local unemployment was still barely below 20 percent.[14] Darcus Howe remembers that James once told him about "the poverty of the English working classes" in this period and "the suffering of it. . . . They had to wrap their feet in cloth."[15]

Yet if James could not help but be struck by the general poverty in Nelson at this time, he was soon distracted by the particular nature of the company he kept, for by 1932, Learie Constantine — or "Connie," as he was known locally — had become something of a local legend. Salem, the Independent Methodist chapel, was perhaps Nelson's spiritual center; the Weaver's Institute, the base of Nelson Weavers' Association, was Nelson's social center; and the ILP's Vernon Street headquarters was perhaps Nelson's political center; consequently, Seedhill, home of Nelson Cricket Club, was arguably Nelson's artistic center.[16] Formed in 1890, and imbued with a democratic spirit, Lancashire League cricket was hugely popular, feeding off and contributing to intertown rivalries, and crowds of eight to ten thousand were common when Nelson played at home. Hundreds of people would even gather to watch the weekday evening practices in the nets.[17] Matches would generally take place at a time and place convenient to almost all, every Saturday afternoon during summer, always starting at roughly 2:00 p.m. and finishing at about 7:00 p.m. (with a fifteen-minute interval between innings), earning it a large, working-class following. Unlike more prestigious matches, where play would regularly stop and start according to the light conditions and in case of rain, Lancashire League cricketers continued playing in all but the worst of conditions, another factor contributing to its popularity.[18]

Constantine's outstanding performances, whether he was batting, bowling, or fielding, not only established Nelson's dominance over the rest of the league, but also inspired people at a time of economic hardship. Constantine's speed earned him the nickname "electric heels," while his short-range catching ability was equally outstanding ("as quick as a cat after a mouse").[19] As one Nelson resident, Ken Hartley, remembered, Constantine's cricket took people away from "the drudgery of cotton weaving and the insecurity that was in the area at that time. . . . He was a light at a time of despondency. The majority of people worshipped him." Hartley recalled that Constantine was perhaps "the first black person to come to Nelson. He lived opposite Whitefield school and the children used to stand outside his house and peer through the window to try and see him."[20] Yet despite the prevailing austerity, Hartley remembered only one notable racist incident, which occurred during a cricket match between Nelson and visitors (and great rivals) East Lancashire in 1929. Jim Blanckenburg, a white South African batsman who had been Nelson's professional from 1925 to 1928 before playing for East Lancashire, turned his back when Constantine tried to shake his hand on coming out to bat. Constantine recalled that he was "hurt, insulted, but above all furious." He remembered, "And that day I bowled 'bodyline' before the term had been invented. . . . I gave him a terrible beating and at the end of it he walked into our dressing room, naked except for a rain coat, and said to our skipper 'Look what that bloody pro of yours has done to me.' I am a black man, but that day he was black and blue."[21]

Constantine himself acknowledged the lack of hostility or suspicion toward him or his family within Nelson, in a speech he gave back home in Trinidad in 1936, which was reported in the *Port of Spain Gazette*. He declared, "In Nelson there are about four negroes. There are three in my family [*laughter*], and Mr. Alfred Charles whom we all know, makes up the quartet, and I may tell you nobody tries to make us feel inferior. . . . In Nelson I can go to the best home and the poorest home and the reception I get in both is very good."[22]

James remembered he "travelled" that first summer in Nelson in Constantine's "orbit" (an "orbit" he never quite left throughout his time in Britain), and he soon warmed to the town of Nelson.[23] Nelson Cricket Club granted him permission to play for them, and on Friday, May 27, the local *Nelson Leader* confirmed that James, a "West Indies student" and "gifted literary and sporting writer," was "practicing at the Nelson nets last night, and created a good impression."[24] A week later, on Saturday, June 4, James duly turned out for Nelson seconds at home against Todmorden. James came into bat at number 3, got out for nothing, and so contributed to Nelson's defeat, but he did redeem himself somewhat with his bowling, taking two wickets in seven overs for sixteen runs.[25] Next weekend, James played in a friendly against Radcliffe, which, thanks partly to Constantine's making fifty, Nelson won. James bowled ten overs, taking one wicket for thirty-five, before coming in to bat (this time at number six) to score another disappointing score (six runs) before being bowled out.[26] However, James remembers that amid all the "discoveries and excitements" of settling in Nelson, "one disastrous consequence" was that Constantine's batting had, like James's, got off to a poor start.[27] Nelson was only just holding its customary spot at the top of the league, and Constantine's form had become a topic of anxious discussion around the town. The *Nelson Leader* noted, "If Constantine could recapture the batting form he showed last season, when he headed the league with an average of 50, there would be little doubt as to the destination of the cup."[28] Though intrigued by cricket's huge local following, seeing at close hand the pressure on Constantine meant that when Radcliffe, after the game, asked James if he wanted to play for them as a professional, he turned them down. James recalled, "I badly needed some money and I loved to play cricket. But my reply was instantaneous: 'Who? Me? To go out there to bat, knowing that they have paid me, and to make nought. No, thank you!'"[29]

The Constantines were well known and respected throughout Nelson, and Constantine "knew cricket officialdom and the Press," and "mill owners, professional men."[30] James found that, cricket aside, conversation with these people did little to change his low opinion of the English. In conversation with the novelist Edith Sitwell in London earlier in the year, James had declared that D. H. Lawrence "would be judged by most people as the finest English writer of the post-war period," and James now may well have been reminded of one of Lawrence's poems, "How Beastly the Bourgeois Is."[31] "The fresh clean englishman," Lawrence wrote, was

Nicely groomed, like a mushroom
standing there so sleek and erect and eyeable —
and like a fungus, living on the remains of bygone life
sucking his life out of the dead leaves of greater life than
his own.
And even so, he's stale, he's been there too long.
Touch him, and you'll find he's all gone inside
just like an old mushroom, all wormy inside, and hollow
under a smooth skin and an upright appearance.[32]

However, wormy old fungus aside, James felt Nelson's Seedhill ground was "as pretty a cricket ground as you could see anywhere." He recalled,

I had imagined a small piece of grass, fighting for its life against the gradual encroaching of cotton factories, menacing with black smoke, machine shops and tenement houses. The ground is nothing of the kind. It is full-size, level and when you sit in the pavilion, you see on three sides a hill rising gradually covered with green grass, clumps of trees, houses here and there, beautiful as it seems only the English countryside can be beautiful.[33]

James would also find himself being increasingly pleasantly surprised as he had the opportunity in Nelson to gradually meet a wider cross-section of English people than had previously been possible in either Trinidad or London. Gloria Valère (née Constantine) remembered, "Our home in Nelson was like Grand Central Station—we had lots of visitors."[34] James remembered, "Some of Constantine's intimate friends who came to the house often found congenial company in me, apart from cricket. . . . These humourously cynical working men were a revelation[;] . . . some of the best friends a man could make I made during my first weeks in Nelson."[35] James also "quite by chance" made friends with Harry Spencer, who had inherited a bakery (with a tea room upstairs), which he ran with his wife, Elizabeth. The Spencers had three children at the same school as Gloria Constantine, and James remembers that Harry Spencer was a "cultivated man" who shared his love of literature, history, and music.[36] James later gave a vivid portrait of Spencer:

Harry Spencer was one of the most extraordinary men I have ever met or hope to meet. He wasn't extraordinary in any dramatic way but he was a man of sterling English character, an intellectual of the first order and a man of great generosity. . . . The bakery and tearoom were in the centre of Nelson and he himself lived with his wife and three children in a detached cottage on the outskirts of Nelson, with a wonderful view of the moor and mountain.

I got to know him early and quite by chance. We at once discovered our common interest in books and music, and a critique of society generally, and before long I spent hours every day at the bakery talking to Harry or reading, and night after night and at weekends I would be at his house where I became a member of the family. He was a shortish, rather stout man and you had to watch him carefully to see the intelligence and alertness of his face. . . . He had a good library, not much but well chosen, and a vast collection of gramophone records—Bach, Beethoven, Mozart and Schubert—classical, in which he and his whole family delighted.

Elizabeth Spencer, "a very gracious woman, devoted to Harry," was also to become a good friend and gave James his "first and few appreciations of English cooking—potatoes, roast beef and Yorkshire pudding, lamb, all sorts of vegetables which she grew herself." James describes how it was through Harry Spencer that he was able to develop his understanding of England and English history, and they even went for trips outside Lancashire, visiting York Minster and Warwick Castle. James recalled, "We were great walkers. On Sundays and public holidays we would set off in the morning at about 9 o'clock and walk ten or fifteen miles, talking all the way about what we saw or the relation between different parts of Lancashire. He would point out to me and talk with immense knowledge of farmhouses, mills, old castles, churches, cathedrals, and what happened there 100, 200, 500, 600 years before."[37]

Through his new friends, James soon discovered something in particular of the living tradition of class struggle and socialism in Nelson's history. As he noted at the time, "Nelson is a town where most of the working people are pretty closely united."[38] A stronghold of the ILP since the 1890s, it had come to be known as "Red Nelson" and even "Little Moscow" since the 1928 lockout designed to break the power of the militant Nelson Weavers' Association.[39] The labels stuck, despite the fact that they owed more to the militant trade unionism of the weavers and a Labour-dominated Council that, driven by local ILP members, often women, instituted an effective "municipal socialist" program of good housing, than to the influence of

FIGURE 2.1 Harry Spencer, 1933. © The British Library Board.
Nelson Leader, February 17, 1933, 13.

Marxism or the tiny local branch of the Communist Party of Great Britain (CPGB).[40] That said, in 1920, the Nelson ILP had been described as "Communist" at the Second World Congress of the Communist International, and as Jeffrey Hill notes, the ILP had "fashioned a socialist culture" in Nelson that "provided entertainment, enjoyment and recreation for politically minded people . . . [and] ensured that socialist politics were as much to do with the nurturing of good comradeship and moral commitment as with electoral decision-making in smoke-filled rooms."[41]

James was so taken by what he soon learned of this local history of working-class solidarity and activism that he related a remarkable story about a recent cinema boycott in Nelson to the readers of the *Port of Spain Gazette*. Cinema was very popular, as "for many, apart from the beauties of nature, an abiding love of the English people, the cinema is the only recreation." Sometime before James arrived, a company who owned several cinemas in Nelson had tried to cut the wages of their local projector operators, who seem to have launched a campaign through their union. "One day

I got into conversation with a quite ordinary person," James remembered, who told him how "the whole town of Nelson, so to speak, went on strike."

> They would not go to the cinema. The pickets were put out in order to turn back those who tried to go. For days the cinemas played to empty benches. In a town of forty thousand people you could find sometimes no more than half a dozen in the theatres. The company went bankrupt, and had to leave. Whereupon local people took over and the theatres again began to be filled. It was magnificent and it was war. I confessed I was thrilled to the bone when I heard it. I could forgive England all the vulgarity, and all the depressing disappointment of London for the magnificent spirit of these north country working people. As long as that is the stuff of which they are made, then indeed Britons never, never shall be slaves.[42]

Such lively stories of working-class history therefore directly challenged James's moralistic and elitist Fabian vision of social change from above. As he remembered, discussions with his new friends "brought [him] down to earth" as previously his "Labour and Socialist ideas had been got from books and were rather abstract."[43] Cedric Robinson has suggested that while in Nelson, "physically remote from the more typical sites of middle class radicalism and organised politics, James was enveloped by a more contemplative work and a more mundane politics."[44] Yet James did not only pass the time engaged in "contemplative work," watching Constantine play cricket, or "enveloped" in discussion of the poetry of D. H. Lawrence in Harry Spencer's teashop. James had read the anticolonial declarations of the British Labour Party while researching his biography on Cipriani, and he soon joined the strong local Labour Party.[45] However, while the Nelson Labour Party may well have been slightly "mundane" politically much of the time, it is likely that in 1932 it was almost certainly a "site" of "radicalism." Since the disaster of the October 1931 General Election, the "forward march of Labour" in Britain had been well and truly halted, as the parliamentary Labour Party was almost completely wiped out and was now retreating in some disarray. Ramsay MacDonald, the former Labour prime minister, Philip Snowden, the chancellor of the exchequer (who had once lived in Nelson), and others had already jumped ship to join the Conservatives and Liberals in a new coalition, contributing to the near destruction of their old party in the general election of October 1931.[46] While MacDonald now became prime minister again at the head of the new "National Government," Labour lost their old leadership, as two hundred of their most experienced MPs (including the then party leader, Arthur Henderson) lost their seats.[47] In the parliamentary seat that included Nelson, David Mayall has described how Labour's majority was overturned and "the monocled, cigar-smoking, bowler-hatted Linton Thorp unseated Arthur Greenwood by a margin of 7,686."[48]

Now with only fifty-two MPs, which included an ILP contingent, some of the new Labour leadership swung to the left dramatically, reflecting the wider party's dismay at the betrayal of MacDonald, and the sense that the 1929–31 Labour government had been brought down by the economic power of a hostile capitalist class, using extraparliamentary means. By 1933, Sir Stafford Cripps, one of the most prominent Labour MPs, would even go as far as to declare that it was wrong to say that "the capitalists will permit the change to be made within capitalism," and he wrote a pamphlet, "Can Socialism Come by Constitutional Methods?"[49] Cripps here repudiated the Fabian Sidney Webb's influential reformist perspective, noting, "It is not now a question of 'the inevitability of gradualness.' The one thing that is not inevitable is gradualness."[50] About the time James joined the Labour Party, the ILP, sixteen thousand strong, had just left it, calling on the working class to unite under the "red banner of revolutionary socialism."[51]

The shift of Labour to the left after the debacle of 1931 was a political expression of the wider economic crisis gripping British and, indeed, world capitalism. As world trade continued to fall long after the Wall Street crash in October 1929, the only thing growing in the British economy were the dole queues, which by August 1932 hit the three million mark. Almost one in four insured workers remained out of work until early 1933.[52] As the British historian Arnold Toynbee noted in 1931, "Men and women all over the world were seriously contemplating and frankly discussing the possibility that the western system of society might break down and cease to work."[53] James had picked up on this ideological crisis in his reading, and while looking around for explanations happened to make the acquaintance of a fellow bibliophile in Nelson, Mr. Frederick Cartmell.[54] James remembered he became "rather friendly" with Cartmell, who owned a small printing business and was "fanatically interested in books and bought regularly books which he had no time to read."[55] In June 1932, the first volume of Leon Trotsky's *History of the Russian Revolution* had been published in England, and Cartmell loaned James a copy.[56] James was eager to understand the October Revolution but recalled in the *History* that Trotsky "was not only giving details of the revolution itself, but he was expounding the Marxist theory of historical materialism." All this naturally appealed to a former History teacher like James, but "Trotsky referred not only to historical events and personalities, but he made references to literature as expressing social reality and social change."[57] Trotsky's references to James's other love, the literary classics that he had devoured in his youth, acted then like a "hook" that ensnared him, and he remembers he "was able automatically and without difficulty to absorb [Trotsky's] argument and the logical line that he presented."[58] In his *History*, Trotsky explained why workers, especially those in Britain, could follow conservative ideas much of the time yet retain the possibility of transformation into agents of their own destiny. One can imagine the thrill James must have felt as he read Trotsky's bold prediction that "Great Britain is headed for gigantic revolutionary earthquake shocks, in which the last fragments of her conservatism, her world domination, her present state machine, will go down without a trace. MacDonald is preparing these shocks no less successfully than did Nicholas II in his time, and no less blindly."[59]

The other book that Cartmell loaned to James later in 1932 was a new single-volume English edition of *The Decline of the West* (originally published in two volumes in 1918 and 1922), by the German Oswald Spengler. H. Stuart Hughes notes that Spengler's work "marked the full formulation of a cyclical theory of historical change and a comparative approach to culture which had been gradually establishing themselves among the implicit presuppositions of early twentieth-century thought."[60] Challenging many Eurocentric tenets from the perspective of global history, Spengler offered "an analysis of the decline of that West-European Culture which is now spread over the entire globe."[61] Spengler raged against "the machine" of capitalism, but while he thought it "in danger of succumbing to a stronger power," unlike Trotsky, Spengler did not see any hope in the international working-class movement.[62] Instead, Spengler pessimistically predicted the rise of a new breed of strong "Caesar-men" like the British imperialist Cecil Rhodes, "the first man of a new age" who "stands for the political style of a far-ranging, Western, Teutonic and especially German future."[63] Given the rising threat of fascism, the work's prophetic theme and title alone assured that it was popular with a wide range of British intellectuals.

Having been encouraged by meeting class-conscious "Western" workers in Nelson, James recalled that he "did not accept the decline that Spengler preached," though James was struck by Spengler's "strong sense of historical movement" and his discussion of "the relation between different historical periods and different classes."[64] James later told an interviewer: "What Spengler did for me was to illustrate pattern and development in different types of society. It took me away from the individual and the battles and the concern with the kind of things that I had learned in conventional history."[65] As such, Spengler's *The Decline of the West* complemented Trotsky's *History*, and James remembered that he "read and reread these two tremendous tomes."[66]

The search for some sort of understanding of this crisis-ridden system led James, while a guest of the Constantines, to give up playing cricket for Nelson and even miss watching them on occasions. James recalled, "I was reading hard. Night after night I would be up till three or four. I must have seriously discommoded that orderly household. Often I was abstracted and withdrawn. Literature was vanishing from my consciousness and politics was substituting itself. That was no easy transition."[67]

Constantine's daughter, Gloria, vividly recalls one incident:

My mother and I were in the living room and his bedroom was directly above the living room and my mother said to me "Do you smell something burning?" and so I said "I think so." She said "Oh my goodness" and so she went up the stairs. There is Nello [James] very busy writing or doing something or reading or doing something, sitting in a cardigan near an electric fire and his cardigan is on fire. And when my mother pointed out to him "Nello, you are on fire" he said "Oh my goodness, oh my goodness" but the thing is he hadn't a clue.

When Gloria was asked by Darcus Howe whether she knew or had any sense that she was in a house with a man of great importance, she replied: "No. Just remember that in our house, in Nelson, my father was the man of great importance." But as for James, "he always treated you, even though you were very small, as a person, he didn't talk down to you."[68]

Arguably, James's political attention at this time was still primarily focused on the West Indies, "back home," as opposed to Britain or Europe. Until he moved in with Constantine, James recalls, "I doubt if he and I had ever talked for five consecutive minutes on West Indian politics. Within five weeks we had unearthed the politician in each other." When James showed the manuscript of his biography of Cipriani to Constantine and told him he hoped one day to get it published, Constantine was again supportive: "Go ahead. Find out what it will cost and I'll pay. When you sell the copies at home you can pay me back."[69] Frederick Cartmell agreed to publish *The Life of Captain Cipriani: An Account of British Government in the West Indies*, and copies were sent back to Trinidad. James now thought it an appropriate time to get in touch with William Gillies, the British Labour Party's first ever international secretary, after being appointed in 1920, whom he was supposed to meet in London. On August 10, 1932, James wrote to "William Gillies Esq.":

> In suggesting that I should call on you Captain Cipriani of Trinidad informed me some weeks ago that he had written to you about me. Unfortunately an attack of writer's cramp caused me to leave London hurriedly and I am likely to be in the North for a considerable time. I have had printed for circulation at home a Life of Captain Cipriani, designed to place before the reader the essentials of the political situation at home. I am hoping to get an English edition which would reach the few who are interested in West Indian affairs. May I send you a copy?[70]

On August 16 Gillies — essentially a party functionary who was later characterized by his successor, Denis Healey, as "a cantankerous Scot who distrusted foreigners and hated all Germans" — replied: "I would certainly be pleased to receive a copy of your Life of Captain Cipriani. It was in April that Captain Cipriani wrote to me about your proposed visit. Now it is August. Towards the end of the month, I shall probably be going on holiday. But, in any event, I should like you to call upon us when you are passing through London."[71]

Gillies duly received a copy of the book and a covering note from James, who promised to visit when he was next in London. James noted he would have made contact in April, but said: "Having to leave London suddenly I decided to conclude and print the first half of my book before writing to you about it."[72]

Now a published author, and with encouraging notices about his book in the Trinidadian press, James ventured outside the Constantine household again. On August 27, 1932, as the cricket season drew to its dramatic close, James went to watch Nelson playing away to local side Rawtenstall, whose team included the legendary veteran bowler Sydney Barnes. Barnes, aged fifty-nine, was playing his last match. James remembers, "I was profoundly impressed by him, both as a cricketer and as a man. Coming home that evening the old journalistic spirit stirred in me." Paying homage to "the greatest of all bowlers," James wrote a report on Barnes's last match and showed it to Constantine, who suggested James send it to a friend of his on the *Manchester Guardian,* the famous cricket writer Neville Cardus, to see if any local papers might be interested. Cardus published the article in the *Manchester Guardian* on September 1 and called James in to see him.[73] As Stuart Hall notes, Cardus discovered that James "had a phenomenal memory and knew the scores every touring team had made since about 1901," and made him an offer he could not refuse, to help cover next year's cricket season.[74] Coupled with the fact that on September 3, Constantine scored fifty runs to ensure victory for Nelson in that year's Lancashire League (getting a standing ovation in the process), celebrations were clearly in order in the Constantine household. James remembers, "There was much rejoicing in our camp."[75]

The Great Lancashire Cotton Strike

It is doubtful that such celebrations lasted long. In August 1932, mill owners across Lancashire started to tear up existing agreements and bring in scab labor to try to restore profitability in the cotton textile industry, forcing cotton workers and weavers to take strike action to save their livelihoods. This was merely the latest in a series of attacks on wages and conditions in the industry since the Great War, and it followed an attempt by employers to force weavers to mind not just the standard four looms but six or even eight for an increase in pay—the "More Looms" system. In early 1931, employers in Burnley had tried to introduce the new system without union agreement but this had sparked a countywide lockout of 100,000 weavers. Under pressure not just from trade unions but also the Nelson MP and minister of health, Arthur Greenwood, employers had been forced to back down within a month. On May 11, 1931, protests in Nelson against the More Looms system (and against local blacklegs, in particular) had culminated in "the Battle of Pendle Street," when two thousand weavers were charged by mounted police. One demonstration held a few days later in solidarity with those arrested at that protest saw over half the town, over twenty thousand people, condemn the violence of the police and the injustice of the More Looms system.[76] On July 24, 1932, the struggle between employers and cotton operatives in Lancashire once again came into the open with a strike in Burnley. By mid-August, the *Nelson Leader* noted that while Nelson was still all quiet on the industrial front, "the scenes that [took] place at Burnley and Brierfield, however [were] unprecedented. . . . Nothing less than guerilla warfare [was] in progress between strikers and police."[77] In the same few days that James secured his job, almost all cotton workers in Nelson were suddenly forced to fight desperately for theirs. On Monday, August 29, 1932, 16,000 Nelson cotton workers (more than 12,500 of them weavers) went on strike, bringing the town to a complete halt. Torrential rain and flooding had initially kept the mood subdued, and, as the *Nelson Leader* noted, "never in the history of the town when a dispute or strike [was] in progress [had] such a tranquil and calm spirit prevailed." While the paper insisted it was just like a "holiday," this was not how either the desperate workers engaged in mass picketing of the mills or the British state, who called up extra foot and mounted police to protect the blacklegs, saw it.[78]

The mass strike, which raged for over a month across Lancashire, was a timely reminder of the power and resourcefulness of the working class for James, something he had not witnessed since striking dockers and their supporters shut down Port of Spain in 1919. On September 8, the Nelson Labour Party organized a demonstration in solidarity with the strikers, and it is likely James joined it, marching behind the Colne Borough band and banners expressing the bitterness and anger of those marching, demanding "Reinstatement for all weavers," "Union pay for all strikers," and "Down with the Means Test." Others proclaimed, "This is a Grand National Government," "1914–18 heroes—1932 zeroes," and "We refuse to starve in silence."[79] As the working people of "Little Moscow" once again proved themselves worthy of their best traditions by throwing themselves behind the strikers, one doubts the validity of Robinson's notion that James was able to "meet with British workers for discussions removed from super-heated circumstances" in Nelson.[80] Indeed, David Renton goes as far as to suggest that "it is hard to think of a town in Britain that was more radical at this time."[81]

In September 1932, while the strike was going on, an English edition of James's *The Life of Captain Cipriani* was published by Cartmell's printing firm, Coulton and Co. While forcefully putting the case for West Indian self-government rather than Crown Colony Government, James, following Cipriani, did not at this stage call for complete independence from Britain, but rather for autonomy for the West Indies within the Empire, autonomy along the lines of that in the white dominions. In some ways, the work was essentially a moral appeal to the British government's better conscience. Yet witnessing the desperate struggles of Nelson's striking weavers had made it all too clear to James that the "National" government simply did not have a "better conscience," and, as he remembered, his "Labour friends made merry with it." Nevertheless, James now saw a way of helping repay Constantine for helping publish it. As he remembers, "The people in Lancashire had an inordinate appetite for asking Constantine to come to speak to them, most often in church and similar organisations. It was something of a strain on him, but he was always ready to oblige." James began to go along with Constantine to these talks about the West Indies and soon took much of the strain off his friend, giving meetings himself. James recalled, "By the winter we were in full cry all over the place. . . . We were educating thousands, including ourselves."[82]

James certainly found speaking on West Indian self-government a political education, as he remembers he would introduce himself as being from the Caribbean and say, "We want independence, you know, and we hope the Labour Party will give it to us."[83] Yet the Lancashire working class were skeptical. James contends, "My audience was not wide but it was interested in politics."[84] Gandhi had visited Lancashire in 1931, and many of these workers knew that even under the last Labour government, those battling for national liberation in India had been imprisoned.[85] Moreover, they were highly cynical, having recently experienced MacDonald's Labour government. In May 1929, millions of workers had voted Labour into power with 287 MPs, establishing it as the largest party in the House of Commons.[86] The promised return to prosperity was soon dashed amid the "Great Slump," as what MacDonald called "the economic blizzard" blew any pledge to tackle unemployment off course. In August 1931, with unemployment now affecting more than one in five workers, MacDonald and Snowden attempted to implement a "solution" to the crisis, making savings by decimating the benefit paid to the unemployed.[87] When a minority of the cabinet rebelled at the apparent attempt to force the working class to pay for the capitalist crisis, the Labour government collapsed in disgrace. As James remembered, when he told the Lancashire workers of his hopes for the Labour Party in 1932, they said, "You make a mistake. Ramsay MacDonald, [Arthur] Henderson, Phillip Snowden, [Herbert] Morrison, they never gave us anything and we put them there; why do you think they would give you any?"[88]

Answers to questions like these demanded serious attention from James, and he remembers that while he "was a Labour Party man," he increasingly "found [himself] to the left of the Labour party in Nelson, militant as that was."[89] He had joined them, in part, as a way of showing solidarity with his comrades back in Trinidad, but now his belief that Labour was the best organization to deliver support for the struggle for West Indian self-government was being challenged. In 1928, Labour had pledged that in "Colonies with a Higher Form of Civilisation," such as the British West Indies, where the population was "culturally more advanced," that "the measure of self-government demanded by the inhabitants of these territories as a whole should be granted immediately." Cipriani, a delegate at the British Commonwealth Labour Conference held that year, had announced on his return to Trinidad: "We have this as a dead certainty, that the Labour Government will stand aback of the claim for self-government by any one of the Colonies asking for it."[90] At a time when ideas of West Indian autonomy and federation were spreading in the West Indies, in 1930, Cipriani moved a resolution in the Trinidadian legislative council, calling for a royal commission to investigate granting "self-government" to the colony.

While the governor of Trinidad was not overtly hostile — recognizing the popular mood — Neal Malmsten notes that "permanent officials at the Colonial Office were strongly opposed to the proposal." In February 1931, Sir Gilbert Grindle, an assistant undersecretary and former head of the West Indies Department in the Colonial Office, was quite unequivocal about the matter: "The vivid imagination of the negro tends to hypnotize him with words that he uses without understanding their meaning. I suggest, therefore, that the despatch should explain what 'self-government' means and tell them plainly they are not going to have it." In any case, Secretary of State Lord Passfield (Sidney Webb) overruled those inside the Colonial Office "who wanted to hold out the hope of a future inquiry." The only positive "action" taken with respect to the West Indies by the Labour government before it collapsed had been the appointment of a commission in August 1929 under the chairmanship of Lord Sydney Olivier to investigate the crisis in the sugar industry.[91]

West Indian nationalists had therefore every right to be aggrieved after the Labour government collapsed in ignominy without fulfilling its pledge. In March 1931, Lord Passfield had mooted the idea of a commission to discuss the possibilities for federation in the West Indies. In February 1932, out of power, Labour's Advisory Committee on Imperial Questions now asked Cipriani to draw up his vision for federation, receiving an angry retort about Labour's record while in government in response:

> What did the Noble Lord Passfield mean to convey by the statement that he would not appoint a Commission to enquire into and report on the Constitution of the British West Indies with a view to granting them Self-Government? Did the Noble Lord find it impracticable to assert his individuality as against his underlings in the Colonial Office? Did His Lordship find it inconvenient to divorce his baronial mantle from his Socialist and Fabian creed?[92]

In September 1932, the colonial secretary Sir Philip Cunliffe-Lister, a "diehard red-neck Tory slave driver," according to the Communist *Negro Worker*, had appointed the Commission for West Indies Closer Union under General Sir Charles Ferguson and Sir Charles Orr that explicitly ruled out looking at the question of self-government. Cipriani warned Gillies in late August 1932 that, as a result, "the Commission's visit [would] only make the situation more farcical than it now [was]," and progressive and labor organizations were likely to boycott it.[93]

Yet as a result of their failures in power, in opposition Labour were determined to try to make some amends, and their national conference in Leicester in October 1932 showed something of the party that James was a member of at that time. The Socialist League had formed to rally what was left of the Left of the Labour Party after the departure of the ILP, and the conference backed public ownership of joint stock banks and passed a resolution without discussion that declared "the main objective of the Labour Party is the establishment of socialism." The conference also endorsed a resolution asking that "on assuming office, either with or without power, definite Socialist legislation must be immediately promulgated, and that the Party shall stand and fall in the House of Commons on the principles in which it has faith."[94] The *Times* reported that "gradualism is dead. . . . The next Labour Government will be all red, and pledged to ride for an ignominious fall if it takes office a day before the country is as Socialist as the Labour Party Conference." Perhaps partially in dismay at this radicalism, Arthur Henderson, no longer an MP, resigned as party leader, to be replaced by George Lansbury, an avowed pacifist who already led the parliamentary Labour Party.[95] Cipriani seems to have been somewhat boosted by this conference, and he extolled the virtues of parliamentary socialism at a meeting of other West Indian progressives in Dominica, a "counter-conference" that committed itself to drawing up an alternative "suggested constitution" for the official commission. He assured his fellow militants: "In the British Labour Party, and Trades Union Congress, alone lie your safety and salvation."[96]

In early November 1932, James traveled back down to London and met up with Gillies, and for the rest of his time in Nelson the two corresponded frequently. The main theme that emerges from their correspondence is the seriousness with which James took his campaigning work for West Indian self-government, seeing to it that Gillies was kept up to date on all the latest political developments. While in London in early November, as the long-awaited Commission for Closer Union set off from London, James met a delegation from Grenada (including Theophilus Albert Marryshow, an elected member of Grenada's legislative council) that had succeeded in forcing the Colonial Office to consider evidence on matters of self-government during the commission's inquiry, even if they could not rule on it.[97] James ensured that Gillies got a copy of the Dominican West Indies Conference proposals for responsible government in a federal dominion.[98] James himself worked to stay informed about quite detailed and complex constitutional and economic matters.

No doubt through Gillies, while in London, James was introduced to Leonard Woolf, husband of Virginia, a Fabian former colonial civil servant and secretary of Labour's Advisory Committee on Imperial Questions.[99] Woolf had drafted the 1928 declaration of the Labour Party with respect to West Indian self-government, and he clearly felt a little embarrassed about the lack of progress since then. As James reported to Gillies, "I have seen Mr. Woolf and he has promised to do all he can."[100] James continued, "Mr. Woolf has consented to consider a pamphlet of 10,000 words dealing with the West Indian question, and I am at work on it. I must thank you for your kind assistance in this matter and hope he will see his way to print it. I shall send you a carbon copy of the M.S.S. I send to him. It may be useful as containing the argument in a concentrated form."[101]

As it happened, Woolf was impressed enough by reading a copy of James's *The Life of Captain Cipriani*, telling James, "I would like to publish this, but not all of it." James replied, "Go right ahead."[102] On January 12, 1933, James reported to Gillies, "I am sure you will be glad to hear that Mr Woolf is likely to publish an abridged edition of the *Life of Captain Cipriani* in the Day to Day series, and that [Kingsley Martin] the Editor of the

N.S.A.N. [*New Statesman and Nation*] has asked me to submit an article on the W.I. political situation."[103]

If James had been at all nervous when first speaking about the West Indies to people in Lancashire, by January 1933 it seems he was in his element and extremely confident. The local ILP in Nelson booked James for a meeting, describing him as "a well-known, intelligent and capable speaker."[104] Indeed, in front of this more politically radical audience James felt free to begin to tentatively generalize about British imperialism as a whole rather than just on its hold over the West Indies. The *Nelson Leader* published a report of a "fine lecture" by James on "Coloured Peoples under British Rule" that he gave to the Nelson ILP on January 22, 1933: "A fairly good audience turned up at the ILP rooms on Sunday evening to hear Mr. James, the West Indian, who is a good friend of Constantines, speak on the above subject. His audience were rewarded by the manner in which the speaker dealt with the subject, and also for the sympathy which he had for the exploited people under British rule, in their demands for independence." We also get a sense of James's disappointment with the Labour Party: "At the outset of his address, he stated that there was no hope of Labour's ideals being realised in this country unless the colonial peoples under British rule were granted independence. Mr. James then went on to deal with three sorts of coloured people who were subject to British rule, i.e. the people in Kenya, Burma and the West Indies." James's reference to Kenya is noteworthy, as it is possibly the first record we have of his discussing Africa at any length in any sort of public forum, certainly in Britain:

> Dealing with Kenya, he [James] said that thirty two years ago the natives were untouched by British rule and white civilisation. They could be classed like European rural districts today. Then the white settlers came, and in order to live, the natives had to pay a poll tax to the settlers. This meant that they had to have money, and in order to get money they had to work for the white settlers. Failing to pay the poll tax, they were punished and subject to criminal law. The natives of Kenya were keenly up against this imposition.

If the *Nelson Leader* reporter has quoted accurately, James's comments constitute a quite remarkable defense of African civilization before the impact of colonialism. The idea that without the benefits of Western "white civilisation" and British colonial officials, Africans could have established a form of society comparable with "European rural districts today" was a provocative challenge to prevailing racist assumptions. Nor was James unaware of the Kenyan people's struggle against the brutal white settlers who had stolen their land. The *Leader* reports, "There were many questions at the close, and there was no doubt that the audience very much appreciated the striking and interesting way in which the address was presented."[105]

James's speech seems to have tapped into the rich vein of anti-imperialism in Nelson. His was an audience, after all, whose grandparents may well have taken part in the boycott of cotton from the Southern states during the U.S. Civil War of the 1860s, and whose parents had objected to schools' being closed to celebrate the relief of Mafeking in the Boer War, on the grounds that for children to associate "rejoicing and holiday-making with war and bloodshed was distinctly immoral." It was an audience who may have marched against British intervention in the Great War, and in Soviet Russia afterward, and who now supported Gandhi's boycott of imported British cotton.[106] Nelson overall must have enabled James to imagine what a "Britain" without empire might look like; this small weaving town, with its pacifist and democratic traditions and socialist culture, was, if not quite fully "postcolonial," certainly the antithesis of anything he had read about before or seen in the sprawling metropolis of London.

This is not to say that James did not encounter any challenges in Nelson to his campaigning against British colonial power. In an article James wrote in 1964 for *New Society*, he described the peculiar relationship between the residents of Constantine's house, on Meredith Street, and the people of Nelson at that time:

> Except for a coloured man who used to push a cart about the street and collect garbage they knew nothing at all about coloured people, had never got into close contact with any. Mr. Constantine was a very distinguished cricketer and local hero; I was obviously a person with education and knowledge more than the average in Nelson. Mrs. Constantine conducted herself with great reserve and dignity. The three of us were very conscious that we were, so to speak, on exhibition. The people of Nelson began by believing that we had something to do with India. When they were made to understand that this was not so, that English was our native language and we had no native religion, they began to look upon us as an entirely unknown sort of people, unknown at least to them, and they began to look upon us as typical West Indians. So much

so that a local acquaintance who was very critical of my pronouncedly pro-Labour attitudes, having visited the West Indies, returned and did a powerful propaganda along the following lines: "All of them are not like Constantine and James. The Constantines and James are exceptional people, but don't think all of them out there are like these."[107]

More important, in the week in which the *Nelson Leader* carried the report of James's meeting, the Nazi leader Adolf Hitler was appointed chancellor of Germany. As a result, when James sent his article on the political situation in the West Indies off to the *New Statesman*, it was rejected. The commission on the West Indies had yet to report, but more crucially the spotlight was now on German politics. The appointment of Hitler may have passed without comment in James's letters to Gillies, but in terms of European politics it was as if an earthquake had hit. James reported with some sadness to Gillies in February 1933: "I have just received a letter from Mr. Kingsley Martin who has an article of mine on the West Indian situation. It says that unfortunately people are not interested and I must keep my eye open for anything in the news which may make an article topical."[108]

Gillies replied, explaining the thinking of the *New Statesman*'s editor and clearly wanting to offer some consolation but also finding it a little hard to elicit much sympathy for James's predicament in the aftermath of the Reichstag Fire: "I have been away on the continent, and since my return have been preoccupied with the German situation. . . . It is quite true that political articles in the *New Statesman* must be topical and alive." Of course, Gillies added, "literary articles may be as dead as mutton."[109] James's enthusiasm for and commitment to the struggle for democracy in the West Indies do not seem to have been dimmed, and he continued his speaking tour about the West Indies. On Sunday, February 19, "Mr. C.L.R. James of Nelson" addressed two "large gatherings" at Charlesworth Independent Chapel (near Glossop), with Constantine presiding.[110] Two weeks later, on another Sunday morning in early March, James was invited to introduce the weekly political discussion class of the Nelson Labour Party. As Nelson Labour Party's paper, the *Nelson Gazette*, put it when advertising the meeting, "Next Sunday Mr. C.L.R. James will deal with the present policy of the Labour Movement, and the speaker will have something of importance to say, and it will no doubt be delivered from an unusual angle."[111] By the time he left Nelson, in late March 1933, the *Nelson Leader*'s "Table Talk" columnist noted, "Mr. James has become a familiar figure in the town, and has also lectured and spoken on various topics from several local platforms."[112] It is perhaps also worth quoting from a letter that James wrote to Gillies on March 12, 1933, just before he returned to London to begin working for the *Manchester Guardian*:

> My pamphlet [*The Case for West Indian Self-Government*] will be out on the 21st of the present month. I have an idea in mind for circulating it among various branches of the Labour Party, as many as I can manage. By the time I have written to them and pay for the transport of the book, profit will have vanished, but it does not matter. I would like to have copies scattered in the right place among all supporters of the movement. Can you recommend me to any publication where I can get a list of the secretaries of the various Labour groups? And if it is not too much to ask, and would not be out of place in your official position, could you give me a line or two recommending the book. Lord Olivier has written a formal letter to me praising it. Someday I hope to go from Labour Party Group to Labour Party Group trying to interest them in the West Indies but I cannot afford that as yet and want to try this means. . . . I have been speaking to the Nelson Labour Party and the Colne and hope to do some more before I leave the North.[113]

The correspondence with Gillies not only reveals James to be a committed activist with respect to anticolonialism but also an intellectual who, while loyal to the Labour Party, was also thinking seriously about his relationship to the international Communist movement. In the context of the Great Depression, the growing menace of fascism, and a Labour government that had so manifestly failed to represent the labor movement, a political radicalization took place among many in British society. As James later remembered, "It was this period of disillusionment with British capitalism which preceded a wave of sympathy for Stalinist Russia and the skilfully propagated 'success' of the Five Year Plan" as an alternative to the crisis-racked West.[114] Accordingly, the CPGB emerged from its isolation, when it had just over 2,500 members in November 1930, mostly in core bases of Scotland and South Wales, to grow to 9,000 members nationwide in 1932, a result of its work among the millions of unemployed, a figure that was to grow further.[115] The Nelson CPGB was small, but the members threw themselves into the struggles of the cotton weavers with an energy that put most Labour Party members to shame. Even back home in Trinidad, while

James's *The Life of Captain Cipriani* was "a grand success," it was also facing some criticism for its moderate tone, and one old friend even asked why James did not call for "a classless society, a communist society."[116] James himself must have puzzling over the very same question, not least because at this time the international Communist movement took questions of imperialism and racism rather more seriously than the British Labour Party. Since March 1931 the Scottsboro case, which saw nine black boys charged with the alleged rape of two white girls on a train in Alabama, had made headline news internationally.[117] At a time when all but one of the boys were facing the death penalty, the Communist Party in America were at the forefront of organizing their legal defense, through an organization they had founded in 1922, International Labour Defence (ILD).

Indeed, the ILD was even one of the topics James and Gillies had discussed when they met in November 1932. James himself does not seem to have previously heard of the organization, but questions had been asked about it back in Trinidad in the *Port of Spain Gazette*, after Vivian E. Henry, TWA secretary, showed support for it on a visit to Europe. In June 1932, Ada Wright, mother of one of the accused "Scottsboro Boys," spoke in London as part as a European speaking tour of the ILD, a meeting attended by "a large number of white and coloured workers."[118] It seems possible that Henry was among those inspired, and in early July 1932, he had attended a conference in Berlin organized by German Red Aid, a group affiliated with the ILD.[119] While leading members of the Labour Party had stressed their support for the campaign to free the Scottsboro Boys, its members were forbidden from involvement in Communist-led groups such as the ILD. Gillies took care to warn James—and clearly, he hoped, through James, Henry also—about the hidden agenda of the ILD:

> With regard to the International Labour Defence, I have very little doubt as to the identity of this organisation. In this country, the International Labour Defence (British Section) is one of the ancillary organisations of the British Communist Party. It was formerly known as the International Class War Prisoners' Aid (British Section), or, on the Continent, the Red Aid. But there appears to have been a change of name, and with regard to that point, enquiries are being made. The change of name may not be unconnected with the fact that membership of the International Class War Prisoners' Aid is incompatible with membership of the Labour Party.[120]

At this time, relations between Labour and the CPGB, having steadily deteriorated during the 1920s, were particularly sour, largely as a result of the current Communist policy of "class against class," which argued that the leaders of Labour were "social-fascist labour bureaucrats."[121] James seems to have been persuaded by Gillies's anticommunism to some extent. In a letter sent on November 10, James informed Gillies: "[I have] written to Captain Cipriani about Henry's visit to Europe and the dangers of his getting entangled with the Communist Party. This, however, I did quite unofficially."[122] Unofficial or not, James's letter came too late for Henry, who had already got himself "entangled."[123] Gillies wrote to James on November 21: "The lady who called here told me that Mr. Henry had gone to Moscow. As an international Congress of the 'Mopr' organisations is being held in Moscow from November 10 to 25, it is probable that the lady was right. Is it not so? The 'Mopr,' made up of the initials of the Russian title, is another name by which this organisation is known on the Continent." Gillies added, "Therefore, do not be surprised if your organisation [the TWA] is now being attacked as Bolshevik, or as one having Bolshevik affiliations."[124]

James seems to have found the information Gillies sent to him about the ILD and its links to the Communist International quite fascinating, for although he was reading Trotsky while he was in Nelson, he still had much to learn about the contemporary British and European Left.[125] In a letter James wrote to Gillies in February 1933, for example, he innocently confused the Labour Party's *Labour Magazine* with the CPGB's *Labour Monthly*.[126] While James certainly did not see himself as a "Bolshevik" at this time, he did regard British colonialism as a far greater "danger" than Communism. It is perhaps worth citing a letter Captain Cipriani wrote to Gillies in November 1932 to remind us of why anticolonialists such as James were bitterly opposed to the British government:

> It would be well to remind the Home Government that the time has long since past when we in the Colonies are going to sit still and swallow everything that is pushed down our throats. . . . We are sick and fed up to the back teeth of all this mawkishness and if you do not help us to run and administer our own affairs then we will be bound to make every effort on our side to free ourselves from this rotten form of industrial and economic slavery in the way that seems most satisfactory and profitable to ourselves. I had at one time a great deal of confidence in the Labour Party, I still have a great deal of confidence in many of its

members, but you will pardon me when I say that frequent and repeated disappointments have shaken that confidence to its very foundations and so say all of us. The Englishman's word is no longer his bond, we the small peoples of the Empire realise that we are there for only one thing, the exploitation and oppression of the English imperialist and foreign capitalist.[127]

Overall, it had not taken long for the young writer "Ishmael," having debarked from the ship in Plymouth and boarded the far bigger ship of Britain, to sense that not all was well on board. If the HMS *Britannia* was not quite the *Pequod* Ishmael boarded under the monomaniac Captain Ahab, during the Great Slump of the 1930s it might as well have been. As Eric Hobsbawm has written of British capitalism at this time, "Never did a ship founder with a captain and crew more ignorant of the reasons for its misfortune or more impotent to do anything about it."[128] How ironic that James should find one of the few sections of the crew that did not feel either ignorant or impotent amid the crisis in a northern industrial town named after Britain's greatest admiral, Lord Nelson.[129] In *Mariners, Renegades, and Castaways*, James wrote that Ishmaels "are dangerous, especially when they actually leave their own environment and work among workers or live among them."[130] The ordinary working people of Red Nelson certainly helped James become "dangerous." On James's eightieth birthday, in 1981, E. P. Thompson suggested that his friend was like Tom Mann, in that he intended to "grow more dangerous" as he grew older.[131] Thompson was right. In his *Eightieth Birthday Lectures*, when someone suggested to James that the British working class was somehow too "backward" and not "educated" enough for socialism, the great socialist would point out that on the contrary it was his working-class friends in Nelson that had "helped to educate [him]."[132]

Perhaps even more strikingly, James gravitated toward revolutionary politics while avoiding what Isaac Deutscher called the "vulgar Marxism" of orthodox Communism. Even some who later worked politically with James, like Cornelius Castoriadis, assumed that he simply must have come under Moscow's spell at some point.[133] After all, a fellow member of the TWA, Vivian Henry, had been recruited into the networks around the Communist International when he visited Britain around the same time. Unlike Henry, James did not go to Moscow but settled in the "Little Moscow" of Nelson, where he had become acquainted not with Josef Stalin but with

Leon Trotsky.[134] In any case, while James left Nelson to begin professional work as a cricket reporter, despite still harboring dreams of making it as a novelist, he did not now try to ingratiate himself with the literary elite in Bloomsbury on his return to London. Instead, he vividly once recalled: "Hitler came to power in 1933 and . . . the contemporary world had been swept into politics, political life. . . . I got swept into politics."[135]

C. L. R. James, Race, and Revolutionary Politics

"I had not been in Europe two years before I came to the conclusion that European civilization as it then existed was doomed," James later recalled.[1] In general terms, it should be noted that such a conclusion was of course far from unusual at the time. The Wall Street crash in 1929 had been a critical factor in the plunge of Europe, a continent irrevocably scarred by the destruction of the Great War, into a devastating economic crisis that had profound political and ideological consequences, most strikingly leading to the triumph of Hitler's Nazis in Germany in 1933 on the back of mass unemployment. James's political radicalization in general, and his orientation toward Marxism in particular, was an entirely understandable reaction to the worst crisis in the history of capitalism. In 1933, E. H. Carr would declare Marx had "a claim to be regarded as the most far-seeing genius of the nineteenth century and one of the most successful prophets in history."[2] As Stuart Macintyre has noted of this period, "Erstwhile critics such as [G. D. H.] Cole, [Harold] Laski and even the Webbs revised their anti-Marxist attitudes, and Cole wrote that 'To look around on the world today with seeing eyes is to be a Marxist, for Marxism alone explains what is going on.'"[3] The hopes raised by the Russian Revolution, and the apparent success of the First Five-Year Plan in enabling the Soviet Union to avoid the nightmare of unemployment, meant that Communism offered a serious, alternative way out of the crisis, and one that, unlike fascism, stood, theoretically at least, for more, not less, democracy in the process. As Carr once noted, he had been born in 1892 and so "grew up, not in the high noon but in the afterglow of the great Victorian age of faith and optimism, and it [was] difficult for [him] even today to think of a world in permanent and irretrievable decline."[4] In turning to Marxism, James, the "Victorian with the rebel seed," was in similar fashion affirming his optimism, his faith in the potential for humanity to progress.

Yet if in general James's turn to revolutionary politics was quite understandable, his precise political and intellectual evolution here perhaps demands closer attention. At a time when the appeal and attraction of Soviet Communism was perhaps at its height among intellectuals, James returned to London from Nelson in March 1933 having read and reread the first volume of Trotsky's *History of the Russian Revolution*, before joining the minuscule British Trotskyist movement just over a year later. Clearly, the importance of reading Trotsky's masterful three volumes of historical analysis cannot be underestimated, and it shaped him profoundly as it did many others. "I had plunged into a river from which I was never to emerge," James recalled. He remembered,

> In 1933 I began to work as a cricket reporter. . . . I bought Volume I of the *History of the Russian Revolution* . . . but during the summer of 1933 when I was making some money Volumes II and III became available and I bought them intending to read them when the cricket season was over in September. By the end of 1933 I had re-read Volume I . . . and had read Volumes II and III as I had never read any books before except *Vanity Fair* and Kipling's *Plain Tales From the Hills*.[5]

Moreover, alongside James's turn toward Trotsky's brand of revolutionary Marxism had gone a radicalization away from any identification with imperial Britain and toward a militant vision of Pan-African liberation. As Hitler took to the world stage, proclaiming the supremacy of the Aryan race, James found himself more and more openly declaring solidarity with the oppressed of the earth. Tensions emerged between James's identification of himself as "British" and his developing revolutionary "black internationalism," expressed through his loyalty to not just an increasingly anti-imperialist vision of "West Indian self-government" but also his growing commitment to more radical transnational identifications with black Africans and other people of African descent. James's early turn toward Trotskyism would be critical in enabling him to advance and develop a Marxist perspective on black and colonial liberation struggles across the African diaspora amid the changing relationship of the Soviet Union and the Communist International to such questions during the 1930s. This chapter will therefore examine how James in Britain first came to embrace what Kent

Worcester has called "class struggle Pan-Africanism," before moving on to a discussion of how that form of militant black internationalism manifested itself in practice.[6]

The League of Coloured Peoples

In March 1933, as Learie Constantine was helping James move from Nelson to London, he introduced his friend to Dr. Harold Moody, a Jamaican who had been resident in London since 1904. In 1931 Moody had founded the League of Coloured Peoples (LCP), and he now invited James to join.[7] Roderick Macdonald has noted that the LCP "may lay claim to embodying the first conscious and deliberate attempt to form a multi-racial organisation, led by Blacks, although with a membership that for its first ten years was predominantly white." The fact that no white person was ever elected to the LCP executive marked it out from both its larger American counterpart, the National Association for the Advancement of Colored People (NAACP), as well as the liberal Joint Council to Promote Understanding between White and Coloured People in Great Britain. "The League of Coloured Peoples has as its object the purpose of stating the cause of the Black Man," declared the opening editorial of the first issue of its journal *The Keys* (July 1933).[8]

From March 24 to 26, 1933, James attended the LCP's first weekend conference at High Leigh, Hoddesden, Hertfordshire, along with over forty others from countries including the Gold Coast, East Africa, Sierra Leone, the United States, and from across the West Indies. Among the speakers on the Saturday was LCP secretary Stephen Thomas, a West African barrister and lecturer at the London School of Economics, who spoke on the "West African" and "deplored the fact that there was but little contact between the Africans in various parts of Africa itself, and even less contact with their brothers and sisters in other parts of the world." That afternoon, James, described as a "brilliant young man" who had recently published *The Life of Captain Cipriani* and *The Case for West Indian Self-Government*, spoke eloquently in the speech "The West Indian," and it is perhaps worth reproducing some of *The Keys* report of his speech:

> Mr. James began by showing how the black man in the West Indies had been shorn of all African civilization and had been engulfed by Western civilization. This meant that there was no spirit of nationalism, which

gave force to democratic movements in other countries. To offset this, the similarity in language, religion and education, with schools open to all races on equal terms, meant that there was no clash between a Caste or Tribal system, and modern democratic ideas.... The greatest problem among the Negroes in the West Indies was an internal one—based on varying shades of complexion. Any united movement in the West Indies had to be based on the black masses, or it was doomed. The working people were splendid material and showed their true worth in the late war.... The officials were not very keen however in raising the standards and educational requirements. They felt that as long as the West Indies was agricultural, no education for the masses was needed.... Only absolute freedom would give the pent up energies of the West Indian the necessary outlet. Crown Colony Government was a cancer eating into the very vitals of the nation. There was a definite need of a West Indian consciousness, and a pride in the matters that pertain to our group.

James's militant nationalist speech sparked a "lively discussion," and he doubtless joined in other debates on "the Indian student," "the East African," and "co-operatives in Africa." The official report of the conference noted: "Speakers from various parts of the world had expressed the need for unity and cooperation, because this was a very critical period in the history of our race."[9] Though not overtly political, in 1933 the LCP supported the Scottsboro Boys campaign and condemned the recent revival of lynching in America.[10] Involvement in the LCP must have further opened James's eyes to racism in Britain and internationally, while constituting in itself a new multiracial community of resistance. James would soon become a member of the LCP executive, and he later recalled that "there was some propaganda, there was agitation." As James remembered, "Moody would be able to speak now and then to a member of Parliament, he would get a letter in the papers, and anything in those days mattered because there were too few black people around, and here was somebody who wasn't an insignificant person, who was a well-established medical practitioner."[11]

Such "middle-class respectability" was much prized among LCP members as part of their ideology of "imperial Britishness," alongside what Anne Spry Rush has called their "missionary-like faith in the benign quality of Britain's civilising mission." Indeed, "the League valiantly attempted to reconcile its ideal Britain, devoted to justice and fair play, with the finding that, as one member from South Africa noted, 'the treatment of coloured people in London almost forces one to believe that colour bar is the policy of the British Empire.'" Moody's concern with cultivating pride in "Britishness" and the "Christian" empire among black colonial subjects can be seen, for example, in July 1933, when the LCP presented a highly decorated copy of *The Keys* to the Prince of Wales.[12] One wonders what the Prince of Wales might have made of James's description of Crown Colony Government as a "cancer."

Nonetheless, James at this point still shared much of the middle-class ideological worldview of other league members when it came to Britishness and in May 1933 would publicly stress that though committed to agitating for "full democratic control" for West Indians, "there [was] no treason in this." James elaborated on his position:

> The West Indian Negro in the West Indies is the most loyal subject in the British Empire, and any move towards giving the island to any other country would immediately cause revolution. But perhaps you will allow me to say that the coloured West Indian of decent up-bringing and good education on holiday or studying for the professions in England is often treated in such a way that he loses much of the goodwill which he brought with him. Englishmen who respect the Empire would do well not to forget that it is the West Indians studying in England who will be moulding West Indian political opinion in the future.[13]

In August 1933, James wrote a "shocking exposure" titled "Slavery To-day" for *Tit-Bits* magazine as part of the wider commemoration in Britain accompanying the centenary of the official abolition of slavery across the British Empire: "In 1833, the Act of Abolition involved no more than 700,000 slaves. *Today, a century after, there are more than 5,000,000 slaves, distributed throughout fifteen different areas of the world.* This, then, is what we have to face a century after the Emancipation. Five million fellow human beings still in bondage and sentenced to a lifetime of servitude and suffering."

James declared "some direct *personal* interest" in the suffering of "the shackled who [had] no future" as he was "the great-grandson of a freed slave." He reasoned, "Although I am still a young man I knew personally a great-aunt of mine who had been a slave in her early days, and I have often heard her speak of what slavery meant in those days before the Abolition." James went on to indict the continuing horrors of slavery for many Africans, noting "there *are still thousands of slaves within the British Empire.*" Yet

Mr. C. L. R. James, law student
and writer, is a member of The
League of Coloured Peoples

FIGURE 3.1 C. L. R. James, 1933. © The British Library Board.
All rights reserved. *Tit-Bits*, August 5, 1933, 16.

James, despite his own private research on the Haitian Revolution, "the only successful slave revolt in history," declared in public that the best hope for liberation from the barbaric bondage of slavery lay with making an appeal to the better conscience of the British government, in order to force the League of Nations to act:

> Britain led the way one hundred years ago, and by an interesting coincidence it was British efforts a few months ago which have led to the setting-up of a Permanent Commission of the League of Nations to deal with slavery. . . . In that there is a weapon close at hand which can end the evil. But first we must set our own house in order. We owe that at least to the memory of Wilberforce and the other pioneers whose work we are celebrating today. Then pressure must be brought to bear on the League to see that all nations who tolerate slavery are indicted, with no concealment and respect to none. Public opinion, ten times more powerful now than it was in 1833, will do the rest. It worked a miracle then, it can do so again.[14]

Defending African Art

In mid-May 1933, *The Listener*, the official journal of the British Broadcasting Corporation, had advertised that "a representative exhibition of African sculptures and textiles [was] at present on view at the Lefèvre Galleries" in London, and carried an article on "Negro Art" by Stanley Casson, a Fellow of New College, Oxford, and an expert on classical antiquities, author of *The Technique of Early Greek Sculpture* (1933). As Casson noted, "The present exhibition at the Lefèvre Galleries affords a unique opportunity to study African art at first hand."[15] James took the opportunity and later noted that the exhibition "was the first real impact that Africa had on [him]," because before then he "was completely unaware that Africa had artistic structures and traditions of its own."[16] James recalled the visit:

> I was about thirty-two years old and for the first time I began to realise that the African, the black man, had a face of his own. Up to that time I had believed that the proper face was the Graeco-Roman face. If a black man had that type of face he had a good face, and if he didn't, well, poor fellow, that was his bad luck. . . . I went to this exhibition, I bought the catalogue, I bought some books.[17]

Those books were to prove necessary to counter Casson's review of the exhibition, "Negro Art." Casson damned African art first with faint praise, and then damned it in more time-honored fashion, noting it "has remained always on the primitive level" and that the work of the "Negro sculptor" is the work of what he "might call a grown-up primitive." Casson continued, "And by primitive art I mean art that is produced by men who have the minds of simple children and the hands of grown-up men."[18] The letters page of *The Listener* soon carried a response to Casson from one "C.L.R. James" from "Hampstead," in London, defending African art:

> It is inconceivable to me how anyone looking at the Pahouin Venus in the present exhibition in the Lefèvre Galleries, some of the masks in the British Museum, and figures like those on p. 95 and p. 103 of Guillaume and Munro's book on *Primitive Negro Sculpture*, can continue to base his criticism on the theory, daily more and more discarded by anthropologists, that the mind of the African, in his so-called "primitive" condition, was the mind of a child.[19]

The next issue of *The Listener*, June 7, 1933, saw Casson reply, noting, "Mr. James has heaved the heavy anthropological brick at my head." Casson went on, "Will Mr. James come off his high horse and tell me exactly what modern anthropologists really think about Negro art, if they think much? In the meantime, if he will read *L'Art Primitif*, by G.H. Luquet, in [Paul] Rivet's *Biblioteque d'Anthropologie*, he will learn much to his advantage, as this is a solid anthropological work. From it, it is quite clear that Negro adult minds and child minds are alike."[20]

Casson was clearly trying to call James's bluff here, trusting that his critic would bow in deference to his knowledge of anthropology, particularly the work of French anthropologists. But James was having none of it:

> First, is Mr. Casson quite clear in his own mind about what he means by the term "primitive" Negro? There is a general belief that Negroes in Africa before the coming of the slave-traders were everywhere savage. Among books of the early voyagers which will disprove this and testify to the standard of civilisation many had reached, is [Richard] Hakluyet's *Voyages to Guinea*. But there is an even greater complication. Two important groups of African people have remained untouched by European civilisation until comparatively recent times. The Routledges in *With a Prehistoric People*, described the Kikuyus of Kenya, who until western

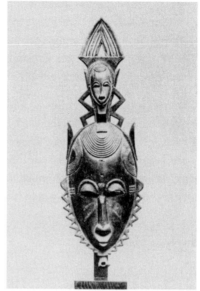

FIGURE 3.2 Ivory Coast figure, fifteenth century.

FIGURE 3.3 Ivory Coast mask, Mossi, fourteenth century.

civilisation touched them, lived a life, in the opinion of Mr. McGregor Ross, superior to that of many modern European peasants. [Emile] Torday and [T. A.] Joyce, in their *Notes Ethnographiques . . . sur les Peoples . . . Bushongo,* have described the Bushongo who founded a vast empire, excelled in industry and art, and showed, in Emil[e] Torday's own words, "high social and political organisation and culture." Their great period goes back at least three hundred years, yet up to half a century ago or less, they were quite unknown. Were they "primitive" Negroes? I do not believe that the adult Bushongos, for instance, had the minds of children. And even if it is admitted that some of these Negro tribes who produced fine work were of the most primitive type, yet [Alexander] Goldenweiser's chapters on the mentality of early man in his book *Early Civilisations,* and Chapter 4 of Franz Boas' *The Mind of Primitive Man* [1911], are a warning to those who make dogmatic statements about the workings of the primitive mind. Goldenweiser quotes Wundt: "This, however, does not imply that within the narrow sphere that constitutes his world the intelligence of primitive man is inferior to that of cultural man." It does not help at this stage for Mr. Casson to say that "artistically" the Negro has the mind of a child. That statement by itself means nothing. Lafcadio Hearn says that great artists are men who go through life retaining the freshness of outlook of children. That is a very different sort of remark from Mr. Casson's sweeping statement that Negro adult minds and child minds are alike.[21]

One gets some sense of the breadth and depth of James's reading in this letter, which quotes from the work of the Hungarian anthropologist Emile Torday, the American anthropologist Alexander Goldenweiser, and the legendary German antiracist anthropologist Franz Boas.[22] Casson was to have the last word, but was conciliatory, ending the debate on the grounds that he "must leave Mr. James to his researches."[23]

Studying Marxism

It was dangerous advice, for although James was a member of the LCP and also the Labour Party, his principal object of research was increasingly Marxist theory. James used to frequent Student Movement House in Russell Square, in central London, and at this "official society for students mainly from abroad," James remembered that many of the students "were believers in Marxism but for the most part they were supporters of Stalin and the Communist Party."[24] He also recalled meeting black colonial seamen in London "who were involved in the transportation of [the Communist publication] Negro Worker to the islands of the West Indies" around this time.[25] Reading Trotsky's History alongside odd discussions with left-wing international students and politically radical black seamen ensured that James began to pick up something of the intensity and importance of the controversy between the exiled former Soviet commissar for war and those with loyalty to Stalin over the nature of the Russian Revolution and Marxism itself, and he remembered he realized he needed to undertake his own "serious and concentrated study" of both.[26] James had the good fortune to now come across a left-wing bookshop in central London called Lahr (on 68 Red Lion Street), which Jonathan Rose has described as "a mecca for down-and-out Nietzscheans and scruffy poets" during the 1930s.[27] Here James found and bought two volumes of Leninism by J. V. Stalin, which he carefully proceeded to read "pencil in hand." James remembers that Stalin's book was heavy going: "Practically from the first page Stalin's factual history, his analysis and his style appalled me but I was trained in searching into [and] balancing antagonistic accounts of historical events. Both Trotsky and Stalin referred continuously to Lenin. Obviously I had to read Lenin[,] . . . whom I read in the popular series of *Selected Volumes*." Moreover, Trotsky, Stalin, and Lenin "continuously referred to Marx." James soon realized that even more study was now necessary:

> So in accordance with my ingrained habits which I had brought from the Caribbean I bought Marx seeking as usual what Othello called "the ocular truth." I gobbled up Volume I of *Capital*, for quite a while tackled volumes II and III and at that time did not get very far with them. But I read and re-read *The Eighteenth Brumaire of Louis Bonaparte*, the *Communist Manifesto* and other early pamphlets of Marx as were available.[28]

With all this intensive independent reading in the summer of 1933, James soon made the acquaintance of the owner of Lahr, a German anarchist called Charlie Lahr. Lahr, according to David Goodway, was "very probably the last" in the line, "stretching back to the late eighteenth-century," of "great London radical booksellers-cum-publishers."[29] Lahr soon became interested in James's research program. James remembers, "[Lahr] would put aside a book or pamphlet for me he knew or thought would interest me. . . . Through Charlie I was made acquainted with pamphlets and publications of the American Trotskyist movement, also with similar publications in French."[30] By now, James remembers he "was reading hard and was already a long way towards becoming a Trotskyist."[31] After his study of Marxism and the Russian Revolution, James recalled: "I realised the Stalinists were the greatest liars and corrupters of history there ever were. No one convinced me of this. I convinced myself."[32]

Clearly this is not the place to reiterate all the fundamental issues on which Trotsky's Marxism differed from that of the official "orthodox Communist" movement, including his defense of revolutionary internationalism as opposed to the construction of "Socialism in One Country," his defense of classical Bolshevik strategy and tactics, as outlined at the first four congresses of the Communist International, and so on. Nor can we examine in detail how Trotsky continued to develop and enrich Marxist theory during this period, as for example with his outstanding analysis of the resistible rise of Adolf Hitler.[33] Yet it is important to stress the impact two aspects of Trotsky's Marxism would have made on James: first, Trotsky's unrepentant commitment to the principle of anti-imperialism, and second, his development of the Marxist theory of permanent revolution, and perhaps just as crucially, and linked to this, of uneven and combined development under capitalism.

Some sense of how Trotsky's Marxism must have helped to shake James out of any residues of his earlier commitment to parliamentary socialism might be gleaned from a brief quote from the conclusion to Trotsky's *Where Is Britain Going?* (1925):

> The cold cruelty displayed by ruling England in its relations with the Hindus, Egyptians, and Irish, which has seemed to be an arrogance of race, will in the case of civil war reveal its true class character when directed against the proletariat. . . . In the decisive struggle against the proletariat, the English bourgeoisie will receive the most powerful support from the bourgeoisie of the United States, while the English proletariat will draw its strength in the first place from the working class of Europe and the subject nations in the British colonies. The character of the British empire will inevitably impart to this gigantic struggle the scale of a worldwide conflict. It will be one of the most impressive spectacles of world history. The destinies of the English proletariat will be bound up in this struggle with the destinies of all mankind. The entire world situation and the role of the English proletariat in production and in society assures it of the victory, provided its leadership be truly and resolutely revolutionary.[34]

One gets here a sense of how Trotsky's vision of world history, of the specter of looming revolutionary upheaval across the British Empire, might have inspired James. Its limitations as a guide to formulating a feasible strategic orientation with respect to how the 1930s actually unfolded aside, it is worth noting that Trotsky's anti-imperialism flowed from his Marxist understanding of the world system. Of particular relevance here is the theory of permanent revolution, which Trotsky himself had done so much to develop in opposition to the dominant evolutionist orthodoxy of the Second International, based initially on the experience of how the tiny working class in backward, czarist Russia had created the world's first workers' council or "Soviet" during the revolution of 1905.[35]

In a work published first in 1930 as *Permanent Revolution*, Trotsky not only provided a summary of the theory as outlined in his previous work *Results and Prospects* (1906), but also unrepentantly stated for the first time what he had left only implicit before, namely the universal applicability of the Marxist theory of permanent revolution.[36] Trotsky noted:

With regard to countries with a belated bourgeois development, especially the colonial and semi-colonial countries, the theory of the permanent revolution signifies that the complete and genuine solution of their tasks of achieving *democracy and national emancipation* is conceivable only through the dictatorship of the proletariat as the leader of the subjugated nation, above all of its peasant masses. . . . No matter what the first episodic stages of the revolution may be in the individual countries, the realization of the revolutionary alliance between the proletariat and the peasantry is conceivable only under the political leadership of the proletarian vanguard.[37]

Trotsky condemned the Stalinist "stages" model of revolution (first "democratic" then "socialist") as "lifeless," and he exposed the Second International orthodoxy of a division between "civilised" and "other" countries as irredeemably Eurocentric.[38] Moreover,

the above-outlined sketch of the development of world revolution eliminates the question of countries that are "mature" or "immature" for socialism in the spirit of that pedantic, lifeless classification given by the present [1928] programme of the Comintern. . . . Backward countries may, under certain circumstances, arrive at the dictatorship of the proletariat sooner than advanced countries, but they will come later than the latter to socialism.[39]

Whereas the Marxist theory of permanent revolution during the 1920s became the defining original sin of "Trotskyism" for orthodox Communists as the rising Stalinist bureaucracy sought to isolate Trotsky's Left Opposition, for the Trinidadian James, who would have first read a brilliant concrete account of the theory in Trotsky's *History of the Russian Revolution*, things were somewhat different. Indeed, as Neil Davidson notes, Trotsky in his *History* transformed permanent revolution from a strategy "lacking a complete theoretical basis" into a fully developed theoretical model applicable globally and based not only on "the theory of uneven development" (which dated back to the Enlightenment) but also what he called "the law of combined development."[40] As Trotsky put it,

the laws of history have nothing in common with a pedantic schematism. Unevenness, the most general law of the historic process, reveals itself most sharply and complexly in the destiny of the backward countries. Under the whip of external necessity their backward culture is compelled to make leaps. From the universal law of unevenness thus derives another law which, for the lack of a better name, we may call the law of *combined development*—by which we mean a drawing together of the different steps, an amalgam of archaic with more contemporary forms. Without this law, to be taken of course in its whole material content, it is impossible to understand the history of Russia, and indeed of any country of the second, third or tenth cultural class.[41]

In other words, were one wanting to better understand the history of a tiny Caribbean island like Trinidad or Haiti, it was not enough to simply point to the obvious and talk about how their economic, political, and cultural "backwardness," in comparison to Britain or France, for example, illustrated the "unevenness" of development under capitalism. Colonialism had materially blocked the possibility of such countries enjoying what Trotsky had called "the privilege of historical backwardness," which had seen countries like Germany and Japan "skipping over intermediate steps" on the path to capitalist modernity. To understand "backward" societies in the colonial world, one had to look in concrete detail at how, to quote Davidson, "the archaic and the modern had melded or fused in all aspects of these social formations, from the organisation of arms production to the structure of religious observance, in entirely new and unstable ways."[42]

For James, Trotsky's discussion of "the law of uneven and combined development" must have helped explain like nothing else the "amalgam of archaic with more contemporary forms" that he noticed in colonial Trinidad, and it reinforced his growing sense that if there was hope for the Caribbean, it lay with the working class. When faced with implicitly racist accusations about how black people in the Caribbean were somehow "primitive" and not yet "ready" for self-government, James would always instinctively reply with examples from his experience of how "Western" and "modern" the working people and their democratic politics and culture actually were. Now Trotsky's *History* had allowed James to more fully make sense of his early life in what he would later call the "heterogeneous jumble" of Trinidad, with its division between town and country, and between a more rural north and a more industrialized and developed south around the oil fields. Moreover, while James had grown up a "country bumpkin," the Marxist theory of permanent revolution could help explain why a "modern" labor movement around the nationalist Trinidad Workingmen's Association had grown so rapidly in just over a decade after the Great War, and pulled behind it radicalizing intellectuals like himself with its energy and resolve.[43] As James would later declare, "In analytical power and imaginative audacity" Trotsky's development of the Marxist theory of permanent revolution was "one of the most astounding productions of the modern mind. . . . After Marx's discoveries political thinkers were limited to the use of his method. It has never been better used."[44]

A Meeting with George Padmore

Yet within a few months of moving to London, James's developing sympathies for Trotsky's Marxism were soon given their first serious test. One day in the summer of 1933, James heard that George Padmore, a legendary leading black figure of international Communism and author of a classic study *The Life and Struggles of Negro Toilers* (1931), would be speaking in central London, on Gray's Inn Road.[45] Padmore was the head of the International Trade Union Committee of Negro Workers, located within the Profintern, the Red International of Labour Unions, and he edited their paper, *Negro Worker*. He had just escaped from Nazi Germany, where he had been imprisoned following Hitler's seizure of power, the passport Padmore had courtesy of being a British colonial subject enabling him to get deported.[46] Hitler's victory gradually led to an abandonment of the Communist International's extremely sectarian "class-against-class" line, and the tiny Communist Party of Great Britain (CPGB) was now trying to initiate a United Front against fascism with the two other main British working-class organizations, the Labour Party and the Independent Labour Party (ILP). While the ILP agreed to talks, the Labour leadership felt unity with Communists would undermine what was left of their electoral credibility and in any case that the real enemy was less fascism per se but "dictatorship" and "extremism," including Communism. Labour's "anti-Communist anti-fascism" led them to attack the CPGB's new front organizations, refusing to be drawn into what William Gillies in a Labour Party pamphlet published in 1933 called "the Communist Solar System." By mid-1933, Gray's Inn Road had become, in the words of Reginald Reynolds, home to the headquarters of "a whole network of satellite organisations in the 'Communist Solar System,'" and if James was loyal to Labour, he might well have resisted going to see Padmore.[47] However, James remembers, "I was going to every meeting in those days and the race-aspect of the matter was an added attraction," not least because Labour never seemed to hold any meetings on the colonial question.[48]

James would not regret his decision. As he remembered, he turned up at the meeting hall to find "about seventy or eighty people, about half of them white, and about five minutes before the time in walked my boyhood friend Malcolm Nurse." The two had not seen each other for almost a decade, since Nurse had left Trinidad for America, and they had lost contact long ago. James remembered, "We knew each other at once. He came and said, 'Hello, how are you?'" It quickly became apparent that the legendary "George Padmore" was in fact none other than Nurse himself. A little stunned, but also "amazed and delighted," James assured his old friend that they would "talk afterwards," and now found a seat as "George Padmore" took the stage. James recalled Padmore's speech: "He spoke to the audience about struggles all over the world. Although he was a very good speaker, he was not a great orator; but what he had was authority. I was struck by the admiration and awe with which the audience listened and looked at him." Padmore briskly dealt with personal questions about his courage in the face of danger and the risks he took. "It was part of his profession, that was all."[49] C. A. Smith, chair of the London ILP and author of a pamphlet published in 1926, The Crime of Empire, later remembered James's and Padmore's "laughing uproariously" at the meeting's end.[50]

After what must have been the most exhilarating public meeting James had ever attended, the two went for a meal and James vividly recalled how they ended up returning to his flat and talking "till about four o'clock in the morning." James said, "He told me: 'You were here in 1932 March, April, May?' I said yes." James continued, "He said: 'My God, man, I was here in 1932 looking for people to carry to Moscow to help to train them to organise blacks. If I had seen you I would have asked you.' I told him: 'Well, boy, if you had seen me and asked me to go to Moscow the day after I had landed in London I would have gone.'"[51]

James recollected, "That was how we just missed each other."[52] In September 1932, Padmore had briefly visited London after trying to organize the first "World Congress of Seamen" in difficult circumstances in May in Hamburg, but by then James was in Nelson.[53] After meeting and talking to the inspirational Padmore (who returned to his Profintern post in France in August 1933, soon after this encounter), it seems likely that James had finally decided that he was a no longer merely a socialist, but a revolutionary socialist, a "communist." Yet, it must have also made James aware of

FIGURE 3.4 George Padmore, 1937.

how much he still needed to know, and his sympathies for "Trotskyism" must have been challenged. How could the "Stalinist" movement be so bad if such a good friend could rise so high in it, so soon after joining it in America in 1927?[54]

Joining the Trotskyist Movement

"I was a cricket reporter for the *Manchester Guardian* while I educated myself politically," James remembered of the summer of 1933, clearly enjoying a job that ensured him ample free time to read.[55] While trying to measure James's political radicalization through his writings on cricket would be problematic, to say the least, there does seem to be some evidence of it. On August 14, 1933, while reporting Lancashire's game against Hampshire at Old Trafford, James attempted to apply a class analysis (of sorts) to some of the Hampshire players: "Boyes, long, slim, and graceful, fielded at short leg with aristocratic boldness and easy skill. Captain Philip Mead had little to do, but it was pleasant to watch his good-humoured proletarian amble from slip at one end to slip at the other. Kennedy supplied the solid, bourgeois virtues of length, flight and spin. . . . He remained a dangerous bowler, never degenerating into negative theories."[56]

By now, James himself was certainly rethinking his own "solid, bourgeois virtues" and was in the process of "degenerating" nicely into Marxism, a "negative theory," albeit at the pace of a "good-humoured proletarian amble." Having independently orientated toward Trotskyism, James seems to have been further aided in his degeneration in 1933 by an Englishman called Geoffrey Bagot. James remembered that Bagot was not an organized revolutionary but "was interested in Trotskyism and spoke to [James] about it," particularly with respect to history.[57] James remembered that he and Charlie Lahr had by now formed "a curious partnership," with Lahr answering James's growing number of questions about politics and the labour movement in Britain, particularly leading figures within it. James recalled, "Charlie would instruct me usually of some scandalous betrayal which all political persons of the left knew and talked about." That James should have learned much about the hypocrisy and failings of many Labour Party leaders and trade union bureaucrats in Britain from discussions with a German anarchist might surprise some. Yet "Charlie did not so much argue a political issue. He disseminated information." Particularly instructive for James was Lahr's analysis of Hitler's rise to power. James recalled, "Of Germany I knew nothing concrete except the music of Bach, Haydn, Mozart and Beethoven and the philosophy of Kant and Hegel."[58]

The summer of 1933 also saw James's return to Nelson, and during one visit Harry Spencer, after listening to his good friend enthuse over the latest book he had received from France and how it fit into his plans to write about the Haitian Revolution, asked, "Why are you always talking about this book—why don't you write it?" When James explained he was saving up to visit the archives in France, Spencer gave James ninety pounds to enable him to get "on to France" that winter.[59] Yet it was arguably James's experiences in Paris, outside the libraries and archives, that hold the final clue to his political development. In February 1934, Paris was experiencing massive civil unrest as the far right hoped to emulate Hitler's success the year before, through exploiting the growing protests of the middle class and blaming "corrupt" financiers and Jews. On February 6, 1934, the fascists called a huge demonstration against the recently formed, left-of-center government under the Liberal Radical Party's Eduard Daladier. The vicious fighting that ensued with police led to Daladier's resignation, his replacement by a right-wing Liberal, and proof that through force the French fascists could deliver political change. The social democratic Socialist Party, happy to line up behind the still-governing Radical Party, did nothing. The French Communists were still following Stalin's line of a "Third Period," wherein socialist revolution, not counterrevolution, was imminent, and their paper L'humanité carried the headline "No panic" and declared that the choice between the fascists and the existing government was like the choice between "plague and cholera."[60]

Yet just as James might have wondered about whether he would have to rely on his British passport to escape from a fascist prison cell as Padmore had, workers in Paris instinctively felt the need for unity against the fascists, something only a minuscule group of Trotskyists were arguing for. On the night of February 10, 1934, James has described how he witnessed "fierce fighting" and "men were killed." He later recorded how "the proletariat, the stock of 1789 and the 10th August, 1792, of 1830, of 1848 and 1871, came out in their thousands, whether Socialist or Communist." On February 12, the main union federation, the General Confederation of Labour, called for a general strike and at the last minute the Communist Party called for a demonstration, albeit separate from that held by the main Socialist Party and the General Confederation of Labour. Instead of the two demonstrations showing their traditional animosity toward each other, on meeting, workers spontaneously and gloriously came together to sing antifascist slogans. James noted, "It was in the streets that French parliamentarism was saved. The coup had failed."[61] Coupled with the inspirational but ultimately unsuccessful uprising by the Social Democratic Schutzbund in Vienna, by then under Dollfuss's dictatorship, James left France exhilarated at seeing fascism being resisted at last.[62]

Meanwhile, back in Britain, encouraged by Mussolini's and Hitler's success, Sir Oswald Mosley had since 1932 put himself forward as national "saviour" to the crisis, pouring almost one hundred thousand pounds into his new British Union of Fascists (BUF).[63] By the spring of 1934, Mosley's BUF enjoyed an air of respectability among some sections of the British establishment and was beginning to be seen as a legitimate part of the British political scene. Indeed, the "Blackshirts" had the sympathy and even the admiration of some elite figures, most famously the media baron Lord Rothermere.[64] Having seen the sort of "fight" that the official social democratic and Communist parties had put up against fascism in France, James on his return to Britain felt that he "wanted to meet some Trotskyists."[65] When he finally ran into some of these elusive individuals "distributing a pamphlet" at a Labour Party meeting in London in summer 1934, James joined the revolutionary movement at last. James remembers, "There were some people from Oxford and Cambridge who . . . brought some criticism to the official Trotskyists and they couldn't answer. So on the same night I joined I had to speak on behalf of Trotskyism."[66] If James was pleased to see the "official Trotskyists," we can only imagine how happy they were to see him.

The Impact of "Black Paris"

Looking back at his six months spent researching the Haitian Revolution in France, during the winter of 1933 and spring of 1934, James was always very proud that, as a black colonial subject from the British Caribbean, he was able to surprise librarians at La Bibliothèque Nationale with his knowledge of the French language.[67] Very early on into his historical researches in Paris, James had the good fortune to meet Léon-Gontran Damas, a black student and poet from French Guiana. James recalled Damas's attitude to him at the time: "If you are working on the Haitian Revolution, this is the kind of material which you need; I know Paris and sources of material very well and I put my knowledge at your disposal." James remembered that Damas helped him become "aware of rapid ways in which to get the materials [James] wanted and needed for examination" in La Bibliothèque Nationale and the Archives Nationales. And Damas also took James "to bookshops which specialized in collecting and selling documents about the colonial revolution and Caribbean history."[68] James accordingly covered ground "at a tremendous rate" in various archives, bookshops, and libraries by the banks of the Seine.[69] Intellectually, the experience also led James to radicalize "at a tremendous rate," discovering, for example, the French philosopher Henri Bergson:

> I remember my first break with the philosophy of rationalism. It was Bergson, 1934. His work had come at the turn of the century. And it was startling to me on two counts.
> (1) He attacked the abstractions of Understanding, their mechanical categorisation, etc., and opposed to this, Intuition.
> (2) Humour, he said, was the fulfilment of the desire to see the snob

and the aristocrat humbled. So that the well-dressed man slipping on a banana peel was his classic example of humour. It is still individualistic, as it would be in this philosopher, but I remember it broke me with morbid and melancholy philosophy speculation.[70]

Rationalism, which was championed by the Enlightenment, has been defined as an attempt to "reconstruct reality by insisting that only those aspects of the world which conform to preconceived canons of reason have any true substance; the rest is insubstantial illusion bound to be condemned to oblivion as rationality gains ground against error and superstition."[71] Bergson had been part of a wider revolt against "positivism" and "naturalism" that swept Europe during the 1890s, rejecting the tendency to discuss human behavior through analogies drawn from natural sciences and seeking instead to explain and understand what had previously been dismissed as "superstition" and the "irrational." For the Hungarian Marxist philosopher Georg Lukács, who was also inspired by Bergson before he became a Marxist, Bergson therefore stood outside of "the main philosophic tradition" for which "the reified world appears henceforth quite definitively . . . as the only possible world, the only conceptually accessible, comprehensible world vouchsafed to us humans." Instead, Bergson represented an attempt to "radically question the value of formal knowledge for a 'living life.'"[72]

That James found reading Bergson liberating should not really surprise us, as Bergson's stress on "intuition" was to prove an inspiration to several black colonial subjects in France during the 1930s, including Léopold Senghor (later president of Senegal). Against the white supremacist claims of European imperialism, Senghor drew courage from Bergson's argument that "the objects of discursive reason were only the superficial surface that must be surpassed, by *intuition*, in order to have a deeper vision of the *real*."[73] James's and Senghor's invocation of Bergson also reminds us that for many black colonial subjects twentieth-century Paris was more than just an intellectual center of the West. Invoking Walter Benjamin's description of Paris as the "Capital of the Nineteenth Century" in *The Arcades Project* (1939), Jonathan P. Eburne and Jeremy Braddock suggested in 2005 that it was also a "Capital of the Black Atlantic." This manifested itself not only in "the transatlantic circulation of ideas, texts, and objects" that resulted from those black writers from across the African diaspora having visited Paris, but also in "the Benjaminian sense of a wish image of diasporic imagination," where "black Paris" became a mythological space of tolerance and enlightenment with respect to race.[74] In Paris during the early 1930s, black journals such as *La revue du monde noir* and *Légitime défense* flourished and were important precursors to the Negritude movement, which was born in 1935. Léon-Gontran Damas (alongside Léopold Senghor and the Martinican poet Aimé Césaire) would be central to the development of the philosophy of Negritude.[75] Though never part of the Negritude movement himself, James got a taste of the heady atmosphere of "black Paris" as a racialized space when he met the Haitian military historian Colonel Auguste Nemours, "an enthusiastic admirer of Toussaint but exceptionally fair," who was keen to explain Haiti's war of independence to him "in great detail, using books and coffee cups on a large table."[76]

James returned to Britain inspired by his experiences, and in March 1934, he visited Nelson and gave a lecture titled "The Negro," which was reported at length in the *Nelson Leader*. In this meeting, James denounced French colonialism in Africa as being even worse than the British in South Africa, noting that "between 1911 and 1926 3,250,000 natives died in French Equatorial Africa. Big holes were dug and the natives were thrown into them and blown up with dynamite." Yet James contrasted the level of racial prejudice in France with that of Britain positively:

> The average person in England did not understand the negro. They saw him only dancing and kicking his heels like a half-crazy lunatic; the screen always presented him in an unfair position. People could not get away from the idea that he was fit for nothing better than the role of shoe-black or railroad porter. . . . If hearers went across the Channel and investigated conditions in France . . . they would find negroes in the French Cabinet, in the ranks of retired naval and army men, in the professions, universities and colleges. France had already disregarded scientific theories, and judged the negro on results.[77]

For the "African Revolution"

James's speech in Nelson on "the Negro" also gives some indication of his new, militant Pan-Africanist politics. According to the correspondent of the *Nelson Leader*, James noted that African people had never simply been passive victims in the face of the ravages of the slave trade, but had organized resistance. Seemingly referring to the aforementioned Bushongo of the Kasai, James noted, "These people established themselves right in the centre of Africa, and, having formed a kingdom, were able to resist all encroachments. The result was they had formed a civilisation which showed what Africa would have been able to achieve had it remained free from foreign interference. In fact their moral code might have served as an example to the rest of the world."[78]

After highlighting the immorality of the European slave-trading powers, James noted the devastating impact of colonialism in Africa, beginning with the situation in South Africa, where Europeans had been "for about 300 years, and the natives had no prospects after 300 years." Yet after discussing the barbarism of British rule in South Africa, and the repressive pass laws crushing the spirit of the people, James predicted that "there was going to be a tremendous revolt in Africa someday." James then moved on to discuss the East African state of Kenya, where white settlers were not creating a "civilisation," but destroying one. Apparently, James "was amazed at the atrocities committed by Englishmen who had the opportunities of education and upbringing, and who ought to know better." Yet his reading of Marxism meant that already by March 1934 James "did not lay the blame on individuals, but on the system which permitted these things to happen. It was an economic question."

> "I have spoken seriously because it is a serious question," said Mr. James in conclusion. "Although it is a racial question on the surface, it is a political and economic question below. I have spoken without hostility because some of the truest friends of the negro are white men. I don't think you can do very much; the forces that control these things are far more powerful than you are, but the situation is not entirely hopeless. I think everyone here will realise that we are living on the eve of great changes. This is a transition period, and great things must come out of it, and it is possible that the negro may look forward to receiving better treatment than he has had in the past."[79]

James's cautious optimism about the "great changes" ahead, after having heard George Padmore speak on "the coming revolt in Africa," and after his experiences in black Paris, meant that by 1934 he could now clearly see an alternative strategy for Pan-African liberation than that of trying to win the British Labour Party to a formal commitment to anticolonialism. In 1933, the Labour Party had published a policy report outlining future colonial policy, which explicitly ruled out self-government for "the primitive communities of Africa" and even seemed to retreat somewhat from their previous pledge for West Indian self-government.[80] While one can imagine James's growing frustration as a Labour Party member, he was also tiring of the politically moderate approach of the LCP, with their middle-class "respectability" and stress on black colonial subjects' always asserting their "Britishness" when campaigning against racism and colonial oppression.

The decisive issue concerning James's break with the LCP leadership seems to have been the controversial issue of Aggrey House. In 1932, Moody had quietly joined the Colonial Office's hostel committee, which had just bought a ten-year lease on a house on 47 Doughty Street, in central London, which they planned to open up as a "club" for "all coloured people," a meeting place between "black and white" and "a door to the English home and English life."[81] By the time Aggrey House opened, in March 1934, the truth had come out that it was not just Moody but also the British state that was financing it. The West African Students Union (WASU), who had themselves already successfully set up an independent hostel in Camden for African students ("Africa House"), put out a leaflet, *The Truth about Aggrey House: Government Plan for Control of African Students*, which denounced "this scheme of Imperialism." In March 1934, WASU held a protest meeting, with the support of a whole range of organizations, including several Communist-backed groups, such as the National Council for Civil Liberties, the New India Political Group, the Negro Welfare Association (NWA), and the League Against Imperialism (LAI), and the Africa House Defence Committee was formed to show solidarity with the existing student-run African hostel. Despite his position as a leading LCP member, James had no problem deciding which side he was on in this dispute, joining those defending Africa House and successfully proposing a motion calling for "a complete boycott of Aggrey House by all students of African descent in London."[82] His tenure on the LCP executive had lasted barely one year.

From this point on, James, the Trinidadian Trotskyist, would be a figure at the heart of the tiny, militant Pan-African milieu in London, and he embraced their radical "black internationalism." As a "black Bolshevik" now himself, James worked closely with the anticolonial and anticapitalist agitators and activists around Communist-backed organizations such as the LAI and NWA.[83] The NWA had been formed in 1931 and was led by the Barbadian Communist Arnold Ward, whom James later recalled as "a slow speaking working class type," "utterly devoted to the cause."[84] James also appears to have made the acquaintance of the radical poet, editor, publisher, and journalist Nancy Cunard, whose flat at 9 Heathcote Street, in central London, was a popular meeting place for Pan-Africanists. When Cunard decided to move to black Paris in 1934, to finish compiling her monumental 855-page anthology *Negro*, it is not perhaps a complete coincidence that James now moved into 9 Heathcote Street from Hampstead.[85] When Cunard's *Negro*—a remarkable fusion of Pan-Africanism and Communism—appeared in 1934, there was a passing reference to James as a "writer."[86] Since moving to Britain, however, as James later recalled, events in the outside world had intervened, and would continue to intervene, to ensure that "fiction-writing drained out of [him] and was replaced by politics."[87]

Resisting Mussolini's "Civilising Mission"

In early 1935, the murderous intentions of the dictator of Fascist Italy, Mussolini, to conquer the East African state of Ethiopia (then called Abyssinia) were declared. Together with Liberia, Ethiopia was one of the last areas of Africa free from European control, its armies having heroically defeated Italy at the battle of Adowa, in 1896. Since 1932 Mussolini had been preparing Italian troops for their role in the proposed glorious resurrection of the "Roman Empire." In order to justify such nineteenth-century-style empire building, the ideology of "humanitarianism" was deployed by the Fascist regime alongside open, old-fashioned racism, and promises were made to end slavery in Ethiopia and free the two million enslaved. In time-honored fashion, the criminal invasion and occupation of a sovereign nation was declared to be, as Mussolini himself put it, "a war of civilization and liberation."[88]

This is not the place to examine the full reaction in Britain to Mussolini's war plans in all its complexity or to Fascist Italy's barbaric war. It might be worth noting that Winston Churchill, who had been "charmed" by Mussolini's "gentle and simple bearing" when he met him in 1927, was persuaded that British imperial interests were not endangered by Italy's plans and so continued to marvel at the man he had hailed in 1933 as a "Roman genius."[89] Such a stance was quite widely shared in British government circles (and Conservative opinion more generally), and some hoped that the acquisition of African territory by the likes of fascist Italy and Nazi Germany might act as a safety valve for European stability. This feeling among conservative and upper-class opinion extended to even the leading figure of the official antislavery movement in Britain, Lady Simon, who was married to a senior cabinet minister and took Mussolini's rhetoric about "civilization and liberation" at face value.[90]

Yet for Africans, and for people of African descent like James, the specter of Mussolini's Blackshirts spearheading yet another European imperial "civilising mission" in Africa filled them with both horror and rage. Indeed, across the African diaspora an international explosion of protest now erupted, and Robert Weisbord has noted that "perhaps no single event in the twentieth century more clearly illuminated the nexus between diaspora blacks and continental blacks than the Italian-Ethiopian war." This was because of the collective memories Ethiopia evoked, with both "an impressive cultural tradition traceable to ancient Axum and a uniquely successful resistance to the European intrusion in Africa in the latter part of the nineteenth century."[91] The great-grandson of slaves, James needed no lectures from Mussolini about the sufferings of the enslaved—James had even written about Ethiopia in his article "Slavery Today" (1933).

Robert Hill has drawn attention to how Italy's invasion of Ethiopia "marked the turning-point of nineteenth-century and post-war Black nationalism and paved the way for the emergence of an explicitly political Pan-Africanism," noting "the contribution of C.L.R. James would prove to be one of the essential factors in clearly establishing the changed outlook."[92] Through the LCP, James had met Amy Ashwood Garvey, and as Italian war drums began to beat ever louder, James remembered that both of them "felt that there ought to be an opposition" in Britain to Mussolini's looming war and that she had "a unique capacity to concentrate all the forces available and needed for the matter in hand."[93] Together they revived an ad hoc committee formed in 1934 to aid the Gold Coast Aborigines' Rights Protection Society (ARPS) deputation to England.[94] James became chair of the resulting International African Friends of Abyssinia (IAFA).[95] They soon gathered around them in London a quite remarkable group of figures from across Africa and the Caribbean, as Padmore later recalled:

> Among the sponsors of this IAFA were the two representatives of the ARPS Messrs [George A.] Moore and [Samuel R.] Wood and Dr. J[oseph]. B. Danquah who was secretary of the Ofori-Atta led delegation

from the Gold Coast. The officers of the IAFA were Mr. C.L.R. James of Trinidad as chairman; Dr. Peter Milliard of British Guiana and the Hon. T. Albert Marryshaw of Grenada as vice-chairmen; Mr. Jomo Kenyatta as honorary secretary; Mrs. Amy Ashwood Garvey, former wife of the famous Negro leader, as honorary treasurer. They, together with Mr. Sam Manning of Trinidad, Mr. Mohammed Said of Somaliland, and the author [Padmore] formed the executive committee.[96]

The IAFA's first public meeting to protest the looming war was held in London on July 23, 1935, and *West Africa* described how it was "crowded" with "men and women of African descent." The meeting sent "resolutions of sympathy with Abyssinians in their resolve to maintain independence" and began a fund to either "send an ambulance" or "found a permanent hospital if there is no war."[97]

Such an expression of solidarity with African people was sorely lacking among many leading British politicians and commentators, who openly declared for Fascist Italy's proposed "civilising mission." Lord Hardinge of Penshurst described the people of Ethiopia as "a savage and barbarous enemy" and so, as Lord Stanhope, undersecretary of state for foreign affairs, told a Foreign Office official, it would be wrong to sell them arms, as that "would be going back on the White Man everywhere." On July 15, 1935, the *Daily Mail* asserted, "The British public take no interest whatever in the slave-owning Abyssinian Empire. And in this war which now seems inevitable their sympathy is wholly with the cause of the white races, which Italy is so finely upholding." The *Mail's* foreign editor, Ward Price, went further, following Churchill in declaring Mussolini a "genius" and warning that if the British opposed Italy's expansion "to one of the last and most backward of independent nation states, we should be hindering the progress of civilisation." The possibility of an Ethiopian victory was too alarming to consider. The earl of Mansfield feared that "should Italy lose, it would be at once a great encouragement to all that stands for mischief and sedition among the coloured races of the world."[98] On the anti-imperialist British Left, such racism was often effectively ridiculed. As Reginald Reynolds put it:

> In short the ring is cleared for a straight fight between Italian aeroplanes and Ethiopian huts. . . . Of every Ethiopian child who is killed, we shall be able to say "that is a blow struck against slavery"; and when Italian

Fascism has reduced the whole land to the slavery of empire, our newspapers will no doubt applaud the destruction of thousands of human lives and the soul of an ancient nation as another victory of civilisation.[99]

On Sunday, July 28, 1935, the IAFA held its second public meeting at the Memorial Hall, Farringdon Street. As *West Africa* reported, "A crowded meeting of sympathisers with Abyssinia, was held, presided over by Mrs. A. A. Garvey, of the West Indies. The speakers represented several African territories." The report continues:

> The first speaker was Mr. C.L.R. James, a West Indian writer and journalist, one of whose short stories was adjudged among the best of a recent year. He surveyed the history of Abyssinia's intercourse with foreign Powers. His plea may be summarised as follows: Africans and persons of African descent all over the world have always looked with zealous pride at Abyssinia, which, alone of ancient African kingdoms, still maintains independence. They therefore viewed with alarm and indignation the desire expressed on behalf of Italy, of conquering Abyssinia and the concentration of Italian troops and armaments on the Abyssinian frontiers. . . . Mr. James expressed the belief that many Africans would be willing to offer themselves for the frontline, or for any auxiliary form of service in the event of war.[100]

From the reports of this meeting, one also gets some insight into how James reconciled his frantic political activity with his professional work reporting cricket. On Monday, July 29, readers of the *Manchester Guardian* would have read James describe an incident that took place during the match between Hampshire and Lancashire at Southampton, played on the Saturday: "The dullness of the innings was enlivened by music from a loudspeaker, a brass band, singing, and periodical discharges from a gun, with all of which . . . the local Conservative party made demonstration in the stadium next door." While "it sounded far more exciting than the cricket[,] . . . the gunfire next door continued with no regard for the batsman's concentration," nearly leading one Lancashire batsman, Paynter, to be dismissed by a "political diversion." "Cricket," James noted wryly, "should be kept well away from politics." A mere ten pages later, readers of that Monday's *Manchester Guardian* might then have been somewhat startled to discover a report noting that at the IAFA meeting the previous evening, their beloved cricket reporter "gave a lucid history of the European treaties with Abyssinia" and declared that "Abyssinia is a symbol of all that Africa was and may be again, and we look on it with a jealous pride."[101]

In fact it seems that James had suffered from a "cricket diversion" during the IAFA launch meeting, as, possibly still thinking about Paynter's batting, he remembers, "I got myself into a blunder. . . . Being a Marxist I was naturally opposed to the League of Nations, but in the excitement of forming the organisation we passed a resolution demanding . . . that the League of Nations take steps against the Italian Government."[102] It was not altogether surprising that such a liberal proposal succeeded in getting passed, for the IAFA was a broad organization that included in its leadership quite politically moderate, classically reformist figures such as the two members of the Gold Coast ARPS delegation, George A. Moore and Samuel R. Wood.[103] Moreover, as James remembered, "Lord Robert Cecil, a League of Nations maniac, instituted a private poll. It gathered over eleven million votes for collective security and over six million for an armed League of Nations."[104] In late June 1935, a month earlier, the results of this "Peace Ballot" were announced, and it showed that many people in Britain were deeply unhappy at Tory foreign policy and the prospect of another war. In part as a response, in July 1935, pragmatically thinking of British colonial possessions in East Africa, the new Tory prime minister Stanley Baldwin took the opportunity to dramatically steal the wind from Labour's sails, claiming that "collective security" through the league was now "the sheet-anchor of British policy."[105] The Soviet Union had also recently joined the League of Nations, in September 1934 — despite having been famously described as a "thieves' kitchen" by Lenin — and so now in Britain even the CPGB joined the clamor and called for League action. As James remembered, "There were certain political elements who were extremely glad that our organisation, which was pretty widely known among the limited circles who were interested in these matters, could be included among those who were urging the intervention of the League of Nations."[106]

Yet had the Tory national government, the Labour and Liberal opposition, or the CPGB wanted to, they would not have been able to cite the IAFA as supporting their position for long. Thanks in no small part to the clear political lead now given by James, the IAFA soon reversed their position with respect to calling for league sanctions, and they voted to reject "any appeal to the League of Nations." As James remembers, "Most of us who were in the organisation and who were supporting it, had a conception of politics very remote from debates and resolutions of the League."[107] This comes through well in testimony from Kingsley Martin, editor of the *New Statesman and Nation*, who described the IAFA public meeting at Memorial Hall in his "London Diary" column:

> The meeting was not a big affair — a couple of hundred coloured people, and perhaps fifty white. But I have never seen an Albert Hall meeting which impressed me as so significant an omen as this little gathering in Farringdon Street, called to enlist support for the Emperor of Abyssinia. Mussolini has appealed to the war spirit and declared a white crusade against Black barbarism. Naturally, the response is Black defiance of white Barbarism.
>
> The speakers came from the West Indies, the Gold Coast, Kenya, Somaliland and Abyssinia itself. When they expressed a hope that the League of Nations or the British Government would see justice done, the audience was silent or ironical. When they declared that coloured people everywhere would fight and die free men rather than submit to the subjugation of the last independent native kingdom, the meeting yelled with enthusiasm. . . . You only had to say the word "civilization" to get this meeting jeering. Soon it was persuading itself that Abyssinia was the centre of the civilization, and Europe of barbarism.[108]

As James put it in a letter to the *New Statesman* the next week,

> There are some amongst our Society, including myself, who believe that the only final guarantee for Africa, as for the rest of the world, is the international socialist order. There are others who believe that Ethiopia must be supported because God said so in the Bible. But whatever our views, we are in this struggle as one, in that we stand by Ethiopia, and that we will do all that we can to help her. And most of us are fortified by the knowledge that in conflict with Italian Fascism we are with the stream of history and not against it. History will judge and the verdict will not be long delayed.[109]

On Sunday, August 25, 1935, the IAFA held a mass meeting in Trafalgar Square, London, resolving to defend Ethiopia from "the latest and most brutal example of European Imperialism in Africa" and demanded a lifting of the embargo on selling arms to that country, "a wicked and deliberate discrimination." As well as James himself, described by the British journalist Hannen Swaffer as a "West Indian orator" who was "an expert on the history of Abyssinia's treaties" and spoke "with eloquence and with

FIGURE 3.5 C. L. R. James speaking in Trafalgar Square, mid-1930s.
Used by permission of Anna Grimshaw and Socialist Platform.

an honest fervour," the IAFA could call upon a remarkable range of talent and experience. Testament to the way James's organization had revived the Pan-Africanist movement in Britain is the fact that for speakers they could also call upon Amy Ashwood, "a fluent speaker"; Padmore, who in August 1935 had returned to Britain; and Jomo Kenyatta, a Kenyan nationalist representing the Kikuyu Central Association, who had been close to the CPGB.[110] Another former Communist, the Barbadian seamen's organizer, Chris Braithwaite, who used the pseudonym "Jones" to avoid victimization, also addressed the rally.[111] James's militant speech epitomized the strength of feeling of those present at the rally: "We are not motivated by anti-White feeling[,] . . . but the question of Ethiopia has brought about a union of sentiment between black men in Africa, America, the West Indies and all over the world. Ethiopia's cause is our cause and we will defend it by every means in our power."[112]

As the *Daily Herald* reported the rally:

Ringing cheers greeted the declaration of Mrs. Ashwood Garvey, wife of Marcus Garvey, the famous leader of the Negroes, that, "No race has been so noble in forgiving, but now the hour has struck for our complete emancipation. We will not tolerate the invasion of Abyssinia." . . . On the platform were the three young sons of the Abyssinian Ambassador, Dr. Martin, and beside them stood coloured seamen, students, actors, musicians, doctors and in, in his colourful costume and plumed head-dress, a well-known racing tipster, waving the flag of Abyssinia. Every speaker was coloured. "We don't want war," said the chairman in open-ing the meeting, "but if Mussolini continues in his Imperialistic aggres-sion, we shall rise like one man in all parts of the world, and we shall in-flict such a disaster on Fascism that it will never be able to raise its head again."[113]

T. Ras Makonnen, born George Thomas Nathaniel Griffith in British Guiana but now claiming Ethiopian ancestry, happened to be passing through London for the first time in his life and had heard about the rally:

I had noticed in an evening paper an announcement of a big meeting in Trafalgar Square the next day, so I went along. A number of people spoke. . . . I passed my card forward saying that I was an Ethiopian and I would welcome an opportunity to speak. At once I was invited to come forward, and from the plinth at Trafalgar Square I dramatized the whole scene. I linked up the struggle in Ethiopia with the larger struggle against imperialism in Africa. Across the square I pointed to South Africa House and linked its significance with the present con-flict. And what else does one see from the centre of the square? Napier, Kitchener, outstanding British war-lords, and towering above them all was Nelson. But what of the English that the black and brown colonials knew about—the Shelleys, Byrons and Keats—all tucked away in some gallery or church? So one could see that Britain had really glorified those who had made its empire, and not its scholars. . . . After the meeting people came up and we introduced ourselves, and went off to Lyons Corner House for the usual tea.[114]

By August 1935 the IAFA had need of an official headquarters, and Amy Ashwood offered her own residence at 62 New Oxford Street, where she ran her International Afro Restaurant.[115] Africans from across the diaspora felt Ethiopia was, in the words of Makonnen, "the black man's last citadel," and he remembered "letters simply poured into our office from blacks on three continents asking where they could register."[116] Perhaps most strikingly, the IAFA seems to have seriously considered organizing an "International Brigade" from Britain to go and fight fascism in this last citadel of Pan-African pride. The British foreign secretary, Sir Samuel Hoare, had argued on August 1, 1935, that if Italy invaded Ethiopia it would "inevitably lead" to "the formidable unsettlement of the great coloured races of the world." The IAFA were determined to do their bit to prove this Tory correct, and James remembered that their desire to go and fight Mussolini created "something of a political stir."[117]

That an established cricket journalist like James, who had no military experience, should himself be willing to risk death fighting for Ethiopia requires additional explanation. Robin D. G. Kelley suggests, "As a Black man who probably felt a tinge of pride in Ethiopia's legacy, and whose admiration for Africa ran much deeper than anti-imperialism, he felt obligated to defend the place of his ancestors."[118] James's Pan-Africanism comes through strongly in a letter he would later write to his friends and comrades in the ILP, published on June 3, 1936, in the ILP's weekly paper, the *New Leader*. James explained that he hoped to join the Ethiopian army to make contact with "the masses of the Abyssinians and other Africans." As he put it, "I did not intend to spend the rest of my life in Abyssinia, but, all things considered, I thought, and I still think, that two or three years there, given the fact that I am a Negro and am especially interested in the African revolution, was well worth the attempt."[119]

Yet James's speeches in August 1935 also give a sense of how his desire to fight in Ethiopia reflected the way his study of the Haitian Revolution clearly fired his imagination about how the coming war against Italian imperialism might be won. Toussaint—whose memory had been saluted at the IAFA's public meeting on July 28, where "Wordsworth's sonnet to the black hero of Haiti" had been read out loud—had organized the defeat of the European armies through a ruthless guerrilla war waged from the mountains of Haiti.[120] The Ethiopians' victory at Adowa in 1896 had also been achieved in a similar manner, through adopting a "scorched earth" strategy and retreating into the mountains, before falling on the isolated and overstretched Italian army.[121] As James now put it to an IAFA public meeting on August 16, 1935, should the Ethiopians find themselves unable to get to grips with the Italians in conventional combat, the IAFA would "look to them to destroy their country rather than hand it over to the invader. Let them burn down Addis Ababa, let them poison their wells and water holes, let them destroy every blade of vegetation."[122] Could James's research on Haiti have inspired him to seriously consider the possibility that history could repeat itself, that the Ethiopians—an army made up in part of slaves—could humiliate the vastly more militarily powerful European forces as had the rebel slaves on Saint Domingue?[123]

James's Marxism also comes through in the letter written in June 1936 to the *New Leader*, where he noted that by joining the Ethiopian army, he "would have had an invaluable opportunity of gaining actual military experience on the African field where one of the most savage battles between Capitalism and its opponents [was] going to be fought before very many years." James had doubts about whether the Ethiopian emperor had the necessary strategic and tactical skills necessary to lead a guerrilla army to victory over Mussolini's forces. James insisted, "As long as the Emperor was fighting Imperialism I would have done the best I could," but should the Emperor have surrendered, "I would have identified myself with those bands, hundreds of thousands of them, who are still fighting, and for years are going to carry on the fight against Imperialistic domination of any kind." Just as Toussaint's forces had won the battle of ideas against the invading Napoleonic armies, confusing them utterly by reclaiming the songs of republican and revolutionary France, such as the *Ça ira* and the *Marseillaise*, so now James suggested the same kind of ideological battle would have to be waged in Ethiopia: "I believed also that I could have been useful in helping to organise the anti-Fascist propaganda among the Italian troops."[124] James did not end up going to fight for the liberation of Ethiopia from "imperialist domination of any kind." Despite British government pressure on the Ethiopian government to ban British subjects serving in their army, the Ethiopian regime was initially welcoming of the IAFA offer.[125] However, the British Foreign Enlistment Act of 1870 forbade British subjects to join forces of countries—in this case, Italy and Ethiopia—that maintained friendly relations with Britain, and IAFA members were persuaded by the Ethiopian Minister in London that their efforts on behalf of Ethiopia would be better directed from Britain.[126]

October 1935 marked the start of Mussolini's barbaric war, and on the night of the attack, 1,200 people packed into an ILP rally in London's Memorial Hall to hear James—chair of not only the IAFA but also of the ILP's Finchley branch—put the case for Ethiopia alongside the party chair James Maxton, MP, and the *New Leader* editor Fenner Brockway.[127] Though many people in Britain reacted in disgust to Mussolini's invasion, few did more than James to rally solidarity with the Ethiopians while the war was going on. One of the advantages of James's often close relationship with the ILP, which despite a decline in membership remained a more substantial and significant organization during the 1930s than is often realized, was that because of its deep, historic roots in the British working-class movement, it provided a platform for him to engage with socialist activists across the British Isles.[128] James wrote searing articles in the *New Leader* putting the case against Mussolini's war and European imperialism in Africa more generally.[129] In the autumn of 1935, the ILP organized a national lecture tour, which took James across England, to, among other places, Southampton, Norwich, Coventry, Nottingham, and also up to Scotland—and for the first time to South Wales.[130]

James's outstanding abilities as an orator stayed in the memory of all who had the fortune to hear him. Over seventy years later, one young ILP member at this time, Len Edmondson, could still remember James as "a very good, very able speaker," addressing one such meeting at the ILP-owned Westfield Hall, in Gateshead, in the northeast of England.[131] Brockway remembered that as a "Socialist orator," James was "immensely popular in the ILP."[132] James's solution to the crisis was very clear, based on his revolutionary Marxist politics of liberation from below. The idea that the League of Nations, dominated by the Great Powers of Britain and France, who had carved up most of Africa between them already, would decisively act to defend the people of Ethiopia from Mussolini was mistaken. James argued that to call for action by the League of Nations, "to come within the orbit of Imperialist politics is to be debilitated by the stench, to be drowned in the morass of lies and hypocrisy." Instead of appealing to the major European imperialist powers to impose League of Nations sanctions on Fascist Italy, James urged an alternative strategy—"workers' sanctions"—international industrial action to stop Mussolini's war machine: "Workers of Britain, peasants and workers of Africa, get closer together for this and for other fights. . . . Now, as always, let us stand for independent organisation and independent action. We have to break our own chains. Who is the fool that expects our gaolers to break them?"[133]

It is little wonder that with James in the leadership, the U.S. embassy in London could report in November 1935 that while the IAFA had begun as "slightly anti-imperialist" it was now "showing a tendency to move further towards the left."[134] In Ireland, Nora Connolly, daughter of the legendary socialist James Connolly, who had been murdered by the British in the Easter Rising of 1916, read a report of James's meetings in South Wales and invited him to address the Irish Citizen's Army. Accordingly, in December 1935, James remembered he had "a tremendous meeting" on Ethiopia in Dublin, while also apparently taking the opportunity to go horse riding in Phoenix Park.[135] Robert Alexander notes that James's meeting represented "the first exposition of Trotskyist ideas in Ireland."[136] When Anna Grimshaw later asked James about the visit, he "said that he didn't really understand what it meant to be revolutionary until he went to Ireland. The English 'revolutionaries'—Marxists, Trotskyists, ILPers—were of a very different kind" than the Irish revolutionaries who "really understood armed struggle and revolutionary conflict."[137]

Militant Pan-Africanism after Ethiopia

Africans and people of African descent, especially those who have been poisoned by British imperialist education, needed a lesson. They have got it. Every succeeding day shows exactly the real motives which move imperialism in its contact with Africa, shows the incredible savagery and duplicity of European imperialism in its quest for markets and raw materials. Let the lesson sink in deep.[138]

So wrote James in early 1936 in an article for the LCP journal *The Keys*, "Abyssinia and the Imperialists," as the full depth of British and French complicity in the barbarism of Mussolini's war on the people of Ethiopia became known. Given a free run by the major European powers and with advanced military technology, particularly aircraft, Fascist Italy had effectively declared "mission accomplished" by March 1936. However much heroic resistance the Ethiopians mounted to the Italian invasion, without international aid and modern arms, the odds facing them were insurmountable. While rebels did retreat to the mountains to conduct a guerrilla war, the Italians used poison gas bombs extensively to terrorize the rest of the population, even targeting the Red Cross and hospitals. The leader of a mobile Red Cross hospital commented: "This isn't war—it isn't even slaughter. It's the torture of tens of thousands of defenceless men, women and children with bombs and poison gas."[139]

The mighty efforts of black, radical activists internationally in solidarity with Ethiopia had been to no avail. As Weisbord has noted, "Regrettably, the black world had the will but not the power to stem the tide of fascist aggression. Perhaps the greater tragedy is that the white world which had the power lacked the will."[140] Those Pan-Africanists with hopes that at least one country within the "white world" — the Soviet Union — might have mustered the necessary willpower to rally international solidarity with Ethiopia were to see them dashed. Leaving the major imperialist powers aside, the betrayal of Ethiopia by the Soviet Union — which by the 1930s was inexorably spiraling down into counterrevolution and Stalinist terror — was particularly striking. As war loomed in 1935, Trotsky observed that it was "an irony of history" that "in the international arena, the government of the Soviet Union has become a conservative power. It is for the status quo, against change. But it has not lifted a finger for the status quo in Ethiopia."[141] In fact, come war the Soviet bureaucracy did lift a finger, but only to tell the Ethiopians where they could go. The economic interests of the Soviet oil industry came before any notion of rallying international working-class solidarity through the Communist International. As Trotsky later remarked, while Litvinov "expressed his gratitude to the diplomats of France and England for their efforts 'in behalf of peace,' efforts which so auspiciously resulted in the annihilation of Abyssinia, oil from the Caucasus continued to nourish the Italian fleet."[142]

This betrayal of Ethiopia was merely one of the most visible demonstrations of the way the Soviet government had steadily abandoned world revolution, in favor of building up "Socialism in One Country." After Hitler had come to power, Stalin had moved to try to make diplomatic approaches with Britain and France for reasons of national security, and the theorists of the Communist International accordingly now drew a distinction between the "Democratic Imperialist" countries of Britain, America, and France on the one hand and the "Fascist Imperialist" powers of Germany, Italy, and Japan on the other. In August 1933, Padmore made what he retrospectively justified — with no small justification — as a principled resignation from the Communist International over their sidelining of support for anticolonialist struggle against the supposedly "democratic" and "peace-loving" British and French colonial dictatorships in Africa. After surviving a vicious Stalinist witch hunt, Padmore had worked in Paris with

Francophone Pan-Africanists in an attempt to organize a "Negro World Unity Congress" in July 1935, but when this failed to get off the ground, Padmore left for London, turning up at the door of James's flat in August 1935, and quickly throwing himself into IAFA activity.[143] Padmore's talents, experience, and range of contacts (which included W. E. B. Du Bois and Nancy Cunard) soon made him the natural national organizer of the IAFA. While James traversed the British Isles on his speaking tour, Padmore ensured that the IAFA developed its organizational links in all directions, including with a similar new organization in France, Comité de Défense d'Ethiopie.[144]

As far back as October 1935, in an editorial "Soviet Russia Aids Italy," the black American journal of the NAACP, *The Crisis*, had noted that "the Soviets are raking in good capitalist profits selling wheat and coal tar to Italy for use in the war against Ethiopia." *The Crisis* accordingly branded the Soviet Union guilty of shameless and hard-boiled "opportunism" and its protestation of "self-determination for small nations" and "love for the downtrodden, exploited black people" so much "pious flub-dub."[145] When the news broke that the Soviet Union had sold oil to Mussolini, many black activists broke with orthodox Communism and organizations like the LAI overnight. Padmore recalled, "The few Africans in London who were associated with the League [against Imperialism] through affiliated membership of the Negro Improvement [Welfare] Association, headed by Arnold Ward, a West Indian, severed their association with the Communists and helped to form the International African Friends of Abyssinia."[146]

There was an understandable tendency among black revolutionary activists who had just had their faith in the Soviet Union and orthodox Communism shattered to now turn to a primarily cultural Pan-Africanism. It is telling, for example, that Kenyatta would now adopt Kikuyu dress, despite the cold climate of Britain.[147] More worryingly, many radical black activists in Britain were so disgusted at the betrayal of the Soviet Union that they began to retreat from revolutionary politics altogether, and they fell back into lobbying and placing demands on the British government. This tendency even affected someone of the caliber of George Padmore, as can be seen from his generally authoritative and impressive study *How Britain Rules Africa* (1936), which he had been working on since 1934.[148]

Padmore stated at the outset of *How Britain Rules Africa* that "very little is known about the effects of the capitalist economic system upon the native populations, a subject upon which we hope to throw some light." As

Padmore put it, "Our chief aim is to throw light into dark places" and in colonial Africa "everywhere we shall see stark imperialist oppression and exploitation, allied with racial ignorance and arrogance, swaggering about without the least sign of shame." Padmore deployed the term "colonial Fascism" to describe places such as Kenya and South Africa, in order to highlight the problematic nature of the Communist International's turn in 1935 toward liberal "anti-fascism" through building newfangled "Popular Front" alliances at the expense of anticolonial work. "The Colonies are the breeding-ground for the type of fascist mentality which is being let loose in Europe today," Padmore asserted, and the "brutality and barbarity" apparent in places like South Africa and Kenya reminded Padmore "of conditions in [Nazi] Germany." Padmore dedicated his work to "The Youth of My Race — The Vanguard of the New Africa" and ended it with a proto-Fanonian rallying cry for Pan-African liberation: "As far as Africa is concerned the way is still dark, the goal is not yet in sight, but about one thing Africans have no doubts, and that is: The future belongs to the oppressed. The future of Africa belongs to the Blacks, for they are the most oppressed of the earth."[149]

"Never was a book more timely," James declared in his review of *How Britain Rules Africa*. James praised Padmore's work, noting that "as a picture of Africa today, economic and political, it is a masterpiece of reliable information, knowledge and understanding, and easily the best book of its type that has yet appeared."[150] James was not uncritical, however, because while Padmore had drawn heavily on Lenin's *Imperialism* for analysis, the comment that "as far as Africa is concerned the way is still dark, the goal is not yet in sight" suggested he no longer seemed to have an answer to Lenin's crucial question "What Is to Be Done?" or at least, if he did, it was not particularly Leninist. Indeed, Padmore's epilogue noted that

> since the war, the more enlightened and far-sighted sections of the ruling classes of Europe with colonial interests in Africa have been appealing to the Blacks to co-operate with them. Africans welcome this gesture, for they want to co-operate and live in peace with all peoples, irrespective of race, colour and creed. But how can there be co-operation with those who seek to destroy them? . . . Let those who preach co-operation demonstrate their sympathy with Africa in *deeds*, not words; for Africans have had too many empty promises made them in the past, and the present is far from being reassuring.[151]

James publicly rebuked the reformist logic implicit in his friend's perspective:

> It is on the future of Africa that the author, himself a man of African descent, is grievously disappointing. He heads one section "Will Britain Betray Her Trust?" as if he were some missionary or Labour politician. In the true tradition of Lenin, he insists on the rights of the African people to choose their own development. But, astonishingly, he welcomes the appeal of "enlightened far-sighted sections of the ruling classes of Europe with colonial interests in Africa" to co-operate with Africans. That is madness. How does the lion co-operate with the lamb?
>
> Africans must win their own freedom. Nobody will win it for them. They need co-operation, but that co-operation must be with the revolutionary movement in Europe and Asia. There is no other way out. Each movement will neglect the other at its peril, and there is not much time left. The great cracks in the imperialist structure are widening day by day.[152]

In March 1936, the staging of *Toussaint Louverture*, James's anti-imperialist play about the Haitian Revolution, at London's Westminster Theatre, not only symbolized the Ethiopian resistance to Italian imperialism on the British stage but also must have helped counteract the tendency among Pan-Africanist radicals to abandon revolutionary politics in this period. James's own vision of Pan-African liberation was again restated in a lecture on "Economic Organisation in the Tropics," given to the LCP at their third annual weekend conference, again at High Leigh, in Hoddesden, on Saturday, April 4, 1936. As *The Keys* reported,

> [James] begun by pointing out how appropriate it was for the Conference to begin by considering the economic problems. For economics was at the root of the matter in Africa. Europeans might talk as much as they liked about going to Africa to civilise the African, but it was important for Africans to realise that what took white men to Africa in the first place was the desire for profits, and that the nations of Europe would remain in Africa only so long as profits could be obtained.
>
> To secure profits they needed land and labour. Mr. James went on to illustrate the vileness into which white men in Africa had been led by their greed for land, and the measures, at times little short of slavery, which were practiced to compel a sufficient number of Africans to

apply to white men for work. That situation, in his view, was destined to worsen, for as Japan drove British Imperialists out of the East, and as their hold on India weakened, they would be driven increasingly to invest their capital in Africa.

Africa's problem, said Mr. James, was the same as the problem of every other part of the world. What we saw in Africa was capitalism in its vilest form. In Africa, as elsewhere, it was producing its own destroyer, the native proletariat, who were destined sooner or later, in company with their revolutionary comrades elsewhere, to establish a free Africa.

Unsurprisingly, James's unrepentant Marxist perspective on the situation—"what we saw in Africa was capitalism in its vilest form"—was followed by a "long and lively" discussion, during which "Mr. James was cross-examined on his view of the imminence of revolution in Africa, and on the theory that revolution could be an instrument of social progress."

After lunch, the controversy continued when Dr. Norman Leys, the Christian socialist and British authority on Kenya (where he had served as a government medical officer for twenty years) together with James "led a vigorous attack" on the philosophy underpinning talks by George Brown, a lecturer from America "who had just returned from sociological investigations in Liberia," and the British journalist Leonard Barnes, a former member of the Colonial Service and author of *The Duty of Empire* (1935). Brown and Barnes "seemed to suggest that the essential features of tribal organization could be retained" and progress in Africa still be made, but for Leys and James "the tribe, dominated by superstitious custom and narrow loyalties, belonged to the past, and could never stand up to the spread of education and transport facilities." *The Keys* notes that "round this central problem the conference ranged itself into two groups which, at teatime, were still unable to agree."[153] Members of the LCP were equally fiercely divided by the question of the relationship of religious missionaries to imperialism.[154] James's refusal to romanticize the old tribal networks around chiefs in colonial Africa and to counterpose instead struggles of the "native proletariat" reinforces the extent to which his Pan-Africanism was quite different in character from that of Kenyatta, for example.[155]

In order to help win such arguments and stress the continuing relevance of agitating for social revolution, James felt the pressing need for an accessible, comprehensive work in English that would present the Marxist critique of the Stalinized Communist International that Trotsky had done so much to develop, above all in his draft statement delivered in 1928 in response to the Sixth Congress of the Communist International, "The Third International after Lenin." In early 1936, James had been introduced by Fenner Brockway to the publisher Fredric Warburg, and, as he remembered, Warburg wanted "to publish some books about the Left." As James recalled, "Warburg . . . sends to tell me that he wants to see me. . . . I am invited to go to the country with him and his wife. . . . They take me down to play cricket. He says, 'James, I want you to write a book about African Socialism.' I tell him, 'No, that is not the book for me.'"[156]

The book that James convinced Warburg to publish instead would be James's pioneering anti-Stalinist history of "the rise and fall of the Communist International," *World Revolution, 1917–1936* (1937), no mean achievement given this was destined to be one work on the Communist International that few orthodox Communists would be rushing out to buy.[157] The title seems to have been chosen as a direct repost to the leading CPGB theorist Rajani Palme Dutt's recent *World Politics, 1918–1936* (Left Book Club choice in July 1936), an examination of the world of "official politics" that focused on the Great Power relations between states as they had evolved, discussing, for example, "the New Power-Relations after the War" and with the ubiquitous homage to Russian state power, "the Victory of Socialism in the Soviet Union."[158] Contra Dutt, James kept his attention firmly focused on the political activity and development of the "international revolutionary movement against Capitalism."[159]

As a historian who was simultaneously researching the interplay between the French Revolution and the Haitian Revolution, James was well suited to explore the ramifications of the international for the national with respect to the Russian Revolution. If the Haitian revolutionary leader Toussaint Louverture ultimately failed, James would write in 1938 in *The Black Jacobins*, "it is for the same reason that the Russian socialist revolution failed, even after all its achievements—the defeat of the revolution in Europe."[160] In *World Revolution*, James powerfully demonstrated how the defeat of, above all, the German revolution of 1918–23 led to the rise of a blood-soaked "terrorist regime" of Stalinist bureaucrats in the Soviet Union itself, a dictatorship that was not only "a caricature of socialism," but also a "revolting tyranny," a "political tyranny without parallel in Europe."[161] He also tracked the resulting implications of the rise of the Stalinist bureaucracy for Soviet foreign policy, detailing for example, how and why initial support for "workers' sanctions" on fascist Italy to stop the war on Ethiopia in Communist International propaganda and agitation became steadily replaced by support for action by the League of Nations alone.[162]

With the publication of *World Revolution*, James became, as Martin Upham notes, "the first British Trotskyist to make a substantial theoretical contribution."[163] When they finally met in 1939, Trotsky told James he had written "a very good book," though it was marred by "a lack of dialectical approach, Anglo-Saxon empiricism, and formalism which is only the reverse of empiricism." Trotsky thought James had failed to adequately track the degeneration of the Communist International from 1917 to 1936 carefully enough, in particular with respect to the failure of the German revolution in 1923 and the Chinese revolution in 1927. Whereas James had provocatively headed a chapter "Stalin Kills the 1923 Revolution," Trotsky felt "the German revolution had more influence on Stalin than Stalin on the German revolution."[164] James had perhaps been a little too deeply influenced on matters relating to the German labour movement by his German anarchist friend Charlie Lahr. James recalled Lahr's concrete knowledge had helped him

> penetrate more profoundly than usual not so much into the political arguments and conflicts but into the actual feeling of the different social organisations in Germany before Hitler. I do not hesitate [in chapter 12, "After Hitler, Our Turn"] . . . in showing that the Communist International deliberately manoeuvred Hitler into power. . . . There is a sense of journalism from day to day in the chapter which is the result of my constant seeking out Charlie as events happened from day to day.[165]

Trotsky was understandably less impressed with the specificities of this aspect of James's argument, noting that he could not "agree that the policy of the International was only a materialisation of the commands of Moscow," while the idea that Stalin had a "plan" to "allow fascism to come into power [was] absurd . . . a deification of Stalin."[166]

By the time of the publication of *World Revolution*, in April 1937, the Moscow Trials were in full swing, and the leaders of Western Communist parties were busy dutifully following orders to intensify their "campaign in the press and among the masses against Trotsky and Trotskyism as a terrorist agency, a gang of wreckers, subversives, spies, and accomplices of the German Gestapo."[167] Whereas the far-from-tranquil circumstances in which James had written *World Revolution* undoubtedly accounts for some of its weaknesses and limitations, it nonetheless represented a timely intellectual defense of the Trotskyist movement amid this growing atmosphere of slander, hysteria, and hatred. Despite Communist denunciation of *World Revolution* as "objectively fascist," Warburg remembers it "sold moderately well" and "became a kind of Bible of Trotskyism."[168] The veteran British socialist Raymond Postgate described it in the *New Statesman* as "unique of its kind" and "very badly needed," while a reviewer in Postgate's new left wing monthly FACT noted, "We welcome Mr. James's illuminating essay[,] ... a careful, disciplined anti-Stalinist history of the course of the revolution since 1917."[169] Indeed, even some British Communists of the 1930s were intrigued enough to risk a brief look. Tom Kemp, who was later to break with the CPGB after 1956 and join the Trotskyist movement, recalled that "back in the 1930s, worried about the Moscow Trials, I had a surreptitious look at [Trotsky's] *The Revolution Betrayed* or C.L.R. James's *World Revolution* in the public library, only to hastily put it away if a friend approached."[170] Outside Britain, the British colonial authorities, with James now under surveillance as a threat to imperial "security," naturally moved to censor *World Revolution*, forbidding the export of the work to India, though Al Richardson, in his illuminating introduction to the republication of the work in 1993, noted it was smuggled in and so made some impact.[171]

Fight

From October 1936, James also took on editing *Fight*, the journal of the Marxist Group—the name of the small, British Trotskyist group of which James was a leading member, and that operated first inside and then outside the ILP as an independent group from late 1936. *Fight* came out on a more or less monthly basis, and James's first editorial reiterated that "this journal stands for the old principles of international Socialism," including standing "for the support of colonial toilers against capitalist oppression and tyranny, but through their own revolutionary struggles and not through the League of Nations." Accordingly, James noted, "We shall devote space in every issue to the colonial question."[172] As well as reporting on various anticolonial struggles, in the second issue of *Fight*, published in December 1936, James reprinted an extract from a speech Lenin made in 1920 at the Second Congress of the Communist International, which stressed the possible significance of the "peasant Soviets" that emerged during the Russian Revolution for the future "development of backward peoples." For Lenin, "Peasant soviets, the soviets of the exploited, are applicable not only to capitalist countries, but can be adapted also to pre-capitalist conditions. . . . With the assistance of the proletariat of the advanced countries the backward nations can arrive to the Soviet form of organisation and through certain stages pass on to Communism, obviating the capitalist stage. . . . All working masses, including those of the remotest nationalities, are susceptible to the Soviet idea."

For James, as he stressed to readers of *Fight*, "Lenin had a profoundly original conception of the development of backward people," and it seems Lenin's discussion of "peasant Soviets," together with the Marxist theory of permanent revolution, constituted the theoretical basis underpinning how James imagined how the coming African revolution might unfold and develop.[173] While James accepted that colonial Africans in revolt had "a real chance of success only when British Imperialism [was] being attacked at the same time by the British revolutionary workers," in the meantime he reiterated there was "a lot that [could] be done." James noted,

> Some of the African peoples, the Kikuyu of Kenya for instance, have representatives in London. Negro seamen live in London and can make contacts with Kenya and other parts of Africa. We can build up a real solidarity by fighting the cause of Africans, Indians, and other colonials here and by letting them know that we look to them to help us in the struggle. . . . A revolutionary movement in this country can never achieve final success unless in close understanding and cooperation with the revolution in the colonies.[174]

The International African Service Bureau

Though the IAFA itself had disbanded after "major combat operations" had finished in Ethiopia and after others in April 1936 had formed the broader Abyssinian Association to continue the campaign against the Italian occupation, the questions Mussolini's invasion and occupation had raised about Africa and imperialist domination in general were more relevant than ever as Europe headed once again toward war.[175] Accordingly, from about June 1936, Padmore had tried to launch a new broad organization, the "Pan-African Federation." As well as referring to a publication, *Voice of Africa*, published by the "Pan-African Congress (British section)," Special Branch files mention Kenyatta's speaking at London meetings of this in June 1936 with Makonnen and the veteran West African Pan-Africanist Robert Broadhurst, who had been involved in Pan-African Congresses organized in London in 1911 and 1921.[176] On July 31, 1936, Padmore convened a public meeting of the Pan-African Federation at Memorial Hall, on Farringdon Street. Alongside Padmore, the platform of speakers included Arthur Creech Jones and William Mellor, from the Labour Party; Fenner Brockway, from the ILP; Dorothy Woodman, secretary of the Union of Democratic Control; and the Indian nationalist Krishna Menon.[177] Makonnen managed to secure the Pan-African Federation a place to meet, by renting a basement flat on 2 Calthorpe Street, and he remembers that various black people in London "came around simply because we provided a base and a talking point where the coffee pot was almost always on the stove. . . . The movement gradually proceeded."[178]

Padmore would also soon benefit from one remarkable piece of good luck, recovering a large discarded stock of his rare and valuable study *The Life and Struggles of Negro Toilers* (1931) from the CPGB's "Workers' Bookshop" when it moved to a new location in 1936.[179] However, selling books to contacts at various and assorted meetings was no substitute for having an effective organization, and many in the Pan-African Federation were impressed by the impact Menon's India League had managed to make in Britain.[180] As Makonnen remembers, "We were out to create a movement. . . . The existing African and West Indian organizations in England at the time were very mild, and also one could see a useful parallel in the Indian League with its powerful expatriate Indian nucleus working in close conjunction with the Labour Party intellectuals."[181]

There seem to have been a number of preparatory meetings of what was then known as "the Pan African Federation, known as the Pan Afro Group," in April 1937, including one attended by two key black American activists in the National Negro Congress, the young academic Ralph Bunche and Max Yergan.[182] Yet more critical in importance still was the recent arrival in London of Isaac Theophilus Akuna Wallace-Johnson, of Sierra Leone. A Communist, Wallace-Johnson was a former seaman who was now secretary of the West African Youth League and a towering giant of African trade unionism.[183] In May 1937, just as the LAI was finally wound up, the International African Service Bureau for the Defence of Africans and People of African Descent (IASB) was now launched, holding regular open-air meetings on Sunday afternoon in Hyde Park. In the first issue of its monthly news bulletin, *Africa and the World*, in July 1937, the IASB declared its aims and objectives:

> The International African Service Bureau is an organisation representing the progressive and enlightened public opinion among Africans and peoples of African descent. It supports the demands of Africans and other colonial peoples for democratic rights, civil liberties and self-determination.
>
> One of the chief functions of the Bureau will be to help and enlighten public opinion in Great Britain, especially the working and middle classes, as to the true condition in the various colonies, protectorates and mandated territories in Africa, the West Indies and other colonial areas. In this way we hope than the people of England will be in a better position to raise their voices in protest against abuses and injustices which obtain in many colonies.[184]

Makonnen remembers that the IASB was neither "large" nor "highly-organised" but "it came together in an informal way." "Padmore was there, James, Babalola Wilkie from Nigeria and perhaps another thirty fellows. But there wasn't any clear membership."[185] They had support from several key ILP intellectuals, including not only Reginald Reynolds and Ethel Mannin, but also the independent Marxist F. A. Ridley, author of *Mussolini over Africa* (1935).[186] By the time the IASB held its first quarterly meeting in an Indian restaurant on September 7, 1937, the group, while in debt, could report steady progress (including, for example, pressuring sympathetic MPs to ask a total of twenty-three awkward questions in Parliament since May).

Makonnen drew up a constitution, limiting "Active Membership" to "Africans and peoples of African descent, regardless of nationality, political creed or religious faith, who accept its aims and abide by its Constitution." The leadership that crystallized around Padmore, who became chair, and James was also very strong. Wallace-Johnson, who became general secretary, had been the editor of a paper called *West African Sentinel*, and now in Britain, in October 1937, he launched a journal for the IASB, *African Sentinel*, "a Journal devoted to the interest of Africans and peoples of African descent, all over the world." The initial idea seems to have been that it would accompany the news bulletin *Africa and the World*, which James had helped edit, but *African Sentinel* soon replaced the earlier bulletin. Amy Ashwood was vice president, with Broadhurst treasurer. "Associate Membership" was declared "open to Europeans and members of other races who sympathise with the aims and objects of the Bureau," and by now the IASB had an impressive list of patrons, enabling the group to take offices on Gray's Inn Road. Patrons included not only Nancy Cunard, Mary Downes, F. A. Ridley, Victor Gollancz, Sylvia Pankhurst, and Dorothy Woodman but also four Labour MPs (Philip Noel-Baker; D. N. Pritt, K. C.; Ellen Wilkinson; and future Labour colonial secretary Arthur Creech Jones).[187]

The first issue of *African Sentinel* clearly spelled out the independence of the IASB, but, reflecting the diversity of its patrons, noted in the section "Our Policy" that though the group owed "no allegiance or obligation whatsoever to any organisation or group in this or any other European country," it aimed as far as possible to be "constructive, fair and liberal in [its] views and opinions." As the *African Sentinel* declared:

> Our main objective is to serve as a medium of information between the Colonial and European public — the British in particular — as well as to create a connecting link between the Africans at home (in Africa) and the Africans abroad (in the West Indies, United States of America and other Western countries) by the transmission of messages and information, news and views, from one to another, in the most accurate and concise forms. The fundamental cause for which we are out and which is to advocate and defend, as far as it may be possible, the cause of the oppressed sections of humanity, and particularly of the great majority of Africans and peoples of African descent who are scattered all over the face of the globe.[188]

James remembers, "Padmore was tireless. . . . He had wide connections while he had been an official of the Comintern" with radical black Pan-Africanists and "despite the vicious lying attacks that the Communists spread about him . . . from Africa, the Caribbean and elsewhere they came to him and his organisation in a ceaseless stream."[189] Brent Hayes Edwards has convincingly stressed the importance here of Padmore's continuing close political relationship with Tiemoko Garan Kouyaté, the Paris-based Sudanese ex-Communist and Francophone Pan-Africanist, a relationship dating back to 1929, in shaping the IASB's subsequent strategic vision and organizational form.[190] Moreover, thanks in the main to Wallace-Johnson, a whole host of West African radicals were brought onto becoming at least nominal members of the IASB executive.[191]

One remarkable aspect of the IASB was the leading role played by West Indians rather than Africans. Kenyatta, Wallace-Johnson, and Broadhurst aside, the leadership was dominated by West Indians, above all Padmore, James, Amy Ashwood, Makonnen (publicity secretary), and Chris Braith-waite (alias "Jones"), organizing secretary.[192] Indeed, James would later de-scribe the IASB as "the most striking West Indian creation between the wars."[193] Bill Schwarz has drawn attention to this, wondering at "the hubris of this tiny group of West Indians, in the IASB and its forerunners, in turn-ing their attention to the entire stage of Africa, believing they had it within their grasp to organize the emancipation of a continent."[194] There are in-deed striking historical parallels with the work of a Trinidadian nationalist of an earlier generation, Henry Sylvester Williams, who had founded an "African Association" in London, which called the world's first Pan-African conference in July 1900. But a charge of "hubris" made against the IASB seems misplaced, for as the group explicitly acknowledged in 1938, "We know our limitations." As *International African Opinion* put it:

> We know that we cannot liberate the millions of Africans and peoples of African descent from their servitude and oppression. That task no one can do but the black people themselves. But we can help to stimu-late the growing consciousness of the blacks, to give them the benefit of our daily contact with the European movement, to learn from the black masses the lessons of the profound experiences that they accumulate in their daily toil, to point out certain pitfalls that may be avoided, to co-ordinate information and organization, to do an incessant propaganda in every quarter of Britain, exposing evils, pressing for such remedies as are possible, and mobilizing whatever assistance there is to be found in Europe for the cause of African emancipation.[195]

Makonnen recalled how they settled on the name "Service Bureau": "We had naturally considered the possibilities of reviving Du Bois's pan-African movement, but it seemed safer to operate under the umbrella of service rather than risk a frontal attack by taking a bolder Pan-African title. The idea therefore was to emphasize service to people of African descent in as many ways as possible—educational, economic, co-operative and political."[196]

In other words, they did not even regard themselves as worthy successors to the now more or less defunct movement around W. E. B. Du Bois, which had organized Pan-African conferences in London in the past, let alone arrogantly assume they could organize the liberation of Africa. Rather, the IASB raised the case for and built solidarity with liberation struggles across the African diaspora. James remembers their "main weapon was propaganda," and through public meetings, composing resolutions and statements, pressuring MPs, and firing off letters to the British press they "prevented anyone being able to say that people were 'satisfied' with the colonial situation or 'apathetic.'" By 1938, the IASB, thanks to the fundraising talents of Makonnen, had also managed to raise the necessary money to rent a new base at 12a Westbourne Grove, "the upper floor of a large building where [members] held meetings and had rooms for strangers visiting London."[197] Aside from holding their own meetings, the IASB also held large rallies in Trafalgar Square on a fairly regular basis, while on "Empire Day," May 24, 1938, the group organized an anticolonial exhibition at London's Conway Hall.[198]

A History of Negro Revolt

Testimony to the growing profile of the IASB in 1937 came when the British socialist historian Raymond Postgate asked Padmore for a piece on "Negro revolt" for his left-wing monthly review FACT. It is perhaps revealing of Padmore's own politics, and also that in 1937 his new work *Africa and World Peace* had been published, that, claiming pressures of IASB activity, he instead referred Postgate to James. James, who was just putting the finishing touches to *The Black Jacobins* and was by this time "within Padmore's circle of associates, the most articulate theoretician of Pan-Africanism," according to Manning Marable, wrote what became *A History of Negro Revolt* rapidly, finishing by April 1938.[199] Padmore was a critical source of support, and James recalled how Padmore "brought his great knowledge of Africa to bear" and the two "had a marvellous time putting in a number of provocative statements which [they] knew Postgate would object to. But by putting in those and then agreeing to take them out, much really good stuff was sure to get in." James paid tribute to Padmore in *A History of Negro Revolt*, noting: "The files of the *Negro Worker* give many accounts of these revolts, and *The Life and Struggles of Negro Toilers*, by George Padmore, contains a great deal of coordinated information which is not easily available elsewhere."[200]

A History of Negro Revolt was a fast-paced and sweeping study, in which James portrayed and analyzed from a Marxist perspective an incredibly rich and diverse range of social movements and black liberation struggles across the African diaspora dating from the Haitian Revolution, in the process helping to recover an almost submerged revolutionary tradition. Like *World Revolution*, *A History of Negro Revolt* inevitably suffered a little in places from the rushed circumstances of its composition, and many have echoed Worcester when he suggested that it is "marred by a distracting degree of sloppiness both at the level of presentation and theory."[201] Yet whatever the work's weaknesses and limitations, what stands out today above all, as Michael O. West and William G. Martin have noted recently, is how it represents a "pioneering and exceptional" contribution to the historiography of revolutionary "black internationalism."[202]

Recalling the writing of *The Black Jacobins*, James noted that "historical in form, it drew its contemporaneousness, as all such books must, from the living struggle around us, and particularly from the daily activity that centred around Padmore and the African Bureau."[203] The same and more could be applied to the writing of *A History of Negro Revolt*, which in its discussion of contemporary struggles across Africa and the Caribbean often relied directly for information on the IASB's supporters in the colonial world. Particularly critical here was the rather overlooked role played by Chris Braithwaite, IASB organizing secretary, an important "class struggle Pan-Africanist" in his own right who was perhaps the critical lynchpin of an anticolonial maritime subaltern network in and around the imperial metropolis of interwar London. Through his contacts as chair of the Colonial Seamen's Association, which he had helped found in 1935, Braithwaite was key to the distribution of IASB literature into colonial Africa and the Caribbean. James recalled that they "tried all ways" to get their banned "subversive" publications into the colonies. James remembered, "We had one or two people who worked on the waterfront. They gave the pamphlets to seamen and people in boats. . . . We got it around, to my astonishment and delight."[204] The contacts Braithwaite and others made in turn fed information and reports back to London. One very clear example of this can be seen in James's discussion of the heroic arc of labor rebellions that swept the British Caribbean during the 1930s, when the Caribbean background of leading members of the IASB and their contacts with activists in places such as Trinidad and Jamaica enabled the IASB to effectively rally solidarity in Britain itself.[205]

FIGURE 3.6 Chris Braithwaite, circa 1940. Used by permission of the Braithwaite family.

Perhaps some of the most important and original sections of *A History of Negro Revolt* emerged when James focused his attention on colonial Africa and the "series of revolts, which [had] never ceased" since the European "scramble" for the continent in the 1880s, up to and including the general strike in the Gold Coast (now Ghana) in 1937. James's stress on agency here made the work very different from, for example, Padmore's *How Britain Rules Africa*, which provided relentless detail over four hundred pages of the exploitation of African workers through charting the precise structural differences in terms of capital formation and imperial rule that marked each individual colony. As James noted succinctly, "The difference between the native under Belgian imperialism plain and simple, and Belgian imperialism carrying out the mandate of the League of Nations, is that the Belgian Government presents a report at Geneva on the working of the mandate. The native, however, is not likely to know this."[206]

Despite the problems of censorship about uprisings in the colonial world, through the IASB's contacts, James, for example, managed to piece together a brief portrayal of "the extraordinary women's revolt" against the implementation of an unfair new tax in the British colony of Nigeria in 1929. Though what is now known as the "Women's War" was bloodily repressed, James noted this was a spontaneous rebellion, "the strength and vigour" of which were "a shock to the Europeans." As James described it:

> Thousands of women organised protest demonstrations against the Government and its chiefs and at Aba, the capital of the Eastern Province, the women who sold in the market, faced with the possibility of a tax which would destroy their small profits, organized a revolt. The writer is informed by Africans from Nigeria that the actual happenings in Aba have been suppressed in all official reports. The women seized public buildings and held them for days. The servants refused to cook for their white masters and mistresses and some of them made the attempt to bring the European women by force into the markets to give them some experience of what work was like. . . . A detachment of soldiers suppressed the revolt, shooting at the black women as they tried to escape across the river. Martial law was proclaimed and the Governor called a meeting of the African editors of Lagos threatening them with imprisonment if they published news of what was happening at Aba.[207]

The Copperbelt Mineworkers' Strike of 1935

James concluded *A History of Negro Revolt* with an account of the spontaneous mass strike of copper miners in Northern Rhodesia (what is now Zambia) in May 1935, an anticolonial struggle that James thought of immense historical portent and significance. The Copperbelt miners had struck in protest at an increase in the poll tax at a time of rising economic insecurity, a strike that was bloodily repressed, with six miners left dead and twenty-two wounded. Frederick Cooper has drawn attention to the creativity of the miners and their supporters during this strike: "The Northern Rhodesian mineworkers strike of 1935 was organised without benefit of trade unions, and it spread from mine to mine, from mine town to mine town, by personal networks, dance societies, religious organisations, and eventually mass meetings. The movement embraced nonminers in the towns, women as well as men."[208]

One can imagine the growing excitement for a "class struggle Pan-Africanist" and revolutionary Marxist like James in Britain as he gradually learned more and more about what had actually taken place. The movement was centered around the "native proletariat"—Copperbelt miners—yet the remarkable manner in which the struggle had spread seemed to almost suggest something akin to Lenin's vision of "peasant soviets." For James, the parallels between the glorious self-activity and capacity for improvisation displayed by the supporters of the striking Copperbelt miners and the enslaved Africans who had made the Haitian Revolution were compelling. "Should world events give these people a chance, they will destroy what has them by the throat as surely as the San Domingo blacks destroyed the French plantations." James made such a statement after noting that the official *Report of the Commission Appointed to Enquire into the Disturbances in the Copperbelt, Northern Rhodesia* (1935), a commission chaired by Sir Alison Russell, had found that "the Watch Tower Movement has some influence among the Rhodesian natives."[209] In *How Britain Rules Africa*, Padmore had described how the "Watch Tower Movement" of Jehovah's Witnesses and others was "one of the most formidable organisations of tribal-'religious' character" in Africa: "The *Watch Tower Movement*, although originating in Nyasaland, has widespread ramifications into the Belgian Congo, Northern Rhodesia and Tanganyika. Much of its activities is so interwoven in the tribal life of the people that it is difficult for Europeans to keep track of its underground activities."[210]

For James, the "Watch Tower Movement" was a symbol of the coming African revolution: "It is difficult to say exactly the true influence of the Watch Tower. The writer has been informed by Negro sailors that its influence is widely spread throughout Africa, and that it is the most powerful revolutionary force in Africa today." Using such sources as well as the detail in the Russell Commission, James went on to spell out a pioneering Marxist analysis of the appeal of this millenarian movement based on "Revelations of St. John the Baptist" in the Bible to those suffering under European colonial domination: "The Watch Tower bases its teaching on the second coming of Christ . . . [and declares] all the governments which are ruling the world, especially Great Britain and the United States of America, are organisations of Satan, and that all churches, especially the Protestant and Roman Catholic churches, are emissaries of Satan. Religion thus becomes a weapon in the class struggle."

James described how Watch Tower preached "a transparent doctrine" in colonial Africa, "a fierce resentment against all the imperialist Powers." "It does not seek to distinguish between the Fascist and the democratic imperialisms. To the vast body of Africans in Africa such a distinction is meaningless." Watch Tower saw Great Britain as the "blasphemous name" of the seventh head of "the Beast," which represented the ruling powers of the world under the control of the devil, "given authority over every tribe, people, language and nation." The League of Nations was a "false prophet" born of the devil, and the British Empire another beast that "exercised all the authority of the first beast on his behalf, and made the earth and its inhabitants worship the first beast. . . . He deceived the inhabitants of the earth." As James commented, "The gentle Jesus, meek and mild, of the missionaries cannot compete with the Watch Tower God." He continues: "Such are the ideas moving in the minds of these African copper miners. They are absurd only on the surface. They represent political realities and express political aspirations far more closely than programmes and policies of parties with millions of members, numerous journals and half a century of history behind them."[211]

In September 1938, *A History of Negro Revolt* was published, and James remembered it "could be seen on all bookshops and railway stalls."[212] Nonetheless, he recalled that "the book has a peculiar history": "Postgate's name got the book sold in book-stores all over the country. When they found out what was in it some of them carefully hid it. There were places we went to where we found they had hidden it — they put it under a lot of other books, but when you asked for it they would say, yes, we have it."[213]

Such self-censorship in the "dark heart" of imperial Britain was perhaps not so surprising. At the end of *The Black Jacobins*, James would describe colonial Africa as a "vast prison," and in *A History of Negro Revolt* James described how "the African bruises and breaks himself against his bars in the interests of freedoms wider than his own."[214] James stressed that a mass prison breakout was not just necessary but in certain conditions possible as there were so few white people who could act as guards around. Given that "the real basis of imperialist control in Africa [was] the cruisers and aeroplanes of Europe," the looming interimperialist war provided real possibilities for African revolutionaries. "If, for instance a revolt began in the Congo and spread to South Africa, East Africa, West Africa, the Africans could easily overwhelm the whites if these could no longer receive assistance from abroad."[215] Many other black writers naturally dreamed of a postcolonial Africa during the 1930s. The black American "literary Pan-

Africanist" George S. Schuyler even went as far as to imagine "a tale of black insurrection against Italian Imperialism," a "revolt in Ethiopia," the rise of a new "black Internationale," and the emergence of a "great new civilization in modern Africa," a "black Empire," in a set of Afrocentrist stories written during the 1930s.[216] However, few "organic intellectuals" of the Pan-African movement outside the colonial world itself did more than James in not only tirelessly working for African emancipation but also, in *A History of Negro Revolt*, excavating and recovering the concrete historical foundations and actual precedents in world history for the coming "African Revolution." As James put it, "Though dimly, the political consciousness immanent in the historical process emerges in groping and neglected Africa. If Toussaint wrote in the language of '89, the grotesquerie of Watch Tower primitively approximates to the dialectic of Marx and Lenin. This it is which lifts out of bleakness and invests with meaning a record of failure almost unrelieved."[217]

International African Opinion

After completing the manuscript of *A History of Negro Revolt* in April 1938, James felt that he now had the confidence, based on his political knowledge and historical and theoretical understanding of the anticolonial struggle in Africa, to be able to take on more responsibility for IASB affairs when Wallace-Johnson returned to Sierra Leone. Alongside his editing of the British Trotskyist publication *Fight*, James now took on editing what had been the *African Sentinel* but was now relaunched as *International African Opinion*, with the motto "Educate, co-operate, emancipate: Neutral in nothing affecting the African Peoples."[218] Makonnen would later remember that in the early stages of putting together IASB publications, "like many papers" of its kind, the editorial collective "would sometimes concoct letters purporting to come from the Congo and many other places."[219] By the time of the launch of *International African Opinion*, the experience and contacts of Padmore and Braithwaite, and the network around Wallace-Johnson, who was now back in Sierra Leone, meant that from the beginning the new journal began to circulate in a serious manner among colonial Africans. James now aimed to try to use the journal and IASB publications more generally to help ideologically arm the anticolonial networks around the group. He envisioned *International African Opinion* not as a "literary journal or giver of advice from the mountain-tops," but "a journal of action" that aimed to be "a living weapon in the struggle" and his editorials gave it a much more militant "class-struggle" outlook. As he put it in his first editorial,

> We base ourselves upon the great masses of the people. The individual achievements of a few black men do not and cannot solve the problems of the blacks. One of our most important tasks is to make clear to the black intellectuals and other members of the middle class, that in the present state of world affairs there is no way out for them by seeking crumbs from the tables of their imperialist masters. They must identify themselves with the struggle of the masses.

James declared, "We shall be merciless to those blacks who in pursuit of their own narrow interests so frequently betray the great masses of the Negroes, the large majority of them are the working poor."[220] As Brent Hayes Edwards notes, James's editorials recalled "earlier work such as Kouyaté's 'Vox Africae' and Padmore's editorial stance in the *Negro Worker* in its effort at a theoretical articulation of the complex relations between radical intellectual work in the metropole and black mass resistance in the colonies themselves."[221] The British authorities certainly regarded *International African Opinion* as "inflammatory," and like previous IASB material suppressed it from open sale.[222]

James's last editorial for the journal before he left for America in October 1938 noted "War Springs from Capitalist Rivalry" and "Only African Freedom Ensures Lasting Peace" and gives a flavor of the kind of revolutionary politics he was trying to inject into the IASB, and through the IASB to black anticolonial activists across the African diaspora, on the eve of another looming inter-imperialist war: "If we must fight, then Africans and peoples of African descent will fight for themselves, confident that in taking this course we, like the Blacks of San Domingo, will be playing an historical role in liberating not only ourselves but other sections of oppressed humanity. . . . Peace and Empire are irreconcilable. Imperialism must be destroyed."[223]

Thanks in no small part then to James, Padmore remembers that many black intellectuals around the IASB in Britain "held Marxist views on economic and political problems, although they were never members of the British Communist Party." By May 1938, the CPGB had retreated from offering British colonies independence and were merely committed to supporting interim democratic charter rights, but ever since the Communist International's turn to the "Popular Front" in 1935, James, Braithwaite, and Padmore used to go to CPGB meetings to expose their "pretensions at being revolutionists."[224] As James remembered, they would speak about the struggles of French and British colonial subjects who now had been forgotten as Britain and France were declared grand "peace-loving democracies" and bulwarks against fascism. James recalled, "While I would ask a question, and Padmore might say a word or two, it was Chris Jones [Braithwaite] who made a hell of a row."[225] Indeed, "at the shortest notice, he [Braithwaite] could generate indignation at the crimes of imperialism and the betrayals of Stalinism as to shock into awed silence hundreds of British people in the audience."[226] The close links these IASB members had with the ILP ensured that their uncompromisingly anti-imperialist argument reached a small but significant audience on the British Left, and influenced many, including George Orwell.[227]

One of the most famous interventions by IASB activists came in mid-July 1938, at the London Conference on Peace and Empire, an event organized by the India League in conjunction with the London Federation of Peace Councils. "The subject peoples are no longer docile and capable of being used to suit the purposes of imperial powers," Nehru declared to his thousand-strong audience in the Albert Hall.[228] Yet the full profundity of such a lesson was clearly lost on most of those in attendance. Most of the British Left at this time would have tended to agree with the distinction articulated at the conference by the British Labour politician and prominent advocate of the Popular Front Sir Stafford Cripps, who conceded that while India was strong enough to have freedom now, Africa for some time would have to be governed by "trusteeship" under some sort of international mandate. Cripps was accordingly heckled from the conference floor by IASB members and then savaged in the journal *International African Opinion* by James:

> It is clear that Sir Stafford Cripps has the typical vice of many European Socialists, even revolutionaries. He conceives Africans as essentially passive recipients of freedom given to them by Europeans. Possibly Sir Stafford thinks that the British working class will gain freedom by the ballot-box and the speeches of Major Attlee and himself. Thinking Africans know that ultimately they will win theirs, arms in hand, or forever remain slaves. . . . They will organise themselves, create armies, develop leaders. We have an historic parallel. The half-brutish and de-

graded slaves in San Domingo in 1791 joined the French Revolution. In six years illiterate slaves were Generals of division and able administrators. . . . The African slaves will do the same and more at the prospect of a new existence. Without them and the other colonial masses, the British worker can win at most only temporary success. Is it to leaders and people like these who have conquered their liberty in blood and sacrifice that Sir Stafford will offer his "trusteeship"?

On the question of imperialism, Cripps's speech revealed that it was actually the European working-class movement that was "backward." As James wrote of Cripps:

Sir Stafford is also a victim of one of the crudest of bourgeois sophistries. . . . Any sort of "trusteeship" will be needed only by exploitation. The European movement is indeed backward when Sir Stafford can make these proposals without a protest being made. . . . The surest way to lay up infinite trouble, not only for Africans but for Europeans, is to encourage reactionary ideas like trusteeship for backward peoples. The bureaucratic mentality which displays itself so blatantly in regard to people abroad can be trusted to show itself at home. It must be fought by Africans and European workers alike in their common interests.[229]

Overall, if Paul Robeson, the black American singer and star of the stage and screen, could in 1953 declare he had "discovered Africa" and come to consider himself "an African" in London, his home from 1927 to 1938, in part through studying African languages and folksongs at what is now the School of Oriental and African Studies, the same was fundamentally true for James, though he of course undertook no formal academic study.[230] Rather, James developed his Pan-Africanism in Britain through independent reading related to his researches into the Haitian Revolution, discussions with the likes of Padmore, and organizing alongside African activists such as Wallace-Johnson and his compatriot from Sierra Leone, Robert Broadhurst, a man Wallace-Johnson once described as "the Grand Old Man of African nationalism."[231] Some, like Kenyatta, would go on to play leading roles in the process of decolonization after the Second World War. It might be enough to surmise here that against the idea that James "had a long way to go to come to terms with the distinctive African contributions to human civilization" once he had become a Marxist, it seems that his experience during the 1930s only served to strengthen his initial feelings about the human capabilities of African people as a whole, feelings he had developed growing up in the Caribbean.[232] As James concluded in *The Black Jacobins*, a work written with Pan-African resistance to European colonialism at the very forefront of his mind,

> the imperialists envisage an eternity of African exploitation: the African is backward, ignorant. . . . They dream dreams. . . . The blacks of Africa are more advanced, nearer ready than were the slaves of San Domingo. . . . Imperialism vaunts its exploitation of the wealth of Africa for the benefit of civilisation. In reality, from the very nature of its system of profit it strangles the real wealth of the continent — the creative capacity of the African people. The African faces a long and difficult road and he will need guidance. But he will tread it fast because he will walk upright.[233]

FOUR

"The Humbler Type of Cricket Scribe"

C. L. R. James on Sport, Culture, and Society

C. L. R. James's *Beyond a Boundary* (1963) was once famously hailed by John Arlott as "arguably the best book ever written about cricket. . . . It is not only a warm and human book, but the most profound and searching discussion ever propounded on the game, if only for the reason that the writer was the most erudite, intellectual and also humanly perceptive person who ever devoted himself to its study."[1] As a profoundly insightful and influential meditation on the aesthetics and history of cricket, the work has secured for itself the status, as Stefan Collini has noted, of a "minor classic":

> That unclassifiable work—part autobiography, part cricket history, part cultural meditation, part nationalist polemic—was remarkable for its strong sense of form, despite the apparent heterogeneity of its subject-matter. A discussion of the ethical teaching of Dr Arnold, the Victorian headmaster, seemed to lead ineluctably into an argument for making Frank Worrell the first black man to captain the West Indian cricket team. It was a book by someone who was passionate about cricket, but who never lost sight of the truth that there were far more important things to be passionate about.[2]

This chapter is not going to dwell at any length on *Beyond a Boundary* as a seminal discussion of the contradictory and complex relationship between colonialism and cricket, and how the quintessentially English game of cricket came to so profoundly shape the culture of the Caribbean.[3] The origins of *Beyond a Boundary* of course lie in James's growing awareness of the injustices of colonial rule as they manifested themselves while he was busy playing, watching, and reporting cricket in colonial Trinidad. Given that all sections of Trinidadian society had cricket clubs that regularly played each other, from the "white and wealthy" Queen's Park to the "totally black and with no social status whatever" plebians' Stingo, it was easy to compare all the top players at close range.[4] James never failed to be shocked and outraged at continually seeing quality black players, like the Stingo player and docker Telemarque, who deserved inclusion in the West Indian national side, left out by openly ignorant and racist white selectors.[5] Moreover, the simple fact that both the white and wealthy and the totally black played cricket regularly against each other cast light on the totality of society. One moment both teams would be on the pitch, "playing with a straight bat," treating the other as equals and offering each other consolation ("bad luck") only to then return to all the old deference and racism in the pavilion. Given this, together with the state repression of overtly political anticolonial activism, it is not surprising that some cricket matches took on immensely powerful symbolic significance, not least when the island's best "black" team, that of Shannon (with cricketers like Learie Constantine and Wilton St. Hill), played Queen's Park.

James recalls, "I had always seen cricket in a manner beyond the ordinary. Chiefly in the writings of C. B. Fry, who to this day I know as one of the finest of writers—non-intellectual writers of the twentieth century. He analysed cricket with an insight and a severity and yet with a breadth of view that you don't find normally. I had been trained on him. I had been brought up on his books."[6]

The inspiration for James of a figure like Charles Burgess Fry, a brilliant all-rounder who played for and captained England, notwithstanding, Bill Schwarz has noted that "one of the great paradoxes" of *Beyond a Boundary* "is that James's most 'English' work . . . could not have been imagined into existence without the work of great theoretical labour sustained in the United States." In a fine article on James's *American Civilization* (written around 1949–50), a work in which—as might be expected—cricket did not feature at all, Schwarz nonetheless explored how "the conceptual structure of *Beyond a Boundary* directly derives from the political and intellectual insights developed in the United States":

> *American Civilization* served James as a preparatory, experimental exercise—his *Grundrisse*, to draw an analogy from Marx scholarship—which made *Beyond a Boundary* possible. . . . In both we can witness James explicitly interrogating the precepts of a civilisation. And in both we can see a historical method peculiarly his own coming into effect.

. . . The achievement of James's ten-year labour of striving to think be-yond Trotskyism lie in both *American Civilization* and *Beyond a Bound-ary*, where the reader can follow his discovery that there were "large areas of human existence that my history and my politics did not seem to cover."[7]

James's work was not simply one remarkable product of his method-ological and theoretical shift. Andrew Smith, author of *C. L. R. James and the Study of Culture*, has suggested that "it was his [James's] time immersed in America's very different sporting culture that gave him the distance and point of comparison out of which he would finally produce *Beyond a Boundary*." Yet Smith has also usefully drawn attention to how "the basis of *Beyond a Boundary* had been worked out some quarter of a century be-fore the book was published," before James's fifteen-year-long American sojourn, while he was in Britain.[8]

For five of the seven summers James spent in Britain during the 1930s, he worked as a cricket reporter, "the first West Indian, the first man of colour, to serve as cricket reporter for the [Manchester] *Guardian*," and he was possibly the first black professional sports reporter in British history.[9] Yet aside from one superb article by Smith, James's early cricket writing has oddly failed to attract much scholarly attention despite his reputation as one of the outstanding theorists of the game.[10] In 1986, a dozen of some of James's finest articles, first for the *Manchester Guardian* (1933–35), working with Neville Cardus, and then for the *Glasgow Herald* (1937–38), were re-published as part of a wider collection of his writing on his beloved game, entitled simply *Cricket*.[11] In a review, Stefan Collini thought that though the author of *Beyond a Boundary* had "certainly earned his right" to such a vol-ume, republishing James's early journalism did "little justice to the author of that deeply pondered, carefully crafted work." For Collini:

In general, if such ephemera are to bear reprinting so long after the events they describe, the author must either be a distinguished stylist in his own right or else rise to a level of analysis that transcends the local detail. James's early *Guardian* pieces meet neither of these criteria. Per-haps he consciously disciplined himself to write in a manner he thought appropriate to the stiffer social world of English cricket, perhaps his role as Cardus's understrapper did not permit much adventurousness, either practically or psychologically. Certainly, some of the writing has a slightly dated, *Boy's Own* ring to it now: reporting a run-out, for example, he wrote "Leyland could not get back in time and had to go: it was a grave loss to the English eleven."[12]

Yet it is possible that the dozen selected essays in *Cricket* do not do James's early cricket journalism full justice. James, after all, wrote nearly 140 brief reports for the *Manchester Guardian* over three seasons, and fifty lengthier columns for the *Glasgow Herald* over two seasons. Though James modestly described himself in this period as "the humbler type of cricket scribe," contemporaries certainly commended his pieces highly enough. Fredric Warburg, for example, found them "splendid."[13] James's cricket journalism during the 1930s affirms the importance of this relatively neglected sphere of his existence to our understanding of his work in this period.[14] Smith's findings demonstrate how many of James's "central arguments that he develops in that book . . . are already discernible" in his early cricket writing, not least "his sense of the relationship between cricketing technique and a wider historical zeitgeist . . . and his passionate defence of the sport as art."[15]

Cricket Reporting in Britain

In *Beyond a Boundary*, James recalls his time as a cricket reporter in Britain during the 1930s as "happy days," noting, "If I were writing the usual type of cricket reminiscences I would have plenty to say."[16] He covered all levels of games, as he followed Lancashire around the country, doing battle over the course of three days against other county sides, and as he covered national celebration matches such as "Gentlemen" versus "Players," "England" versus "the Rest," and "North" versus "South," as well as the thrilling heights of the 1938 test series between England and Australia. Relentless practice allowed James to hone his technique, and he recalled that he was soon in "good form": "When I went round English cricket grounds reporting the matches of the Lancashire team, or when I watched all the Test matches through the season of 1938, these were times when I could sense the course of an over from the way the batsman stood waiting between balls."[17] As James wrote in 1937, "You can usually tell a great batsman even when he makes only ten runs, though few of us can reach that height of perspicacity which enabled the late Sydney Parson, after watching Victor Trumper make 1 and 0 against Essex in 1899, declare that he was the finest batsman which had ever come from Australia."[18]

From about the 1880s, as Matthew Engel notes, "Lancashire cricket began to occupy, if not quite a central position, then at least an honoured corner of the pages of *The* [Manchester] *Guardian*." A tradition was born, "and the great certainties of late Victorian and Edwardian England ran through *The Guardian's* cricket reports, which were often splendidly Lancashire chauvinist." Engel observes,

> If there was a golden age as far as the *M.G.* was concerned, it began after the war when a young man who had been serving as a reporter, drama critic and [C. P.] Scott's personal assistant fell ill with a pulmonary condition and, by way of convalescence, went at the news editor's suggestion for a few days in the sun at Old Trafford. And Neville Cardus, "Cricketer" as he was bylined after 1920, began to give the discerning readers of Manchester the best and most enjoyable cricket reports the world has ever seen. . . . The "Cricketer" era exactly spanned the inter-war period; in 1940, feeling redundant in Manchester shorn by war of both good cricket and good concerts, Cardus sailed to Australia and did a stint as music critic of the *Sydney Morning Herald*. He wrote about cricket on and off for *The Guardian* until his death in 1975, aged eighty-five.[19]

Ramachandra Guha has noted, "Modern cricket writing was founded, more or less, by Neville Cardus. . . . In his writing, the portrayal of character and the evocation of context take precedence over the analysis of technique." Guha argues that many of the best English cricket writers who followed "were all writers first and cricket writers second. It was Cardus who showed them that cricket could be a vehicle for literature. Without him, they might instead have made a career writing poetry or plays." Though Guha does not explicitly suggest the same was true of James, who had been a sports journalist in Trinidad and had grown up on the Victorian tradition of cricket literature epitomized by Ranjitsinhji's *The Jubilee Book of Cricket*, he does rightly note that Cardus was "read, but not copied or avoided, by the Trinidadian historian and revolutionary."[20] As James later wrote of Cardus, "his vivid darting style" ensured that "the *Manchester Guardian* held a unique position in the journalism of cricket." The very tradition of "cricket literature" that James consciously embraced complicates his own later suggestion that in Britain, "fiction-writing drained out of [him]."[21]

Even though during the 1930s, the "golden age" of the *Manchester Guardian*, James tended to be a cricket reporter somewhat in the shadow of Cardus, his writing offers us a unique take on the game during this critically important decade. Mike Cronin and Richard Holt note of the interwar period: "Cricket became entrenched as one of the cornerstones of Englishness and the accompanying centrality of the Empire within such a vision. Cricket, the test matches that were played between England and her colonial nations, and the values of fair play that were enshrined in the game, all combined to make the sport a powerful symbol of empire."[22] As one English cricket correspondent noted in 1937, "Today cricket has developed far beyond the imagination of its early players. . . . The fortunes of a few flannelled men upon a green field are responsible for the state of mind of thousands of people in different quarters of the earth. The game has become a business, a means of livelihood to hundreds, and the principal item of news in the daily journals of the British Empire."[23]

For James, a black colonial subject coming from one of the far-flung corners of the empire, to be employed in such a prestigious post as a journalist on two leading daily journals of imperial Britain was a tremendous personal achievement. "It was a great feeling," he later recalled, "to sit beside *The Times* in the Number One seat allowed to the *Manchester Guardian* at Old Trafford," Lancashire's home cricket ground.[24] More crucially it also allowed him an opportunity to cast his gaze over a custom and practice that was not just arguably the "national game" in the imperial metropolis but since its "golden age" had become the game of English-speaking peoples across the empire. If, as Keith Sandiford has suggested, "the story of imperial cricket is really about the colonial quest for identity in the face of the colonisers' search for authority," then James's cricket journalism may come to be seen not only as distinctive in its own right but also as a crucial first draft for a new writing of the history of the game in the 1930s.[25]

The 1933 West Indies Cricket Tour

In April 1933, James started as the *Manchester Guardian*'s cricket correspondent, which initially involved covering the early preparations for the West Indies tour of 1933. His "work" was to watch the visitors, many of them old friends, practicing in nets, though he did cover one early match in May, in which the West Indies took on Northamptonshire.[26] The 1933 tour was only the second time that the West Indies had officially played a test series in England, and James wrote about their team not just for the *Manchester Guardian* and the *Port of Spain Gazette*, but also for *The Cricketer* and *The*

Keys. The series he wrote on "West Indian cricket" from May 6 to June 24, 1933, in *The Cricketer* is particularly noteworthy, as he introduced English readers to the Caribbean, noting cricket there was organized in a more amateur fashion than in England. James commented, "The league cricketer in the North of England today with his good ground, his highly organised system of matches, his experienced professional and his enthusiastic (and generous) crowds enjoys advantages which not one in twenty of international West Indian cricketers enjoy. Yet if West Indians lack artificial aids Nature is on their side. We can play and often do play right through the year."[27]

Yet it was a quite different "natural" advantage that many English commentators now feared the visitors may look to exploit. The English side had just returned from defeating Australia in what became known as the infamous "Bodyline" test series of 1932–33, when Douglas Jardine, the public-school- and Oxford-educated Marylebone Cricket Club captain, instructed fast bowlers Harold Larwood and Bill Voce, both former Nottinghamshire coal miners, to bowl at the "body" of Australian batsmen, or so Australians claimed. This tactic of "fast leg theory," as the English cricket establishment euphemistically dubbed it, forced batsmen to either take evasive action from balls aimed less at their leg than at their body and head, or attempt to fend the ball away with the bat, possibly giving catching chances to the fielders deliberately massed close to the batsman on his leg side. As Jack Fingleton, one of the Australian team members, later put it, "bodyline" amounted to nothing less than "a revolution against [Donald] Bradman," designed to intimidate Australia's outstanding batsman, whose astonishingly high run rate had been central to Australia's away victory over England when they had previously met in 1930. As a tactic, however, bodyline "succeeded," because England regained the Ashes with a four to one margin, but it was also widely condemned by the Australians as a "revolution against cricket," or at least the spirit of fair play, and the storm cloud of controversy it blew up is still remembered today.[28]

In the run up to the first test in late June 1933, many English commentators fell into hypocritical hysteria about how dangerous the West Indian fast bowlers Learie Constantine and E. "Manny" Martindale might be on a fast pitch. James was quick to defend his compatriots, noting that what they bowled "was not body-line because there was only one man forward short leg on the on side," and thus not intimidating. However, James feared that West Indies cricket officialdom might change their bowling line out of deference. As James insisted,

Whether [Jack] Grant [the West Indies captain] will allow himself to be frightened by these English critics is an important question. If he breaks the morale of his fast bowlers by expressing doubts as to whether the tactics of Constantine and Martindale are fair, the West Indies should flay him alive. The English had no mercy on the Australians. Now that the tour is over and the Ashes won, nearly every English writer and cricketer with the most bare-faced effrontery condemns body-line bowling, but when the Australians protested they shrieked to high heaven that there was nothing in it and the Australians were merely squealing. This is our chance and if weakness and a lack of sense of realism in the high command makes us lose it, then our blood be upon our own head.[29]

James's concerns that the "high command" may let the side down echoed Constantine's critique in *Cricket and I*. Constantine noted:

Of all Test playing combinations the West Indies team alone is composed of men of different race. And there lies a difficulty which I believe few of the West Indian selectors themselves realise. . . . Test Match cricket today is no sort of game. It is a battle. And to win you need not only the strenuous efforts of individual players: the work of each player must be backed by a sense of solidarity, of all the others supporting him, not only actually but so to speak in the spirit. The lack of this is the chief weakness of the West Indies team in big cricket. . . . Until all members of a West Indies side realise that every consideration must give way before the necessity of uniting in spirit and in truth to win through a series of Test Matches the West Indians will not play the cricket that I know they can play. Much depends on the players, much more depends on the leadership, which must itself be above pettiness, sympathetic, and yet be strong, and command respect from all in the team.

The problem, as Hilary McD. Beckles explains, was that it was "the ideological position of white cricketers and administrators that contest with England was essentially a non-political event in which 'cousins' exchanged mutual admiration."[30] In 1923, for example, H. B. G. Austin, the white captain of the West Indies side touring Britain, said that he hoped his team "were worthy to belong to the Mother Country," declaring there was "no more patriotic part of the Empire than the British West Indies, and . . . they wanted, they demanded to be left with the Flag under which they bred."[31] A decade on, little had changed. The 1933 team contained any number of black players who could have captained the side, including Constantine himself, Martindale, Ben Sealey, and George Headley, but it was captained by G. C. "Jack" Grant, a Cambridge Blue. Beckles notes that Grant "supported the view that England was the motherland that deserved loyalty and respect from all its colonies in all areas of life," a view many black players in the side did not share, and "this divided and weakened West Indies cricket. The division was political, and had to be removed by political means."[32]

In general, James was hopeful about the West Indies prospects, reassuring his readers in the *Port of Spain Gazette*:

> After watching cricket here and carefully weighing my words, I have no hesitation in saying that in cricket, as in many other things, West Indians are among the most highly gifted people one can find anywhere. The English have money, thirty times our population, vast organisation, every conceivable advantage. Yet with all that, we could hold our own. Our trouble is that we have not yet learned to subordinate everything to winning. Under modern conditions to win you have got to make up your mind to win. The day West Indians White, Brown and Black learn to be West Indians, to see nothing in front to right or left but West Indian success and the means to it, that day they begin to be grown up. Along with that it will be necessary to cultivate any number of fine speeches, noble sentiments and unimpeachable principles. But these you must indulge in before the struggle, cricket or whatever else it may be, and also after the struggle is over.[33]

In June 1933, the publication of Constantine's *Cricket and I* was a timely aid to this "struggle." As James later noted, "To the West Indians it was the first book ever published in England by a world-famous West Indian writing as a West Indian about people and events in the West Indies."[34] In his preface to the work, Cardus declared, "Constantine is a representative man: he is West Indian cricket, just as W.G. Grace was English cricket."[35] The influence of James, who had ghostwritten the work, could be seen in some of the "noble sentiments and unimpeachable principles" that ran through the work. The work stressed that "Trinidad is a Crown Colony, that is to say it is governed by the Colonial Office officials in England, and a movement for throwing off this yoke is gathering strength." Constantine's autobiography also made note of the "political upheavals" at the time of the French Revolution, "not only in France but in the West Indian island of Hayti which belonged to the French."[36]

The 1933 test series allowed James to study up close "the other West Indian master of the period" aside from Constantine, the naturally outstanding young Jamaican batsman George Headley, who had been born in 1909. James recalled, "I watched the West Indies in the nets at Lord's in 1933 before the tour began. George never to my knowledge practised seriously. He fooled around playing the ball here and there. It was his first visit to England, but he was as sure of himself as if he were in Jamaica."[37] As James informed readers of the *Manchester Guardian*, Headley was "as great a master of style as he is of runs. . . . At the wicket no one can miss his mastery. He is of that type which uses a bat as if it is an extension of the arm. Ease, poise, balance, he has them all."[38] While James doubtless regularly met with the West Indies team socially, he did not get to cover the full tour itself, as most of his cricket reporting for the *Manchester Guardian* instead involved covering the county matches of Lancashire.[39] In late June 1933, for example, rather than being able to follow the first test between England and the West Indies at Lords, James found himself up in Manchester, watching "dull cricket" and "Warwickshire's stolid batting" at Old Trafford.[40] However, James's job meant he did get to see more of Britain than just London and Lancashire, and that summer he visited the cricket grounds of, among other places, Birmingham, Northampton, Harrogate, and Scarborough.[41]

England won the first test by an innings and twenty-seven runs, and the second test began at Old Trafford on July 22, 1933. Once again, James was forced to miss out, having to cover "Lancashire at the Oval" in London instead.[42] The West Indies batted first, making 375 all out, thanks to a spectacular 169 from Headley. Now as England came out to bat, Grant, the West Indies captain, ordered Martindale and Constantine to try bodyline. While the Old Trafford pitch was not as suited to bodyline as the hard Australian wickets, facing such tactics for the first time, England first suffered, falling to 134 for 4. An inspired 127 from Jardine, his greatest innings and only Test century, rallied England to a total of 374. In the second West Indian innings, Clark bowled bodyline back to the West Indians, and though the match ended in a draw, it had been the highest-profile game in which bodyline was bowled in England. In mid-August, England took their revenge in the third and final test at the Oval, winning by an innings and seventeen runs, and so taking the series by 2–0. James once again was elsewhere, watching Lancashire play Hampshire.[43] Later, he remembered how "the body-line upheaval shocked everyone and made the cricket world pull itself up and tread carefully. . . . Jardine soon went, never to return."[44]

What Should They Know of Cricket Who Only Cricket Know?

If bodyline was "not cricket," then what *was* cricket? For James, as he put it once in the *Glasgow Herald*, it was first and foremost "a spectacle, an exhilarating competition, demanding physical fitness, skill, and judgment, pleasing alike to players and watchers."[45] Yet it was also to be distinguished from what he called "a multitude of ruder sports."[46] As Smith notes, "cricket has had a certain superficial 'literary' association ever since it was wrenched from its Georgian and pre-Georgian origins and reconstituted as part of a distinctly bourgeois project of self-definition and pedagogical reproduction in the British public schools."[47] As a life-long avid reader of English "cricket literature," and of course the product of a "British public school," it is perhaps not surprising that James followed the tradition represented by Cardus in seeing cricket as an art, like drama or opera. James would, for example, regularly make references in his writing to Shakespeare, whether describing the dismal weather ("All the morning, a heavy, gloomy mist, such as one would associate with Macbeth's blasted heath, hung over the ground") or the activity of the players themselves ("Like Bottom, they were transformed—but into Lions").[48] As Smith notes, "In many respects, James's willingness to treat cricket with the kind of interpretative parameters usually reserved for 'higher' forms of culture, i.e., for practices whose intellectual status is precisely opposed to such 'bodily' pursuits as sports, would have been no great surprise to his readers."[49]

One hot day in August 1934, James found himself watching Lancashire play Kent down at Dover, amid

> the sun and gaiety, the tents, summer dresses and music of the Dover festival. . . . What a wonderful day and setting for cricket it was! The Dover ground is one of the most beautiful in England and was at its best: flag-topped tents to either side of the sleek, green turf, a belt of trees and rows of houses shading into the rolling downs and surrounding the pavilion, high-rising terrace after terrace dotted with people looking lazily on.

While the match itself was sadly "limpid," James took the opportunity to philosophize:

> The ancient Athenians had terraced seats in the open air, and if they looked on at Aeschylus and Sophocles, they had their Olympic Games too. What would an Athenian have thought of the day's play? Probably

that the white-flannelled actors moving so sedately from place to place were performing the funeral rites over the corpse of a hero buried between the wickets. Watson and Iddon, from their garb and movements, he would have supposed to be the priests waving the sacrificial wands with solemn dignity.[50]

Players moving "sedately" and batsmen batting with "solemn dignity" did not make for a dramatic spectacle. As James would put it a few years later, "For successful cricket you want a great batsman[,] . . . fast bowlers who will send wickets flying[,] . . . exceptionally neat and clean wicket-keeping which makes the spectator wonder how on earth he manages to do it[, and] . . . fine fielding. . . . And, finally, you want that touch of the unexpected the uncertain fellow, whom you are hoping will come off today and do the impossible."[51]

If none or even just some of these elements are present, it is manifestly the case that cricket can for long periods resemble some sort of funeral. Even if one is watching a great batsman, like Don Bradman, demolishing all who stand in his way, the game can still sometimes feel flat, as James noted when the Australians played H. D. G. Leveson-Gower's eleven at Scarborough in September 1934: "After the first excitement, this sort of thing becomes slightly monotonous. A bowler bowls, Bradman makes a stroke, not a single fieldsman moves, and the ball is returned from the boundary. The essence of any game is conflict, and there was no conflict here; the superiority on one side was too overwhelming. . . . [The match] threatened to degenerate into boredom, if not misery.[52]

Ideally, in a cricket match, James noted, "a dual process is going on. As the batsmen master the bowling, bowlers are finding out their weaknesses."[53] Accordingly, when Bradman returned to England for the 1938 Ashes test series, things were set for an intriguing clash between two more or less equal sides. As James put it,

The eagerly awaited cricket season of 1938 is with us at last, and on the news Don Bradman takes only second place to the arbiters of Europe's destiny. Some fortunate youth, having hit Bradman's wicket with a ball, becomes as important as if he had hit a statesman's head with a bomb. . . . England v Australia is an event. He is a poor creature who knows anything about the game and does not feel a slight shiver of joyful anticipation as he speculates on the surprises, the great innings, the dramatic catches, and the inspired spells of bowling which this season will bring forth.

Cricket then was a game, but also more than a game. Of course, "England v Australia is neither a war nor a revolution," the Marxist historian of the Communist International reminded his readers. "Cricket was and remains a game—a wonderful game—the practice, history and very jargon of which enshrine in a truly extraordinary manner the spirit and tempers of the English people."[54] One wonders what some of the Scottish readers of the *Glasgow Herald* might have made of this formulation, but James's view that "the spirits and tempers of the English people" were enshrined in a sport, the game of cricket, was also an explicit challenge to those for whom cricket was nothing more than a game. The imperial poet Rudyard Kipling in *The Islanders* (1904), after observing the mess the British had made fighting the Boers, rails against "flannelled fools at the wicket and muddied oafs in goal," urging public schools to teach boys not cricket or football but how to ride and shoot so they would be better prepared in future for the real game of colonial warfare.[55] In the 1950s, amid decolonization, James would later be inspired by Kipling's question "What should they know of England who only England know?" in order to imagine a future postcolonial English society. In a pertinent challenge to Kipling's talk of "flannelled fools" James would ask in *Beyond a Boundary*, "What do they know of cricket who only cricket know?"[56]

The "Englishness" of Cricket

James's formulation that "the practice, history and very jargon" of cricket "enshrine in a truly extraordinary manner the spirit and tempers of the English people" was in an important sense a rather traditional stance. Leaving Kipling aside, as Anthony Bateman has argued, during the era of Victorian colonial expansion, "both cricket and English Studies were crucial institutional manifestations of an attempt to create a new collectivist idea of Englishness."[57] By the time James arrived in Britain, the connection between Englishness and cricket was all but hegemonic, and the game had become a social mainstay of rural life in particular. As Ross McKibbin notes, "In so far as cricket was played and followed throughout the country by all social classes and by both men and women, it was the most 'national' of all sports."[58] For all his West Indian nationalism and Marxist internationalism,

James seems to have had no qualms about immersing himself in the intricacies of the composition and performances of the English team in order to write his columns on "English cricket" for the rather "pro-Establishment" and Unionist *Glasgow Herald*. James declared that he thought Walter Hammond was "a master in his prime, and he will make centuries for England yet," while "all who have seen [Denis] Compton agree that he has the makings of a great player."[59] On the other hand, Jim Smith was "an admirable bowler and wise" but the "village whirlings of his bat have never been looked upon as serious."[60] Yet occasionally these discussions seem to move beyond the objective and balanced, as though James was consciously playing up to the anticipated sympathies of his Scottish readers toward the English team, itself perhaps indicative of the entangled nature of Britishness. So in May 1937, James praised Charlie Barnett, England's opening batsman: "We ought to have henceforth and for years to come a No. 1 of the old-fashioned type. He hit Hampshire for a terrific century last week. It is good to see an England opening batsman scoring a century in an hour."[61] The "we" in the passage is quite remarkable, and indeed other articles by James in the *Glasgow Herald* were headed as if he could be counted on as a firm stalwart of England, whether it be in phrases like "Farnes is back in our team" or "our bowling and fielding [are] the best in years."[62]

Of course, in another sense, the position James found himself in was quite remarkable. In June 1937, with the test series against New Zealand looming, James notes, "The England team will be chosen in a few days, and I propose here to select 13 players who might be in attendance on Saturday week."[63] Selecting his dream England team was hardly usual behavior for a black Trinidadian, and James did not think it appropriate as a colonial subject to cow before the "mighty" England selectors. When they picked a different England line-up than the one he had suggested, James commented, "The Selection Committee have said no to all the insidious wooing of the lovers of adventure and speculation. . . . Orthodoxy is the order of the day."[64]

Anyone but England?

James's apparent "unconditional but critical" support for England did not mean that he was now any sort of enemy of the "underdog." Early on in the 1937 season, James predicted that Yorkshire, "an extraordinarily fine side" from "the rain-sodden North," would be champions come the end of the season. Yet, as James put it, if anyone beats Yorkshire, "it will be welcomed nowhere so much as in this column. The more often champions are beaten the better for everybody." Other possible champions were Gloucestershire and Middlesex. James continued, "But probable or possible champions are not by any means the most interesting counties. They are what I call the sharp-shooters, who go around playing good cricket (more or less) and seizing their chance every now and then to bring down the mighty from their seat."

The sharp-shooters James had in mind were county sides like Essex, Somerset, and Kent, and he recalled the "glorious licking" Essex gave to Yorkshire in August 1935, "bowling them out first innings for 31 and winning in two days by an innings and over 200 runs."[65] So when New Zealand did better than expected in the 1937 test series, James was quick to historically situate England's disappointing performance:

> There is gloom in the council chambers and in the offices of the scribes, and wherever the wise ones congregate. All credit to New Zealand. Cowrie is a very fine bowler, and their batsmen hit the ball. But of John Stuart Mill it was said that his eminence was due to the flatness of the surrounding company. Surely New Zealand did so well because England did so badly. The curious thing is that this disappointing form is not new. . . . During the last 10 years—since 1926, in fact—the England team has never played up to form, and has been subject to catastrophic collapses. They collapsed against India at Lord's. At Manchester the Indians in the second innings showed a complete mastery of the England bowling. The West Indian bowlers seemed able to get right in among the early England batsmen, and often the recovery was made after six wickets had fallen. These were teams that should never have been anything else but thoroughly beaten from lunchtime on the first day. Some of their men would show good form, but that these teams should be challenging the England team as they did in a reasonable number of games was, and remains, inexplicable to anyone who considered the merits of the various players without prejudice.
>
> What is the explanation? There is none that I can think of. It most certainly is not a question of sheer cricketing ability. These touring sides are properly trounced by one or two of the best counties and often have to fight for their lives against counties which are merely good. . . . That

it is the sheer merit of West Indian, Indian, or New Zealand bowlers is not true. For, if it were, county batsmen could not make so many runs against them as they do.[66]

That such a fervent anti-imperialist could be apparently "stuck" for even one possible reason as to why Indian and West Indian cricketers performed better than expected against the England team is perhaps a little puzzling. Smith notes, "It is hard at this point, and elsewhere in these articles, not to be somewhat thrown by James's apparently wholesale mimicry of the alternate churlishness and arrogance of English imperial opinion."[67] The *Glasgow Herald* was far from a radical paper, and perhaps James feared losing his job through offending some of his more conservative readers if he went too far in his cricket columns. Yet it is perhaps worth noting that after filing that report on Tuesday, August 4, 1937, James spent the rest of that week putting together a "Special West Indian Edition" of the IASB newsletter *Africa and the World*, in solidarity with the heroic arc of labor rebellions sweeping across the British Caribbean. That Saturday, August 8, James had heckled a meeting held by Marcus Garvey in Hyde Park, demanding that Garvey express his support for striking workers in the Caribbean.[68] That Sunday, James spoke in Trafalgar Square alongside Padmore, Kenyatta, Braithwaite, and Wallace-Johnson at a mass rally to launch a "Trinidad Defence Committee."[69] When James came to write his next column on Tuesday, August 11, he was certain to find space to praise the "sublime impudence" so often displayed by those playing England at international cricket:

Let me draw a far-fetched comparison. Did any military expert in his senses believe that the new untrained levies of the French Revolution could have defeated the professional armies that were moving on France in the autumn of 1792? And now, to bring the analogy nearer home, I believe that New Zealand, the West Indies, and India do so well against men better than themselves because they have the dash and fire of young men, on tour, with their reputations to make and not very much to lose. With an impudence that is almost sublime these raw teams attack the England side and play over their normal form. I believe there is a lesson to be learnt.[70]

Seeing Cricket Historically

As a Marxist closely engaged in studying the Great French Revolution in order to write *The Black Jacobins*, James is surely not displaying English nationalism as such, but rather a kind of historical awareness and consciousness. For example, on the August Bank Holiday of 1938, James visited the Oval to watch Nottinghamshire play Surrey alongside fourteen thousand other "Ovalites," noting, "One could not keep from seeing it for the historic game that it was, one of the strongest strands in the English cricket tradition." James set the scene:

> Notts v Surrey at the Oval on August Bank Holiday. He would be a poor historian of English social life who, having a large canvas, failed to find a space for some reference to this fixture. W. G. Grace was in his day the best known of all Englishmen, and as such has his place in the annals of the country.
>
> Pelham Warner related in his account of his cricketing life how Arnold, of Rugby, astonished them by talking one day of [Arthur] Shrewsbury and [William] Gunn. It was the arrogance of youth to be astonished. What would have been astonishing was if Arnold had known nothing about them. Imagine a man today who would say he knew nothing of Don Bradman, or even [Jack] Hobbs and [Herbert] Sutcliffe. Such a man would be in important respects defective. He might know very little about them, he might detest them, taking them as symbols of flannelled folly. But he should know that they existed, and should be clear that Hobbs and Sutcliffe were not a kind of sauce, nor Bradman something for tired feet. England in the nineties knew Shrewsbury and Gunn. Hundreds of thousands must have seen them at the Oval on Bank Holiday during the last 20 years of the last century. . . . There has been an almost unbroken tradition of some of the greatest batsmen in England playing on August Bank Holiday before a London crowd. It is said that many who never saw another cricket match throughout the year found their way to the Oval that day, met old friends, and at the end of the day's play parted until the next Bank Holiday and the visit of the Notts team. When one thinks of Notts cricket one thinks not of Trent Bridge but of the mining villages which have produced so many of the most famous players. To think of Surrey cricket, however, is to think of the Oval.[71]

James then treated his readers to a brief history of the ground, from its founding in 1845 at the place of an "oval-shaped market garden" to its becoming "one of the permanent homes of English cricket":

> It has more of London in it than Lord's. The huge gasworks are a perpetual reminder of the industrial civilisation in which this small patch of green grass represents the obstinate determination of modern man to prescribe some of the old physical vitality and friendly conflict in the very midst of grime and macadamised roads, crowded flats, and the clang of machinery. Far from giving way before the pace of industrial life, cricket gains ground. The name of Gunn on the scorecard on Monday seemed the beginning of a road on which one could travel for a hundred years. And yet, curious circumstance, few of the great English poets, painters and writers have dealt with this creation and possession of the English people. . . . No one has ever written a sonnet on Notts v Surrey August Bank Holiday at The Oval. Why not?[72]

Such passages also suggest that there was an element of Romanticism to James's appreciation of the game. Indeed, for James, the joy of cricket lay not in any form of rational accounting of statistics or utilitarianism. "'Statistics prove' began a speaker on the wireless the other night, and I turned him off at once," James noted in 1933.[73] On the eve of the first test between Australia and England in June 1938, James returned to "the problem of Bradman" — how could this outstanding batsman be got out? "How it will be solved, what attempts will be made to solve it, provide the nicest problem that has faced cricketers for many years, and will make these matches of singular interest for the spectator who has advanced a little beyond the stage of judging a day's play by the boundaries made or the wickets taken."[74]

James naturally had his own ideas on the Bradman problem and, after watching the great man in 1934, asserted: "Despite all theories of wicket and modern batting, good length and really fast bowling to slips who can catch will deal satisfactorily with most batsmen and, more than anything else, are likely to dismiss Bradman in the vulnerable first five minutes."[75] Now in 1938 James reiterated that Bradman's batting style was liable to give an early chance to the slips. For James this constituted "the heel of Achilles, a very small heel, [James feared], but yet palpable."[76] Covering the tremendous first test at Trent Bridge, James commended the Yorkshire and

England bowler Hedley Verity for at least holding Bradman for a period through a sheer exertion of the will:

> Verity returned to his best form and did a noble piece of bowling. When the ball landed in the spot it beat everything, bat, wicket-keeper, and sometimes slip. It was treated as the spot on the cheek of a beautiful woman. The batsmen patted it tenderly, Brown went behind the wicket, bent down, and had a long squint at it to see exactly where it was in relation to the stumps, while Verity searched perseveringly for it through some long and accurate spells. It held Bradman watchful as a mouse for hours. Once he jumped into Verity like a tiger, and drove fiercely with the obvious intention of distracting him from his aim. But the stroke did not come off, and Bradman retired into the cat and mouse game.[77]

However, the real heroes of the drawn Trent Bridge test, "one of the great matches in the history of the game," were the Australian batsmen, in particular Stan McCabe, who made 232 runs in 235 minutes, one of the fastest double-centuries in test history: "Australia escaped defeat, and once again Bradman saved his side. . . . McCabe's innings has been lauded in prose and will doubtless be celebrated in verse. All the circumstances taken into consideration, it is the greatest piece of cricket I have ever seen or heard of, nor do I expect to see anything comparable for many years to come."[78]

The Role of the Individual

Bradman and McCabe's heroics may have been enough to save a draw in that Test match, and help Australia secure the Ashes overall, but as some compensation England managed to win the final clash at the Oval in August 1938. As James reported, "This last test has been a mixture of epic play, tragedy and farce, and like all structures which do not follow a definitive pattern it leaves behind a feeling of dissatisfaction. . . . What really ruined the match as a match was Bradman's injury. . . . Australia, on a wicket still good, expired without almost a kick. The groundlings shrieked with joy, but does anyone really like to see Caesar on his knees?"[79]

James for one did not. As he put it in his very first article for the *Glasgow Herald* on April 28, 1937:

> We must recognise that exciting cricket depends upon exciting personalities and exciting teams. And exciting personalities are, I think, acci-

dents. Not altogether, perhaps. We live in a standardized age, means of communication multiply, we hear and see the same things, and therefore think and act far more alike than our parents did. The result is a mastery of elementary technique by an increasingly greater number, a general raising of the standard. But the striking personality is perhaps more rare as a result. How many competent novelists are there today! But Dickenses do not abound.

One "Dickens" of the cricket field during this period, one "accidental" great personality, was, of course, Bradman. Invoking William Blake, James asked, "What immortal hand or eye shaped the fearful symmetry of Bradman exactly in 1929?" James answered, "We do not know and cannot know." [80]

In May 1938, in the run up to the looming 1938 Ashes clash, James once again marveled at the mysterious Bradman:

> The thing is stupendous. Bradman's 258 at Worcester is one of those feats the magnificence of which twiddles fingers at the laws of probability. It saddens us at this unchallengeable demonstration of human inequality. Then it raises us to exaltation that we live in an age when such things are done. It encourages the illusion that progress is automatic — the inevitable consequence of the years. It is, in my opinion, one of the finest things this noble cricketer has ever done. . . . At Worcester he has played twice and scored double centuries each time. As Arnold Bennett said of Mr. Lloyd George — "He can rise no higher, he can only fall." [81]

Later that month, after another magnificent display, James again paid homage to the master batsman:

> I have tried to avoid writing about Bradman's innings, and have purposefully left myself little space for it. Saturday, however, set the seal on it. It is the limit of batting. Perhaps he did not drive as much as he might. But the leg-glancing, the cuts, the back-strokes through the covers, the forcing strokes to the on-side, the diversity and the mastery, whole and complete. How could anyone do better except his own marvellous self? William Tell shot the apple off his son's head, but the poor man would have gone to the stake if he had had to hit Bradman's wicket. There may have been greater batsmen. May they sleep in peace. I am no longer interested and discard my former regrets. As Saturday progressed I understood better many things in connection with cricket: for instance, what it meant to be on the same side as Bonaparte, Nelson, or Lenin. [82]

As Smith notes, "It is hard, and probably impossible, to bring to mind another writer of the twentieth century who could have compared, in this way, Don Bradman and Lenin."[83] Whether Bradman appreciated such a comparison is not known, but for James, this really was the ultimate tribute, as shown by the respect he would pay in *The Black Jacobins* to Toussaint Louverture, also fit to join such illustrious company as Bonaparte, Nelson, and Lenin.

James's stress on the importance of great personalities to great cricket comes through well in his discussion of another Australian cricketer, the bowler W. J. "Tiger" O'Reilly: "He is what is rare today in cricket, a truly great bowler; and also what is still rarer, a man of authentic personality. Almost you could say he was a character. But unlike the poet, the great bowler is both born and made." James opined,

> [O'Reilly is] a man of finesse and finger-spin, of individualism and idiosyncrasy, of storms and calms and quick reactions; but this artist's temperament is disciplined and controlled and never runs into extravagance, being rooted in the solid basis of a good, never otherwise than good, an immaculate length. Is he as good as he was? I doubt it myself. Have you ever listened to Chaliapine's gramophone records, those made before the war and those made 10 or 15 years later—the same arias? In dramatic contrast, in portrayal of character, in capacity to put it over, 1930 is beyond all comparison with 1910. But something elemental has gone from his voice. The vibrating timbre, the sheer physical wonder of it, are no more. So it seems to me with O'Reilly.[84]

And yet despite such outstanding players as Bradman, McCabe, and O'Reilly among the Australian side, James spent time discussing England's "meritorious foundation of superior play."[85] As he explained, one can examine in turn the strengths and weaknesses of individual players on each team, weigh them up, and come to some tentative predictions before a match begins: "That is what we can say about material things, such as we can touch and see and reasonably calculate upon. But what about the new spirit which moved through an England team for the first time in so many years and had the Australians on the defensive from the start?"[86] The question of "team spirit" and morale—the relationship of the individual to the collective—was a critical one. It was with this in mind that James insisted on the importance that four Yorkshiremen—Arthur Wood, Hedley Verity, Bill Bowes, and Norman Yardley—played in the fourth test at the Leeds ground, Headingley, recruiting Edmund Burke for good measure to reinforce his argument:

> With those four Yorkshiremen playing together on their home ground the England team would be immensely strengthened morally. These things count in cricket. In fact, if [Len] Hutton and [Maurice] Leyland, two other Yorkshiremen, and [E.] Paynter, their Lancashire neighbour, were playing, England would be as strong as never before in this series. There are bonds light as air but stronger than links of iron, Burke says. And these intangible things can make, and often have made, the difference between victory and defeat.[87]

The young Len Hutton flourished as a player, and it was in part because he had been shaped and disciplined by his experience playing for such an impressive county team as Yorkshire. James wrote of "the youth," Hutton: "The real tough, fighting Yorkshire spirit is there — I can imagine the united will-power of that broad county sharpening Hutton's eyes, guiding his feet, giving power to his elbow, so that he might endure and achieve."[88] James described Hutton's subsequent batting for England: "An iron will drove him on, and it is of such stuff that really great cricketers are made."[89] If England, aside from Denis Compton, had few other outstanding young players coming through, one reason was because they were unfortunate enough to not be playing for a "powerful county" like Yorkshire, noting that playing for a weak county team often stifled their brilliance.[90] There was a dialectical interaction between the individual and the collective, but a team spirit united by bonds light as air would always be ultimately stronger than the iron will of any individual.

Modernity and Tradition

During the summer of 1938, James took time away from covering England versus Australia to watch another, rather different "match of traditions," Oxford versus Cambridge. James observed, "People who have never seen either University or one player still take sides though the spectators do not attire themselves with the glory of yore." James used the occasion to address the question of the decline in cricket at Oxbridge compared to the "golden age" of the 1880s, when promising young players such as Ranjitsinhji, C. B. Fry, F. S. Jackson, and R. E. Foster — "the great amateurs of their time"—progressed as a matter of course into the England team. Yet in 1938, "scarcely anybody [was] looking at this match with a view to finding England players." There was no superficial explanation possible for this change given that "young men develop in much the same way." James observed,

> But the type of cricket has changed, has been steadily changing, and I believe that there is the root of the trouble. A Test in England today is of four day's duration, a significant indication. Such a match is a battle. County games also are more dour. The young amateur goes into an atmosphere far more removed from his ordinary experiences than he did 25 years ago. Hobbs has commented on the sternness of post war games. That and the economic difficulties which prevent young amateurs devoting themselves entirely to cricket are sufficient to account for the change.[91]

In *Beyond a Boundary*, in a chapter entitled (with a nod to Spengler) "Decline of the West," James would develop this theme about the "sternness" and confrontational nature of postwar cricket, insisting that bodyline "was not an incident, it was not an accident, it was not a temporary aberration." As James famously put it:

> It was the violence and ferocity of our age expressing itself in cricket. The time was the early thirties, the period in which the contemporary rejection of tradition, the contemporary disregard of means, the contemporary callousness, were taking shape. The totalitarian dictators cultivated brutality of set purpose. . . . It began in World War I. Exhaustion and a fictitious prosperity in the late twenties delayed its maturity. It came into its own in 1929. Cricket could no more resist than the other organisations and values of the nineteenth century were able to resist. That big cricket survived the initial shock at all is a testimony to its inherent decency and the deep roots it had sunk.[92]

It was perhaps for this reason that James cherished the moments he had with veterans of the game in England, who offered a glimpse of what he called in 1937 "an older and freer style of cricket" as opposed to "these wretched times we are in."[93] On September 8, 1937, James told readers of the *Glasgow Herald* about an incident that had happened to him at the weekend:

I happened to be playing in a village match last Saturday against a scratch team. Their captain told me that he had on his side a man who used to play for Middlesex 40 years ago. He was certain that I didn't know him or hadn't heard of him, one of the brothers Douglas, J and R.N. Of course I had heard of them. They used to come into the Middlesex team in August with another good player, C.M. Wells. J. Douglas, I learnt, was 64, but loved the game and still played well enough. Naturally I was anxious to see him, and saw enough of him to see many things.

"I could see another generation at work," James declared, regretting the fact that his lack of luck with the bat meant he did not actually get to face up to Douglas himself. James admitted, "My span of life, alas, did not allow much sampling of the other sides bowling." But might not modern technology be used to preserve such glimpses of the past? James pondered the question:

> Whether the cinema people ever take anything except those snippets that we see in the newsreels, I don't know. The M.C.C. [Marylebone Cricket Club] might do worse than have newsreels of selected periods during the coming tests taken, and put aside for reference. It would cost very little and, without particularising, I am certain that, any things now being stored in more serious spheres are likely to be of less interest in 30 years time. I would cheerfully spend a few hours watching a county match, or a Test match for that matter, between two teams of, say, 1899. How high exactly did [Hugh] Trumble toss the ball? Tom Richardson's off break. What did Clem Hill, the left-hander, do with it? Did those batsmen consistently drive the half-volley, whoever bowled it? Always fascinating questions for all cricketers, they suddenly become doubly so by the glimpse of the vigorous and courageous man shaping as he did 40 years ago, defying time.[94]

Yet James was far from a nostalgic, conservative reactionary. "People who grumble about 'the spirit of the players in the good old days' are senile or short-sighted."[95] As he reminded his readers, "You cannot turn the clock of history backwards, even if it were desirable to do so."[96] Instead, throughout his writing there is a careful critical examination of the changes that had transformed and were transforming classic cricket into the modern game, offering encouragement and warnings in equal measure. Aside from Bradman and Headley, James freely admitted that "the standard is not what it was" compared to the "golden age," but "we must remember that the level of a game cannot be stationary." James praised the smaller English county sides like Northamptonshire and Essex: "The smaller fry . . . who under so many difficulties [kept] the game going." Overall, "the financial question" remained but the game of cricket was in a generally healthy, even "a flourishing condition," in England at least.[97]

James detested aspects of the modern game, in particular the fashion for batsmen to play safe with the forward defensive in the face of spin or whenever in any doubt, "that long defensive questing forward stroke which is the ugliest stroke in cricket."[98] Yet he also declared, "One of the great strokes of the modern age, due ultimately, I expect to the prevalence of bowling that swings late, is to get back on his wicket and play the pitched-up ball through the covers as it rises off the pitch. It is safer than the old-fashioned, grandiloquent, left foot forward and full-blooded swing. It is in its own way quite as beautiful."[99] During the second Ashes test at Lord's in 1938, James observed, "Bradman is a genius, and therefore a law unto himself. Hammond is a classic batsman who has adapted the classic game to modern conditions. Brown is a modern batsman—post war to his bootlaces; back on the wicket first and watching the ball from there, very strong at pushing and glancing all the way from wide mid-on to fine leg, a master of the slicing stroke off a fast bowler behind point."[100]

James's approach to modernism within cricket was encapsulated in his discussion of the changed format of *Wisden's Almanack*, the cricket fanatic's bible, in 1938:

This years issue is symptomatic of the determination of those connected with the game in any shape or form not to let things go on in the old way. *Wisden's* is transformed, and the transformation is admirably done. It retains its dignity, yet is much more handy for reference, running straight from page 1 to the end with a new index that facilitates easy reference. Births and deaths and obituaries are placed at the end instead of at the beginning; there is more co-ordination in the arrangement of facts. In the actual matter provided there are more articles than usual of general interest, such as [A. P.] Freeman on bowling and G. O. Allen on wickets. This is indeed welcome, for an integral part of the chronicles of the time is what the players of the day think of their technical problems. . . . In arrangement, production, and matter, *Wisden's* is definitely an improvement. But one tribute may be paid to the old *Wisden's* under the editorship of Mr. Sidney Pardon—that beautiful prose style he wrote is gone. Its greatest distinction was that he never over-wrote, never sought to dazzle, but achieved elegance by a strenuous simplicity in which scholarship and a fine mind were not so much obvious as implicit. The new *Wisden's* is a sign of the times: so, alas! is the absence of style.[101]

Accordingly, as the 1938 season began, James disapproved of the widespread media "hype" being created around the looming Ashes clash, particularly given the way European fascist regimes had recently tried to use sporting occasions for political aims and to further racist ideological aims:

> Too much "ballyhoo" will affect the game. 1938, we agree, is not 1888. But yet it looks as if these Test matches are going to be played in an atmosphere of publicity and artificial tension which will sensibly affect players and spectators. Selection and rejection, successes and failures, may achieve a significance out of all proportion to their importance, and prejudice a balanced view. Luckily, none of the great nations of Europe as yet produce Test teams; else there would be fierce disputes as to whether the matches should be played under the auspices of the League [of Nations] or not. It is good that these games should awaken public interest—they deserve it. But there can be too much of a good thing, and unfortunately, too much of a bad thing. What is to be done? Nothing drastic, and certainly no Society for ye Preservation of ye Ancient Spirit of ye game of Cricket. But cricketers, from the highest to the lowest, regular spectators, and other minor satellites, such as the humbler type of cricket scribe, can cheerfully refuse to play up to the highest notes. By passive sabotage and stolid debunking a surprising deal of good can be done.

> "Let all lovers of the game bear in mind what has happened to the Olympic Games," James warned, reminding his readers of how the Nazis had successfully used them in Berlin in 1936 for propaganda purposes. Yet, as a revolutionary socialist, James remained optimistic about the future of cricket: "That cloud of doubt being duly noted and charted, 1938, we can see, is likely to be a memorable year in the history of the game. Last year was one of the best seasons we have known for years, and this year the possibility of excitement and pleasure are enormous. We have all the elements of a great season. But the greatest of these is—weather permitting. May it permit!"[102]

Beyond the Boundary

A key reason James was optimistic about cricket's "inherent decency" in the face of totalitarianism was that he saw the audience, the spectators of the matches, not as passive, objective onlookers but as civilizing subjects in their own right. James was invariably tolerant at those rare moments when the boundary between the spectators and the players was crossed. In 1934, covering Lancashire playing Kent, James commented that "the game of cricket flourishes in Kent": "Here again, as in Southend, the little boys were playing all over the field during the interval, and the Kent team were in their places and Hopwood was taking guard while the field was still dotted with people going back to their places. Does this lighthearted attitude make for a lower standard of cricket? Kent can point to Woolley, Freeman, Ames, Chapman, Valentine, Levett, Marriott. How many counties today can show such a list?"[103]

In early August 1938, on a day off from covering the test matches, James relayed how he "strolled into The Oval [the day before] to see some of Surrey and Middlesex, these old London rivals. . . . There was a fair crowd, but how peacefully the match proceeded! [James] sat in the crowd on the stone tiers . . . [and] spectators wandered in steadily, men on a week's holiday, and their wives, out for a day in the sun." Then the monotony was suddenly broken:

> [An] unemployed-looking man next to me got into conversation, and asked me if I had seen the tests. I told him all, whereat he was enormously impressed, as I knew he would be, but he soon floored me completely by telling me that he had been a professional cricketer for 20 years until muscular rheumatism put an end to his career. That was the most exciting piece of play I experienced between the start and the lunch. My friend left and so did I.[104]

For James, as he explained to his readers in 1938, "the crowd" was "an integral part of any cricket match." This was particularly apparent in some places, for example at Yorkshire's home ground, Headingley, where the crowd was rarely passive. "They are certainly keen in Yorkshire," James noted, "the Leeds crowd is unique." "How it appealed!" "Cricket at Lord's is one thing and at Leeds it is another, and long may the Leeds crowd flourish."[105] While covering the fourth Ashes test at Headingley in July 1938, which Australia won by five wickets, James noted with just a tinge of regret about England's batting collapse during the second innings that "the last five English wickets went down without one batsman playing for death or glory." James reported, "Perhaps this was the best that could be done. But if one were to ask the thousands of Yorkshiremen who thronged the ground—How do you prefer your Bill Bowes? Playing back elegantly to O'Reilly or swinging his bat at him? The shout would be unanimous—'Swinging the bat, of course.' And I think they would be right."[106]

It was to be the first Ashes test in mid-June 1938, which was marked by heavy barracking by Nottingham's Trent Bridge crowd of the Australian opening batsmen Jack Fingleton and Bill Brown, that prompted James to his greatest elucidation on what he called "the crowd militant":

The crowd refused to practise non-intervention, and those who study mass psychology should have been present at Trent Bridge. On Friday and Saturday when England battered the Australians and then got them out the crowd went from delirium to delirium. It saw a catch in every bumped ball from an Australian bat and an lbw [leg before wicket] every time the ball touched an Australian pad. It heaved deep sides of regret when these baseless expectations bore no fruit. It punctuated with howls of glee the quick dismissal of the Australians on Monday. The superb stroke play and courage of McCabe giving a relish to the feast. But as McCabe manoeuvred Fleetwood-Smith from harm's way and smote his gallant way to the second century the crowd entered into the spirit of the thing and cheered each successful evasion almost, but not quite, as if England were saving the game.

It barracked when Fingleton and Brown were playing slowly, and there is no valid reason why a crowd should not barrack when it wants to. You cannot treat 30,000 people at a match as if they are children in a kindergarten. The barracking *was* unintelligent. But Fingleton and Brown made an appeal against the light at half-past five, reason for which was invisible to mortal eyes except theirs. When Chester approached Emmott Robinson to consult him, that sturdy Yorkshireman signified his negative when still a yard from Chester. He refused, so to speak, to discuss the matter, and the crowd was quick to see it. When it barracked as the bowler was going up to bowl it was interfering with the game, and Fingleton was quite within his rights to refuse to go on until the interruption had stopped.

But the crowd reasserted itself before the end of the day, and carried off all the honours. The occasion for this splendour was the dismissal of Fingleton. The greatest catch in the game, a long stretching left-handed effort at first slip sent back Fingleton, and the time was a quarter past six. Would Bradman come? He means everything to the Australian side, and I would wager that more than one of his men must have offered to go instead. "He would be a fool to come", whispered a wise and experienced critic at my side. And then in the gathering darkness came the Australian captain, striding down the pavilion steps as jauntily as ever, and never so much the "Don" as in this brave gesture.

Practically the whole ground stood up and greeted him with roars and roars of applause that lasted almost all the way. The barrackers appreciated his courage, and wanted to let him know also that the little unpleasantness with Fingleton was merely an interlude. It was the biggest moment of a game which had many, and if only a crowd could be as unintelligent as to barrack Fingleton and Brown when they were saving the game, what else but a crowd could so spontaneously and generously lift up all hearts and justify humanity?[107]

It is here that we arguably finally see the real meaning behind James's formulation that "the practice, history and very jargon" of cricket "enshrine in a truly extraordinary manner the spirit and tempers of the English people." There is more to James's formulation than an intervention into an existing discourse about "Englishness," for the key word is not "English" but "people." As Smith notes, what distinguished James when it came to understanding cricket was "the fact that he [understood] it to be serious and significant *because of,* and not despite, its status as a popular activity." In the spontaneous generosity of the Trent Bridge crowd toward the Australian captain we see, as Smith notes, "a glimpse of the universal."[108]

Cricket and Marxism

For James, it is clear that his work as a cricket journalist traveling around the length and breadth of England, covering matches at every level, meant, as he put it (albeit in a different context) in *Beyond a Boundary,* he "expanded [his] knowledge of cricket and, as always with cricket, of life in general."[109] It would be mistaken to suggest that already by the 1930s James could stake a claim alongside Antonio Gramsci, Georg Lukács, and Leon Trotsky as an outstanding cultural theorist of the classical Marxist tradition.[110] But as McKibbin notes, "Sport was one of the most powerful of England's civil cultures," and the articles James wrote on cricket in this period arguably go as profoundly to the heart of the question of "national culture" in England as anything else written by a Marxist in this period.[111] Of course, James did not go out of his way to flag this aspect of his writings up. As Smith writes, "While it is thus certainly true that his reading of cricket is irreducibly historical it operates only on the basis of a careful reading of the forms of cricket itself. . . . He insisted that anyone seeking to understand the game in social terms had first to understand the game in its own terms."[112] It is perhaps for this reason that many of James's comrades in the Trotskyist movement never seemed to show much appreciation for his cricket journalism, so much of which was apparently obsessed with the particular styles and favorite strokes of individual players on the England team and so on, without understanding how after attending to the specific intricacies James was then able to rise from the concrete to the general.

In 1925, in *Where Is Britain Going?*, Trotsky had suggested that any future "British Revolution" would "inevitably awaken in the English working class the most unusual passions, which have hitherto been so artificially held down and turned aside, with the aid of social training, the Church, and the press, in the artificial channels of boxing, football, racing, and other sports."[113] Such an analysis of sport was of course far more sophisticated than the position the official Communist movement was to take subsequently, which went from a crude denunciation of sport as "bourgeois" as part of the "class against class" Third Period "line" taken in the late 1920s and early 1930s, and then embracing sport in an uncritical manner during the Popular Front period and thereafter.[114] James would famously later take issue with Trotsky's argument that the popularity of a sport like football or cricket was ultimately an expression of alienation under capitalism, an "artificial channel" into which the "unusual passions" of the British working class were "turned aside." For James, as we have seen, cricket in Trinidad with all its racial injustice and divisions had illuminated the question of politics though exposing some of the hypocrisy of British colonial rule, and his lifelong study of the game revealed that in both the metropole of imperial Britain and in a colony like Trinidad cricket represented not merely a diverting dramatic spectacle but part of the popular culture of society. Apparently James and Trotsky discussed cricket when they met in 1939, and in *Beyond a Boundary*, James made his disagreement with Trotsky on this question explicit: "Trotsky had said that the workers were deflected from politics by sports. With my past I simply could not accept that. I was British."[115]

In James's cricket articles of 1937 and 1938, it is perhaps possible to detect a subtle challenge to the existing Marxist analysis of sport as formulated by Trotsky. "We live in a serious age, and there are many estimable people who despise cricket and lovers of cricket," James wrote in July 1937, perhaps thinking of some of his more serious comrades on the far left. Yet in an appreciation of the Australian fast bowler E. A. McDonald, who had tragically recently died in a car accident, James proudly defended his love of the game. Declaring Ted McDonald "the greatest of modern fast bowlers," James wrote, "I confess freely that I looked, and still look, on a man like McDonald with open-eyed admiration." As James concluded:

> The splendid physique, trained and adapted to endurance and highly skilful performance, is not only the enjoyment of millions of modern people. All through the ages humanity has admired such men. That most intellectual of peoples, the Greek, gave their athletes a high place, a thing our modern "high-brows" might remember. And I cannot conceive of a time when McDonald and his kind will not fill the eye and minds of their fellows with admiration and a generous envy of their natural gifts developed by patient toil to such strength and endurance and skill.[116]

Christopher Hitchens once noted James's cricket writing reminded him "of what Lionel Trilling once said about George Orwell—that 'he must sometimes have wondered how it came about that he should be praising sportsmanship and gentlemanliness and dutifulness and physical courage. He seems to have thought, and very likely he was right, that they might come in handy as revolutionary virtues.'"[117] In any case, James held fast to his idea that cricket, because of its "inherent decency" and "deep roots," would, if not quite help make a socialist revolution, at least have a fair chance of surviving one. In 1938, the inspirational Kent and England batsman Frank Woolley announced his retirement, and James paid his tribute in an article titled "Cricket Is Losing a Supreme Artist." As James noted of Woolley:

> The foundations of his style were laid in another age. Whatever his virtues, no batsman of the modern school will ever play like Woolley, as no modern historian will ever write like Gibbon. . . . He was one of the great cricketers of his time, but he was more than that. He gave to thou-

COLOURED "STARS" APPEAR AT SEEDHILL

SERVICES RENDERED FOR WORTHY OBJECT

CONSTANTINE'S XI

Back row: ~ ____ ,). E. Constantine, G. Headley, Achong, E. St. Hill. Seated: E. A. Martindale, Amarsinh, L. N. Constantine, Ald. J. Robinson (the Mayor), Dr. P. Millyard, A. Charles, C. L. R. James.

Photo: D. C. Holmes.

On behalf of the Nelson Mayor's Distress Fund, an interesting cricket match was played on the Seedhill ground on Tuesday afternoon. The Nelson team opposed a side captained by Constantine, the latter including several professionals figuring in the Lancashire League and the Central Lancashire League.

Batting first, Nelson scored 162 for seven in two hours and 12 minutes and then declared. Constantine figured in the unusual role of wicket-keeper, and did his job well. Some good hitting was seen when Constantine's eleven was batting, the former Nelson professional scoring a typical 50, being caught out

next ball. Amarsinh hit up 46 in 25 minutes, beautifully straight driving a ball well out of the ground. Constantine's eleven replied with 142 for seven, when rain drove the players off the field.

Nelson: J. Kerrigan c Millyard b St. Hill 3; H. Thomason c Headley b Amarsinh 13; E. Bradshaw b Charles 29; R. C. Hawkwood c Headley b Achong 12; H. Dibb c Charles b Achong 14; A. J. Birtwell not out 31; Amarsinh b Headley 9; R. Wood not out 31; extras 13; total (for 7 wkts. dec.) 162.

Constantine's XI.: Amarsinh c Ideson b Birtwell 46; Headley run out 11; St. Hill b Knowles 1; E. Constantine c Dibb

b Bradshaw 18; A. Charles b Knowles 0; L. N. Constantine c Amarnath b Hawkwood 50; Achong not out 6; C. L. R. James not out 0; extras 3; total (for 7 wkts.) 142.

Bowling Analysis.

Nelson innings: Amarsinh 7—1—12—1; St. Hill 7—2—9—1; Achong 11—1—32—2; Dr. Millyard 4—2—9—0; A. Charles 7—2—18—2; C. L. R. James 4—0—11—0; E. Constantine 4—1—5—0; Headley 5—0—13—1; J. Kirk 5—0—40—0.

Constantine's XI's innings: Amarnath 4—0—10—0; R. Wood 2—0—16—0; A. J. Birtwell 6—0—40—1; D. Knowles 9—2—52—3; E. Bradshaw 3—0—17—1; C. Hawkwood 1.2—1—4—1.

FIGURE 4.1 Learie Constantine's charity cricket XI, 1938. © The British Library Board. All rights reserved. *Nelson Leader*, August 19, 1938, 13.

sands and thousands of his countrymen a conception of the beautiful which artists struggle to capture in paint and on canvas. . . . They recognised in him something beyond the average scorer of runs, some elegance of line and harmony of movement which went beyond the figures on the score-board. That, indeed, will give him his place in the game, a place higher than many who won more matches for their side. . . . He is fifty-one. Think of it, fifty-one! This means by the same reckoning that Compton, if he does as well, will have reached similar eminence in 1968. What wars and revolutions will have rolled by!

Yet thanks to players like Woolley, James was confident cricket would survive "the epoch of wars and revolutions": "For if the game of cricket were ever put on trial for its life, its advocates would bring Grace and Bradman and Ranjitsinhji and a few others as evidence on behalf of the defence. But they would bring Woolley too. And if they were clever advocates they would play him as their strongest card. For if he could not win the sympathy of the jury then what other cricketer could?"[118]

FIVE

"There Is No Drama Like the Drama of History"

The Black Jacobins, Toussaint Louverture,

and the Haitian Revolution

In early 1936, Winston Churchill decided to pay a rare visit to the theater in London's West End. Churchill had read "some unappreciative descriptions" of a play, a historical drama set in the Napoleonic period, and admitted to initially feeling "discouraged" from going. Churchill recalled,

> However, upon the advice of Mr. Edward Marsh, a high connoisseur and keen supporter of the living stage, I went last night to see this remarkable play. In my humble judgment as a life-long but still voracious reader of Napoleonic literature, it is a work of art of a very high order. Moreover it is an entertainment which throughout rivets the attention of the audience. . . . If it be the function of the playwright as of the historian "to make the past the present, to bring the distant near, to place the reader in the society of a famous man, or the eminence overlooking a great battle," this is certainly discharged.

Those lines, written in a letter to the *Times* and coming as they did from the former chancellor of the exchequer, meant that despite weak reviews, the play in question, *St. Helena* by R. C. Sherriff and Jeanne de Casalis, was swiftly granted an extended run in another theater. Churchill was no doubt greatly satisfied, for he clearly found its portrayal of the last years in exile of the former French emperor Napoleon Bonaparte on the island of Saint Helena deeply moving. "There is a grandeur and human kindliness about the great Emperor in the toil which make a conquering appeal," Churchill insisted. "Nor need the sense of inexorable decline and doom sadden unduly those who have marvelled at Napoleon's prodigious career."[1]

Yet Churchill, that "voracious reader of Napoleonic literature," for some reason failed to muster the energy to go and see another historical drama on London's West End, one which had opened a month after he had written to the *Times*, and one which also featured a portrayal of Bonaparte. Set on the island of Saint Domingue, as opposed to that of Saint Helena, that play was *Toussaint Louverture: The Story of the Only Successful Slave Revolt in History*, a panoramic dramatization of the Haitian Revolution of 1791–1804. Then again, *Toussaint Louverture*, written by C. L. R. James in 1934 and staged by the prestigious Stage Society on March 15 and 16, 1936, at the Westminster Theatre, was not just "another historical drama," but the first time for almost a century that a play explicitly about the Haitian Revolution had been performed on the British stage.[2] After seeing James's play, one would have found it rather difficult to detect any particular "grandeur" behind Bonaparte's ruthless determination to restore slavery on the French colony of Saint Domingue, after the enslaved of that colony had already died in their thousands to liberate themselves from their conditions of barbaric bondage. As for the "human kindliness" of Bonaparte, any readers of Churchill's letter who had seen James's play would have no doubt been bemused to learn of the emperor's proposed plans once his highly feared, professional armies had destroyed the exhausted rebel army of former slaves: "I shall not leave an epaulette on the shoulders of a single nigger in the Colony." If the audience of James's play in 1936 had left the theater feeling a "conquering appeal" for anybody, it would surely have not been for the "great Emperor" Bonaparte, but for a former slave of the French Empire, the great Haitian revolutionary leader Toussaint Louverture. Indeed, with the legendary black American artist Paul Robeson in the starring role as Toussaint, words like "grandeur" and "human kindliness" could not fail but be utterly redeemed and gloriously invested with new content and new meaning. As James would note in his magisterial history of the Haitian Revolution, *The Black Jacobins*, whereas the life story of Toussaint "does not approach the greater dramatic creations, in its social significance and human appeal it far exceeds the last days at St. Helena."[3]

To attempt to do justice to "the making" of either James's historical drama *Toussaint Louverture* or his masterful epic *The Black Jacobins* — one of the grandest "grand narratives" ever written — in one chapter would be to do an injustice. Nevertheless, the linking of the two works not only reminds us that they should be seen together as companion pieces of historical literature, each complementing each other, but also allows us to explore at greater length some of the forces and passions shaping both works. James's *Toussaint Louverture*, the production of which was the first time black professional actors had ever performed on the British stage in a play written by a black playwright and the only time Robeson starred in a play by a writer of African heritage, was only published for the first time in 2013, and the scholarship on that work remains in its infancy.[4] *The Black Jacobins* on the other hand has long won for itself the status of a classic, and, as James Walvin notes, not only "remains *the* pre-eminent account" of the Haitian Revolution "despite the vast accumulation of detail and argument advanced by armies of scholars" since, but also stands as the ideal "starting point" for understanding the experience of slavery in general.[5] James's insights, developed in partnership with Eric Eustace Williams, his fellow Trinidadian, former pupil at Queen's Royal College (QRC), and author of another classic study *Capitalism and Slavery* (1944), have become an established subject of research. However, if *The Black Jacobins* has since helped raise "armies of scholars" who have revisited the great battlefield of Haiti armed with James's work, far fewer have been concerned with understanding how James himself came to write such a powerful work of revolutionary history. Yet *The Black Jacobins* stands as a fine culmination and conclusion to the work of James in imperial Britain over six years; indeed, it was James's finest single intellectual achievement in this period of his life.

The Historical Philosophy of the Young C. L. R. James

Before James even went to QRC, he had from a young age already begun to find some sort of meaning in European literature and history from his voracious reading. He remembered "an English history book by a man called [Cyril] Ransome. It was dry fact but [he] read it from cover to cover over and over again. The English always won the battles." His natural instincts with the underdog, James "resented it fiercely" and "used to read and reread the few battles they had lost," in the process cultivating "a fanatical admiration for Napoleon."[6] The young James now perhaps had a "hero" to imagine while reading Thackeray's *Vanity Fair,* "a Novel without a Hero," set in Britain during the wars with Napoleonic France. In the QRC library, James was excited when he "found all sorts of books on history and classical studies."[7] One school friend, William Besson, recalled that James would read "history and literature" in class "instead of doing the class work": "I remember him reading [J. R.] Green's *English History* which the ordinary run of students like myself did not read."[8]

John Richard Green's *Short History of the English People* (1874) offered a radical liberal take on the nationalist rewriting of national histories that marked the nineteenth century in general. As Green notes in his preface, "The aim of the following work is defined by its title; it is a history not of English Kings or English Conquests, but of the English People." As Raphael Samuel observes, Green "preached a kind of democratic evolutionary gospel, believing that great men counted for comparatively little in the story of the nation and that the 'real life' of the English lay in 'their ceaseless, sober, struggle with oppression, their steady, unwearied battle for self-government.'"[9] James would later always insist that those who grew up on tiny Caribbean islands instinctively grasped a sense of the "totality" of society, from top to bottom, rulers and ruled, in a way that was harder in larger societies such as Britain. As he puts it to Stuart Hall, West Indians had the advantage in that they "kept on seeing the whole thing as a whole."[10] "People's history" such as that espoused by Green therefore perhaps came almost naturally to someone like James.

During the 1920s, James would slowly develop his philosophy of history itself, as he revealed in a 1967 interview with Richard Small:

I read an enormous amount of history books[,] . . . chiefly the history of England and later, histories of Europe and ancient civilization. I used to teach history, and reading the lot of them I gained the habit of critical judgement and discrimination. . . . I remember three or four very important history books. These were a history of England by G.K. Chesterton and some histories of the seventeenth century by Hilaire Belloc. These books violently attacked the traditional English history on which I had been brought up and they gave me a critical conception of historical writing.

James remembered that as a teacher of both English and History in Trinidad he used to tell his students that to understand "the historical development" of any given period one had to get "some idea of the economic circumstances, you must also get some idea of the political circumstances and you must get to know the literary circumstances."[11] It is perhaps interesting here to note that in his autobiography *My Life*, Trotsky described how when he was young he too once held to "the theory of multiple factors," economic, political, cultural, and so on, to explain social change, noting that it was then "the most widely accepted theory in social science." "People denote as 'factors' the various aspects of their social activity, endow this concept with a supra-social character, and then superstitiously interpret their own activity as the result of the interaction of these independent forces." What this theory left out, Trotsky explained, was that it was human agency that changed society, not the "multiple factors which were supposed to dwell on the Olympus of history and rule our fates from there." For Trotsky, his grasp of this truth came initially through reading the "old Italian Hegelian-Marxist," Antonio Labriola, in particular his *Essays on the Materialistic Conception of History* (1896).[12] James had no such luck—such Marxist classics were absent from the QRC library. However, James's articles for *The Beacon* in 1931 reveal that James had already independently arrived at a sense of the fundamental importance of human agency in history before reading any Marxism.

In the article "The Problem of Knowledge" in March 1931, James stressed the importance that historians not be narrowly concerned with politics but open to the cultural movements of their day, admitting he found it remarkable that the great Whig historian Thomas Babington Macaulay, author of a *History of England*, "who died in 1859, had no good word to say of Shelley, Keats, Wordsworth and the whole Romantic Movement, the most fascinating problems in the world." James revealed a general despair with the "absurdities" of various contemporary leading "philosophers, especially philosophers of history," taking to task, for example, Henry Thomas Buckle's *History of Civilisation in England* (1857–61) for allowing "his prejudices to blind him to the truth" despite being "a historian writing a history of civilisation." James savaged Buckle's "preposterous theory of the Nordic races being stimulated to extra effort by the cold climate of the North, while the Italians, Spaniards and Greeks of the South were enervated by the climate thus accounting for the nineteenth-century supremacy of Northern Europe." James then moved on to discuss "the rise, decline and fall of the Roman Empire, which was certainly the greatest European organisation of the early world and, comparatively speaking, is perhaps 'the greatest panorama in the history of mankind.'" Yet Edward Gibbon's *The History of the Decline and Fall of the Roman Empire* (1776–88) also disappointed James:

> What was the cause of this decline? I do not know, but I shall tell you what I do know. Gibbon was an atheist, and he attributed it to the adoption of Christianity. . . . We learn a lot about Gibbon. . . . We learn many interesting facts about Roman History, but what we want is some authoritative and positively convincing presentation of the reasons why

this great empire collapsed. That we do not get nor are we ever likely to get. To say that it was due to a variety of causes . . . is merely a beginning of the question.[13]

How to move past an explanation based on "a variety of causes"? In the summer of 1931, James reviewed an edited collection of Mahatma Gandhi's writings, observing that "the most amazing thing" about Gandhi was the fact that "over two hundred millions of men [were] behind him." As James noted,

> If he wished he could turn India into a seething confusion of riot and bloodshed which would be unparalleled even in this century of violence. What is the secret of this power? . . . It is this personal sincerity [of Gandhi], this unquestioned integrity of soul, which has so caught the imagination of the Oriental people to whom he belongs and made him the wielder of power such as few men in history have handled. . . . There is something in common between Gandhi and these men, some secret well of power, something which Western civilisation doesn't understand and against which its militarism, its political organisation, its mastery of the physical forces of nature, are quite powerless.

The abstract and determinist notion of the theory of "multiple factors" shaping historical development simply couldn't explain the power of the mass movement around someone like Gandhi, which proved that human beings were fundamentally at the heart of making history. James noted that reading about Gandhi had provided James "the solution of a historical problem which has in the past caused [him] some difficulty": "Whether great men make history or are but the crests of inevitable waves of social evolution. I am now more than ever inclined to believe that they shape the environment more than the environment shapes them."[14]

The Memory of the Haitian Revolution in the British Caribbean

James's questioning of the "militarism" of "Western civilisation," which had already turned the twentieth century into a "century of violence," is also illuminating given that he had already begun to independently research the rich, hidden history of the Caribbean. James remembers he was "one of the pioneers" in introducing "West Indian history" in school, something not then on the official curriculum.[15] One friend from this period, the writer Ralph de Boissière, later recalled how James's early "opposition to colonialism had a solidly grounded historical base, something that none of [James's peers] possessed," and "C.L.R. delivered telling blows with history."[16] In particular, James recalls "reading everything" he could on the Haitian Revolution, but aside from a couple of works by British writers during the 1850s, including Rev. J. R. Beard's little 1855 biography of Toussaint, he was grievously disappointed on finding no books of "serious historical value" while in colonial Trinidad. James remembered his reaction on reading a recent "very bad" biography of Toussaint, Percy Waxman's *The Black Napoleon* (1931): "What the goddam hell is this?" James recalled, "I was tired of hearing that the West Indians were oppressed, that we were black and miserable, that we had been brought from Africa, and that we were living there and that we were being exploited."[17]

Nonetheless, James made effective use of Waxman's biography as part of his counterblast to the racism of Dr. Sidney Harland in his article "The Intelligence of the Negro" (1931), which was notable for being the first time James wrote about Toussaint's astonishing achievements. "I would have far preferred to write on Toussaint" rather than on Harland's "arrant nonsense," James noted with a slight pang of regret toward the end of his article.[18] Robert Hill has rightly emphasized the importance of "the overriding vindicatory nature" of James's discussion of Toussaint in 1931, remarking that "in the context of the domination of European colonialism, vindication was never a personal luxury. It was also a cultural and ideological necessity."[19]

The collective memory of the Haitian Revolution and its legacy in the rest of the Caribbean was highly contested. In Trinidad, the white elite had been predominantly French at the time of the Haitian Revolution, and the "Haytian Fear" was real. By the second half of the nineteenth century, as Bridget Brereton notes, "fear of violence from the African Trinidadians receded" for the British elite, and one governor, A. H. Gordon, in 1869 described them as "the quietest and most inoffensive people it has ever been my lot to meet with."[20] A kind of silencing about the event took place accordingly in the discourse of the island. This silence was rudely interrupted in 1887, when James Anthony Froude, the famous English "man of letters," a historian, biographer, and friend of Thomas Carlyle who was to end his life as Regius Professor of Modern History at Oxford University, visited the British West Indies.[21] On his return to Britain, Froude wrote *The English in the West Indies, or the Bow of Ulysses* to try to counter the increasingly popular argument that the West Indian colonies should now be given home rule or self-government, and his method—his "historical philosophy"—was quite simply the most crude and blatant racism against black people imaginable. Racism necessarily underpinned the "intellectual" legitimizations of British colonial rule in the West Indies, before and subsequently, but it was customary to express this in "respectable," restrained and sophisticated terms.[22] Yet as Eric Williams once noted of Froude, "no British writer, with the possible exception of Carlyle, has so savagely denigrated the West Indian Negro."[23]

According to Froude, those Africans who had gone through the barbaric horrors of the slave trade and colonial slavery at the hands of the English should count themselves "lucky" to have escaped Africa: "In no part of the globe is there any peasantry whose every want is so completely satisfied as Her Majesty's black subjects in these West Indian islands. They have perfect liberty, and are safe from dangers, to which if left to themselves they would be exposed, for the English rule prevents the strong opposing the weak." Unfortunately, despite generations of English rule, for Froude, black people in the West Indies were still "poor children of darkness," and "if left entirely to themselves, they would in a generation or two relapse into savages." There were "two alternatives" facing "all the English West Indies—either an English administration pure and simple" or "a falling eventually into a state like that of Hayti, where they eat the babies, and no white man can own a yard of land." Froude was not at all silent about the Haitian Revolution—he detested everything it represented.[24]

Yet Froude's racist tirade had been famously and gloriously countered almost immediately by a black Trinidadian schoolmaster, John Jacob Thomas. Despite being in ill health, Thomas had traveled to England and in 1889 published for the benefit of an English audience an exposure of both Froude's fraudulent racism as well as his audacity in damning a people about whom he knew nothing. In *Froudacity: West Indian Fables Explained*, Thomas noted Froude's "oft-repeated predictions about West Indian Negroes degenerating into the conditions of their fellow-Negroes in the 'Black Republic'" and that "the West Indies degenerating into so many white-folk-detesting Haytis, under our prophet's dreaded supremacy of the Blacks, is the burden of the book." Thomas accordingly tore into Froude's racism toward the people of Haiti and, in a devastatingly powerful conclusion to his book, notes that "cannibalism and the hideous concomitants" were for various reasons "relatively minor and restricted dangers to man's civilisation and moral soundness." Far more "fatal and further-reaching dangers to public morality and happiness" were caused by the poison of racism, "the circulation of malevolent writings whereby the equilibrium of sympathy between good men of different races is sought to be destroyed, through misleading appeals to the weaknesses and prejudices of readers."[25]

As a supporter of West Indian self-government, James was almost certainly aware of and inspired by Thomas's brilliant vindicatory counterblast to Froude. Yet what remains striking about Thomas's *Froudacity* was the comparative silence about Haiti in comparison with the British West Indies, possibly on the grounds that it was more important to put a clear case for self-government by avoiding plunging into complicated historical controversies. Yet Froude had made repeated references to Haiti, and at one point he even wrote a brief "history" of the Haitian Revolution. It is possible that James as a historian felt a certain frustration while in colonial Trinidad with this silence of the democratic movement on the question of Haiti. After all, as James later demonstrated regarding Froude's racist "analysis" of the Haitian Revolution, "every sentence that Froude [wrote was] absolutely and completely wrong. *Every single sentence*."[26] On arriving in England in 1932, James continued to research the Haitian Revolution: "I began to look for materials and found only the same shallow ones I had read in the Caribbean. I immediately began to import books from France which dealt seriously with this memorable event in French history."[27]

Commemorating Antislavery in Britain

The summer of 1933 in Britain saw the centenary anniversary of the official declaration of the abolition of slavery throughout the British Empire. As J. R. Oldfield has noted, "The centenary is best understood as a rolling programme of events that was intended to mark Emancipation (1 August 1834), as well as the passage of the Emancipation Bill in 1833. . . . It seems likely that over 250 commemorative events were put on between March 1933 and November 1934." Oldfield continues, "Just as remarkable as the size and scale of these celebrations [were] their range and diversity," including not only lantern lectures, church services, and meetings but at least seventeen performances of a specially commissioned pageant play, *Slavery*, or *Towards Freedom*. First performed in London in October 1932, the play ranged chronologically from 500 AD to the present day, though it "came dangerously close to reinforcing what was rapidly becoming a standard or orthodox view" by placing the Tory MP for Hull, William Wilberforce, center stage. As one character representing "Liberty" notes, "he caused the abolition of the slave trade."[28]

We can follow the course of the national debate created around the issue through *The Listener*, which ran a series of articles on "Slavery, 1833–1933," to coincide with a lecture series on BBC National Radio. The BBC series began in late April 1933 with "The Crime of Slavery" by Sir John Harris, parliamentary secretary to the Anti-slavery and Aborigines Protection Society and author of *A Century of Emancipation* (1933). This was followed by "Britain's Efforts to Abolish the Slave Trade," by Charles Kingsley Webster, professor of international history at the London School of Economics, while Reginald Coupland, Beit Professor of Colonial History at Oxford University and author of *Wilberforce* (1923) and *The British Anti-slavery Movement* (1933), commented on "The Emancipation of the Slaves." Coupland was followed by the Rt. Hon. the Viscount Cecil of Chelwood, who had helped set up the new Permanent Slavery Commission at the League of Nations, and then Lady Simon, author of *Slavery* (1929). The theme of all of these self-satisfied experts can be summarized by one quote from Coupland, who noted with pompous pride that after abolishing the slave trade in 1807, "Britain once more led the way in abolishing slavery itself."[29]

By the 1930s, this invented tradition of an abolitionist British state fundamentally committed to liberty had become one of the oldest and most cherished myths of British nationalism. Reinforced by works such as the American Frank J. Klingberg's *The Anti-slavery Movement in England: A Study in English Humanitarianism* (1926) and the British imperial historian C. M. MacInnes's *England and Slavery* (1934), this dominant view of abolition in Britain had held sway for over a century. It can be best perhaps summed up by a phrase beloved by the likes of Coupland, originating with the Victorian writer William E. H. Lecky. In his *History of European Morals from Augustus to Charlemagne* (1869), Lecky had remarked that "the unweary, unostentatious and inglorious crusade of England against slavery may probably be regarded as among the three or four perfectly virtuous pages comprised in this history of nations."[30]

It was this mythological and self-serving narrative that had helped ideologically legitimize Britain's first taking the "lion's share" of Africa in the European imperialist "scramble" for that continent in the late nineteenth century, giving a supposedly abolitionist British state the moral high ground necessary to undertake Victorian "civilising missions" among non-Europeans. After the Great War, this myth was steadily refashioned into a new, sophisticated, imperialist, and paternalist doctrine of "trusteeship," which counterposed "good government" in the colonies to the rising demands among the colonized for immediate "self-government." In 1923, Coupland had insisted that Wilberforce "more than any other man . . . founded in the conscience of the British people a tradition of humanity and of responsibility towards the weak and backward black peoples, whose fate lay in their hands. And that tradition has never died. . . . British rule in Africa has been true to the principle of trusteeship."[31] Or as Lady Simon put it, "Wilberforce was not the first to put forward the ideal of trusteeship for the backward races, but he was one of the first to put it into active and vigorous practice."[32]

It was this idea that the "backward races" of the British West Indies still needed British "trusteeship" that James was determined to counter when, on the evening of May 29, 1933, he found himself sitting down in the BBC National Radio studios to give the sixth and final talk in the slavery series. James's talk was published in that week's *The Listener*, under the title "A Century of Freedom." In it James, the "great-grandson of a freed slave tells how, since emancipation, the West Indian Negro has been able to attain to high positions of trust and responsibility in Trinidad and the West Indies."[33] As James remembered of his broadcast, "I visualized my audience as people who had to be made to understand that West Indians were a Westernized people. I must have stressed the point too hard, in fact I know I did. Colonial officials in England, and others, began their protests to the B.B.C. almost before I had finished speaking."[34]

James's talk, stressing the growth and development of the educated West Indian middle class, was published back home in the *Port of Spain Gazette* and praised by the paper's regular columnist, "Carton," who noted the addresses on slavery up to then had "been among the best of the 'talks' of the present year," but amid a "goodly company Mr. James competently held his own." Carton continued, "Mr. James did not mince the situation, and he never descended to a gibe in the midst of his plain-speaking. The broadcast could not have been better done. . . . I suppose Mr. C.L.R. James is the only West Indian who, up to the present, can claim that he has addressed an audience of millions! To do this is only possible by the microphone, and from one of the great broadcasting centers of the world."[35]

Though stressing that West Indians were more than "ready" now for self-government and democracy, perhaps aware that he was speaking as a member of the League of Coloured Peoples and from such a prestigious platform, James did little to challenge the elitist and mythological historical narrative that had been previously presented. Not only was there no mention of Toussaint or the Haitian Revolution, but James also chose to play down the significance of all earlier slave rebellions and revolts in the Caribbean altogether: "The emancipation from slavery [in 1833] is the greatest event in the history of the West Indies. For the average West Indian Negro it is his Magna Carta, Bill of Rights, Independence Day, and French Revolution, all in one."[36] In early August 1933, in his article on "Slavery Today" for *Tit-Bits* magazine, James not only paid tribute to "the memory of Wilberforce" but went even further in his praise for the British Parliament's passing of the act in 1833, making the astonishing statement that for West Indians, "our history begins with it [the act]. It is the year One of our calendar. Before that we had no history."[37] After his major shift toward revolutionary Marxism and militant Pan-Africanism in the seminal year of 1934, James would never make such statements ever again, in order to compromise with "imperial respectability," and would that year put the finishing touches to a play that in part set out to tell British audiences the truth about abolition.

Resurrecting a Revolutionary:
C. L. R. James's *Toussaint Louverture*

"The play was conceived four years ago and was completely finished by the autumn of 1934," James informs us in his author's note in the original 1936 program of *Toussaint Louverture*.[38] In the course of writing *Toussaint Louverture*, James had become a Trotskyist, and one can detect the influence of Trotsky's masterful *History of the Russian Revolution* in the play. As Trotsky had noted,

> Thousands and thousands of books are thrown on the market every year presenting some new variant of the personal romance, some tale of the vacillations of the melancholic or the career of the ambitious. The heroine of Proust requires several finely wrought pages in order to feel that she does not feel anything. It would seem that one might, at least with equal justice, demand attention to a series of collective historic dramas which lifted hundreds of millions of human beings out of non-existence, transforming the character of nations and intruding forever into the life of all mankind.

"The history of a revolution," Trotsky had written, "is for us first of all a history of the forcible entrance of the masses into the realm of rulership over their own destiny."[39] James's stress on the agency of the masses of black slaves in lifting themselves out of nonexistence during the "collective historic drama" of the Haitian Revolution was to be the great underlying theme of his play *Toussaint Louverture*. As James notes in his stage instructions at the outset of Act 1, Scene 2 of *Toussaint Louverture*, the moment the enslaved of Saint Domingue had gathered in 1791 to plot their rising in the depths of the forest, "they, the Negro slaves, are the most important character in the play. Toussaint did not make the revolt. It was the revolt that made Toussaint." James's play shows the transformation of the black masses themselves during the liberation struggle, from being "nearly naked" and "dirty and unkempt," scattered in groups and living in fear of their white masters at the start of the play, to forming what James describes as "a solid mass . . . in dress and bearing . . . a civilised people" at the moment of final victory.

In the Haitian Revolution, the ideals of the Enlightenment, of liberty, equality, and fraternity, became a material force to be reckoned with, embodied in the rebel slave army. During their mighty collective struggle for freedom, long-held and cherished beliefs in kingship, rooted in ancient tribal tradition, began to be transcended. James's play was accordingly concerned with the vital question of revolutionary leadership, and in particular the heroic commander of the rebel slave army. It was Toussaint who had been central to ensuring it was the new ideas that triumphed over the old, and so the making of "the only successful slave revolt in history."[40] James's play ends with Dessalines performing what Paul B. Miller has described as "one of the most revolutionary symbolic and enlightened gestures in the history of the struggle for independence in the Americas. Eager to differentiate the revolutionary army from the French enemy, Dessalines designs a new flag by removing the white from the French tricouleur."[41]

"There is no drama like the drama of history," James reflected in *The Black Jacobins*, after recording the cruel death of Toussaint, whose "life work" had been "the maintenance of liberty for all" at the hands of the French state in the Fort-de-Joux, a freezing-cold prison in the Jura mountains, in April 1803.[42] While *Toussaint Louverture* had allowed James full artistic freedom to portray the life, character, and tragic death of the heroic revolutionary personality, it should not be forgotten that in many ways *The Black Jacobins* also had at its heart a biographical portrait of Toussaint.[43]

Toussaint, James insisted, "dominated from his entry until circumstances removed him from the scene. The history of the San Domingo revolution will therefore largely be a record of his achievements and his political personality."[44] As James put it,

> The revolution had made him; but it would be a vulgar error to suppose that the creation of a disciplined army, the defeat of the English and the Spaniards, the defeat of Rigaud, the establishment of a strong government all over the island, the growing harmony between the races, the enlightened aims of the administration — it would be a crude error to believe that all these were inevitable. At a certain stage, the middle of 1794, the potentialities in the chaos began to be shaped and soldered by his powerful personality, and thenceforth it is impossible to say where the social forces end and the impress of personality begins.[45]

Such a critical stress on the importance of Toussaint's revolutionary leadership challenges the assumption that James's *Black Jacobins* was somehow about attempting to demonstrate that "the lack of specially-trained leaders, a vanguard, did not hold back the movement of the San Domingo revolution."[46] There are lots of possible influences shaping James's emphasis of the importance of Toussaint himself here. For example, in 1937, Secker and Warburg had published *Bonaparte*, by the great Soviet historian Eugene Tarlé, which James consulted while writing *The Black Jacobins*.[47] In his introduction, Tarlé distinguished his Marxist approach to writing biography from the "romantic or idealistic conceptions of history" as well as "that species known as the 'heroic school,'" which ascribed to Napoleon "the role of 'creator' of his epoch." Nonetheless, "the man . . . presents one of the most extraordinary phenomena in world history":

> For us, the Napoleonic empire is the birth of the stubborn conflict of new social and economic forces, a conflict which did not begin with Napoleon or end with him, and whose basic significance consisted in the victorious assault of the middle class against the feudal and semi-feudal order in France and Europe. This struggle was complicated by the simultaneous conflict between the French and the economically more powerful English commercial and industrial groups for control of the more backward countries. This, and the wars of national liberation which followed, succeeded in placing Europe on the road of "free" capitalism. It does not mean, however, that we should underestimate the gigantic per-

sonality standing in the centre of this dual conflict and imposing upon it the impress of his tragic destiny.[48]

James's debt to Trotsky is also fundamental in this context, for Trotsky's *History* explicitly stressed the crucial role played by Lenin in making the October Revolution after arriving back in Russia from exile in April 1917 during a revolutionary situation: "The role of the personality arises before us here on a truly gigantic scale. It is necessary only to understand that role correctly, taking personality as a link in the historic chain. . . . From the extraordinary significance which Lenin's arrival received, it should be inferred that leaders are not accidentally created, that they are gradually chosen out and trained up in the course of decades, that they cannot be capriciously replaced."[49]

Many commentators, from Isaac Deutscher onward, have challenged Trotsky's stress on personality and the role of the individual in history, arguing that it "goes so strongly against the grain of the Marxist intellectual tradition," as laid down most famously by Plekhanov.[50] Anthony Maingot has accordingly accused James in *The Black Jacobins* of "voluntarism" (as opposed to "orthodox Marxism" and "materialism"), asserting that "for Engels . . . there were no indispensable heroes." Yet it is worth remembering that if Engels really "depersonalized history," as claimed by Maingot, then the question might be asked why, for example, Engels spent time discussing "the magnificent figure" of Thomas Müntzer, "the soul of the entire revolutionary movement in Southwestern Germany" during 1525, in *The Peasant War in Germany*.[51] Engels's portrayal of Müntzer, like Trotsky's of Lenin, doubtless shaped how James imagined Toussaint, but in any case, as one writer—almost certainly James himself—wrote in *Fight* in June 1937, "Revolutionary Socialists accept the materialist interpretation of history. They see a man himself in terms of the nation, the epoch, the class and the family to which he belongs. Nevertheless they recognise the role of the individual. On the October Revolution was the imprint of Lenin. The character of the counter-revolution is in the rude, disloyalty of Stalin."[52]

C. L. R. James, Eric Williams, and the Destruction of the Myth of Abolition

When James resigned his prestigious post as a lecturer in English and History at Trinidad's Government Training College in order to come to Britain, the job was initially offered to one of his former students at QRC, Eric Williams. However, Williams had also been training, with James's help, for a Trinidadian Government Scholarship to study at Oxford University, and when he successfully won this, electing to study modern history, he followed in James's footsteps, also arriving in Britain in 1932.[53] James has described meeting Williams, "congratulating him on his scholarship" and saying that he was glad to see that Williams "had broken out of the law and medicine routine and was going in for history." James told Williams: "You need not be afraid of the future. Trinidad and Tobago in 15 years will be a very different place from what it is now."[54] The young Williams worked hard for his degree in modern history, which involved studying Latin, French, European history from 700 to 1789, and political economy, while he took a special subject in British colonial history from 1830 to 1860.[55] As James remembered, "Williams used to come to my house in London and spend his vacations with me. Frequently I used to go up to Oxford and spend some time with him. . . . He used to send me his papers from Oxford on Rousseau, on Plato and on Aristotle for my comments."[56] James also recalls spending free evenings on pub crawls around London with Williams and his student friends, which he could enjoy so long as he had "Marx, Jane Austen or H.G. Wells in [his] pocket."[57]

In 1935, Williams graduated with first-class honors, a tremendous achievement. "I had come, seen and conquered — at Oxford!" At the start of the new term in September 1935, Williams enrolled in another course in philosophy, politics, and economics, in order to try to win an All Souls Fellowship.[58] However, he was unsuccessful in winning a fellowship, and so he abandoned his PPE course in 1936 to return to historical scholarship. Mussolini's war on Ethiopia drew Williams for the first time into the political arena, and he recalled he "led the fight at Aggrey House against Italian imperialism, and advocated League of Nations support for Ethiopia."[59] By summer 1936, James's historical research on Haiti was very advanced, and he recalled:

> [Williams] came to me, as he usually did, asking me questions. He said, "I am to do a doctorate. What shall I write on?" . . . I told him, "I know exactly what you should write on. I have done the economic basis of slavery emancipation as it was in France. But that has never been done in Great Britain, and Britain is wide open for it. A lot of people think the British showed good will. There were lots of people who had good will,

but it was the basis, the economic basis that allowed the good will to function." He said, "Do you think it will be good?" I said, "Fine." He said, "Well, what shall I say." I said, "Give me some paper!" and I sat down and wrote what the thesis should be with my own hand, and I gave it to him. He must have copied it down, and took it to the Oxford authorities. Later he told me they said it was fine. And he went from there.[60]

Whatever input James had in formulating the primary thesis, clearly such a topic appealed to Williams, and in what was one of the most important decisions of his life and career he now began to work on the thesis "The Economic Aspect of the Abolition of the West Indian Slave Trade and Slavery," "of all the chapters in British colonial history, the least known." His tutor for his doctorate was Vincent Harlow, a historian of seventeenth-century Barbados, and "the premier colonial scholar at Oxford."[61] James remembers whenever he now went over to France for research purposes, Williams "would go with [him]."[62]

There was more than anticolonialist politics and James's Marxism turning the two West Indians toward a focus on the social and economic realities of colonial slavery in the Caribbean. Williams was right to note that "no work of scholarly importance had been done in England" on the abolition of the Atlantic slave trade and slavery in the British Empire and that "British historians wrote almost as if Britain had introduced Negro slavery solely for the satisfaction of abolishing it."[63] However, outside England there had been work done. In 1905, there had been important insights into the abolition of the slave trade in a German work of economic history by Franz Hochstetter, a work that Williams in particular thought highly of.[64] As for James, he later told Stuart Hall that while in France he came across French historians who "had made it clear, that the movement toward the abolition of slavery came from the capitalistic element who were tired with the poor production of . . . feudalism and slavery." James recalled, "I had learnt this in France, I didn't discover it."[65]

Critically important for both James and Williams was a 1928 work by an American historian, Lowell Joseph Ragatz, *The Fall of the Planter Class in the British Caribbean, 1763–1833: A Study in Social and Economic History.* Like many other white American professors in the 1920s, Ragatz was personally racist.[66] Yet Ragatz understood the need to examine the social and economic history of the Caribbean, and he traced a quite amazing, long-term, structural decline of the West Indies from the 1750s to the 1830s. In the 1750s, West Indian sugar planters "were the conspicuously rich men of Great Britain," often absentee landlords like the Lascelles family, who owned Harewood House: "Sugar was king. They who produced it constituted the power behind the throne, and the islands on which their opulence and commanding position had been reared were regarded by all as the most valued of overseas possessions."[67] However, by the 1820s, the position of this once powerful planter class in the British Caribbean could not be more different, as the beneficial monopoly of trade with Britain became a stranglehold, "the dwindling returns from their decayed properties all but completely engrossed by creditors." "The sugar colonies themselves, sunk into social and economic stagnation, were viewed with hostile eyes and their value to the homeland was commonly questioned. . . . Never in imperial history [had] there been a more striking contrast."[68] The impact Ragatz's thesis made on James and Williams should not be underestimated. James thought it "yet another of those monumental pieces of research into European history which American scholarship is giving us in such profusion."[69] When the revised version of Williams's thesis was eventually published, he dedicated it to Ragatz, "whose monumental labours in this field may be amplified and developed but can never be superceded."[70]

In 1935, Reginald Coupland gave a lecture on "The Meaning of Wilberforce." He contended, "The conscience of all England was awakened. That, in a word, is how the slave system was abolished. Not because it was good policy or good business to abolish it—it was neither, it was the opposite— but simply because of its iniquity."[71] In 1933, James had written that "the slave trade is the one trade which has never felt a slump."[72] James did not retreat from that argument in *The Black Jacobins*, noting that "profits were always high," but he simply points out that "nothing, however profitable, goes on forever."[73] After reading Ragatz, it seemed clear that the British had partly abolished the slave trade because they were slowly realizing that slavery itself was not as profitable as free labor, nor the old mercantilist system as potentially profitable as free trade. As James contended, "The rising industrial bourgeoisie, feeling its way to free trade . . . were beginning their victorious attack upon the agricultural monopoly which was to culminate in the Repeal of the Corn Laws in 1846. The West Indian sugar-producers were monopolists whose methods of production afforded an easy target, and Adam Smith and Arthur Young, the forerunners of the new era, condemned the whole principle of slave-labour as the most expensive in the world."[74] James then tore into Coupland and his ilk with typically devastating wit: "Those who see in abolition the gradually awakening conscience of mankind should spend a few minutes asking themselves why it is man's conscience, which had slept peacefully for so many centuries, should awake just at the time that men began to see the unprofitableness of slavery as a method of production in the West Indian colonies."[75]

Coupland's ilk were "a venal race of scholars," who, because "profiteering panders to national vanity, [had] conspired to obscure the truth about abolition." In a few pathbreaking paragraphs, and for arguably the very first time in the English language, James, in the words of Roger Anstey, propounded "an ingenious explanation of how humanitarian motives were subordinated to economics in the Younger Pitt's conduct of abolition in the 1790s."[76] For this section, James had doubtless been helped more than he acknowledged by Williams, who spent two years undertaking doctoral research in the Public Record Office, Parliamentary Papers, Hansard records, Colonial Office papers, Foreign Office papers, and the Chatham papers.[77] Williams's Oxford thesis, finished in 1938, included a detailed discussion of the British parliamentary debates around the abolition of the slave trade, showing the importance of not only economic considerations but also of Pitt's disastrous attempt at the recolonization of revolutionary Saint Domingue. In London, Williams had associated himself with the Pan-African radicals around the IASB, and the radical, democratic, and antiparliamentary streak that ran through Williams's thesis meant that it almost failed for political reasons. Coupland, one of Williams's examiners, during the Great War had "published as a morale-booster the war speeches of Pitt," and as Williams recalled,

> All the dice were loaded against me, for at Oxford, I had committed the unpardonable sin—I had challenged the British interpretation of the abolition of slavery. . . . I still recall, how I was told, in unambiguous language, that if I persisted in my analysis of Pitt's policy in respect of slavery and the slave trade in the war with France, not only would my thesis be failed, but in the opinion of the spokesman, rightly be failed.[78]

Certainly its exposure of the moral hypocrisy and bankruptcy of parliamentarians such as Pitt meant Williams found it impossible to find a publisher for his thesis in 1939, at a time when the British imperial war machine was on the brink of another great war for "democracy." Even Fredric Warburg, who just the year before had published James's *Black Jacobins*, which had contained in condensed form the essence of Williams's argument, now drew back, sensing perhaps a rising mood of British nationalism. As Williams recalled, "Warburg ... told me: 'Mr. Williams, are you trying to tell me that the slave trade and slavery were abolished for economic and not humanitarian reasons? I would never publish such a book, for it would be contrary to the British tradition.'" [79]

In 1944, when Williams's thesis was published in America in an expanded and much revised form as *Capitalism and Slavery*, he would rightly praise James for having presented "in a general way the relationship between capitalism and slavery" in *The Black Jacobins*. However, Williams erred slightly when he followed this up by declaring that "the thesis advanced" in *Capitalism and Slavery* is "stated clearly and concisely and ... for the first time in English" in *The Black Jacobins*.[80] In *Capitalism and Slavery*, Williams went further than he did in his Oxford thesis, and he now tried to suggest that colonial slavery had made possible the breakthrough in England of modern capitalism, which in turn then killed slavery because of free trade and the profitable advantages of free labor.

For James, the enormous profits from slavery and the slave trade did of course help "enrich British capitalism" and French capitalism and so help bring down the old aristocracy and its colonial monopoly in France. Indeed, "slavery and the colonial trade were the fount and origin and sustenance" of France's "thriving industry and far-flung commerce." In *The Black Jacobins*, James asserted, "Long before 1789 the French bourgeoisie was the most powerful economic force in France, and the slave-trade and the colonies were the basis of its wealth and power. The slave trade was the economic basis of the French Revolution. 'Sad irony of human history,' comments Jaurès. 'The fortunes created at Bordeaux, at Nantes, by the slave trade, gave to the bourgeoisie that pride which needed liberty and contributed to human emancipation.'" [81]

Yet James in *The Black Jacobins*, in an outstanding application of the "law of uneven and combined development," clearly demonstrated—in a way that Williams did not—that Atlantic slavery and the slave trade, the plantations and the slave ships, were fundamentally modern, capitalist institutions in themselves, things which did not just enrich but had been themselves formed by "the French bourgeoisie" and "the British bourgeoisie." James described the plantations as "huge sugar-factories" and the slaves as a proto-proletariat, "closer to a modern proletariat than any group of workers in existence at the time and the rising was, therefore, a thoroughly prepared and organised mass movement." When they rose as "revolutionary labourers" and set fire to the plantations, James compared them to "the Luddite wreckers."[82] Vindicated in his views about the essential modernity of the West Indian working class by the demands advanced and tactics adopted during the recent Caribbean labor rebellions, James described the most militant rebels of the Haitian Revolution as "revolutionaries through and through . . . brothers of the Cordeliers in Paris and the Vyborg workers in Petrograd."[83] It was James's grasp of the modernity of Atlantic slavery and so also of the slave experience and slave resistance, as much as his understanding of the class dynamics of abolition, that made *The Black Jacobins* such an outstanding advance on all previous scholarship.[84]

For James, the battle over abolition was not simply between the dynamic industrial bourgeoisie of Britain on the one hand and the stagnant West Indian sugar-planter class and their representatives in Parliament on the other, itself "but one stage in the successive victories of the industrial bourgeoisie over the landed aristocracy."[85] It was also a struggle between two factions of the British capitalist class — "the British bourgeois" who were the "most successful of slave-traders" against "those British bourgeois who had no West Indian interests," who now "with tears rolling down their cheeks for the poor suffering blacks . . . set up a great howl for the abolition of the slave trade."[86] As James had written in *A History of Negro Revolt*, "The abolitionists it is true worked very hard, and Clarkson, in particular, was a very honest and sincere man. But that a considerable and influential section of British men of business thought that the slave-trade was not only a blot on the national name but a growing hole in the national pocket, was the point that mattered."[87] James's *The Black Jacobins* did not dishonor the memory of the historic contribution made by "those millions of honest English Nonconformists who listened to their clergymen and gave strength to the English movement for the abolition of slavery," people whom "the sons of Africa and the lovers of humanity will remember with gratitude and affection." Yet James damned those he called, invoking a phrase of Cecil Rhodes, "the 'philanthropy plus five per cent' hypocrites in the British Houses of Parliament."[88]

The slave trade and colonial slavery in the Americas had been seen as so natural and essential to the success of the emerging global capitalist system and the making of the modern world that very few Europeans even questioned it, let alone agitated for its end. It was to be the Haitian Revolution that began in 1791 that, to paraphrase Walter Benjamin, "blasted open the continuum of this history," forcing the French to abolish slavery

across their vast empire in 1794, within three years of the revolution's beginning, and forcing the British to abandon their participation in the highly
profitable Atlantic slave trade in 1807, only three years after the revolution's
end.[89] W. E. B. Du Bois had noted the importance of the Haitian Revolution in passing, in his doctoral thesis on the *Suppression of the Slave Trade*,
completed in 1897. Yet James, in 1938, for the first time historically demonstrated that it was indeed the Haitian Revolution that had essentially
"killed the West Indian slave-trade and slavery."[90] Through a skillful use of
sources and the insights of other historians, including even the likes of Sir
John William Fortescue, the Tory military historian, James elegantly destroyed some of the most cherished assumptions of British nationalist historiography.[91] In *The Black Jacobins*, James did not just "effectively for the
first time" give "slaves an agency," he made the emancipation from slavery
and the slave trade the act of the enslaved themselves.[92] Indeed, "the black
Jacobins of San Domingo were to make history which would alter the fate
of millions of men and shift the economic currents of three continents."[93]

Romanticism and Revolutionary History

In his important and insightful work on "the tragedy of colonial enlightenment," *Conscripts of Modernity*, David Scott stresses how *The Black Jacobins*
is "above all, a literary-historical exercise in revolutionary Romanticism . . .
a modernist allegory of anticolonial revolution written in the mode of a
historical Romance." It is perhaps worth dwelling here on how what Scott
calls "Romanticism and the longing for anticolonial revolution" might have
shaped James's work.[94] Without wishing to distract any attention from the
importance of what might be called "the four Williams" — Hazlitt, Shakespeare, Thackeray, and Wordsworth — to the young James's life-long love of
English literature, one writer among the many he read in Trinidad is often
somewhat overlooked.[95] This was the American novelist James Fenimore
Cooper, author of vivid accounts of native American tribes fighting for sur-
vival against British and French colonialism, such as *The Deerslayer*, *The
Pathfinder*, *The Last of the Mohicans*, and *The Prairie*.[96] Though often simply
seen as a writer of "adventure stories," the Hegelian Marxist theorist and literary critic Georg Lukács more properly termed Cooper's writings classical
"historical novels," and he recognized Cooper as the only worthy follower
of the great Sir Walter Scott in the English language. Scott himself had experienced the tumult of the revolutionary wave of 1789–1815, and as Lukács

noted in *The Historical Novel* (1937), Scott's vision of history was therefore one of "an uninterrupted series of such revolutionary crises." "The important thing" for Scott in his historical novels was "to lay bare those vast, heroic, human potentialities which are always latently present in the people and which, on each big occasion, with every deep disturbance of the social or even the more personal life, emerge 'suddenly,' with colossal force, to the surface."[97] Anyone, whether a revolutionary or a reactionary, who had experienced living through the period 1789–1815, as Scott had done, would have found it difficult to imagine the history of humanity as an essentially unchanging process, free of conflict and crisis.

In a fundamental sense, the collective experience of the Great French Revolution gave birth to the discipline of "History" itself, as a science out of literature, in what Engels called the "triumph of realism."[98] If the earthquake that had just shaken the ancien régime to its very foundations was to be explained and understood, then a new approach to explain change in society was necessary. In the 1820s, pioneering French liberal historians such as Augustin Thierry, Adolphe Thiers, François Guizot, and François Mignet brought some order to the inspired frenzy of revolution. To defend the legitimacy of the democratic gains of the French Revolution, they portrayed the rise to power of the "Third Estate" in 1789 as the rational and inevitable triumph of the productive classes over the privileged and corrupt. In passionately championing the upheaval as a bourgeois revolution, these liberal historians put class, and class struggle, at the center of historical analysis for the very first time, and their new materialist analysis now suggested that the whole history of civilization needed to be completely written afresh.[99] Thierry called for a "new history" to replace the traditional dynastic focus on kings and their courts, a popular history that was "alive" instead of accounts of the past that were not only "cold and monotonous" but also "false and contrived."[100] The French Revolution, Thierry noted, has "taught us to understand the revolution of the Middle Ages; to discern the fundamental character of things beneath the letters of the chronicles," and declared that politically identifying with the collective struggles of the people "suggests insights, divinations, sometimes even leaps of genius" to the historian, discoveries "which disinterested scholarship and a purely zealous love of truth would not have led."[101] After the 1830 revolution in France, which saw the rise of liberalism (and liberals like Thiers and Guizot) to power, it fell to more radical French historians such as Jules Michelet and Alphonse de Lamartine, and then the first socialist historians such as Louis Blanc, to now defend the spirit of the Great French Revolution.

Yet whether liberal, radical, or socialist, all of these outstanding French historians had been inspired by Romanticism, and their writings from the 1820s to the 1840s were vivid "rolling historical narratives" in the spirit of Scott's "historical novels." As Thierry noted of Scott, "There is more true history in his novels of England and Scotland than in many compilations that still go by the name of histories." The great writer Alexandre Dumas praised Lamartine for having "raised history to the level of a novel."[102] The French Romantic historians wrote true "livre populaire," books for the people, designed as if to urgently summon their readers to the heights of revolutionary action achieved by their ancestors in the past. For Michelet, whom Lionel Gossman describes as "the greatest of French Romantic historians and one of the greatest historians of all time," history was about a "resurrection de la vie integrale," the resurrection of life in its totality, something he felt was not just a possibility but a burning necessity. Michelet's *History of the French Revolution* (1847–53) was not simply about reclaiming the hidden history of the French people; it aimed to be the gospel of a new religion of humanity.[103]

It was while researching the Haitian Revolution in Paris, James recalled, that he first encountered what he would later term "the French historical school of the French Revolution[,] . . . one of the greatest historical schools of Western civilization." Reading some of these Romantic historians' dramatic accounts clearly succeeded in bringing the Great French Revolution to life like nothing else he had read. James later reflected that to write the history of a revolution one needed not only "scholarship" but also "that respect for the Revolution without which the history of revolution cannot be written," and he always stressed that few writers ever had more respect for the revolutionary spirit than Michelet.[104] However, after the wave of revolution across Europe in 1848, and particularly the workers' uprising in Paris in June 1848, which baffled the likes of Michelet, it was increasingly left to the authors of *The Communist Manifesto* and then socialist historians inspired by Marxism, such as Jean Jaurès, to defend the spirit of revolution.[105] Yet what perhaps needs to be stressed is the extent to which Marx not only built on the materialist foundations laid by the French Romantic historians but was also inspired by the power of their writing. As Engels noted, Marx had a "particular predilection" for French history, and what Marx owed to Romanticism can be perhaps most clearly seen in his dramatic account of

Napoleon III's coup d'état of 1851, *The Eighteenth Brumaire of Louis Bonaparte* (1852).[106]

Yet by far and away the most important intellectual inspiration for James when he came to write *The Black Jacobins* was Trotsky's *History of the Russian Revolution*. Trotsky's biographer, Isaac Deutscher, has argued that "to Marx's minor historical works, *The Class Struggle in France*, *The 18th Brumaire of Louis Bonaparte*, and *The Civil War in France*, Trotsky's *History* stands as the large mural painting stands to the miniature."[107] Accordingly, if there is such a thing, what might be called "the Romantic soul of historical materialism" burns as bright in Trotsky's *History* as it did in Marx's *Eighteenth Brumaire*. As David Scott notes, comparing Trotsky to Michelet, "The old dream of revolution came to be keyed to a new idea of the rhythm of history, a new conception of historical agency, and a new idea of how to self-consciously wrest the future from the past . . . if the tone of Trotsky's narrative is less oracular and the composition less lyrical, less given to rhapsodic flights of poetic flourish than Michelet's, the dominant mode of emplotment nevertheless remains that of Romance."[108]

For James, Trotsky's *History* was therefore "far more than a brilliant history of a great event" but "the greatest history book ever written and one of the most stupendous and significant pieces of literature ever produced in any language." The *History* was "the climax of two thousand years of European writing and the study of history," and Trotsky was the historian par excellence: "In pure style, this materialist, as rigid with fact as Scaliger, is exceeded in no sphere by any one of his ancestors, not by Thucydides in proportion and lucidity, nor by Tacitus in invective, nor by Gibbon in dignity, nor Michelet in passion, nor by Macaulay, that great bourgeois, in efficiency. There is a profound lesson here not only in history but in aesthetics."[109]

James's *Black Jacobins* is also one of the few works of Marxist history that can take their place alongside Trotsky's monumental work, and the spirit at least of Deutscher's discussion of Trotsky's *History* should also be considered with respect to James:

> Whereas Marx towers above the disciple in the power of his abstract thought and gothic imagination, the disciple is superior as epic artist, especially as master of the graphic portrayal of masses and individuals in action. His socio-political analysis and artistic vision are in such concord that there is no trace of any divergence. His thought and his imagina-

tion take flight together. He expounds his theory of revolution with the tension and the *élan* of narrative; and his narrative takes depth from his ideas. His scenes, portraits, and dialogues, sensuous in their reality, are inwardly illuminated by his conception of the historical process. . . . The *History* is his crowning work, both in scale and power and as the fullest expression of his ideas on revolution.[110]

The Haitian Revolution, as Errol Hill noted, "is the most epic of West Indian stories," and James was concerned when writing *The Black Jacobins* to bring alive what he called "the drama of history" through an epic Romantic work that might inspire and instruct those engaged not simply in pursuing "The Case for West Indian Self-Government" but those involved in anti-colonial movements across the African diaspora.[111] That James succeeded in writing a "grand narrative" of great literary power and dramatic quality is not in doubt. As Rosengarten puts it, "It isn't difficult to find pages of *The Black Jacobins* that rival stylistically anything James ever wrote as a novelist, short-story writer, dramatist or literary critic."[112] Robert Hill has gone as far as to suggest that *The Black Jacobins* stands as the *War and Peace* of the Caribbean: "In addition to its significance as the founding text of West Indian historical scholarship, *The Black Jacobins* ranks as the great epic of West Indian literature. Like Tolstoy's *War and Peace*, which describes the epic story of Russia's struggle during the Napoleonic wars, James' account of the Haitian Revolution expresses a parallel national vision for the West Indies."[113]

Marxist Theory, Colonial History, and the Haitian Revolution

Trotsky once remarked that "what has been written with the sword cannot be wiped out by the pen[,] . . . at least so far as the sword of revolution is concerned."[114] This did not of course stop those James called "Tory historians, regius professors and sentimentalists," "the professional whitewashers" of the historical record, devoting themselves for well over a century to use their pens to the task of trying to wipe out all trace of what had been written in blood and fire by Toussaint's black rebel slave army.[115] For Western scholars, before *The Black Jacobins* and for some time afterward, the Haitian Revolution, when it was mentioned at all, was essentially portrayed as Froude had portrayed it, simply as a bloodthirsty and savage race war, without reason or rhyme.[116] James systematically demolished this racist argument in *The Black Jacobins*: "Had the monarchists been white, the bourgeoisie brown, and the masses of France black, the French Revolution would have gone down in history as a race war. But although they were all white in France they fought just the same." James stressed that the Haitian Revolution was fundamentally about class, not race: "The struggle of classes ends either in the reconstruction of society or in the common ruin of the contending classes. The French Revolution laid the basis of modern France, the country as a whole being strong enough to survive the shock and profit by it, but so corrupt and rotten was the slave society of San Domingo that it could not stand any strain and perished as it deserved to perish."[117]

By asserting the relevance and, indeed, centrality of categories of class and class struggle, James for the first time brought cold hard rationality to the history of the revolution, and his outstanding and pioneering Marxist analysis of slavery and the slave experience has stood the test of time.[118] For example, the enslaved themselves were in part like peasants because "they worked on the land" and also "on their private plots," where, in the few moments of respite they had, "hard-working slaves cultivated vegetables and raised chickens to sell in the towns to make a little in order to buy rum and tobacco." The fact that through cultivation "here and there a Napoleon of finance, by luck and industry, could make enough to purchase his freedom," or at least buy some luxuries, shows not only that money circulated among slaves but also that there was an internal slave market operating—in other words, slaves were in part and in a sense like modern consumers. Finally, the enslaved were also like modern workers because they worked and lived together on capitalist plantations, "in gangs of hundreds on the huge sugar-factories."[119] Today, it is the orthodoxy of academic historians who specialize in studying New World slavery to use the terms "proto-proletariat," "proto-peasantry," and "proto-consumers," and though James did not use these terms, he had clearly grasped the essentials of the slave experience in all its diversity, back in 1938.

In a fundamental sense, *The Black Jacobins* was a pioneering work in the tradition of "history from below," or perhaps "history from below-decks," for two-thirds of the people who were to ultimately make the Haitian Revolution began their lives growing up in Africa, before being captured, mostly at a young age, and then enduring the violence and terror of the Middle Passage, across the Atlantic Ocean, to the New World of the

Americas, in chains on European slave ships.[120] The other third were descendants of those who had survived such a crossing, and so in that sense the Haitian Revolution was an "African revolution"—albeit in a Caribbean setting. Marx famously once said, "Men make their own history but not in the circumstances of their own choosing," and it is hard to imagine worse circumstances in which to try to make history than those in which the men, women, and children who were to make the Haitian Revolution found themselves. For Trotsky, the historian of a revolution had to "enter into the nerves" and minds of the masses, as "the revolution is there in their nerves before it comes out into the street." As Deutscher notes, Trotsky's *History* is "therefore to a large extent a study in revolutionary mass psychology."[121] In his later years, James would opine that the great black American historian W. E. B. Du Bois's account of the American Civil War *Black Reconstruction* (1935) was unparalleled as a work of revolutionary history, for in *The Black Jacobins* "there is no understanding of when you go beyond the economic and the social and political and you get deep into the psychology of the people who made the revolution."[122] But this was too modest an admission, for despite the difficulties in getting source material on the importance of African "survivals" for the Haitian Revolution in the 1930s, in *The Black Jacobins* James was arguably able to effectively "enter into the nerves" of the black slaves, painting a convincing picture of how, for them, Haitian Vodou allowed those without "education or encouragement to cherish a dream of freedom."[123] In Haiti, by the 1930s, as Chris Harman observed, "The American occupation was so crude that it led to a number of intellectuals to try to overcome their separation from the vast mass in the countryside. A *Noiriste* (black cultural) movement developed among them which attempted to understand the Creole, voodoo traditions of the peasantry and which sought to explain the political divisions between mulatto and black in terms of class."[124]

One key Haitian intellectual here was Dr. Jean Price-Mars, a diplomat who in 1928 published *Ainsi parla l'oncle*, "The sayings of Old Uncle," a defense of Vodou.[125] It seems that James benefited from a correspondence with Price-Mars while writing *The Black Jacobins*.[126] In any case, James suggestively evoked the "blackness" of the "black Jacobins," stressing that Haitian Vodou—a new fusion of African religions in dialogue with Catholicism—was "the medium of the conspiracy."[127]

Besides Marx and Trotsky, as we have seen, James was inspired by Michelet, as well as modern socialist historians of the French Revolution. James would recognize in particular the influence of Jean Jaurès, whom he remembered showed "a sympathetic understanding of the great mass movements" in France, and also Georges Lefebvre, who coincidently first coined the phrase "history from below."[128] James also read the great anarchist Peter Kropotkin's masterful *The Great French Revolution* (1909) — possibly on the recommendation of his old friend Charlie Lahr — a pioneering volume of history from below that was admired by Lenin and Trotsky.[129] For Kropotkin, the "true fount and origin of the Revolution" was "the people's readiness to take up arms," noting that it was to this that previous "historians of the Revolution had not done justice — the justice owed to it by the history of civilisation."[130] In *The Black Jacobins*, James would praise Kropotkin for having a "more instinctive understanding of revolution than any well-known book" on the French Revolution.[131]

Kropotkin's influence might begin to be detected when James describes the open revolt on the North Plain in Saint Domingue in August 1791, when the enslaved blacks "neglected and ignored by all the politicians of every brand and persuasion" had "organised on their own and struck for freedom at last."[132] Kropotkin's critical stress in *The Great French Revolution* was on the revolutionary violence of the peasantry, for "the insurrection of the peasants for the abolition of the feudal rights and the recovery of the communal lands" in the summer of 1789 was "the very essence, the foundation of the great Revolution" and "the great rising of the rural districts" — the *jacquerie* — which "lasted five years, was what enabled the Revolution to accomplish the immense work of demolition which we owe to it."[133] James effectively brought out the way the uprising of the enslaved on French Saint Domingue resembled the contemporaneous struggles of the French peasantry: "The slaves worked on the land, and, like revolutionary peasants everywhere, they aimed at the extermination of their oppressors. . . . The slaves destroyed tirelessly. Like the peasants in the Jacquerie . . . they were seeking their salvation in the most obvious way, the destruction of what they knew was the cause of their sufferings; and if they destroyed much it was because they had suffered much."[134]

By 1803, after twelve years of fighting for national independence and social liberation, James noted that the black rebel slave army had been forced to burn Saint Domingue "flat so that at the end of the war it was a charred desert." James wrote, "Why do you burn everything? asked a French officer of a prisoner. We have a right to burn what we cultivate because a man has a right to dispose of his own labour, was the reply of this unknown anarchist."[135]

If Marxist writers, above all Trotsky, had helped James understand the way the enslaved blacks acted like a "proto-proletariat" during the Haitian Revolution, then Kropotkin must have been critical to helping James understand the way the rebellious slave army acted like a "proto-peasantry."

The central story of *The Black Jacobins* for James was not, however, revolutionary violence, critical as that was, for "when did property ever listen to reason except when cowed by violence?"[136] Rather, James stressed the transformation of consciousness that took place among the black laborers and black slave army of Saint Domingue as a result of their mighty collective struggle for liberation:

> The revolt is the only successful slave revolt in history, and the odds it had to overcome is evidence of the magnitude of the interests that were involved. The transformation of slaves, trembling in hundreds before a single white man, into a people able to organise themselves and defeat the most powerful European nations of their day, is one of the great epics of revolutionary struggle and achievement. Why and how this happened is the theme of this book.[137]

As James put it, by 1798 and the expulsion of the British from the island, the Haitian Revolution "had created a new race of men." James described the transformation:

> This change had first expressed itself in August 1791 . . . but they were soon formed into regiments and were hardened by fighting. They organised themselves into armed sections and into popular bodies. . . . At bottom the popular movement had acquired an immense self confidence. The former slaves had defeated white colonists, Spaniards and British, and now they were free. They were aware of French politics, for it concerned them deeply. Black men who had been slaves were deputies in the French Parliament, black men who had been slaves negotiated with French and foreign governments. Black men who had been slaves filled the highest position in the colony. There was Toussaint, the former slave, incredibly grand and powerful and incomparably the greatest man in San Domingo. There was no need to be ashamed of being a black. The revolution had awakened them, had given them the possibility of

achievement, confidence and pride. That psychological weakness, that feeling of inferiority with which the imperialists poison colonial peoples everywhere, these were gone.[138]

Yet James's stress on placing the black masses center stage in *The Black Jacobins*, his writing the history of the Haitian Revolution from below for the first time, did not mean that he lacked a grasp of the totality of social relations in which they played their role. In his preface to *The Black Jacobins*, James gives a profound insight into his understanding of historical philosophy and of the advantages of the Marxist theory of history:

> The writing of history becomes ever more difficult. The power of God or the weakness of man, Christianity or the divine right of kings to govern wrong, can easily be made responsible for the downfall of states and the birth of new societies. Such elementary conceptions lend themselves willingly to narrative treatment and from Tacitus to Macaulay, from Thucydides to Green, the traditionally famous historians have been more artist than scientist: they wrote so well because they saw so little.[139]

The "traditionally famous historians," ranging from the irrationalism of the ancient Greeks and Romans up to the English Whigs, were, for James, less historians than primarily "artists," writers of "narrative," as a result of their rudimentary and idealist philosophy of history. Indeed, they often admitted as much. At the start of the twentieth century, the liberal historian G. M. Trevelyan insisted that "the art of history remains always the art of narrative. That is the bedrock."[140] By 1938, James noted there had been a sea change against traditional political narratives about the doings of statesmen and kings. "Today by a natural reaction we tend to a personification of the social forces, great men being merely or nearly instruments in the hands of economic destiny," James commented. This shift toward social and economic history was in part influenced by the mechanical materialist philosophy of Second International Marxism, but it was one that had influenced the likes of Ragatz and had been taken even further by the Annales school in France.[141]

Yet, for James, neither idealism nor materialism by themselves were adequate philosophies of history, and, moreover, "so often the truth does not lie in between." James offered an alternative to both, based on Marx's theory of history, historical materialism: "Great men make history, but only such history as it is possible for them to make. Their freedom of achievement is limited by the necessities of their environment. To portray the limits of those necessities and the realisation, complete or partial, of all possibilities, that is the true business of the historian." James proceeded to suggest how this theory, because it had the human agency of the masses as well as individuals at its heart, was able to explain revolutionary upheavals:

> In a revolution, when the ceaseless slow accumulation of centuries bursts into volcanic eruption, the meteoric flares and flights above are a meaningless chaos and lend themselves to infinite caprice and romanticism unless the observer sees them always as projections of the subsoil from which they came. The writer has sought not only to analyse, but to demonstrate in their movement, the economic forces of the age; their moulding of society and politics, of men in the mass and individual men; the powerful reaction of these on their environment at one of those rare moments when society is at boiling point and therefore fluid. The analysis is the science and the demonstration the art which is history.[142]

It is not too hard to see the influence of Marx on James here, in particular in Marx's insistence that history was a product of the social interaction of human beings, and the dynamic model he set out in his famous preface to *A Contribution to the Critique of Political Economy*, published in 1859. Marx argued that changes in the "forces of production," the ability of humans to control the natural world in order to provide themselves with livelihoods through work, led to low-level changes in the "relations of production," as people were forced to cooperate with each other differently. The sum total of these relationships constituted "the economic structure of society, the real foundation," or what Marx called the "base," and James "the sub-soil." However, "the economic forces of the age," as they progress and develop, do not automatically "mould society and politics" accordingly, so that humanity steadily advances forward. Marx described how a "legal and political superstructure" was erected at every stage by those elements of society who controlled the surplus created in production, the ruling elite, in order to try to freeze the relations of production at that stage at which they perceived it was most beneficial to them. Marx noted that "from forms of development of the productive forces these relations turn into their fetters. Then begins an epoch of social revolution," or, as James put it, "the ceaseless slow accumulation of centuries bursts into volcanic eruption."[143] In the clash between the forces of production and the relations of production, society "becomes fluid" and the class struggle, a hidden molten lava bubbling away like a subterranean fire down below, bursts into the open with "meteoric flares" and "flights above."

History, for James, was then about both the scientific "analysis" of the driving economic forces in society and the artistic "demonstration" needed to reconstruct the resulting class struggle as it arises into the open. In his second chapter, "The Owners," James offered an unsurpassed portrait of the society of Saint Domingue before the outbreak of the French Revolution, from the ruling, white, master-planter class at the top, down through the intermediate class of free colored "mulattoes," and finally to the mass of black, enslaved people in barbaric bondage themselves. It was their labor that ensured that Saint Domingue was in 1789 "the most profitable colony the world had ever known; to the casual eye the most flourishing and prosperous possession on the face of the globe; to the analyst a society torn by inner and outer contradictions which in four years would split that structure into so many pieces that they could never be put together again."[144]

James would later stress that the entire "theoretical basis" of *The Black Jacobins* was the Marxist theory of permanent revolution: "In a period of world-wide revolutionary change, such as that of 1789–1815 and our period which began with 1917, the revolutionary crisis lifts backward peoples over centuries and projects them into the very forefront of the advanced movement of the day."[145]

As Trotsky had noted, the peculiarities resulting from the "backwardness" of Russian historical development had explained the "enigma" that "a backward country was the *first* to place the proletariat in power":

> Moreover, in Russia the proletariat did not arise gradually through the ages, carrying with itself the burden of the past as in England, but in leaps involving sharp changes of environment, ties, relations, and a sharp break with the past. It is just this fact—combined with the concentrated oppressions of czarism—that made the Russian workers hospitable to the boldest conclusions of revolutionary thought—just as the backward industries were hospitable to the last word in capitalist organization.[146]

Trotsky would always stress that "what characterises Bolshevism on the national question is that in its attitude towards oppressed nations, even the most backward, it considers them not only the object but also the subject of politics."[147] Yet during the 1930s, as Michael Löwy has noted, the absence of "further major upheavals on an equivalent scale in the colonial world during Trotsky's lifetime" probably explains why Trotsky "never felt the political exigency to produce a further theorization of permanent revolution in the colonial theatre."[148] James's greatest achievement in *The Black Jacobins* was to make just such a further theorization. James demonstrated that just as "the law of uneven and combined development" under capitalism had meant the slaves of Saint Domingue, suffering under the "concentrated oppressions" of slavery, were soon to be "hospitable to the boldest conclusions of revolutionary thought" radiating from the Jacobins in revolutionary Paris, so the Marxist theory of permanent revolution illuminated not just anticolonial struggles in the age of socialist revolution, but also the antislavery liberation struggle in the age of "bourgeois-democratic" revolution. Trotsky described how the "privilege of historic backwardness" allowed in certain circumstances the "skipping" of "a whole series of intermediate stages. Savages throw away their bows and arrows for rifles all at once, without travelling the road which lay between those two weapons in the past."[149] Now James explained in *The Black Jacobins* how "the San Domingo blacks had an army and leaders trained to fight in the European manner," and so were "no savage tribesmen with spears, against whom European soldiers armed with rifles could win undying glory."[150]

Throughout his study of the Haitian Revolution, James ably demonstrated for the first time that the revolution was not simply an inspiring struggle on a tiny island on the periphery of the world system, but was inextricably intertwined with the Great French Revolution throughout, pushing the revolutionary process forward in the metropole and investing notions of human rights with new meanings and universal significance. In writing about the Haitian Revolution, James rewrote the history of the French Revolution as well. One only has to look at some of the chapter titles of *The Black Jacobins*, such as "Parliament and Property" — would the new "parliament" established by the French Revolution regard enslaved black people in French colonies as more than "property," in light of the Declaration of the Rights of Man and Citizen (1789)? James then followed this up with "The San Domingo Masses Begin" and "And the Paris Masses Complete." James seems to have been again influenced by Kropotkin in his discussion of events in revolutionary France, particularly the "Communism" in Paris between March 1793 and July 1794: "In the streets of Paris, Jacques Varlet and Roux were preaching Communism, not in production but in distribution, a natural reaction to the profiteering of the new bourgeoisie"; this comment essentially summarizes Kropotkin's more detailed discussion of "the Communist movement" in *The Great French Revolution*.[151] Tragically, of course, while the "Parisien masses" were able to exert tremendous influence over the French republic from 1793 to 1794, there were strict material limits on what was possible for them to achieve and the French Revolution itself soon stalled, degenerated, and fell back into reaction. The rise of Napoleon meant a return to the imperial status quo and eventually to the attempted restoration of slavery on Saint Domingue. Though the French armies were gloriously defeated by the rebel army built by Toussaint, he was captured and taken and left to die in a French prison, while the new black nation of Haiti had been once again devastated by having to fight a national liberation struggle through guerrilla war under the leadership of Jean-Jacques Dessalines. In a fundamental sense, the destinies of the two revolutionary struggles, one in the imperial metropolis and one in the colonial periphery, were bound together, and they rose and fell as one.

"To articulate the past historically," Benjamin suggested, "means to seize hold of a memory as it flashes up at a moment of danger."[152] It is perhaps worth quoting at some length from the conclusion of the 1938 edition of *The Black Jacobins*, in which James not only seized hold of the memory of the Haitian Revolution on the brink of a new interimperialist war, but also allowed his Marxist historical imagination free rein to suggest how the dynamics of permanent revolution might underpin political developments in the near future in colonial Africa, based on his analysis of the Copperbelt mineworkers' strike in 1935, outlined in *A History of Negro Revolt*. Some of it will be familiar to readers of the later revised editions, some less so.

> Let the blacks but hear from Europe the slogans of Revolution, and the *Internationale*, in the same concrete manner that the slaves of San Domingo heard Liberty and Equality and the *Marseillaise*, and from the mass uprising will emerge the Toussaints, the Christophes, and the Dessalines. They will hear. The forces of emancipation are at work, far more clearly today than in 1789. In Europe and Asia the forces of revolution, though damped down, smoulder in every country. The great imperialisms arm and prepare to destroy each other. Like the red cockades and white of San Domingo, they arm the blacks of Africa. From the people heaving in action will come the leaders; not the isolated blacks at Guys' Hospital or the Sorbonne, the dabblers in *surréalisme* or the lawyers, but the quiet recruits in a black police force, the sergeant in the French native army or British police, familiarizing himself with military tactics

and strategy, reading a stray pamphlet of Lenin or Trotsky as Toussaint read the Abbé Raynal.

The African revolution will be as merciless as that of Dessalines'. The blacks will know as friends only those whites who are fighting in the ranks beside them. And whites will be there. The white soldiers listening in doubt to the *Marseillaise* coming from the blacks in Crête-à-Pierrot, the Polish nationalists refusing to shoot the black nationalists, even the gesture of Dessalines when he named his blacks The Polish Regiment, these instinctive strivings of 150 years ago are clear-cut political policy today. The white workers in Europe, as indifferent today as the French before August 1792, will recognise their allies in time as did the Paris workers in the hour of danger.[153]

In other words, European imperialism was on the verge of destroying itself in a bloody interimperialist conflict, which would be fought in part by black colonial armies from Africa. Africans and people of African descent had been given false promises and used as cannon fodder by colonial powers during the Great War, and with another war looming the same would happen again. Yet just as the Great War had ultimately ended in the Russian Revolution and a revolutionary wave across Europe, so James expected that any future interimperialist war would be brought to an end sooner or later in similar fashion, through the outbreak of civil war somewhere in Europe. When black Africans, some of whom may have been fighting for one or another imperialist army, heard "the slogans of Revolution" and the singing of the "Internationale" in a concrete manner—encouraging them to rally to the side of the revolution rather than continue to fight for their imperialist overlords—a "mass uprising" would begin, something that would quickly develop into "the African revolution," led by unknown and undreamed-of revolutionary leaders, perhaps nourished on Lenin or Trotsky, thrown up by "the people heaving in action."

James imagined a fluid and confused situation taking place, with some whites immediately fighting in the ranks alongside black Africans in their struggle, while the legacy of racism would mean that other white workers, even in the country in the midst of socialist revolution, would initially show "indifference" but would doubtless recognize their true allies "in time." If other oppressed nationalities fighting in imperialist armies were deployed against the "black nationalist" struggle, they would surely rebel in turn. The Trotskyist James predicted the process of revolution would see the previously "backward" African working people leap to the very forefront of the international struggle, whereby a modern equivalent of "the white soldiers listening in doubt to the *Marseillaise* coming from the blacks in Crête-à-Pierrot" might take place. Whatever happened, the generally correct "political policy" for both the socialist revolution in Europe and "the African revolution" would be far more "clear-cut" than "the instinctive strivings" that had brought together Toussaint's black army of Saint Domingue with the white Jacobins of revolutionary Paris. The two revolutions would increasingly be part of the same process of international permanent revolution, and through this process, Trotsky's Fourth International would play an important role in forging a genuine "World Party of Socialist Revolution" that would be more than simply an aspiration and a name alone.

James's main intended audience for *The Black Jacobins*, then, was not only those fighting for colonial liberation in Africa and the Caribbean but also those fighting for socialist revolution in Europe. James had spent the winter of 1937 down in Brighton, in order to finish writing up his history of the Haitian Revolution, but in his preface to *The Black Jacobins*, written in 1938, he testified to feeling "the fever and the fret" of the Spanish Civil War. "It was in the stillness of a seaside suburb that could be heard most clearly and insistently the booming of Franco's heavy artillery, the rattle of Stalin's firing squads and the fierce shrill turmoil of the revolutionary movement striving for clarity and influence."[154] James clearly hoped that the Haitian Revolution would inspire those Africans and people of African descent who read *The Black Jacobins* to seize the opportunity that would be presented by the looming interimperialist conflict to organize independently and strike out for freedom. However, General Franco's use of Moroccan troops during the Spanish Civil War had demonstrated the acute danger that if material solidarity with anticolonial struggles was not shown by the revolutionary movement in Europe because of the influence of Stalinism or a more general overriding commitment to liberal "anti-fascism" of the Popular Front variety, then colonial troops could all too easily be bribed with false promises of liberation and then used to crush any outbreak of socialist revolution in Europe itself.[155] "The colonial question," then, was ultimately as much a question for European revolutionaries as for the colonized themselves.[156]

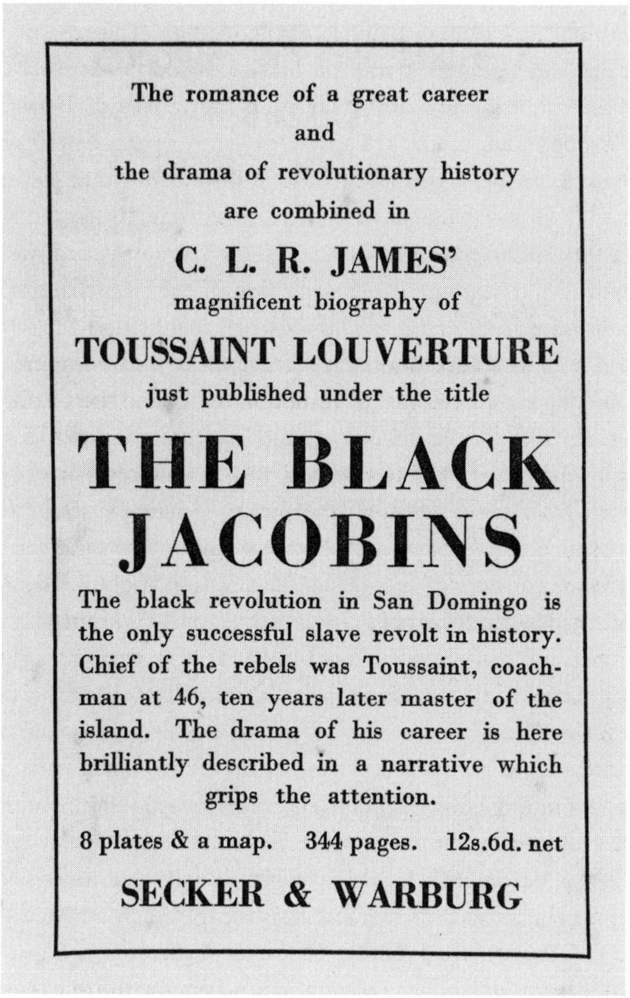

The romance of a great career
and
the drama of revolutionary history
are combined in

C. L. R. JAMES'

magnificent biography of

TOUSSAINT LOUVERTURE

just published under the title

THE BLACK
JACOBINS

The black revolution in San Domingo is the only successful slave revolt in history. Chief of the rebels was Toussaint, coachman at 46, ten years later master of the island. The drama of his career is here brilliantly described in a narrative which grips the attention.

8 plates & a map.   344 pages.   12s.6d. net

SECKER & WARBURG

FIGURE 5.1 Secker and Warburg advertise *The Black Jacobins*, September 1938.
© The Estate of C. L. R. James. Used by permission of the C. L. R. James estate.

"The romance of a great career and the drama of revolutionary history are combined in C.L.R. James' magnificent biography of Toussaint Louverture just published under the title *The Black Jacobins*," Secker and Warburg noted in their promotional material for this "narrative which grips the attention" in September 1938.[157] However, as Peter Fryer pointed out, James "might have been writing in German for all the notice that was taken by historians."[158] Flora Grierson, in the *New Statesman*, dismissed the work because of its "bias," asserting James was "a Communist and wants us to see the worst."[159] Leaving aside the question of quite which "best" bits of the slave experience Grierson had hoped to see highlighted, the awful truth was that if James had actually been a Communist with a capital "C," the work would have received greater attention on publication.[160] As Eugene Genovese noted in 1971, *The Black Jacobins* "deserves to rank as a classic of Marxian historiography but has been largely ignored, perhaps because of the author's Trotskyist politics."[161] There was no "perhaps" about it, though Eric Hobsbawm remembers that "in spite of the author's known Trotskyism" it influenced some of the outstanding constellation of Marxist intellectuals in the CPGB Historians' Group, who were to be central to helping develop the tradition of history from below after the Second World War.[162]

Among those who mattered most for James in the 1930s, as he later told an interviewer, *The Black Jacobins* "was from the beginning recognised as an extraordinary work."[163] Vindication of his efforts came when he asked for the reactions of George Padmore and Paul Robeson: Both Padmore and Robeson told him something similar: "James, I always knew the history was there, that we had it."[164] Copies of *The Black Jacobins* were sent out to IASB contacts in colonial Africa, and in October 1938, Secker and Warburg wrote to I. T. A. Wallace-Johnson, now back in Freetown, Sierra Leone: "At the suggestion of George Padmore, I send you herewith a review copy of C.L.R. James's THE BLACK JACOBINS for review in the West African Standard. I feel sure you will do what you can to promote the book and Padmore thinks you will be able to sell in your district a dozen or so copies. I hope this may be the case."[165]

Padmore himself reviewed James's work, both for Wallace-Johnson's *African Standard* and the Trinidadian publication *The People*, noting, "The author has done justice to his subject." Padmore continued: "He has combined with great skill history and biography without sacrificing one to the other. Mr. James is a real historian, with the sensitive mind of the scholar and an excellent literary style. . . . *The Black Jacobins* is a fascinating story, brilliantly told, and should be an inspiration to Africans and other colonial peoples still struggling for their freedom from the yoke of white imperialism."[166]

When a revised edition of *The Black Jacobins* was published in 1963, it finally began to receive the kind of recognition and attention it deserved amid decolonization and the rise of the New Left and Black Power movements. James added six new paragraphs discussing further the tragedy of Toussaint Louverture in this new edition, while also noting that Toussaint "was attempting the impossible—the impossible was for him the only reality that mattered." The revolutionary energy of the 1960s, epitomized in the slogan "Be realistic—demand the impossible!," thus found its echo consciously or unconsciously in *The Black Jacobins*, helping to make it "a book of the Sixties."[167] For example, Dan Georgakas and Marvin Surkin, in their history of the League of Revolutionary Black Workers (an American organization that was "in many respects the most significant expression of black radical thought and activism in the 1960s," according to Manning Marable), write, "James's ideas were well known to League activists and *Black Jacobins* was the work which struck the deepest chord."[168] The success of the work helped prompt James to rewrite his play *Toussaint Louverture* in 1967, renaming it *The Black Jacobins*, so that other aspects and experiences of the Haitian Revolution might be brought to bear on the new challenges and realities in Africa and the Caribbean now posed by decolonization.

Overall, as the Haitian scholar Michel-Rolph Trouillot once noted, the Haitian Revolution "entered history with the peculiar characteristic of being unthinkable even as it happened. . . . The general silence that Western historiography has produced around the Haitian Revolution originally stemmed from the incapacity to express the unthinkable."[169] For British imperial historians such as Coupland, for example, while there was some sense that "the rebels in St Domingo were preaching Jacobinism throughout the Caribbean," the Haitian Revolution was dismissed as a tragic sideshow, taking place off stage somewhere, in a place "perilously isolated from the civilized world, shut in upon itself by the encircling sea."[170] In a glorious fusion of classical scholarship on the Great French Revolution and Marxist scholarship on the revolutionary process in general, James's *The Black Jacobins* instead painted a vivid panorama of the Haitian Revolution, stressing that it was not simply the greatest event in the history of the Caribbean, but took its place alongside the English Civil War, the American War of Independence, and the French Revolution as one of the great revolutions in world history in its own right. Whereas the greatest victory of the Haitian Revolution was perhaps the revolution itself, and the transformation of consciousness and confidence among the great mass of people who made it, it would also forever transform the world and lay the foundation for the continuing struggle for universal human rights. As James puts it, "The work of Toussaint, Dessalines, Christophe, and Pétion endures in Hayti, but what they did went far, far beyond the boundaries of the island."[171] Indeed, in many ways, the Haitian Revolution went further in its commitment to universal emancipation than any of the revolutions that took place in the age of "bourgeois democratic" revolution; it was, as Paul Foot noted, "perhaps the most glorious victory of the oppressed over their oppressors in all history."[172]

In December 1939, after his move to America and meeting Trotsky for discussions on black liberation, James wrote "Revolution and the Negro" for the Trotskyist journal *New International*. In it, James attempted to bring home some of the main lessons for revolutionary Marxists to be taken from studying the Haitian Revolution:

> The Negro's revolutionary history is rich, inspiring, and unknown. Negroes revolted against the slave raiders in Africa; they revolted against the slave traders on the Atlantic passage. They revolted on the plantations. . . . The only place where Negroes did not revolt is in the pages of capitalist historians.
>
> All this revolutionary history can come as a surprise only to those who, whatever International they belong to, whether Second, Third, or Fourth, have not yet ejected from their systems the pertinacious lies of Anglo-Saxon capitalism. It is not strange that the Negroes revolted. It would have been strange if they had not.
>
> But the Fourth International, whose business is revolution, has not to prove that Negroes were or are as revolutionary as any group of oppressed people. That has its place in agitation. What we as Marxists have to see is the tremendous role played by Negroes in the transformation of Western civilisation from feudalism to capitalism. It is only from this vantage-ground that we shall be able to appreciate (and prepare for) the still greater role they must of necessity play in the transition from capitalism to socialism.[173]

| "To Exploit a Larger World to Conquer"

C. L. R. James's Intellectual Conquest
of Imperial Britain

On November 30, 1938, C. L. R. James addressed a packed rally of the American Socialist Workers' Party in Irving Plaza, New York City, as part of his lecture tour of the United States. James's speech, entitled "Twilight of the British Empire," gives us a glimpse of his revolutionary outlook:

> The British Empire with its 500 million colonial slaves and comparatively small white population is in mortal crisis. The movement for independence in India, the revolution that is surging in the Arab countries and has continued for two years with undiminished vigour in Palestine, the sullen hostility of the African masses, the movement for genuine independence in Egypt, the troubles in the West Indies, all those are symptoms of the increasing unrest which is certain to tear the Empire to pieces under the strain of a world war. . . . The idea that anyone who supports Britain in a war would be supporting democracy, is either criminal hypocrisy or equally criminal stupidity. The British Empire is the greatest instrument of tyranny and oppression known to History, and its overthrow would be a great step forward in human progress. Side by side with the struggle for colonial independence must go the struggle for socialism in Britain. The British labour movement must awaken to reality. Either socialism, with material progress, peace, and fraternal relations between peoples, or empire-increasing racial hatred and imperialist wars.[1]

One of those fortunate to hear James speak after his arrival in America was Martin Glaberman, who remembered thinking he was in the presence of "one of the great orators of the twentieth century." Glaberman recalled, "I was entranced by this tall (six foot, four inch) dark man who kept an audience in his grasp for three hours speaking about the British Empire, striding back and forth across the stage without a podium, without a note."[2] When James left for his lecture tour, the IASB declared "the young historian and labour leader" their "goodwill ambassador." On arriving in New York, James addressed the Association for the Study of Negro Life and History, while in Harlem he was the guest of honor at a testimonial dinner tendered him at the Mimo Club to celebrate the publication with Dial Press of the American edition of *The Black Jacobins*, where he gave an address titled "The West Indies."[3] James's oratorical powers and authority as a speaker derived from his life and recent work in imperial Britain, in particular his efforts to bring the growing resistance against British colonial rule together with the power of the industrial working class in the imperial metropolis in order to hasten the final fall of an empire already in decline.

Empire meant Britain was a place of critical importance for the world during the 1930s, rather akin perhaps to America's position at the center of world affairs today. Any black colonial subject from a tiny Caribbean island in the backwaters of the empire who made the "voyage in" to the "Mother Country" was expected to simply be appropriately awed at the great civilization he found and appreciatively soak up words of wisdom from the great and good before returning home to help serve the colonial project. They were not expected to challenge and demolish the intellectual foundations of the myths on which the whole edifice of British colonialism was constructed, and certainly not in quite the stylish manner of James. By December 1936, George Padmore, after witnessing his friend and compatriot's leadership of the IAFA and the production of *Toussaint Louverture*, could note that James "came to London in 1932 to exploit a larger world to conquer. He has done well."[4]

James would later recall that the colonial subjects in London who came together around the IASB during the 1930s "were able to sense the passing of colonialism" by taking the opportunity to see "what they would not have been able to see from any other point," "to be at the centre of things," "to view colonialism from several stages of development," and so get a "sense of the movement of things."[5] Eric Williams could claim, "I had come, seen and conquered—at Oxford!" when he graduated with first-class honors in 1935, and with the publication of *The Black Jacobins* in 1938, James could with equal legitimacy have claimed that he had come, seen, and intellectually conquered the larger world of imperial Britain. James was perhaps reflecting on what he had personally achieved when in 1938 he championed those anticolonialists "who could combine within their single selves the unrelenting suspicion and ruthless ferocity necessary to deal with imperialism and yet retain undimmed their creative impulse and their respect for the attainments of the very culture they fought so fiercely."[6]

The barriers standing in the way of such a monumental achievement should not be underestimated. As John MacKenzie notes, during the 1930s "a Britain without an Empire seemed almost a contradiction in terms." Empire "was, quite simply, there; a source of pride, not lightly to be put aside, it was also to gain a new economic significance." For the vast majority of British parliamentarians, whether of Right or Left, "the crucial thing now was to exploit it more effectively in a period of increasing world economic difficulty. As in the late nineteenth century, Empire could be portrayed as a means of arresting national decline." Accordingly, during the 1930s "when the professions of marketing, public relations, and propaganda (including censorship) all came of age," the "people who controlled the levers of propaganda" in Britain were "the most fervent exponents of a 'moral' imperialism." Indeed, "popular imperialism seemed to secure dramatic new cultural and institutional expressions," as media ranging from the cinema, the BBC, imperial exhibitions, school texts, juvenile literature to advertising all came into their own and played their part.[7] As James noted in *The Black Jacobins*, the 1930s was truly an "age of propaganda," one that excelled all previous ages "in system and organisation."[8]

If Stalin in 1935 could declare the British Empire "the greatest factor in the world for peace and stability," even the socialist Leonard Barnes, one of the more radical British critics of British imperialism during the 1930s, could not imagine its inevitable decline and fall.[9] "Coronations come and go. But the great British Empire, like the poor (of whom indeed it almost entirely consists), is always with us." Though Barnes felt India would not be held under imperial domination "indefinitely," the most he realistically dared hope and call for in 1937 was "that the great imperial countries should agree voluntarily to some reorganization of their empires in the interests of the economic security of countries less happily situated than themselves." The notion of decolonization in Africa in particular was quite unthinkable. For Barnes, "Colonies in general will have to be brought in to form an integral part of an international collective system. Self-government will be appropriate in some cases, of which India is the most important, but not in others, e.g. some territories of tropical Africa."[10]

Such a consensus about the legitimacy and durability of British power with respect to colonial Africa and the Caribbean was hegemonic among even progressive British intellectuals in the period. The Labour leader George Lansbury declared in 1934 that any future "Socialist Government" in Britain would not "at once withdraw from all the Colonies," a position that was shared by even the CPGB by 1938.[11] For anticolonialist activists, particularly those from Africa and the Caribbean, to educate, agitate, and organize in the "dark heart" of the empire itself was then to undertake an often incredibly dispiriting task. As Flora Grierson bluntly declared in her *New Statesman* review of *The Black Jacobins*, reading predictions of "the coming upheavals" in colonial Africa had "badly shaken" her "faith in Mr. James's intelligence and acumen."[12] Moreover, as A. Sivanandan once eloquently noted of the multitude of "strands" of "black struggles in Britain," such as the 1930s Pan-Africanist movement, strands "woven" together around such activists as James and Padmore, "their pattern was set on the loom of British racism."[13] This included in this period an institutional "Colour Bar," which meant, as Padmore noted in 1938, almost all black people had suffered the "bitter experience" of "looking for apartments and being told constantly, 'We do not take coloured people.'" Yet, as Padmore stressed, such racism was "a reflection of the whole British Imperial policy and the result of jingo education and propaganda which [made] the average Englishman point with such pride to 'the Empire upon which the sun never sets.'"[14] As James apparently told those at an IASB rally in Trafalgar Square on May 8, 1938, "The National Government seldom lost an opportunity to pump the working classes of this country with 'colour prejudice propaganda.'"[15]

Amidst a crisis-ridden decade that saw rising anticolonial movements bloodily repressed internationally, including in India, the Middle East, Africa, and the Caribbean, James recalled "the guardians of imperialism, either directly or indirectly, always had people meeting among the colonial residents and organisations in London seeking to use them or to neutralise them on colonial issues." James recalled that the IASB, "the centre of anti-imperialism and the struggle for African emancipation in London," was "on guard." He recounted, "Colonial people in London found it difficult to be openly pro-imperialist among other colonial people, and as we were always armed with facts and documents, we exercised a sort of moral terror over the feeble-minded."[16] As James would remind his readers with such power and clarity in *The Black Jacobins*, "It was easier to find decency, gratitude, justice and humanity in a cage of starving tigers than in the councils of imperialism."[17] While many Pan-African activists in Britain of course retained their "feeble-minded" identification with imperial Britishness, such a "moral terror" waged by members of the IASB through education and agitation remains remarkable. James recalled that when Marcus Garvey began to suggest in his lectures in Hyde Park that there was a positive side to British and French imperialism in Africa: "Padmore and I used to stand in the audience and we wouldn't crudely attack him, because he was a man of some status, but we would say, 'But that is not so. You didn't use to say so before. Why have you changed your opinion?' And Garvey would say, 'Oh, you boys, you boys!'"[18]

The black population in Britain during the 1930s was not large, but as the historian Winston James notes, the work undertaken by the likes of James and Padmore helped ensure 1930s Britain witnessed "the birth and emergence of a number of new black organisations and a level of black activism that was unprecedented," ensuring that the decade stands as "one of the most crucial decades in the history of black Britain."[19]

It is sometimes easy to forget that James himself on first arrival in Britain in 1932 would had to have included himself among the "feeble-minded" with respect to "anti-imperialism and the struggle for African emancipation," at least by his own later high standards and certainly by those of Padmore. One could point to James's early hopes for West Indian autonomy and "Dominion status" within the wider British Empire, his year-long membership of the LCP executive, his early illusions about the League of Nations, his praise for William Wilberforce, his hopes in the British Labour Party to fulfill its pledges with respect to the colonies, and so on. Indeed, James even seems to have been briefly invited onto the ultra-respectable London Group on African Affairs, a prestigious liberal pressure group whose membership included Harold Moody and Leonard Woolf and which, while officially "non-political and non-sectarian," sought to counter the "dangers of Communism and Indian nationalism" among "unguided" Africans.[20]

Yet while not an inevitability, there is an important sense in which James's natural talents, abilities, and nationalist and democratic political sympathies mean that it is almost impossible to imagine his not breaking with his early identification with imperial Britain and "intellectually conquering" sooner or later. One gets some sense of this from his famous interchange with the novelist Edith Sitwell in London's Bloomsbury district as early as May 18, 1932, when James impressed all with his appreciation and knowledge of the contemporary literary world.[21] It is all too easy to envisage James, had he wanted to, succeeding in making himself a career as a novelist in Britain and remaining throughout the 1930s primarily a literary figure, which is perhaps why so much of recent James scholarship has assumed as a matter of course that this somehow must have been the case. After all, he was more than talented enough as a writer, indeed he had already made a name for himself as such, and one feels he could have networked and cultivated the necessary contacts had he so wished. As he wrote in 1932, "Even though I see the Bloomsbury life for the secondary thing it is, nevertheless both by instinct and by training I belong to it and have fit into it as naturally as a pencil fits into a sharpener."[22] James had plans to write a semiautobiographical novel highlighting "different stages of the form of existence of black people in the Caribbean" and in all likelihood would have ultimately produced a work of literary merit and historic importance at some point about Toussaint Louverture and the Haitian Revolution, whether a play, novel, or biography.[23] Yet after only a few months in Bloomsbury, James left to stay with Learie Constantine up in "Red Nelson," and the rest, as they say, is history.

That James would have radicalized politically to some extent, as a result of living in Britain during the 1930s, in the context of the Great Depression and the rise of fascism, even if he had not stayed in Nelson for ten months at such a critical moment, seems certain, particularly if he had happened to run into his boyhood friend George Padmore again at any point. George Orwell recalled the appeal of the Popular Front–dominated antifascism among writers in England, commenting, "As early as 1934 or 1935 it was considered eccentric in literary circles not to be more or less 'left.' Between 1935 and 1939 the Communist Party had an almost irresistible fascination for any writer under forty. . . . For about three years, in fact, the central stream of English literature was more or less directly under Communist control."[24]

Orwell here overstates the CPGB's actual intellectual allure and organizing power, but it is still all too possible to imagine James's establishing a reputation as simply a "committed" novelist and playwright, and becoming someone feted by Communists and respected by all manner of progressive intellectuals in Britain, particularly those around the likes of Unity Theatre and the Left Book Club. Yet if James had chosen this route, even if he had also begun to break with his earlier identification with imperial Britishness and move toward Pan-Africanism amid the British government's collusion in Mussolini's barbaric war on Ethiopia, it seems almost certain he would have stayed more or less loyal to both the Labour Party and the LCP. Perhaps he would have remained a writer, or maybe ultimately carved out a conventionally successful academic or political career in Britain, America, or Trinidad after the Second World War, during decolonization, in the manner of, for example, W. Arthur Lewis or Eric Williams. One thing, however, is quite certain. If James's dedication to the cause of revolutionary socialism had not been utterly sincere when he left for his lecture tour of the United States in 1938, he would never have ended up going "underground" and living a pseudonymous existence in and among the crisis-ridden American Trotskyist movement for the next fifteen years.

C. L. R. James's Marxism

"The tumultuous thirties," James once recalled, saw "the Great Depression, the success of the first Five Year Plan, the rise of Nazism, the threat of Hitler, the threat, and very real it was, of a Fascist movement in England, the spread of Marxism, the anti-imperialist struggle. . . . All this contributed to making England a seething cauldron of political and social ideas. All traditional conceptions were examined and stripped to the bone."[25] In actuality, 1930s Britain was a relatively stable society that neither constituted "a seething cauldron of political and social ideas" in which "all traditional conceptions were examined" outside the activist milieu nor, under the hegemonic and conservative National Government, was it ever really threatened by a domestic fascist movement. As two other Marxists, Tony Cliff and Colin Barker, later noted of Britain during this period, though:

> Often remembered as the "the red 30s" because of the activities of the unemployed workers' movements[,] . . . the 1930s were also a period of low strike activity, of the greatest Tory vote this century, of workers fighting one another for jobs or scraping before their foremen to keep their jobs, of declining union membership, of despair and demoralisation. In their poverty workers often generated a marvellous sense of solidarity it is true, but often too this was not a fighting solidarity but the solidarity of misery and defeat.[26]

Despite their overly romanticized and dramatized nature, James's comments serve to remind us of the circumstances in which he politically oriented toward Marxism. James's revolutionary socialist politics, forged in the cauldron of Nelson's working-class politics, was critical to shaping the exact form and manner his intellectual conquest of imperial Britain took. He saw more of British society than most other "outsiders," and indeed no doubt also many "insiders," meeting with aristocrats like Edith Sitwell and

Nancy Cunard, reporting the struggles of striking miners in South Wales, covering Test Matches at Lord's, and witnessing firsthand the proud resistance of the working-class communities of East End London and northeast Lancashire to the government and the BUF, respectively, amid appalling levels of poverty and deprivation.[27] James seemed equally "at home" whether at a London concert of the world-famous Austrian pianist Artur Schnabel, chairing a Trafalgar Square rally in solidarity with Ethiopia, or quietly smoking his pipe and enjoying a dram of whisky among his fellow revolutionary socialists in Edinburgh.[28] Unlike almost any other black colonial subject during this period (with the possible exceptions of George Padmore and maybe one or two others around the IASB, like Chris Braithwaite, who had links with the ILP or a past association with the CPGB), James met and got to know hundreds of British working-class militants. Thousands must have heard him passionately and eloquently put forth the case for African emancipation and international socialism against the barbarism of imperialism, fascism, racism, and war. Moreover, it was from his discussions with such working-class audiences that James quickly learned an essential truth about imperialism. As James noted in early 1936, "British Imperialism does not govern only the colonies in its own interests. . . . It governs the British people in its own interests also."[29]

It is worth once again reminding ourselves of the dramatic nature of James's transformation during the crisis of the 1930s from an Arnoldian liberal humanist into one of the most able and important revolutionary socialists in Britain during the Great Depression. To take just one register of this, when James arrived in 1932, as he later told Stuart Hall, though he "had read a lot of history" and "had been concerned about the ordinary person," he was "not at all" a Marxist. James recalled, "I had not read one line of Marx. All I knew was that in the history books of those days you'd see that in 1848 Karl Marx and Friedrich Engels had written *The Communist Manifesto*."[30] In early 1932, James admitted he had read about Lenin and Trotsky and thought their political accomplishments highlighted "the futility of most of the big men in English public life," but for him "Bolshevik Russia" was simply a matter for abstract intellectual speculation, alongside "D. H. Lawrence," "sex," "the Indian question," "British Imperialism," "Abyssinia," "coloured students in London," and "the English people."[31] Six years later, by the time he left for America, he was on the International Executive Committee of the Fourth International, "World Party of Socialist

Revolution," and had won a mandate from that organization to "work out a program on the Colonial question" and begin the work of inaugurating an "International Colonial Bureau" to coordinate putting such a program into practice.[32] Within six months of leaving Britain in late 1938, James would meet Trotsky himself in Mexico for discussions on the history of the Communist International and the strategy and tactics of the black liberation struggle in the United States.

James later wrote that after reading Trotsky's *History*, "the reader is not so much rhetorically exhorted to join up, but as he sees the difficulties and feels the unbounded confidence and unshakeable will which challenges and overcomes them, the knowledge and the power, he becomes part of this wonderful adventure."[33] Marxism not only enabled James to understand the old world in decline, it also gave him the inspiration to fight for the new, and encourage others to do the same. Just as important, however, was that the "new" was out there to fight for. James had seen it in Trinidad in the growth of the TWA out of the mass strike of 1919, in the solidarity on display during the Great Lancashire Cotton Strike of 1932, and then in the French General Strike against fascism in February 1934. James felt that the exploited mass of humanity ultimately had the same interests at heart whether they were in the West Indies or Western Europe, and they were fighting against the same enemy. Marxism, then, for James, was not, as Cedric Robinson once suggested, merely "the prior commitment, the first encompassing and conscious experience of organised opposition to racism, exploitation and domination," something he was to abandon when he found it "ultimately unsatisfactory."[34] Rather, as James wrote to Constance Webb in 1944, "Ten years ago something came into my life and altered its whole course. Everything previous seemed only preparation."[35] While moving from liberal humanism to revolutionary socialism in his attempt to understand the world, James had thrown himself into the struggle to fundamentally change it: "I had plunged into a river from which I was never to emerge."

Trotsky aside, James's subsequent intellectual, personal, and political debts to the activists in the early Trotskyist movement in Britain and internationally were also significant, and like his own activism in this movement deserve further close study in their own right. As James recalled, "I joined the Trotskyist movement and I learned Marxism in the Trotskyist movement."[36] James's Trotskyism meant his Marxism was from the first imbued with the revolutionary, democratic spirit of "socialism-from-below," to use Hal Draper's term.[37] As James put it in his discussion of "Lenin and Socialism" in *World Revolution*, a work he dedicated to "the Marxist Group,"

> The creative capacity of the masses—he [Lenin] believed in it as no other leader of the workers ever did. That creative capacity had hitherto been seen only in revolution. The Soviet system based on the masses in the factories was to organise this creativeness not only for purpose of government but also for production, linking the two closer and closer together until ultimately the all-embracing nature of production by the whole of society rendered the State superfluous.[38]

Yet in part James's stress on the "creative capacity of the masses" was also the result of the circumstances he found himself in during the 1930s. Then as subsequently, Trotskyism was far from the only option available for those inspired by the revolutionary communist tradition flowing from Russia in October 1917, of workers' power and international socialism, but seeking a radical alternative to both Social Democracy and Stalinism. In this period, James met and discussed politics with a fantastic range of Marxists, socialists, and revolutionaries who were outside the Trotskyist movement, perhaps most notably Karl Korsch and Boris Souvarine, a new edition of whose devastatingly powerful biography *Stalin: A Critical Survey of Bolshevism* (1935) James translated into English. Closer to home, aside from the wide range of people whom James met through the ILP, he also met Nora Connolly O'Brien, Sylvia Pankhurst, and Nan Milton, the daughter of the great Scottish revolutionary socialist John Maclean. This work has only touched on some of this rich revolutionary history—for example, his relationship with the German anarchist bookseller Charlie Lahr. However, James's revolutionary activism in the 1930s opens up at every point fascinating glimpses into a subterranean world of far-left politics and an almost forgotten story of heretics, renegades, and dissidents, from surrealist poets who went to fight in the Spanish Civil War to radical Jewish printers living in the East End of London. The seeds of James's later break from the official Trotskyist movement, in 1951, were almost certainly first sown in this period.[39]

James would, however, always register the critical importance during this period of his partnership with his boyhood friend and compatriot George Padmore. Together, James once recalled in tribute to Padmore, they led from the front as ideological agitators in the fight against British imperialist mythology and propaganda during the 1930s: "Traditional England was under fire. And it was the regular habit of a number of us colonials to go to public lectures and meetings of some of the most celebrated lecturers and speakers in England and at question time and during discussion tear them to pieces."[40] The extent to which "traditional England" ever felt seriously "under fire" from anticolonial criticism during the 1930s may be doubted. As Nehru noted in 1936, British officialdom arrogantly had "the calm assurance of always being in the right."[41] James and Padmore's political and intellectual relationship nonetheless remains remarkable and was more mutually beneficial for both than might appear at first sight. James recalled the moment Padmore turned up at the door of his flat out of the blue in 1935, after his break with the Communist International: "As a Trotskyist, full-fledged by this time, the Kremlin betrayal was no surprise to me. But I listened with a great deal of sympathy to all that George had to say," and the slanderous accusations made against Padmore by the official Communists "gave me a first hand inside glimpse of Stalinism."[42] One article in the Communist *Negro Worker* from 1934 had been titled "The Rise and Fall of Padmore," and in 1937 James struck back on his friend's behalf and, with the help of Padmore's partner Dorothy Pizer as typist and secretary, published "The Rise and Fall of the Communist International" in *World Revolution*.[43]

It would not have been at all surprising if Padmore had become so disillusioned after being vilified by the Stalinists to have dropped out of political activity altogether and retreated into research in the British Museum or, worse, into liberal anticommunism. Here, his friendship with James was critical in encouraging him to continue to indefatigably put his inestimable talents and organizational skills to the service of colonial liberation. It must have helped James's research to have someone like Padmore — incredibly knowledgeable about liberation struggles across the African diaspora and a former leading official of the Comintern who had met leading members of the Soviet bureaucracy, including Stalin himself. James recalled, "The play about a successful Negro revolution [*Toussaint Louverture*], the full scale attack on Stalinism [*World Revolution*], must have been very helpful to George."[44] Yet while Padmore's Pan-Africanism now came to the fore of his politics, his disgust at the betrayals of the Soviet Union did not lead him politically closer to James's Trotskyism. Incidentally, Padmore was not only — like James and other political radicals — under surveillance as a threat to imperial "security" by the British state at this time but was also being monitored by agents sent from the Soviet Union.[45] In 1939,

Soviet agents described Padmore as a "Trotskyite" whose activities in the ILP and National Council of Labour Colleges had apparently enabled him "to penetrate more successfully into the ranks of the British working class, to corrupt and stupefy it."[46] In reality, as James recalled, Padmore "would spend time ferreting out and denouncing the perpetual treachery of the Stalinists," and certainly "attended all the Trotskyist meetings, clearing up his mind on Stalinism." However, tellingly, Padmore "never said a word about [James's] Trotskyism," James recalled.[47]

James's support for Trotsky in one sense makes his cultural accomplishments during this period, such as the play and his cricket commentary, even more remarkable, given the dark clouds of reaction that gathered over Europe as fascism, Stalinist terror, and war plunged the continent into what the great Belgian-Russian revolutionary novelist Victor Serge termed "Midnight in the Century." The greater the defeats suffered by the international working-class movement after the Great War, the greater the number of triumphs of fascist and counterrevolutionary dictatorships across Europe, the greater the desperate illusions among many on the Left in the Soviet Union under Stalin, the dictator deified as the new Lenin. In the 1930s, the Soviet Union seemed to represent for many not only the last serious bulwark remaining against fascism but a "new civilisation," the sole society free from unemployment and exploitation amid the greatest economic crisis in the history of world capitalism. Few socialists were willing to face up to the awful truth that the Soviet Union was no longer the land of the October Revolution but was in the midst of a bloody counterrevolution waged by a brutal new ruling Stalinist bureaucracy, and waged in part against that bureaucracy to discipline it into complete subservience to Stalin. Yet, as Serge noted in *From Lenin to Stalin* (1936), "In the struggle between socialism and fascism, socialism will only conquer if it brings greater comfort and dignity to human life." Serge stressed, "It is this aspect which is most prejudiced by the bureaucratic reaction in the U.S.S.R. If we can force this bureaucratic reaction one step backward, if we can prevent it from committing one single crime by showing it as it is, we shall be restoring to socialism and revolution a little of their true grandeur and consequently of their ability to conquer."[48]

Amid Stalin's Great Terror and the "loudspeakers crying out falsehoods, and vast agencies of intellectuals paid to cram people's heads full of lies," Serge declared that the "foremost weapon is the truth," and James was one of those few socialist intellectuals clear-sighted and courageous enough to tell the truth about the crimes and betrayals of the Stalinist bureaucracy and Communist International.[49] As James put it in 1937, the Communist International now represented an "enormous factory for lies and slander" and "Stalinist lies and falsification have spread a miasma over the intellectual life of Europe and America." As he wrote in *World Revolution*, "For suppression, evasion and hard lying the documents of the Soviet Union and the Third International today form, along with British colonial propaganda and fascist demagogy, a trilogy which future historians will contemplate with wonder."[50]

James's growing sense that any authoritarian regime or police state, whatever its particular official ideology (whether "Communist," "fascist," or "democratic"), shared a fundamental common ethos and logic gave *World Revolution* a certain prophetic power. It is not surprising that Orwell, who, like James, had had firsthand experience of British imperial rule (in Burma) and the counterrevolutionary nature of Stalinism while fighting fascism in the Spanish Civil War, was impressed by what he thought a "very able book" when he picked up a copy after returning to London from Spain.[51] Louise Cripps, one of James's friends and comrades in the Marxist Group, recalled that Orwell, presumably while working on what would become his classic *Homage to Catalonia*, in the summer of 1937, met with James and was a "serious enquirer" into Trotskyism.[52] Indeed, as Orwell noted in the *New Leader* in June 1938, when he decided to join the ILP, "at a moment like the present," a period of exceptional urgency, "writing books [was] not enough." Orwell observed, "The tempo of events is quickening; the dangers which once seemed a generation distant are staring us in the face. One has got to be actively a Socialist."[53]

Like Orwell, James strove to convince others of the essential, elementary truth that an individual socialist, no matter how intellectually brilliant or courageous, is, in Serge's words, "nothing if not backed up by an active group which has faith in him and in which he has faith: in other words, a party. Given a party, an intellect, a will, history will be made." For Serge, as for James (if never quite for Orwell), the best hope for building such a collective intellect and will in the 1930s lay with Trotsky, "a revolutionary soul, a brilliant pen" and surrounded by a movement "willing to go through fire with him." The Trotskyist movement, Serge noted, was "still weak, still in the process of birth, and yet a ferment to be feared" by Stalinist bureaucrat and bourgeois alike, as it had a chance of "becoming the germ or one of the germs of a new Bolshevism, in the greatest sense of the word."[54] Stalin, as an Old Bolshevik who had lived through the period of Zimmerwald during the Great War, knew only too well that such a nucleus of revolutionary socialists, given the right conditions, could grow and potentially become significant. Stalin's frantic attempt to destroy such a nucleus forming in the period preceding another great imperialist war in part explains the sheer level of slander and terror his agents directed at Trotsky and his friends, family, and comrades during the 1930s.[55]

The importance of James's contribution as one of the critical "thought-leaders" of early British Trotskyism, given his defense of the political honor and internationalist principles of classical Bolshevism against the Stalinist perversion during this period, is not in doubt. Though distinctly forgotten today, James's *World Revolution* might be best remembered alongside Trotsky's *The Revolution Betrayed* and Serge's *Russia Twenty Years After* (all first published in English in 1937), as part of a classic Marxist trilogy on the destiny and fate of the Russian Revolution. James ably and eloquently played his part alongside the early British Trotskyist movement in defending the organizer of the October Revolution and founder of the Red Army from the tirade of Stalinist slander about "Trotsky-Fascism" during the Moscow Trials at numerous meetings in Britain. James recalls it was a "habit" of his to wreck CPGB-sponsored public meetings that tried to justify what he called "those clumsy, brazen, incredibly impudent falsifications."[56] One can imagine it was very hard for Communist speakers to make out that James, who had made his name opposing Mussolini's war as the IAFA chair, was some sort of "Trotsky-Fascist." James was, after all, one of the best-known black public intellectuals in British politics, and like the Jewish Trotsky, seemed hardly the sort of person Hitler would want running the Soviet Union instead of Stalin.[57] The veteran British Marxist Harry Wicks, with customary generosity, certainly declared his friend and comrade "the outstanding British Trotskyist of the 1930s," noting that "not only was he a good speaker, but his speeches evidenced wide culture and deep reading. Above all, he could think mightily for himself."[58]

Alongside his other intellectual and political achievements outside organized revolutionary Marxist politics, this period of James's life remains remarkable. Among the many outstanding West Indian figures then in Britain, James certainly succeeded in establishing one of the highest profiles.[59] "Even my forgotten novel saw daylight," James remembered. In November 1936, *Minty Alley* (which James had written in Trinidad) was published as if "by accident," as he put it. James recalled Warburg, who had already decided to publish what would become *World Revolution*, "heard me talk about it, asked to see it, and published." There was little publicity for it, and priced at seven shillings and six pence, commercially it was, Warburg remembers, "unsuccessful." However, as James was to later note, "it was the first of the West Indian novels to be published in Great Britain" and so "henceforth the West Indies was speaking for itself to the modern world."[60]

Timothy Brennan has gone as far as to declare this period during the 1930s James's "prolific *anni mirabili*," the period "where his best work had been written."[61] This is not to say that for all its strengths, James's early Marxism was without its limitations, perhaps inevitably, given his training in the persecuted and minuscule early Trotskyist movement. Trotsky's brilliant, pioneering materialist analysis of the resistible rise of Nazism in Germany and Stalinism in the Soviet Union aside, in the main Trotskyism in the 1930s has been seen by historians as a defensive phenomenon. In general, Trotskyists were not attempting to develop Marxist theory in the manner accomplished in this period by Antonio Gramsci in his *Prison Notebooks* but were simply trying to defend Leninist orthodoxy from Stalinist revisionism, and this essential defensiveness also characterized James's *World Revolution*.[62] As Buhle notes, though "the first comprehensive anti-Stalinist history of the Comintern," *World Revolution* was "James's least original major work."[63] While understanding that Lenin "was neither God nor Stalin," at times—as say, in his discussion on the applicability of the Russian "peasant soviets" of 1917 to colonial Africa—James nonetheless perhaps overrelied on the letter of Lenin's writings when conceptualizing politics in the 1930s.[64]

That said, James should still be remembered as one of the most creative and significant Marxist thinkers to emerge in Britain during the Great Depression, and in *The Black Jacobins* and *A History of Negro Revolt* he applied the Marxist theory of permanent revolution to the past and present of the African diaspora with great originality and imagination. His brilliance as a Marxist historian helped ensure the historic lessons of the Haitian Revolution—and the inspirational revolutionary "black Jacobinism" of Toussaint—were part of the collective memory of many of those struggling for black and colonial liberation from the 1930s onward. By advancing understanding of the rich, hidden revolutionary history of Africa and the African diaspora, the West Indian intellectual did more than merely achieve "the intellectual conquest of imperial Britain." As Robert Hill eloquently noted, James only spent "slightly more than six and a half years" in Britain, but in those few years "he added significantly to the emancipation and understanding of the human condition."[65]

In October 1938, James left for America, but, as he remembered, "with the intention of coming back" as he "was well established in Britain." Aside from his commitment to covering the 1939 cricket season for the *Glasgow Herald*, James was also ready to go "underground" and help prepare the British Trotskyist movement for conditions of illegality in case of war.[66] James of course ended up staying in America for fifteen years, a sojourn he would later describe as "marking the most important years of [his] life, intellectually and personally . . . the high water mark."[67] To take just one register of his accomplishments in this period, James's contribution — in partnership with Raya Dunayevskaya and Grace Lee Boggs — to helping develop the theory of state capitalism may well come to be seen as his defining achievement as a Marxist. As Buhle notes, James was "one of the few truly creative Marxists from the 1930s to the 1950s, perhaps alone in his masterful synthesis of world history, philosophy, government, mass life and popular culture," as he attempted to apply the theory of state capitalism to analyze not simply the Soviet Union but the entire world system that emerged in the 1930s and lasted in its full totality until the rise of neoliberalism during the 1970s.[68] The creative manner and style in which James engaged with "the tenets of Leon Trotsky" and transcended many of the limitations of orthodox Trotskyism in order to try to develop Marxist theory to face up to new political realities might stand comparison with his earlier provisional and improvisational engagement with "the tenets of Matthew Arnold."

Yet some have still viewed James's "American years" with a tinge of sadness. Brennan has even suggested that "never after the 1930s was the grace and brilliance of his early writing equalled," before speculating about why James seemingly failed to "rekindle the fire of his brilliantly productive life in Britain," suggesting among other reasons that "he needed social movement to write, and this he did not have in the United States."[69] James himself later admitted: "I *know* that where I could work most concretely would have been *British* politics; the literature, the traditions of Britain are in my bones. I grew up on them." That said, James did also note that his experience and work in America had made him "a world citizen."[70] Moreover, we might remember that the theoretical work James carried out in America was to be critical to the shaping of his seminal study of "the traditions of

Britain" in *Beyond a Boundary*. The publication of that classic work in 1963 more than justified James's statement, in a letter written that year to his friend and fellow West Indian writer V. S. Naipaul, in which James contended: "I believe that, originating as we are within the British structure, but living under such different social conditions, we have a lot to say about the British civilization itself which we see more sharply than they themselves."[71] If *Beyond a Boundary* was to be the culmination of the mature James's thoughts on "British civilization," then this work has attempted to give some sense of just how "sharply" the young James, with his distinctively West Indian perspective that was soon to be complemented by revolutionary Marxism, also saw British society, politics, and culture.

Overall, many writers on James's life and work have either consciously or unconsciously echoed Eric Williams's later casual dismissal of his Marxist belief in "the absurdities of world revolution."[72] Yet there was nothing "absurd" about James's orientation toward revolutionary Marxism during the 1930s, given the anger he felt at both colonialism and a capitalist system in crisis and apparently descending into the barbarism of fascism and imperialist war. If today, despite the contemporary ecological and economic crisis—and the recent return of revolution across the Middle East and North Africa—it still seems "absurd" to talk of world revolution, it is arguably only because, as James once put it, "Western civilisation has forgotten or learnt to distrust the revolutionary temper, the revolutionary spirit, the revolutionary personality built on the grand heroic scale." Yet ever since his conversations with militant cotton textile workers in Nelson, Lancashire, James felt that the "revolutionary spirit" burned "in Europe still in millions of ordinary people. If it did not, civilisation would be at an end, destroyed not by the hydrogen bomb explosions from without, but by the congealing from within."[73] In the 1930s, in the midst of a massive economic crisis, James saw the "congealing from within" in the form of fascism, and one does not have to look far to see the return of that threat today across Europe. Nor, given the intensifying interimperialist rivalries of the contemporary world coupled with the continuing danger of militarism and the proliferation of nuclear weapons, can we forget about the possibility of civilization's being destroyed by "bomb explosions from without."

However, if one just looked at the growth of barbarism in the world then one would surely fall into passivity and despair. James would instead doubtless point us to the mass mobilizations of the global anticapitalist and antiwar movements in recent years, as well as signs of a growing international revival of class struggle itself after decades of defeat, symbols of hope and proof that "the revolutionary spirit" burns still. Those social movements and class struggles in turn could have few greater inspirations for the twenty-first century than C. L. R. James, a "revolutionary personality built on the grand heroic scale" during the world crisis of the 1930s.

NOTES

Introduction

1. Farred, *Rethinking C. L. R. James*, 1.

2. Buhle, *C. L. R. James*, 164.

3. Farred, *Rethinking C. L. R. James*, 11.

4. The quotes here allude to two recent works: St. Louis, *Rethinking Race, Politics, and Poetics*; and Rosengarten, *Urbane Revolutionary*. For my brief review of both, see Høgsbjerg, "Remembering C. L. R. James, Forgetting C. L. R. James."

5. Buhle, *C. L. R. James*, 172.

6. Glaberman, "C. L. R. James," 47.

7. Fryer, *Staying Power*, 336.

8. Glaberman, "C. L. R. James," 47.

9. Farred, *Rethinking C. L. R. James*, 12.

10. Macey, *Frantz Fanon*, 26, 28. On Macey and Fanon, see Lazarus, *The Postcolonial Unconscious*, 161–82.

11. For more on this, see Frassinelli, "Repositioning C. L. R. James."

12. Nielsen, *C. L. R. James*, 105.

13. St. Louis, *Rethinking Race, Politics, and Poetics*, 195.

14. Farred, *Rethinking C. L. R. James*, 11–12.

15. Farred, "The Maple Man," 173–74, 181. In all fairness, one might note that Farred subsequently detected some possible lessons in *The Black Jacobins* for postcolonial Africa. Farred, "First Stop, Port-au-Prince."

16. Buhle, *C. L. R. James*, 4.

17. Buhle, *Tim Hector*, 17.

18. Dance, "Conversation with C. L. R. James" (1980), 119.

19. Buhle, *Tim Hector*, 17.

20. Buhle, "From a Biographer's Notebook," 451.

21. Brennan, *At Home in the World*, 224.

22. For criticism of Tessa Jowell and David Lammy on this score, see Høgsbjerg, "C. L. R. James," 178.

23. Johnson, *Mi Revalueshanary Fren,* 73–74.

24. Craven, "C. L. R. James as a Critical Theorist of Modernist Art," 147.

25. R. Hill, "In England, 1932–1938," 62. In addition James also managed to get his first work *The Life of Captain Cipriani* and his novel *Minty Alley,* both of which he had brought with him from Trinidad in manuscript form, published in Britain in 1932 (with Coulton and Co.) and 1936 (with Secker and Warburg), respectively.

26. R. Hill, "In England, 1932–1938," 61–62.

27. For a highly cynical interpretation of James's life and work in the 1930s in this vein, see Dhondy, *C. L. R. James,* 50–63.

28. St. Louis, *Rethinking Race, Politics, and Poetics,* 94.

29. McLemee, afterword to *C. L. R. James and Revolutionary Marxism,* 217.

30. Warburg, *An Occupation for Gentlemen,* 214. It is also reprinted in Buhle, *C. L. R. James,* 63. On Warburg and the CIA, see Saunders, *Who Paid the Piper?* 111, 175–76, 327–28.

31. McLemee, introduction to *C. L. R. James on the "Negro Question,"* xii.

32. Warburg, *An Occupation for Gentlemen,* 215. James gave de Bayou a copy of *The Black Jacobins* "specially bound in beautiful black morocco."

33. Cripps, *C. L. R. James,* 52.

34. C. L. R. James, *Beyond a Boundary,* 128.

35. Cripps, *C. L. R. James,* 12–13.

36. Sherwood, "Amy Ashwood Garvey," 70; Martin, *Amy Ashwood Garvey,* 136–41; Bush, *Imperialism, Race and Resistance,* 211; Derrick, *Africa's "Agitators,"* 407; Makalani, *In the Cause of Freedom,* 202–3; Duberman, *Paul Robeson,* 192. See also E. Hill, "The Caribbean Connection," 278–79.

37. Derrick, *Africa's "Agitators,"* 407; Jarrett-Macauley, *The Life of Una Marson,* 84. Learie Constantine once suggested that "before World War II, most of London's coloured residents lived in an area of a few hundred yards square, round Tottenham Court Road." Constantine, *Colour Bar,* 65.

38. Derrick, *Africa's "Agitators,"* 407. See also *News Chronicle,* February 25, 1935.

39. Grimshaw, *Special Delivery,* 104–5.

40. Warburg, *An Occupation for Gentlemen,* 214.

41. Van Gelderen, "C. L. R. James — Thinker, Writer, Revolutionary," 42, 44.

42. The National Archives, London, TNA: KV/2/1824/4B.

43. Worcester, *C. L. R. James,* 49.

44. Foster, *W. B. Yeats,* 511. See also Croft, "Ethel Mannin."

45. Reynolds, *My Life and Crimes,* 117.

46. Laughlin, *Letters from London,* 69.

47. Mannin, *Comrade O Comrade,* 133–35, 145.

48. Reynolds, *My Life and Crimes,* 116–17.

49. Huxter, *Reg and Ethel,* 3, 66, 71, 81.

50. Personal correspondence with Julian Harber, November 12 and 15, 2006, and Paul Harber, May 8, 2013.

51. R. Hill, "In England, 1932–1938," 61, 63.

52. On James in Scotland during the 1930s, see Young, *The World of C. L. R. James*.

53. Reynolds, *My Life and Crimes*, 96.

54. Laughlin, *Letters from London*.

55. Worcester, *C. L. R. James*, xv.

56. Le Blanc, introduction to *C. L. R. James and Revolutionary Marxism*, 1.

57. C. L. R. James, *The Black Jacobins*, 102, 344. See also Dubois, *Avengers of the New World*, 172.

1. "We Lived According to the Tenets of Matthew Arnold"

1. Lamming, *The Pleasures of Exile*, 150.

2. C. L. R. James, *Beyond a Boundary*, 70–71.

3. Schwarz, "Crossing the Seas," 12.

4. Neptune, *Caliban and the Yankees*, 27.

5. Rush, *Bonds of Empire*, 10, 20.

6. Gikandi, "The Embarrassment of Victorianism," 158, 167. For more discussions of James's Arnoldianism, see Gikandi, "The Ghost of Matthew Arnold"; Worcester, *C. L. R. James*, 7, 246; and Nielsen, *C.L.R. James*, 152, 173, 175. On James and "colonial Victorianism," see also Høgsbjerg, "'We Lived According to the Tenets of Matthew Arnold.'"

7. Henry and Buhle, *C. L. R. James's Caribbean*, ix.

8. C. L. R. James, "Presence of Blacks in the Caribbean and Its Impact on Culture," 218.

9. Henry, "Africana Phenomenology." See also Henry, "Africana Political Philosophy and the Crisis of the Post-colony."

10. Gikandi, "The Embarrassment of Victorianism," 159.

11. C .L. R. James, "A Century of Freedom."

12. James was born on January 4, 1901. Queen Victoria died on January 22, 1901.

13. C. L. R. James, *Beyond a Boundary*, 37. For more on QRC and "schooling Britons" in the colonial Caribbean, see Rush, *Bonds of Empire*, 21–46, 84–101.

14. C. L. R. James, *Beyond a Boundary*, 31–32.

15. Naipaul, *A House for Mr. Biswas*, 440. During the 1920s, James read Havelock Ellis's *The Psychology of Sex*. Worcester, *C. L. R. James*, 18.

16. E. Williams, *Inward Hunger*, 24.

17. S. Howe, "C. L. R. James," 155–56.

18. C. J. Robinson, *Black Marxism*, 401.

19. Schwarz, "'Shivering in the Noonday Sun,'" 22–23.

20. C. L. R. James, *Beyond a Boundary*, 38–39.

21. James's second wife, Constance Webb, noted that "in London, among friends, he was often called the last of the Victorians." Webb, *Not without Love*, 171.

22. C. L. R. James, *Beyond a Boundary*, 33.

23. On leaving Trinidad in 1932, James wrote, "It is a pleasant thing to be no longer that model of all propriety, a teacher, and that model of subservience, a Government servant." C. L. R. James, "Barbados and the Barbadians," *Port of Spain Gazette*, March 20, 1932.

24. Lamming, *The Pleasures of Exile*, 151. The American labor historian George Rawick thought James a "Victorian hippy." Personal information from Marcus Rediker, November 6, 2007.

25. Rosengarten, *Urbane Revolutionary*, 17.

26. For more on *Vanity Fair*'s influence on James, see A. Smith, *C. L. R. James and the Study of Culture*, 92–100.

27. There is probably more behind James's later remark that it is "Thackeray, not Marx, who bears the heaviest responsibility for me" than meets the eye. In a private letter in 1851, Thackeray summed up his general outlook, noting, "The present politics are behind the world; and not fit for the intelligence of the nation. The great revolutions a coming a coming. . . . The present writers are all employed as by instinct in unscrewing the old framework of society and getting ready for the smash. I take a sort of pleasure in my little part in the business and in saying destructive things in a good humoured jolly way." See C. L. R. James, *Beyond a Boundary*, 47; Greig, "The Social Critic," 47.

28. C. L. R. James, *Beyond a Boundary*, 27, 47. For more on the colonial themes of *Vanity Fair*, see Giddings, *Literature and Imperialism*, 14–15; and C. Hall, "What Is a West Indian?," 42–43.

29. S. Howe, "C. L. R. James," 167. For discussion of the British royalty and colonial Jamaica, see Rush, *Bonds of Empire*, 47–68. In the British socialist periodical *Plebs*, I came across a letter from one E. A. Nash in April 1934 on "Thackeray and Socialism," which noted that "Thackeray's *Barry Lyndon* is, I think, the finest satire of the 'society' of the age that has ever been written. In *Vanity Fair, Henry Esmond, The Virginians, The Newcomes*, etc., he exposes the wholesale jobbery-snobbery-hypocrisy of the ruling classes. . . . All Thackeray's morality showed that he loved humanity, could understand and sympathise with every individual. Personally, when a youth, it was Thackeray's books that turned me to Socialism."

30. E. P. Thompson, *William Morris*, 139. For Marx's appreciation in 1854 of Thackeray's exposure of "political and social truths" about "The English Middle Class," see Baxandall, *Karl Marx and Frederick Engels on Literature and Art*, 106.

31. C. L. R. James, *Beyond a Boundary*, 41. For more on "Afro-Victorianism," see Gikandi, "Pan-Africanism and Cosmopolitanism."

32. Bogues, *Caliban's Freedom*, 13.

33. C. L. R. James, *Beyond a Boundary*, 39–40.

34. S. Hall, "Breaking Bread with History," 24; S. Hall, "C. L. R. James, 1901–1989," 213. It is worth remembering that while James was at QRC, schools in Britain were happily using textbooks such as C. R. L. Fletcher's and Rudyard Kipling's *A School*

History of England (1911), which casually denigrated black West Indians as "lazy, vicious and incapable of any serious improvement." See J. M. MacKenzie, *Propaganda and Empire*, 184; and Fryer, *Black People in the British Empire*, 77–81.

35. C. L. R. James, *Beyond a Boundary*, 40, 43.

36. C. L. R. James, "George Padmore," 253.

37. Springfield, "Through the People's Eyes," 85.

38. Grimshaw, *The C. L. R. James Archive*, 49.

39. S. Hall, "A Conversation with C. L. R. James," 16.

40. Campbell, "Carnival, Calypso and Class Struggle in Nineteenth Century Trinidad," 19.

41. Small, "The Training of an Intellectual, the Making of a Marxist," 55.

42. Bolland, *On the March*, 31.

43. C. L. R. James, *A History of Negro Revolt*, 75.

44. Bolland, *On the March*, 30–32.

45. C. J. Robinson, *Black Marxism*, 363; Campbell, "Carnival, Calypso and Class Struggle in Nineteenth Century Trinidad," 20.

46. Worcester, *C. L. R. James*, 14.

47. Shawki, *Black Liberation and Socialism*, 103, 105.

48. C. L. R. James, *A History of Negro Revolt*, 75.

49. Wynter, "In Quest of Matthew Bondman," 139.

50. Campbell, "Carnival, Calypso and Class Struggle in Nineteenth Century Trinidad," 20; Taylor, "Patrick Alexander Jones ('Lord Protector')."

51. Small, "The Training of an Intellectual, the Making of a Marxist," 56.

52. C. L. R. James, "Without Malice," *The Nation*, February 28, 1959.

53. Grimshaw, *The C. L. R. James Archive*, 49; Small, "The Training of an Intellectual, the Making of a Marxist," 55; Kelley, "The World the Diaspora Made," 114. If James did not get Garvey's *The Negro World* he remembered he "would not die."

54. Bogues, *Caliban's Freedom*, 15. See also Brereton and Thomas-Bailey, "Trinidad and Tobago."

55. S. Hall, "A Conversation with C. L. R. James," 23.

56. Dance, "Conversation with C. L. R. James," 116; Small, "The Training of an Intellectual, the Making of a Marxist," 55.

57. Ryan, *Race and Nationalism in Trinidad and Tobago*, 33–35.

58. C. L. R. James, *Beyond a Boundary*, 117, 119.

59. Sander, *The Trinidad Awakening*. See also Levy, *The Autobiography of Alfred H. Mendes*; and Ramchand, *Life on the Edge*.

60. S. Hall, "Breaking Bread with History," 17.

61. Neptune, *Caliban and the Yankees*, 27.

62. C. L. R. James, *Beyond a Boundary*, 117. The offending article, "Race Admixture," by Dr. Sidney Harland, appeared in *The Beacon*, 1, no. 4 (July 1931), and noted that "while it is not apparent to what extent the negro is inferior in intelligence to the white man, there is little doubt that on the average he is inferior." The controversy is discussed in Scott, *Conscripts of Modernity*, 80–81.

63. C. L. R. James, "The Intelligence of the Negro."

64. Ramcharitar, "The Beacon Short Story and the Colonial Imaginary in Trinidad," 72.

65. Keating, *Matthew Arnold*, 225–26.

66. C. L. R. James, "Discovering Literature in Trinidad," 237.

67. Buhle, "The Making of a Literary Life," 58.

68. Worcester, *C.L.R. James*, 16.

69. Quoted in Sander, introduction to *The Beacon, Volumes I–IV, 1931–1939*, xvii.

70. C. L. R. James, "Michel Maxwell Philip," 87, 103. The "grand style" for Arnold was used "when a noble nature, poetically gifted, treats with simplicity or with severity a serious subject." See Trilling, *Matthew Arnold*, 173. On *Emmanuel Appadocca*, see Cudjoe, *Beyond Boundaries*, 120–30.

71. C. L. R. James, "Michel Maxwell Philip," 94. The classical allusion is from Plutarch's account of the life of Marius.

72. C. L. R. James, "Michel Maxwell Philip," 102–3.

73. C. L. R. James, *Beyond a Boundary*, 117–18; *Negro Worker* (June 1932). On the "Water Riots," see Fryer, *Black People in the British Empire*, 100. The *Negro Worker* was banned in Trinidad in April 1932 under the Seditious Publications Law, and all Communist literature was banned in September 1932.

74. On Arnold and the British working class, see R. Williams, *Culture and Society*, 132–34.

75. Keating, *Matthew Arnold*, 211. As Arnold continued, "Culture says: 'Consider these people then, their way of life, their habits, their manners, the very tones of their voice; look at them attentively; observe the literature that they read, the things which give them pleasure, the words which come forth out of their mouths, the thoughts which make the furniture of their minds; would any amount of wealth be worth having with the condition that one was to become just like these people by having it?'"

76. C. L. R. James, *The Life of Captain Cipriani*, 3. However, in the 1920s James himself was a sports journalist as well as a teacher and so it is perhaps not surprising his teaching colleagues made conversation about cricket with him rather than literature or politics. As James admitted later, there was no one "who talked more about cricket than [he] did in the common-room." C. L. R. James, *Beyond a Boundary*, 125.

77. C. L. R. James, *Beyond a Boundary*, 125.

78. C. L. R. James, *The Life of Captain Cipriani*, 53.

79. C. L. R. James, *The Life of Captain Cipriani*, 4, 6.

80. C. L. R. James, *The Life of Captain Cipriani*, 7.

81. For James's early discussion of the large Indo-Trinidadian population (and Indo-Caribbean population more generally), see C. L. R. James, "Review of *Mahatma Gandhi*"; and C. L. R. James, *The Life of Captain Cipriani*, 10, 16.

82. C. L. R. James, *The Life of Captain Cipriani*, 10.

83. C. L. R. James, *The Life of Captain Cipriani*, 37, 40.

84. See Cudjoe, *Beyond Boundaries*; and Cudjoe, "C.L.R. James and the Trinidad and Tobago Intellectual Tradition."

85. C. L. R. James, *The Life of Captain Cipriani*, 15. In an interview conducted in 1987, James remembered his father as "a philistine of note." When James began writing fiction, his despairing father would ask, "Well, where are you going?" "That is all very well, but what money?" See Buhle, "The Making of a Literary Life," 56–57.

86. C. L. R. James, *The Life of Captain Cipriani*, 13–14.

87. Ramchand, introduction to *Minty Alley*, 13.

88. Keating, *Matthew Arnold*, 226, 233. On empire, Arnold opposed Gladstone's scheme for home rule in Ireland. See Collini, *Arnold*, 89.

89. C. L. R. James, "The Problem of Knowledge."

90. Ramcharitar, "The Beacon Short Story and the Colonial Imaginary in Trinidad," 72.

91. Buhle, *C. L. R. James*, 33.

92. C. L. R. James, "Autobiography, 1932–38," 28. See also Henry, "C. L. R. James and the Antiguan Left," 226.

93. Phillips, "C. L. R. James," 155.

94. Malmsten, "The British Labour Party and the West Indies," 179–82. For more on Lord Sydney Olivier (1859–1943), from 1907 to 1913 a reforming Governor of Jamaica, see Saville, "Olivier, Sydney Haldane (1st Baron Olivier of Ramsden) (1859–1943)"; and for the results of the commission into the sugar industry, see Rich, *Race and Empire in British Politics*, 72, 78; and Lee, *Fabianism and Colonialism*, 210.

95. Breines, "Karl Korsch's 'Road to Marx,'" 46. Interestingly, Breines notes that Korsch's early Fabianism would "serve as the beginning of his later revitalization of the 'subjective factor' within Marxism."

96. For Arnold, the state was the "centre of light and authority," the organ of "our best self." Keating, *Matthew Arnold*, 246–47.

97. C. L. R. James, *Beyond a Boundary*, 117.

98. E. P. Thompson, *William Morris*, 245.

99. C. L. R. James, *Beyond a Boundary*, 167.

100. Quoted in Prawer, *Karl Marx and World Literature*, 81.

101. C. L. R. James, *Beyond a Boundary*, 116–17. Arnold also influenced Oscar Wilde, who in "The Soul of Man under Socialism" argued: "The true perfection of man lies not in what man has but what man is." See Prawer, *Karl Marx and World Literature*, 81. On Wilde and Arnold, see Goodway, *Anarchist Seeds beneath the Snow*, 74.

102. Topham, *Report of the 5th National Conference on Workers' Control and Industrial Democracy*, 55. Intriguingly, Arnold's most famous biographer, Lionel Trilling, was from 1934 a Trotskyist sympathizer while researching Arnold for a Ph.D. Wald, *The New York Intellectuals*, 11, 35, 61, 102.

103. Grimshaw, *The C. L. R. James Archive*, 94.

104. Moses, "Thoughts of C. L. R. James."

2. "Red Nelson"

1. C. L. R. James, *Mariners, Renegades, and Castaways*, 37, 40; Laughlin, *Letters from London*, xxx.

2. C. L. R. James, "The Old World and the New," 210.

3. Laughlin, *Letters from London*, 67, 82, 87, 122.

4. On Constantine, see Howat, *Learie Constantine*; Calder, "A Man for All Cultures"; and Cardus, *Good Days*, 37–41.

5. Fryer, *Staying Power*, 365.

6. C. L. R. James, *Beyond a Boundary*, 114.

7. Worcester, *C.L.R. James*, 27. Gloria Valère (née Constantine) recalls they lived at 3 Lea Green Terrace, Meredith Street. Personal correspondence, September 12, 2006.

8. Liddington, *The Life and Times of a Respectable Rebel*, 384; J. Hill, *Nelson*, 20.

9. Liddington, *The Life and Times of a Respectable Rebel*, 34.

10. Liddington, *The Life and Times of a Respectable Rebel*, 37–38.

11. J. Hill, *Nelson*, 28. For more on women weavers' experiences, see Bruley, "Women and Communism."

12. Liddington, *The Life and Times of a Respectable Rebel*, 357; Stevenson and Cook, *Britain in the Depression*, 66–67.

13. *Nelson Leader*, June 17, 1932.

14. Mayall, "Rescued from the Shadow of Exile," 31. For slightly different figures, and a discussion of underemployment, "one of the chief difficulties in Nelson," and the difficulties woman weavers had in this period, see J. Hill, *Nelson*, 74–75.

15. D. Howe, "Great Lives."

16. For more on how the ILP, which also owned Clarion House, was an important social and cultural phenomenon in Nelson, as well as for more on Salem Chapel and the Weavers' Institute, see J. Hill, *Nelson*, 31, 45–47, 49, 110, 113. Salem—which held strongly supported men's and women's Sunday school classes—was incredibly antiauthoritarian in the sense that "they had no paid ministry" and "not even a chairman or president. Each meeting started with the election of the chair of the meeting who often was a woman. Ministers were designated who had completed a three year (part-time) training and exam. They conducted services, including marriages and deaths, but exercised no authority." Personal information, Eric E. Robinson, February 4, 2010.

17. When Nelson played Bacup in 1930, fourteen thousand watched at Seedhill (Nelson's ground) but eight thousand to ten thousand was far from unusual. See Howat, *Learie Constantine*, 85. For more on Lancashire League cricket, see Genders, *League Cricket in England*, 34–53; and Fowler, *Lancashire Cotton Operatives and Work*, 67–69.

18. See the article on Lancashire League cricket reprinted in the *Port of Spain Gazette*, October 28, 1938.

19. J. Hill, *Nelson*, 120. James had played cricket with Constantine (and Constantine's father) in Trinidad, and once noted of Constantine's catching ability that "his anticipation [was] almost psychic." See *Glasgow Herald*, May 18, 1938.

20. P. Smith, *The Century Speaks*, 46, 133. James recalled his time with Constantine: "The children were always intrigued at our unusual appearance and often came up to make acquaintance." One time James remembered: "A very friendly little boy came up to me, sat on my knee and asked me where was my spear." C. L. R. James, *Beyond a Boundary*, 120.

21. J. Williams, *Cricket and Race*, 46. See also Hartley's reminiscences in P. Smith, *The Century Speaks*, 46. East Lancashire was the name of Blackburn's Cricket Club, and, heavily patronized by the rich, mill-owning Hornby family, had a much more conservative culture than that of Nelson and were seen as somewhat "cuff and collar." See Fowler, *Lancashire Cotton Operatives and Work*, 68.

22. *Port of Spain Gazette*, March 11, 1936. This was a report of a speech, "The West Indian Youth and His Aspirations," which Constantine delivered to the Trinidad and Tobago Literary Club Council on March 9, 1936. Alfred Charles came to play football for Nelson and stayed with Constantine for a time. Personal information, Eric E. Robinson, February 4, 2010.

23. C. L. R. James, *Beyond a Boundary*, 122.

24. *Nelson Leader*, May 27, 1932.

25. *Nelson Leader*, June 10, 1932. Todmorden was a small weaving town like Nelson.

26. *Nelson Leader*, June 17, 1932. Radcliffe was a small spinning town in central Lancashire. The news that James "of Maple C. C." had been admitted to Nelson Cricket Club and had played in this match was reported back home in Trinidad. See *Port of Spain Gazette*, July 1, 1932.

27. C. L. R. James, *Beyond a Boundary*, 124.

28. *Nelson Leader*, July 1, 1932. Constantine's batting average for 1932 (just over twenty runs) was to be by far his lowest in his career for Nelson. For figures on Constantine's bowling and batting at Nelson from 1929 to 1936, see *Port of Spain Gazette*, June 16, 1937.

29. C. L. R. James, *Beyond a Boundary*, 126.

30. C. L. R. James, *Beyond a Boundary*, 115. Nelson Cricket Club was dominated by a committee of Liberals. J. Hill, *Nelson*, 123–24. The possibly surprising friendships the Constantines made with middle-class families in Nelson are noted in Howat, *Learie Constantine*, 80–81.

31. Laughlin, *Letters from London*, 23.

32. Lawrence, *Selected Poems*, 137. In a letter to Constance Webb in 1948, James refers to this poem, which was included in the collection *Pansies* (1929), albeit in a slightly different context: "I remember some poems by D.H. Lawrence. . . . One of them said 'See that British bourgeois, washed and clean and strong. But put him in a situation where a little human understanding are required. He is a good for nothing.'" See Grimshaw, *Special Delivery*, 374.

33. James and Grimshaw, *Cricket*, 5. James's description was originally published in Trinidad's *Sporting Chronicle* on June 19, 1932, and the *Nelson Leader* republished an extract from this on July 8, noting, "Mr. James's description of the Nelson ground will be of interest locally."

34. Personal correspondence with Gloria Valère, September 12, 2006.

35. C. L. R. James, *Beyond a Boundary*, 122, 127.

36. C. L. R. James, "Harry Spencer," 1; C. L. R. James, *The Black Jacobins*, xv. Harry Spencer was elected president of Nelson's Chamber of Commerce in February 1933. See *Nelson Leader*, February 17, 1933, and his obituary in *Nelson Leader*, December 23, 1965.

37. C. L. R. James, "Harry Spencer," 1–3, 5.

38. Laughlin, *Letters from London*, 123.

39. J. Hill, *Nelson*, 77–78, 81, 86; Liddington, *The Life and Times of a Respectable Rebel*, 35.

40. Liddington, *The Life and Times of a Respectable Rebel*, 345. See also J. Hill, *Nelson*, 96–98; and Macintyre, *Little Moscows*, 14. Built with local gritstone, Nelson's new terraced housing was said to be "the best ever built for working class people." Along with the Labour Party, the ILP, the Nelson Weavers' Association, and the nonconformist churches, the Co-op society was also exceptionally strong in Nelson, and "in addition to huge shops in the town centre the Co-op had grocery shops all over town." Personal information, Eric E. Robinson, February 4, 2010.

41. Kendall, *The Revolutionary Movement in Britain, 1900–21*, 423; J. Hill, *Nelson*, 98–99, 110.

42. Laughlin, *Letters from London*, 123–25. There seems to have been another, smaller-scale dispute with a cinema company in Nelson that was resolved in September 1932. See *Nelson Gazette*, September 27, 1932. For how the cinema gradually replaced the music hall as a popular form of entertainment in Lancashire at this time, see Fowler, *Lancashire Cotton Operatives and Work*, 71; and J. Hill, *Nelson*, 115–16. For how cinema had more generally become "an indispensable part of working-class life" in 1930s England, see McKibbin, *Classes and Cultures*, 187, 419–23.

43. C. L. R. James, *Beyond a Boundary*, 122.

44. C. J. Robinson, *Black Marxism*, 374.

45. C. L. R. James, *Beyond a Boundary*, 118, 122. "During the 1930s no party other than Labour had seats on the Council" in Nelson. Personal information, Eric E. Robinson, February 4, 2010.

46. Liddington, *The Life and Times of a Respectable Rebel*, 35.

47. Stevenson and Cook, *Britain in the Depression*, 120.

48. Mayall, "Rescued from the Shadow of Exile," 30.

49. Cohen, *The Failure of a Dream*, 244; Cliff and Gluckstein, *The Labour Party*, 168–69. In January 1933, the *New Statesman* noted Cripps was speaking to the Socialist League on "Can Socialism Come by Constitutional Methods?" See *New Statesman*, January 18, 1933.

50. Pimlott, *Labour and the Left in the 1930s*, 32.

51. Cohen, *The Failure of a Dream*, 15, 73. In Nelson all the Labour Party councillors had been ILP members, but when the ILP voted to disaffiliate, none of the councillors left the Labour Party.

52. Howell, *British Social Democracy*, 47. See also Stevenson and Cook, *Britain in the Depression*, 65.

53. Bogues, *Caliban's Freedom*, 49.

54. Frederick Cartmell, described in his obituary in the *Nelson Leader* as "a courteous man of high standards," had been a tank officer in the First World War and would be a major in and "keen member" of the local Home Guard in the Second World War. Before his retirement, in 1960, Cartmell had been a master printer at the Every Street works of Coulton and Company and then proprietor of the *Nelson Leader*. "He was an avid reader on a variety of subjects, including the history of printing." See *Nelson Leader*, September 19, 1975.

55. C. L. R. James, "Charlie Lahr," 1.

56. Bornstein and Richardson, *Against the Stream*, 111. In a lecture delivered in 1971 at the Institute of the Black World, Atlanta, Georgia, James described how a Nelson bibliophile he met, "Mr. Cartnell [*sic*]," told him about Trotsky's *History*. See C. L. R. James, "Lectures on *The Black Jacobins*," 67. See also C. L. R. James, "Charlie Lahr," 1. James recalls, "Mr. Cantrell lent me many books, among them *The History of the Russian Revolution, Volume 1* by Leon Trotsky and *The Decline of the West* by Oswald Spengler."

57. Quoted in R. A. Hill, "Literary Executor's Afterword," 297.

58. Bogues, *Caliban's Freedom*, 29.

59. Trotsky, *The History of the Russian Revolution*, 119–20. James quoted this particular point of Trotsky's in 1945. See C. L. R. James, "The British Vote for Socialism," 107.

60. Hughes, *Consciousness and Society*, 375.

61. Spengler, *The Decline of the West*, vol. 1, 50.

62. Spengler, *The Decline of the West*, vol. 2, 477–80, 506.

63. Spengler, *The Decline of the West*, vol. 1, 37, and vol. 2, 432.

64. R. A. Hill, "Literary Executor's Afterword," 297.

65. MARHO, *Visions of History*, 270. In 1940, James "hoped that the fog of mysticism [did] not obscure for Marxists the colossal learning, capacity of synthesis, and insight of Spengler's book." See C. L. R. James, "Trotsky's Place in History," 109.

66. C. L. R. James, "Charlie Lahr," 1.

67. C. L. R. James, *Beyond a Boundary*, 124–25.

68. D. Howe, "Beyond a Boundary." James was known by friends and family as "Nello," from Lionel.

69. C. L. R. James, *Beyond a Boundary*, 119, 122.

70. Labour History Archive and Study Centre, Manchester (LHA), William Gillies Papers: WG/TRI/27, James to Gillies, August 10, 1932.

71. LHA, WG/TRI/28, Gillies to James, August 16, 1932; Healey, *The Time of My Life*, 74.

72. LHA, WG/TRI/V29; and LHA, WG/TRI/30, James to Gillies, August 22, 1932.

73. C. L. R. James, *Beyond a Boundary*, 123. The article, "The Greatest of All Bowlers: An Impressionist Sketch of S.F. Barnes," was reprinted back in the Caribbean, in the sporting section of the *Daily Chronicle* of Demerara, September 10, 1932. See *Port of Spain Gazette*, September 13, 1932. The article has since been reprinted in Grimshaw and James, *Cricket*, 7–10. In declaring Barnes one of the all-time great bowlers, James was in keeping with the consensus of contemporary cricket opinion. See, for example, Colonel Philip Trevor's article, "Great Bowlers of All Time," published in the *Strand Magazine* (1928) and reprinted in Allen, *Cricket's Silver Lining*, 39.

74. S. Hall, "C.L.R. James: A Portrait," 6.

75. *Nelson Leader*, September 9, 1932; C. L. R. James, *Beyond a Boundary*, 123. In 1932, Nelson won the Senior League title, the Junior League title, and the Worsley Knockout Cup Competition. From 1929, when Constantine joined Nelson, to 1938, Nelson won the league championship on a record eight occasions, including four consecutive seasons, from 1934 to 1937. Genders, *League Cricket in England*, 42, 46–47.

76. Fowler, *Lancashire Cotton Operatives and Work*, 90–91; Liddington, *The Life and Times of a Respectable Rebel*, 361, 364. One banner read, "Unemployed can't get 4 looms — what about 8 looms?"

77. *Nelson Leader*, August 19, 1932. James knew Burnley, describing it in June 1932 as "about 20 minutes' run from Nelson." See *Nelson Leader*, July 8, 1932.

78. *Nelson Leader*, September 2, 1932.

79. *Nelson Leader*, September 2, 1932; and Liddington, *The Life and Times of a Respectable Rebel*, 380–81. Nelson's Relief Committee had disbanded itself in August 1932 in protest of the iniquities of the Means Test for unemployment benefits. Selina Cooper, a leading socialist feminist in Nelson, addressed the demonstration in September, congratulating the weavers on "the magnificent display of determination and solidarity" and demanded "the abolition of the Means Test, believing it to be . . . deliberately designed by the National Government to crush the workers into complete subjection." Liddington, *The Life and Times of a Respectable Rebel*, 42.

80. C. J. Robinson, *Black Marxism*, 374.

81. Renton, *C.L.R. James*, 47. The strike ended with a compromise, a small cut in pay in return for full union recognition and a promise of no victimizations.

82. C. L. R. James, *Beyond a Boundary*, 119–22.

83. C. L. R. James, *Eightieth Birthday Lectures*, 55.

84. C. L. R. James, "Black Intellectuals in Britain," 158.

85. C. L. R. James, "The British Vote for Socialism," 113. In 1937, James's Trotskyist paper, *Fight* 1, no. 8 (July 1937), noted, "In 1930, when the Indian masses revolted against British Imperialism, the Labour Party shot down the militants and jailed 60,000 of our Indian comrades. On top of this we had the Meerut Trial, when Indian and British workers, after four years without trial, were sentenced to terms of imprisonment ranging from 10 to 12 years. Some were sentenced to transportation for life. The crime these workers had committed was that of supporting strikes, attempting to build Trade Unions, advocating 'depriving the King Emperor of his sovereignty in India.'" For more on the 1929–31 Labour government and India, see Newsinger, *The Blood Never Dried*, 144–47. For how Labour authorized the bombing of villages in Iraq and Transjordan (now Jordan), see *New Leader*, February 11, 1938.

86. Miliband, *Parliamentary Socialism*, 159. The Conservatives had 260 MPs, and the Liberals 59.

87. Howell, *British Social Democracy*, 11, 38.

88. C. L. R. James, *Eightieth Birthday Lectures*, 55.

89. Richardson, Chrysostom, and Grimshaw, *C. L. R. James and British Trotskyism*, 1. Part of James's loyalty to the Nelson Labour Party may have resulted from the way in the 1930s, as Jeffrey Hill notes, it "consolidated a cultural base" and even ran the "Nelson Socialist Dramatic Society." J. Hill, *Nelson*, 111.

90. Malmsten, "The British Labour Party and the West Indies," 176–78, and LHA, WG/BWI/1.

91. Malmsten, "The British Labour Party and the West Indies," 182. Grindle is quoted in Gomes, *Through a Maze of Colour*, xi.

92. See LHA, WG/BWI/1. See also Madden and Darwin, *Select Documents on the Constitutional History of the British Empire and Commonwealth, Volume VII*, 75. On Labour's "Advisory Committee on Imperial Questions," see Owen, "Critics of Empire in Britain," 194–96.

93. See LHA, WG/BWI/7; *Negro Worker* (May 1932).

94. Miliband, *Parliamentary Socialism*, 201.

95. Naylor, *Labour's International Policy*, 26–27. See also Leventhal, *Arthur Henderson*, 208. Henderson returned to Parliament in 1933.

96. Malmsten, "The British Labour Party and the West Indies," 189.

97. See LHA, WG/BWI/12, letter from Gillies to Cipriani, November 7, 1932. T. A. Marryshow, later hailed as "the Father of West Indies Federation," was a black journalist and veteran campaigner for West Indian self-government who had attended the 1921 Pan-African Congress. On Marryshow's visit to Britain in 1932–33, see Whittall, "Creolising London," 310–12.

98. See LHA, WG/TRI/32, letter from James to Gillies, November 10, 1932; and Malmsten, "The British Labour Party and the West Indies," 189.

99. On Woolf, see Cole, "Woolf, Leonard Sidney (1880–1969)."

100. LHA, WG/TRI/32, James to Gillies, November 10, 1932.

101. LHA, WG/TRI/34, James to Gillies, November 17, 1932.

102. Walmsley, *The Caribbean Artists Movement*, 3.

103. LHA, WG/TRI/40, James to Gillies, January 12, 1933.

104. *Nelson Leader*, January 22, 1933.

105. *Nelson Leader*, January 27, 1933.

106. Fowler, *Lancashire Cotton Operatives and Work*, 5, 74. See also Liddington,

The Life and Times of a Respectable Rebel, 255, 277, 358. Antimilitarism ran strong in Nelson during and after the Great War. Richard Bland, a jailed conscientious objector in the Great War, twice became mayor of Nelson. Bland's "mayoral services were held in the Palace Theatre because, whilst a devout Christian, he vowed never to enter a church building again in protest at the churches' support for wars. On the occasion of a royal visit during his second period of office, he resigned the mayoralty rather than receive the monarch's military escort." Joseph Robinson, a weaver and secretary of Salem who also served on the town council for many years, when mayor "refused to include boy scouts in his mayoral procession in rejection of militarism." Personal information, Eric E. Robinson, February 4, 2010. Another mayor, Richard Winterbottom, in the late 1920s banned nationalistic music, including the national anthem, "Rule Britannia," "Land of Hope and Glory," and "God Bless the Prince of Wales," from being played at the local ceremony on Empire Day (May 24). The band was forced to play jazz instead, and a few months later the Nelson Parks Committee had even imposed a ban on military bands in local parks. On Empire Day, and how it was marked in colonial Trinidad, see George Padmore, "What Is Empire Day?" *Negro Worker*, June 1932.

107. C. L. R. James, "Colour: Another View."

108. LHA, WG/TRI/94, James to Gillies, February 23, 1933.

109. LHA, WG/TRI/95, Gillies to James, March 4, 1933.

110. *Nelson Leader*, February 24, 1933.

111. *Nelson Gazette*, February 28, 1933. Sadly the *Nelson Gazette* did not report James's speech.

112. *Nelson Leader*, April 7, 1933. See also the *Nelson Leader*, April 21, 1933, which reported his actual departure. One leaflet survived and was in the possession of Eric E. Robinson, from "The Comradeship of the C[hristian] E[ndeavour] Holiday Homes, Nelson and Colne Group," dated March 19 (no year), which advertised an 8:00 p.m. "Special Study Circle" at 108 Walton Lane, the Robinson family home, with "Mr. C.L.R. James of West Indies" as "Speaker." Christian Endeavour seem to have been very supportive of colonial students in Britain, and in 1935, the Jamaican Dr. Harold Moody, president of the League of Coloured Peoples, was elected president of the British Christian Endeavour Union, "the first time in the history of Great Britain that a coloured man has been made President of an important national organisation." See *The Keys* 3, no. 1 (July–September 1935), 3.

113. See LHA, WG/TRI/96, James to Gillies, March 12, 1933. When *The Case for West Indian Self-Government* did finally come out, the *New Statesman* praised it as "an admirably written pamphlet." See *New Statesman*, April 1, 1933; *Nelson Leader*, April 7, 1933; and *Port of Spain Gazette*, April 19, 1933. On April 7, 1933, the Commission for West Indies Closer Union reported, upholding the governor's traditional powers of certification of legislative councils and veto. See Malmsten, "The British Labour Party and the West Indies," 189; and Madden and Darwin, *Select Documents on the Constitutional History of the British Empire and Commonwealth, Volume VII*, 75.

James's thoughts on the commission after it reported can be seen in the brief article he authored, "West Indies Self-Government," in *The Keys* 1, no. 4 (April–June 1934).

114. C. L. R. James, "The British Vote for Socialism," 114.

115. Thorpe, *Britain in the 1930s*, 42; Stevenson and Cook, *Britain in the Depression*, 153. There were later hunger marches organized from Nelson, on the initiative of the local Communist Party. See Liddington, *The Life and Times of a Respectable Rebel*, 381.

116. C. L. R. James, *Beyond a Boundary*, 122; and Worcester, *C.L.R. James*, 23. For more on *The Life of Captain Cipriani* and its reception in the Caribbean, see Høgsbjerg, "'A Thorn in the Side of Great Britain.'"

117. See Miller, Pennybacker, and Rosenhaft, "Mother Ada Wright and the International Campaign to Free the Scottsboro Boys."

118. Miller, Pennybacker, and Rosenhaft, "Mother Ada Wright and the International Campaign to Free the Scottsboro Boys," 403. See also Pennybacker, *From Scottsboro to Munich*, 33–37.

119. See LHA, WG/TRI/36, Gillies to James, November 28, 1932. In July 1932, it was announced that Vivian Henry had accepted an invitation from the ILD to send two delegates to attend their annual convention in Berlin in November. See *Port of Spain Gazette*, July 2, 1932.

120. See LHA, WG/TRI/35, Gillies to James, November 21, 1932. See also Miller, Pennybacker, and Rosenhaft, "Mother Ada Wright and the International Campaign to Free the Scottsboro Boys," 416. On Gillies's anticommunism during this period, see Pennybacker, *From Scottsboro to Munich*, 49.

121. On the Communist International and "class against class," see Dewar, *Communist Politics in Britain*. See also Padmore, *The Life and Struggles of Negro Toilers*, 6, 60, 107. The Communist Padmore denounced the likes of Lord Olivier as one of many "social fascist politicians" who were aiding "native local labour misleaders and national reformists to keep the masses in submission by making them promises." In Nelson, local Communists in this period regularly described Labour as the "third capitalist party" in Britain. See Liddington, *The Life and Struggles of a Respectable Rebel*, 372.

122. LHA, WG/TRI/32, James to Gillies, November 10, 1932.

123. Makalani, *In the Cause of Freedom*, 184–85.

124. LHA, WG/TRI/35, Gillies to James, November 21, 1932. In fact, the TWA had regularly (without foundation) been accused of being "Bolshevik" since the end of the Great War, something that may have helped prompt Henry to take the opportunity to go to Moscow to see "Bolshevism" for himself. MOPR stood for Russian Red Aid, and on this world conference in Moscow, which was attended by Ada Wright, see Pennybacker, *From Scottsboro to Munich*, 39–40.

125. As James replied to Gillies on November 30, 1932, "Thanks very much for the information about the International Labour Defence. I shall find out for certain which conference Henry attended. As soon as I do so I shall let you know." LHA, WG/BWI/14. Henry's speech at the ILD conference was published in the *Negro Worker*, under the title "Class War in the West Indies," *Negro Worker* (February–March 1933). Henry was sadly much less radical a figure when the "class war in the West Indies" reached a much higher level during the mass strike in Trinidad of 1937. As general secretary of the Trinidad Labour Party (formerly the TWA), he described it as a "regrettable" action taken by "irresponsible" workers and instead urged workers to "constitutionally advocate for their equitable and legitimate due." Jacobs, "The Politics of Protest in Trinidad," 43.

126. LHA, WG/TRI/42, James to Gillies, February 1, 1932. Gillies, of course, was quick to clarify matters.

127. LHA, WG/TRI/81, Cipriani to Gillies, November 30, 1932. That said, Cipriani was very far from embracing revolutionary politics, telling Trinidadian workers on May 19, 1933, to put their faith in "peaceful evolution" as "violence was the way of the Communists and not of socialists." Ryan, *Race and Nationalism in Trinidad and Tobago,* 40.

128. Hobsbawm, *Industry and Empire,* 212.

129. The name was originally taken from an early nineteenth-century coaching stop, the Nelson Inn, commemorating the famous naval hero, making it "probably the only English town of any size to be named after a pub." J. Hill, *Nelson,* 9–10.

130. C. L. R. James, *Mariners, Renegades, and Castaways,* 40.

131. Thompson, "C.L.R. James at 80," 249.

132. C. L. R. James, *Eightieth Birthday Lectures,* 55.

133. Castoriadis, "C.L.R. James and the Fate of Marxism," 277.

134. James's orientation toward Trotskyism might have been accelerated dramatically if he had attended a Nelson meeting on the "turmoil" in Germany, a lecture organized by the early British Trotskyist, Henry Sara, on March 12, 1933. See *Nelson Leader,* March 10, 1933. On Sara, see McIlroy, "Sara, Henry Thomas William (1886–1953)."

135. Walmsley, *The Caribbean Artists Movement,* 3.

3. "Imperialism Must Be Destroyed"

1. C. L. R. James, *Mariners, Renegades, and Castaways,* 154.

2. Carr, *What Is History?,* lxxviii.

3. Macintyre, *A Proletarian Science,* 94.

4. Carr, *What Is History?,* liii.

5. C. L. R. James, "Charlie Lahr," 1–2.

6. Worcester, *C. L. R. James,* 42. On black internationalism, see Edwards, *The Practice of Diaspora*; West, Martin, and Wilkins, *From Toussaint to Tupac*; and Makalani, *In the Cause of Freedom.*

7. Makalani, *In the Cause of Freedom,* 201.

8. Macdonald, "Dr. Harold Arundel Moody and the League of Coloured Peoples," 291–93. It seems James addressed the Joint Council to Promote Understanding between White and Coloured People on May 2, 1933, on "Self-Government for the West Indies." See TNA, KV/2/1824/1Z. The overt masculinity of black politics in this period, seen here in the LCP's championing of the "Black Man," is explored in Stephens, *Black Empire.*

9. "Conference Report," *Keys* 1, no. 1 (July 1933): 3–8.

10. See Geiss, *The Pan-African Movement*, 346.

11. Macdonald, *The Keys*, 9. James is listed as being on the 1933–34 LCP Executive in *Keys* 1, no. 3 (January 1934).

12. See "Editorial," *Keys* 1, no. 2 (October 1933): 21; and Rush, *Bonds of Empire*, 111.

13. C. L. R. James, "A Century of Freedom."

14. C. L. R. James, "Slavery Today." Italics as in original.

15. *Listener*, May 17, 1933.

16. Rosengarten, *Urbane Revolutionary*, 138.

17. C. L. R. James, "The Old World and the New," 207.

18. *Listener*, May 17, 1933.

19. *Listener*, May 17, 1933. One special branch report, dated March 3, 1937, noted James spent time at 29 Willow Road in Hampstead during 1933. TNA, KV/2/1824/7A.

20. *Listener*, June 7, 1933. Paul Rivet was to become a leading antiracist anthropologist. See Barkan, *The Retreat of Scientific Racism*, 326, 328.

21. *Listener*, June 14, 1933. T. A. Joyce was the keeper of ethnography at the British Museum, and from 1905 he produced commentaries on Emile Torday's trips to the Congo Free State and elsewhere. See Coombes, *Reinventing Africa*, 132–34. In 1938, James would describe Torday as "one of the greatest African scholars of his time." See C. L. R. James, *The Black Jacobins*, 339.

22. For more on Boas, who had worked in America since 1887, see Barkan, *The Retreat of Scientific Racism*, 78. James may have also benefited from knowledge of the work of the Jamaican dentist and sculptor Ronald Moody, younger brother of Harold Moody. See Walmsley, *The Caribbean Artists Movement*, 1–2.

23. *Listener*, June 21, 1933.

24. C. L. R. James, "Charlie Lahr," 2.

25. A. MacKenzie, "British Marxists and the Empire," 154.

26. C. L. R. James, "Charlie Lahr," 2.

27. Rose, *The Intellectual Life of the British Working Classes*, 303.

28. C. L. R. James, "Charlie Lahr," 2. Othello actually refers to "the ocular proof."

29. Goodway, "Charles Lahr." Born Karl Lahr in the Rhineland in 1885, he had chosen internment at London's Alexandra Palace over fighting for the kaiser in the Great War, and though briefly a member of the CPGB on its formation in 1920 he had left over Kronstadt and founded his bookshop.

30. C. L. R. James, "Charlie Lahr," 2–3.

31. C. L. R. James, "Writings from *The Nation*," 291.

32. Widgery, "C. L. R. James," 123.

33. James would later describe reading Trotsky's "succession of articles," on the struggle against fascism in Germany, as being "like a series of powerful searchlights in the prevailing darkness." C. L. R. James, "Trotsky's Place in History," 102.

34. Trotsky, *On Britain*, 148.

35. There is a sizeable existing literature on Trotsky and the Marxist theory of permanent revolution, dating from *Results and Prospects* (1906) through to *The Permanent Revolution* (1930), written in the light of the defeated Chinese revolution of 1925–27. See Trotsky, *The Permanent Revolution and Results and Prospects*; and also Hallas, *Trotsky's Marxism and Other Essays*, 21–36; Molyneux, *Leon Trotsky's Theory of Revolution*; the first part of Löwy, *The Politics of Combined and Uneven Development*; and Dunn and Radice, *100 Years of Permanent Revolution*.

36. Molyneux, *Leon Trotsky's Theory of Revolution*, 40–45.

37. Trotsky, *The Permanent Revolution and Results and Prospects*, 276–77.

38. On Marx and Engels themselves, see Nimtz, "The Eurocentric Marx and Engels and Other Related Myths"; and Anderson, *Marx at the Margins*.

39. Trotsky, *The Permanent Revolution and Results and Prospects*, 279. See also Löwy, *The Politics of Combined and Uneven Development*, 85.

40. N. Davidson, "From Uneven to Combined Development," 21.

41. Trotsky, *The History of the Russian Revolution*, 27–28.

42. Trotsky, *The History of the Russian Revolution*, 27; N. Davidson, "From Uneven to Combined Development," 22–23.

43. C. L. R. James, *Beyond a Boundary*, 31, 34. The early chapters of *Beyond a Boundary* might be read as a demonstration of how "the law of uneven and combined development" shaped an individual life, and James's descriptions of growing up in Trinidad seem to have echoes of Trotsky's descriptions in *My Life* of his own childhood growing up in what is now Ukraine.

44. C. L. R. James, "Trotsky's Place in History," 94.

45. C. L. R. James, "The Old World and the New," 208.

46. Hooker, *Black Revolutionary*, 23, 30. See also Fryer, *Staying Power*, 334.

47. Reynolds, *My Life and Crimes*, 99. On Gillies's pamphlet *The Communist Solar System: The Communist International*, see Pennybacker, *From Scottsboro to Munich*, 49, 293; and Newman, "Democracy versus Dictatorship," 70–71, 86.

48. C. L. R. James, "Writings from *The Nation*," 291; MARHO, *Visions of History*, 269.

49. C. L. R. James, "Towards the Seventh," 240; C. L. R. James, "Writings from *The Nation*," 291.

50. Hooker, *Black Revolutionary*, 26–27.

51. C. L. R. James, "Towards the Seventh," 240.

52. C. L. R. James, "George Padmore," 254.

53. Hooker, *Black Revolutionary*, 26.

54. As Isaac Deutscher once noted, unlike those who joined the Communists in the 1930s and afterward, those who joined in the 1920s "went into a movement in which there was plenty of scope for revolutionary idealism. The structure of the party was still fluid; it had not yet gone into the totalitarian mould. Intellectual integrity was still valued in a communist; it had not yet been surrendered for good to Moscow's raison d'état." See Deutscher, *Heretics and Renegades*, 10.

55. C. L. R. James, "Writings from *The Nation*," 291.

56. *Manchester Guardian*, August 14, 1933.

57. C. L. R. James, "Charlie Lahr," 2.

58. C. L. R. James, "Charlie Lahr," 3–4, 7.

59. C. L. R. James, *The Black Jacobins*, xv.

60. Harman, *A People's History of the World*, 494. As James wrote two years later, "The utter imbecility of all Stalinism was never more completely shown than in the actions of the Communist Party of France in this grave crisis." C. L. R. James, *World Revolution*, 379.

61. C. L. R. James, *World Revolution*, 381.

62. Harman, *A People's History of the World*, 493.

63. Stevenson and Cook, *Britain in the Depression*, 225.

64. As James remembered, "For months the *Daily Mail* was a Fascist organ." C. L. R. James, "The British Vote for Socialism," 114. By July 1934, the BUF would have a membership of up to fifty thousand. See Stevenson and Cook, *Britain in the Depression*, 234. After the violence of the notorious BUF rally at Olympia in June 1934, both respectable support and membership began to fall away.

65. Widgery, "C. L. R. James," 123. See also C. J. Robinson, *Black Marxism*, 375.

66. Richardson, Chrysostom, and Grimshaw, *C. L. R. James and British Trotskyism*, 12.

67. S. Hall, "Breaking Bread with History," 19.

68. C. L. R. James, "My Knowledge of Damas Is Unique," 131–32. I am indebted to Bart Miller for this reference.

69. C. L. R. James, *The Black Jacobins*, xv. The original 1938 bibliography details the Paris archives James visited during the 1930s. C. L. R. James, *The Black Jacobins* (1938), 317.

70. James, Dunayevskaya, and Lee, *State Capitalism and World Revolution*, xxii. For more on Bergson, see Hughes, *Consciousness and Society*, 115–18, 121–22, 341.

71. Rees, *The Algebra of Revolution*, 4.

72. Lukács, *History and Class Consciousness*, 110; Arato and Breines, *The Young Lukács and the Origins of Western Marxism*, 27.

73. See Wilder, *The French Imperial Nation-State*, 246, 257–58, 262.

74. See Eburne and Braddock, "Introduction," 732–33.

75. Césaire first coined the term "Negritude" in the March 1935 issue of the French journal *L'etudiant noir* (The black student). See Césaire, *Discourse on Colonialism*, 12. In his subsequent visits to Paris to research the Haitian Revolution in the 1930s, James recalled that Damas "was not concerned about educating [James] into the realities of Negritude because [Damas knew James] was busy with [other] work which would help the emancipation of Black people." C. L. R. James, "My Knowledge of Damas Is Unique," 133. For James's thoughts on Negritude, see MARHO, *Visions of History*, 270.

76. C. L. R. James, *The Black Jacobins*, xvi, 329. For more on James and Nemours, see Forsdick, "The Black Jacobin in Paris," 17–18, 21.

77. *Nelson Leader*, March 16, 1934.

78. *Nelson Leader*, March 16, 1934. On the Bushongo, see B. Davidson, *Africa in History*, 158–59.

79. *Nelson Leader*, March 16, 1934.

80. Rich, *Race and Empire in British Politics*, 78–79. See also LHA, WG/BWI/77 [Advisory Committee on Imperial Questions], "West Indies Labour Party Policy" (July 1938).

81. It was to be named after the Gold Coast scholar Dr. J. E. Kwegyir Aggrey, and Moody hoped this would become the new LCP headquarters. Adi, *West Africans in Britain*, 57. See also Whittall, "Creating Black Places in Imperial London."

82. Adi, *West Africans in Britain*, 59–60, 62, 64, 85, 193–97. The NWA was affiliated to the LAI and ITUC-NW and was, as Adi notes, in many ways a forerunner to the IASB. On the LAI, see Saville, "The League against Imperialism," and S. Howe, *Anticolonialism in British Politics*.

83. TNA, KV/2/1824/1Z.

84. C. L. R. James, "Notes on the Life of George Padmore," 36. For more on Ward, see Pennybacker, *From Scottsboro to Munich*; and West, Martin, and Wilkins, *From Toussaint to Tupac*, 167–68, 172.

85. Chisholm, *Nancy Cunard*, 272; Pennybacker, *From Scottsboro to Munich*, 53; and see, for example, TNA, MEPO 38/9/17a; TNA, MEPO 38/9/19B; and TNA, KV/2/1824/1Z. James gives his address as 9 Heathcote Street in a letter to the *New Statesman*, March 28, 1936.

86. Comma, "Folklore in Trinidad," 486. On *Negro*, see Edwards, *The Practice of Diaspora*, 309–18.

87. C. L. R. James, *Beyond a Boundary*, 149.

88. The quote from Mussolini was from a speech at Pontinia, December 18, 1935, quoted in the *Times*, December 20, 1935. See Padmore, *Africa and World Peace*, 153. See also Ed Keen's interview with Mussolini in the *Daily Herald*, August 24, 1935.

89. Gilbert, *Winston S. Churchill, Vol. 5*, 226, 457. See also Brendon, *The Dark Valley*, 271.

90. Lady Simon had heard James lecture on Africa in Colne, Lancashire, to the Sunday Lecture Society in March 1935, before setting off to Italy to meet with Mussolini in April 1935. Pennybacker, *From Scottsboro to Munich*, 126–33, 145.

91. Weisbord, *Ebony Kinship*, 89. See also Lewis, *Marcus Garvey*, 168–75; Naison, *Communists in Harlem during the Depression*, 138–39, 155–59; C. J. Robinson, "The African Diaspora and the Italo-Ethiopian Crisis"; Weisbord, "British West Indian Reaction to the Italian-Ethiopian War," 35; and Yelvington, "The War in Ethiopia and Trinidad."

92. R. A. Hill, "In England, 1932–1938," 69.

93. Richardson, Chrysostom, and Grimshaw, *C. L. R. James and British Trotskyism*, 5–6; C. L. R. James, *Beyond a Boundary*, 250.

94. For more on the Gold Coast ARPS deputation, see Rohdie, "The Gold Coast Aborigines Abroad."

95. Fryer, *Staying Power*, 340, 345. See also Bush, *Imperialism, Race and Resistance*, 240.

96. Padmore, *Pan-Africanism or Communism?*, 145. On Marryshow's 1935 visit to Britain, see Whittall, "Creolising London," 331–33.

97. *West Africa*, July 27, 1935. See also Adi, *West Africans in Britain*, 67–70; and Sherwood, "Ethiopia and Black Organizations in the UK 1935–36."

98. Waley, *British Public Opinion and the Abyssinian War*, 23–24, 76.

99. Reynolds, "Italy Returns to Abyssinia," *Keys* 2, no. 4 (April–June 1935): 85.

100. *West Africa*, August 3, 1935.

101. *Manchester Guardian*, July 29, 1935; and *Manchester Guardian*, July 30, 1935. Of course, by Monday, James himself was back in Southampton to see "the match between Hampshire and Lancashire here continue in a minor key."

102. C. L. R. James, "Black Intellectuals in Britain," 158. See also *Times*, July 29, 1935; and Asante, *Pan-African Protest*, 46.

103. Alan MacKenzie describes how on September 5, 1936, for example, in a speech to a WASU gathering, Moore "denounced the injustices of the [British] colonial administration yet fervently pledged West Africans' allegiance to the Crown and the Empire, 'this great commonwealth of nations of which we are proud to be members, *and on which, we pray God*, the sun may never set.'" MacKenzie, "British Marxists and the Empire," 213.

104. C. L. R. James, "The British Vote for Socialism," 114.

105. Waley, *British Public Opinion and the Abyssinian War, 1935–6*, 20.

106. C. L. R. James, "Black Intellectuals in Britain," 158.

107. C. L. R. James, "Black Intellectuals in Britain," 158–59.

108. *New Statesman and Nation*, August 3, 1935.

109. Quoted in *New Statesman and Nation*, August 10, 1935.

110. See Hannen Swaffer's article in *Daily Herald*, August 24, 1935. See also TNA, KV/2/1824/7A; and Waley, *British Public Opinion and the Abyssinian War*, 115.

111. For a brief introduction to Braithwaite, see Høgsbjerg, "Mariner, Renegade, Castaway."

112. *Nottingham Evening Post*, August 26, 1935.

113. *Daily Herald*, August 26, 1935. The racing tipster was Prince Ras Monolulu, born Peter McKay in St. Croix. See Makalani, *In the Cause of Freedom*, 206–8.

114. Makonnen, *Pan-Africanism from Within*, 113–14.

115. Derrick, *Africa's "Agitators,"* 335–36.

116. Makonnen, *Pan-Africanism from Within*, 116–17.

117. Zilliacus, *Abyssinia*, 6; C. L. R. James, "Black Intellectuals in Britain," 158–59.

118. Kelley, "The World the Diaspora Made," 109.

119. *New Leader*, June 3, 1936. The letter is reprinted in C. L. R. James, "Black Intellectuals in Britain," 158–59.

120. *New Statesman*, August 3, 1935; C. L. R. James, *The Black Jacobins*, 248.

121. Wilson, *Russia and Black Africa before World War II*, 57–58.

122. Asante, *Pan-African Protest*, 46.

123. I discuss this possibility further in Høgsbjerg, "C. L. R. James and Italy's Conquest of Abyssinia."

124. *New Leader*, June 3, 1936.

125. *Daily Gleaner* (Jamaica), August 7, 1935; and *Nottingham Evening Post*, August 26, 1935.

126. See Asante, *Pan-African Protest*, 46.

127. *New Leader*, October 4, 1935.

128. On the ILP, see Cohen, *The Failure of a Dream*.

129. James's articles in the *New Leader* were published on October 4, 1935, then on December 13, 20, and 27, 1935, and January 3, 1936. He also wrote longer polemics in the ILP journal, *Controversy*. See C. L. R. James, "ILP Abyssinian Policy," *Controversy* (October 1935), and his contribution to "Italy and Abyssinia: Should British Workers Take Sides?," *Controversy*, special supplement no. 1 (1936).

130. Bornstein and Richardson, *Against the Stream*, 177; and Archer, "C.L.R. James in Britain, 1932–38," 61. For more on James's subsequent well-known battle with the ILP leadership over Ethiopia, see A. MacKenzie, "British Marxists and the Empire," 202–21; and Flinn and Cohen, "The Abyssinia Crisis, British Labour and the Fracturing of the Anti-war Movement."

131. Edmondson also heard James speak at "an 'open' meeting" in the North-East, and remembered George Padmore's "coming to speak several times in this area and staying with people named Winter. . . . Padmore always referred to James as 'My very good friend,' and James did likewise." Personal information received from Len Edmondson via Helen Harrison, February 7, 2006.

132. Brockway, *Towards Tomorrow*, 129.

133. C. L. R. James, "Is This Worth a War? The League's Scheme to Rob Abyssinia of Its Independence," *New Leader*, October 4, 1935, reprinted in C. L. R. James, *At the Rendezvous of Victory*.

134. Martin, *Amy Ashwood Garvey*, 144.

135. Richardson, Chrysostom, and Grimshaw, *C. L. R. James and British Trotskyism*, 3; and C. L. R. James, *The Future in the Present*, 226.

136. Alexander, *International Trotskyism*, 568.

137. Crossey and Monaghan, "The Origins of Trotskyism in Ireland," 54. James put Nora Connolly in touch with Trotsky (then in Norway) and invited her to London to address a meeting to the Marxist Group on Ireland: "I went to meet her and invited her to come over here and speak, and she did. Coming from the railway station we crossed the river by Parliament, and she said, 'You should have done away with that years ago, it is easy from the river.' So I said, 'Yes, we are revolutionaries, but bombing the Houses of Parliament is useless.' 'You're talking of something that you know nothing about!' She instinctively saw the revolutionary possibilities. From this side of the river you could bomb the Houses of Parliament and get away with it." Richardson, Chrysostom, and Grimshaw, *C. L. R. James and British Trotskyism*, 4.

138. C. L. R. James, "Abyssinia and the Imperialists," 63. The original article appeared in *Keys* 3, no. 3 (January–March 1936).

139. Sbacelli, *Legacy of Bitterness*, 55; Brendon, *The Dark Valley*, 279.

140. Weisbord, *Ebony Kinship*, 110.

141. Trotsky, *Writings, 1935–6*, 5.

142. Trotsky, *The Revolution Betrayed*, 195; Padmore, *Africa and World Peace*, 153–54.

143. C. L. R. James, "George Padmore," 255; C. L. R. James, "Writings from *The Nation*," 291. Leslie James has recently detailed some of the intricacies and complexities of Padmore's break in 1933 with the Communist International. See L. James, "'What We Put in Black and White,'" 65–97.

144. Edwards, *The Practice of Diaspora*, 246–47, 276, 298.

145. "Editorials," *Crisis* 42, no. 10 (October 1935): 305. That issue of *The Crisis* also carried Padmore's account of his break with the Communist International, "An Open Letter to Earl Browder," leader of the American Communist Party.

146. Padmore, *Pan-Africanism or Communism?*, 330.

147. Gikandi, "Pan-Africanism and Cosmopolitanism."

148. James proofread Padmore's work and was thanked in the preface. See Padmore, *How Britain Rules Africa*, 17. For more on Padmore as a writer, see Polsgrove, *Ending British Rule in Africa*.

149. Padmore, *How Britain Rules Africa*, 1–4, 396.

150. C. L. R. James, "'Civilising' the 'Blacks.'"

151. Padmore, *How Britain Rules Africa*, 391–92.

152. C. L. R. James, "'Civilising' the 'Blacks.'"

153. "The Annual Conference," *Keys* 4, no. 1 (July–September 1936): 4–6; and "The Third Annual Conference," *Keys* 3, no. 4 (April–June 1936): 48. See also Bellamy, Saville, and Wylie, "Leys, Norman, Maclean (1875–1944)"; and Saville, "Barnes, Leonard John (1895–1977)."

154. "The Annual Conference," *Keys* 4, no. 1 (July–September 1936): 12. James's view of missionaries was not favorable: "The imperialists strive to keep him [the African] ignorant. They educate him through missionary schools which confuse him with talk about suffering and obedience and the life to come." See C. L. R. James, "'Civilising' the 'Blacks.'"

155. James saw some Kikuyu customs as indefensible, such as female circumcision and cliterodectomy, which Kenyatta supported in the face of missionary pressure. See Drake, "Mbiyu Koinange and the Pan-African Movement," 176; and Frederiksen, "Jomo Kenyatta, Marie Bonaparte and Bronislaw Malinowski on Clitoridectomy and Female Sexuality." On James's fraternal but difficult relationship with Kenyatta, see C. L. R. James, "Notes on the Life of George Padmore," 30–31, 36; and his critical appreciation of Kenyatta's work *Facing Mount Kenya* (1938) in C. L. R. James, "The Voice of Africa," *International African Opinion* 1, no. 2 (August 1938): 3.

156. See C. L. R. James, "Lectures on *The Black Jacobins*," 70–71.

157. For more discussion of *World Revolution*, see Høgsbjerg, "'A Kind of Bible of Trotskyism.'"

158. Dutt, *World Politics*.

159. C. L. R. James, *World Revolution*, xxv.

160. C. L. R. James, *The Black Jacobins*, 230.

161. C. L. R. James, *World Revolution*, 301, 409, 411–12.

162. See C. L. R. James, *World Revolution*, 387–89.

163. Upham, "The Marxist Group in the ILP (1933–1936)."

164. C. L. R. James, "Discussions with Trotsky," 60–64.

165. C. L. R. James, "Charlie Lahr," 8–12. See also the discussion in C. L. R. James, *Notes on Dialectics*, 38, 149.

166. C. L. R. James, "Discussions with Trotsky," 60–64.

167. The secretariat of the Executive Committee of the Communist International sent out desperate memorandums in February 1937 calling for campaigns among "the broadest popular masses," aimed at the "entire smashing of Trotskyism." Trotskyists were now not only apparently "the most dastardly enemies of the USSR" but "warmongers" and "enemies of the people's liberty" and the "independence of nations." Chase, *Enemies within the Gate?*, 192, 202–3.

168. Warburg, *An Occupation for Gentlemen*, 214–15. See also Mannin, *Comrade O Comrade*, 5; and Bornstein and Richardson, *Against the Stream*, 219. Worcester reports that James felt it was "a piece of work which was recognised everywhere as worthwhile." Worcester, *C. L. R. James*, 246.

169. Raymond Postgate, "Du Côté de Chez Trotsky," *New Statesman*, May 8, 1937; H. L. Beales, "Critics of Stalinism," *Fact* 3 (1937): 95–98.

170. Brotherstone and Pilling, *History, Economic History and the Future of Marxism*, 305.

171. Bornstein and Richardson, *Against the Stream*, 264; A. Richardson, introduction to *World Revolution, 1917–1936*, xiii.

172. C. L. R. James, "Editorial," *Fight* 1, no. 1 (October 1936): 2–3.

173. C. L .R. James, "Lenin on the Development of Backward Peoples," *Fight* 1, no. 2 (December 1936): 12–13. See also Lenin, *Report of Commission on National and Colonial Questions*, 284–89.

174. C. L. R. James, "Kenya," *Fight* 1, no. 3 (January 1937): 12–13.

175. Waley, *British Public Opinion and the Abyssinian War*, 115. In 1937 Padmore brought out (with Secker and Warburg) *Africa and World Peace*, which argued that the growing tensions in Europe were an extension of the colonial rivalries of the imperialist powers.

176. Derrick, *Africa's "Agitators,"* 337–38, 387–88. In 1935 Padmore had apparently tried to launch a "Pan-African Brotherhood." On Broadhurst, see Sherwood, "Broadhurst, Robert."

177. *New Leader*, July 31, 1936. James was at this time in Paris at the First International Conference for the Fourth International and so must have missed this meeting.

178. Makonnen, *Pan-Africanism from Within*, 118; Derrick, *Africa's "Agitators,"* 387–88.

179. Hooker, *Black Revolutionary*, 23.

180. George, *Krishna Menon*, 51–57; Owen, *The British Left and India*, 239–59. James attended a meeting of Menon's India League in December 1936.

181. Makonnen, *Pan-Africanism from Within*, 117.

182. Derrick, *Africa's "Agitators,"* 338; Makalani, *In the Cause of Freedom*, 211–12. Bunche was in London from February to September 1937. See Pennybacker, *From Scottsboro to Munich*, 90–94, 304.

183. Derrick, *Africa's "Agitators,"* 388. On Wallace-Johnson, see Spitzer and Denzer, "I.T.A. Wallace Johnson and the West African Youth League," 445–52. On Wallace-Johnson's Communism and the IASB, see Makalani, *In the Cause of Freedom*, 211–15.

184. "What Is the International African Service Bureau?," *Africa and the World* 1, no. 1 (July 6, 1936): 1.

185. Makonnen, *Pan-Africanism from Within*, 122. Babalola Wilkey, or Wilkie, was a Nigerian called Edward Sigismund who briefly became IASB general secretary after Wallace-Johnson's return to Sierra Leone. In 1939 Wilkey was expelled for the alleged misappropriation of funds. See Fryer, *Staying Power*, 346; and, for a fuller list of apparent members, Derrick, *Africa's "Agitators,"* 388–89, 418; and A. MacKenzie, "British Marxists and the Empire," 232.

186. Francis Ambrose Ridley was to become great friends with Padmore. See Morrell, *The Gentle Revolutionary*, 10; *Socialist Leader*, March 18, 1950; and *Socialist Leader*, and May 8, 1965.

187. Makonnen, *Pan-Africanism from Within*, 118; "The International African Service Bureau," *African Sentinel* 1, no. 1 (October–November 1937): 4; Fryer, *Staying Power*, 345. On James's relationship with Pankhurst, see Romero, *E. Sylvia Pankhurst*, 213, 259.

188. "Our Policy," *African Sentinel* 1, no. 1 (October–November 1937): 1.

189. C. L. R. James, "Black Intellectuals in Britain," 161. See also Padmore, *Pan-Africanism or Communism?*, 147.

190. Edwards, *The Practice of Diaspora*, 241–305. For James's meeting with Kouyaté in Paris in 1938, see MARHO, *Visions of History*, 269–70.

191. West African radicals on the original executive included Nnamdi Azikiwe, J. J. Ocquye, F. A. Bruce, Louis Mbanefo, Elsie Duncan, K. Sallie Tamba, O. Mandoh, and E. Domanya. See Spitzer and Denzer, "I.T.A. Wallace Johnson and the West African Youth League," 447; and Derrick, *Africa's "Agitators,"* 389. Another Nigerian was Adetokunbo Adegboyega Ademola. See C. L. R. James, "Lectures on *The Black Jacobins*," 69.

192. Fryer, *Staying Power*, 341, 345.

193. C. L. R. James, *The Black Jacobins*, 310.

194. Schwarz, "George Padmore," 140.

195. *International African Opinion* 1, no. 1 (July 1938), quoted in Edwards, *The Practice of Diaspora*, 300–301.

196. Makonnen, *Pan-Africanism from Within*, 117–18.

197. C. L. R. James, "Writings from *The Nation*," 292–93; Hooker, *Black Revolutionary*, 55; C. L. R. James, "Black Intellectuals in Britain," 161.

198. Hooker, *Black Revolutionary*, 53.

199. Hooker, *Black Revolutionary*, 54; Marable, *Black Leadership*, 91. For more on the *Fact* series, see Postgate and Postgate, *A Stomach for Dissent*, 198–99.

200. C. L. R. James, "Notes on the Life of George Padmore," 37; C. L. R. James, *A History of Negro Revolt*, 53.

201. Worcester, *C. L. R. James*, 40. For a critical contemporary review by a fellow IASB member, William Harrison, a black American student at the London School of Economics, see "Negro Life and Letters," *International African Opinion* 1, no. 4 (October 1938), cited in Whittall, "Creolising London," 285–86.

202. West, Martin, and Wilkins, "Haiti, I'm Sorry," 87. See also Høgsbjerg, "The Black International as Social Movement Wave."

203. C. L. R. James, *Nkrumah and the Ghana Revolution*, 66.

204. Richardson, Chrysostom, and Grimshaw, *C. L. R. James and British Trotskyism*, 6. The second issue of *African Sentinel* reported, for example, that *Africa and the World* had been banned in Sierra Leone and the Gold Coast under the "sedition laws." "This Sedition Business," *African Sentinel* 1, no. 2 (November–December 1937): 7.

205. See Høgsbjerg, "'A Thorn in the Side of Great Britain.'"

206. C. L. R. James, *A History of Negro Revolt*, 37, 55–56.

207. C. L. R. James, *A History of Negro Revolt*, 45–46.

208. Cooper, *Decolonization and African Society*, 58.

209. C. L. R. James, *A History of Negro Revolt*, 81–82. See the *Report of the Commission Appointed to Enquire into the Disturbances in the Copperbelt*, 42–51.

210. Padmore, *How Britain Rules Africa*, 365.

211. C. L. R. James, *A History of Negro Revolt*, 82–84.

212. C. L. R. James, "Black Intellectuals in Britain," 160.

213. C. L. R. James, *The Future in the Present*, 70.

214. C. L. R. James, *The Black Jacobins*, 303; and C. L. R. James, *A History of Negro Revolt*, 85.

215. C. L. R. James, *A History of Negro Revolt*, 84–85.

216. See Schuyler, *Black Empire*; and Schuyler, *Ethiopian Stories*.

217. C. L. R. James, *A History of Negro Revolt*, 85.

218. Fryer, *Staying Power*, 346. James was assisted by William Harrison. See Padmore, *Pan-Africanism or Communism?*, 150. For more discussion of *International African Opinion*, see Edwards, *The Practice of Diaspora*, 299–305; and Quest, "George Padmore's and C. L. R. James's *International African Opinion*."

219. Makonnen, *Pan-Africanism from Within*, 120.

220. C. L. R. James, "Editorial," *International African Opinion* 1, no. 1 (July 1938): 2–3.

221. Edwards, *The Practice of Diaspora*, 300.

222. Bush, *Imperialism, Race and Resistance*, 223.

223. C. L. R. James, "Editorial," *International African Opinion* 1, no. 4 (October 1938): 2. As an antiwar IASB pamphlet dated September 1938 stressed, *Europe's Difficulty Is Africa's Opportunity*. Hooker, *Black Revolutionary*, 53.

224. Padmore, *Pan-Africanism or Communism?*, 148. See the CPGB statement delivered in May 1938, "Peace and the Colonial Question," discussed in Owen, *The British Left and India*, 244. Wallace-Johnson remained close to the CPGB in Britain. Makalani, *In the Cause of Freedom*, 213–15.

225. MARHO, *Visions of History*, 269. See also Richardson, Chrysostom, and Grimshaw, *C. L. R. James and British Trotskyism*, 6. "Chris Jones was a very fine comrade. Chris would get himself into a temper and explode and make a revolution at the back of the hall."

226. C. L. R. James, "Notes on the Life of George Padmore," 36.

227. See, for example, Orwell's famous article "Not Counting Niggers," in *The Adelphi* in July 1939, republished as Orwell, "Review of *Union Now* by Clarence K. Streit."

228. Pennybacker, *From Scottsboro to Munich*, 197, 252; see also Cohen, *The Failure of a Dream*, 143.

229. C. L. R. James, "Sir Stafford Cripps and 'Trusteeship,'" *International African Opinion* 1, no. 3 (September 1938): 3.

230. Foner, *Paul Robeson Speaks*, 351–53.

231. Sherwood, "Broadhurst, Robert."

232. The quote is from Bogues, *Caliban's Freedom*, 46.

233. C. L. R. James, *The Black Jacobins*, 303–4.

4. "The Humbler Type of Cricket Scribe"

1. Arlott, "C. L. R. James."

2. Collini, "Radical on the Boundary."

3. On these themes, see also Stoddart and Sandiford, *The Imperial Game*.

4. C. L. R. James, *Beyond a Boundary*, 56.

5. C. L. R. James, *Beyond a Boundary*, 77.

6. S. Hall, "A Conversation with C. L. R. James," 27.

7. Schwarz, "C. L. R. James's *American Civilization*," 129, 131. See also R. A. Hill, "Literary Executor's Afterword," 326–27.

8. A. Smith, "'Beyond a Boundary' (of a 'Field of Cultural Production')," 95.

9. Buhle, *C. L. R. James*, 42.

10. A. Smith, "'A Conception of the Beautiful.'"

11. See James and Grimshaw, *Cricket*, 4–68. The collection *Cricket* has since been republished. See C. L. R. James, *A Majestic Innings*.

12. Collini, "Radical on the Boundary." The quote about Maurice Leyland was from the *Manchester Guardian*, September 12, 1934, reprinted in James and Grimshaw, *Cricket*, 50.

13. *Glasgow Herald*, April 27, 1938; Warburg, *An Occupation for Gentlemen*, 215.

14. This chapter will mainly use articles from the *Glasgow Herald*, but many of James's articles from the *Manchester Guardian* still remain unexcavated by scholars.

15. A. Smith, "'Beyond a Boundary' (of a 'Field of Cultural Production')," 95.

16. C. L. R. James, *Beyond a Boundary*, 149. In May 1938 James would move from central London to 59 Boundary Road in North West London, close to Lords, dubbed "the Mecca of cricket" by Cardus. TNA, KV/2/1824/34A. Cardus, *English Cricket*, 17.

17. C. L. R. James, *Beyond a Boundary*, 44.

18. *Glasgow Herald*, May 19, 1937.

19. Engel, *The Guardian Book of Cricket*, 11, 13.

20. Guha, *The Picador Book of Cricket*, xiii–xiv; C. L. R. James, *Beyond a Boundary*, 38.

21. C. L. R. James, *Beyond a Boundary*, 123, 149, 179.

22. Cronin and Holt, "The Imperial Game in Crisis," 119.

23. Kilburn, *In Search of Cricket*, 108. Jim Kilburn was the cricket correspondent of the *Yorkshire Post* from 1934 to 1976.

24. Hamilton, "Profile."

25. Stoddart and Sandiford, *The Imperial Game*, 1.

26. *Manchester Guardian*, April 19 1933; May 8–10, 1933. Northamptonshire won.

27. James and Grimshaw, *Cricket*, 13.

28. Fingleton, *Cricket Crisis*, x. Christopher Gair has detailed how bodyline was used by the English against Australia in the third test in Australia in January 1933, described by *Wisden* as "probably the most unpleasant [Test match] ever played" and a "disgrace to cricket." See Gair, "Beyond Boundaries."

29. James and Grimshaw, *Cricket*, 34. This article, "Chances of West Indies in First Test," was published in the *Port of Spain Gazette* on June 15, 1933. It is worth remembering that Constantine and Martindale were both black, and Grant, the captain, was white. Martindale was later the first West Indian to make Lancashire his permanent home, after playing in the Lancashire League for Burnley in 1936.

30. Beckles, "The Political Ideology of West Indies Cricket Culture," 152.

31. J. Williams, *Cricket and Race*, 50.

32. Beckles, "The Political Ideology of West Indies Cricket Culture," 152. Neither James nor Constantine blamed Grant personally. See James and Grimshaw, *Cricket*, 34.

33. James and Grimshaw, *Cricket*, 35.

34. C. L. R. James, *Beyond a Boundary*, 124. See also the review in the *Times Literary Supplement*, November 16, 1933.

35. Constantine, *Cricket and I*, xi.

36. Constantine, *Cricket and I*, 27–28.

37. James, *Beyond a Boundary*, 139, 145–46. On Headley, see also James's essay published in 1967 in James and Grimshaw, *Cricket*, 190–202.

38. *Manchester Guardian*, April 18, 1933, reprinted in James and Grimshaw, *Cricket*, 10–12.

39. The LCP held a reception for the team at the Waldorf Hotel on June 23, and a "dance to the cricketers" on September 13. See "The Second Mile-Stone," *Keys* 1, no. 1 (July 1933): 16.

40. *Manchester Guardian*, June 26, 1933.

41. *Manchester Guardian*, May 8, 1933; *Manchester Guardian*, May 22, 1933; *Manchester Guardian*, July 7, 1933; *Manchester Guardian*, September 11, 1933.

42. *Manchester Guardian*, July 24, 1933.

43. *Manchester Guardian*, August 14–16, 1933.

44. C. L. R. James, *Beyond a Boundary*, 187, 189. Jardine was widely condemned for using bodyline against India, an emerging team without a Bradman, and lost the captaincy, becoming something of a pariah in the cricket world. See Gair, "Beyond Boundaries," 96.

45. *Glasgow Herald*, June 2, 1937.

46. *Glasgow Herald*, August 25, 1937.

47. A. Smith, "'A Conception of the Beautiful,'" 49.

48. *Glasgow Herald*, July 25 and 28, 1938.

49. A. Smith, "'A Conception of the Beautiful,'" 49.

50. *Manchester Guardian*, August 20, 1934. Reprinted in James and Grimshaw, *Cricket*, 39–41. For a similar passage, see C. L. R. James, *Beyond a Boundary*, 156.

51. *Glasgow Herald*, June 2, 1937.

52. *Manchester Guardian*, September 10–11, 1934.

53. *Glasgow Herald*, June 22, 1938. As Smith notes, "There is, one senses, something appealingly dialectical about this from James's point of view." Smith, "'A Conception of the Beautiful,'" 52.

54. *Glasgow Herald*, April 27, 1938.

55. Thornton, *The Imperial Idea and Its Enemies*, 91.

56. The Kipling quote comes from his poem "The English Flag" (1891). *Beyond a Boundary* had the working title "Who Only Cricket Know." See James and Grimshaw, *Cricket*, 70. For my take on James's writing of *Beyond a Boundary* amid decolonization, see Høgsbjerg, "Facing Post-colonial Reality?"

57. Bateman, "'More Mighty than the Bat, the Pen . . . ,'" 41.

58. McKibbin, *Classes and Cultures*, 332.

59. *Glasgow Herald*, June 2, 1937.

60. *Glasgow Herald*, June 1, 1938.

61. *Glasgow Herald*, May 12, 1937. Republished in James and Grimshaw, *Cricket*, 56–58.

62. *Glasgow Herald*, July 20 and 25, 1938. It is possible that these headings were inserted by a subeditor.

63. *Glasgow Herald*, June 16, 1937.

64. *Glasgow Herald*, June 24, 1937.

65. *Glasgow Herald*, May 5, 1937. Kilburn explained this "catastrophe" for readers of the *Yorkshire Post*, noting "the plain truth is that good fast bowling on a fast bowler's wicket where the ball bounced high instead of drifting sullenly was far too much for batsmen quite unused to such happenings," something Essex exploited fully while correspondingly there was "the complete inability of the Yorkshire bowlers to find virtue in the same piece of turf." Kilburn, *In Search of Cricket*, 167, 173.

66. *Glasgow Herald*, August 4, 1937.

67. A. Smith, "'A Conception of the Beautiful,'" 62.

68. Lewis, *Marcus Garvey*, 269.

69. "Activities of London Committee," *Africa and the World* 1, no. 4 (September 1, 1937): 10.

70. *Glasgow Herald*, August 11, 1937.

71. *Glasgow Herald*, August 3, 1938.

72. *Glasgow Herald*, August 3, 1938. For the history of Oval, James drew upon H. S. Altham's "admirable" *The History of Cricket*, which "brings the great history of the game moving once more before our eyes."

73. *Manchester Guardian*, April 18, 1933. Reprinted in James and Grimshaw, *Cricket*, 10.

74. *Glasgow Herald*, June 8, 1938.

75. *Manchester Guardian*, September 11, 1934.

76. *Glasgow Herald*, May 11, 1938.

77. *Glasgow Herald*, June 16, 1938.

78. *Glasgow Herald*, June 16, 1938. For more on McCabe's innings, see Bright-Holmes, *The Joy of Cricket*, 72.

79. *Glasgow Herald*, August 26, 1938.

80. *Glasgow Herald*, April 28, 1937. Reprinted in James and Grimshaw, *Cricket*, 53–55.

81. *Glasgow Herald*, May 4, 1938.

82. *Glasgow Herald*, May 18, 1938.

83. A. Smith, "'A Conception of the Beautiful,'" 60.

84. *Glasgow Herald*, August 31, 1938.

85. *Glasgow Herald*, August 23, 1938.

86. *Glasgow Herald*, June 22, 1938.

87. *Glasgow Herald*, July 20, 1938.

88. *Glasgow Herald*, June 24, 1937.

89. *Glasgow Herald*, August 26, 1938.

90. *Glasgow Herald*, July 14, 1937.

91. *Glasgow Herald*, July 7, 1938.

92. C. L. R. James, *Beyond a Boundary*, 186.

93. *Glasgow Herald*, May 12, 1937.

94. *Glasgow Herald*, September 8, 1937.

95. *Glasgow Herald*, June 2, 1937.

96. *Glasgow Herald*, July 14, 1938.

97. *Glasgow Herald*, June 2, 1937.

98. *Glasgow Herald*, September 1, 1937.

99. *Glasgow Herald*, July 14, 1937.

100. *Glasgow Herald*, June 27, 1938.

101. *Glasgow Herald*, May 4, 1938.

102. *Glasgow Herald*, April 27, 1938. The Third Ashes Test at Old Trafford in July 1938 had to be abandoned due to rain.

103. *Manchester Guardian*, August 21, 1934.

104. *Glasgow Herald*, August 10, 1938.

105. *Glasgow Herald*, July 25, 1938.

106. *Glasgow Herald*, July 28, 1938.

107. *Glasgow Herald*, June 16, 1938.

108. A. Smith, "'A Conception of the Beautiful,'" 49, 64.

109. C. L. R. James, *Beyond a Boundary*, 248.

110. Neil Lazarus has argued that "in his writings about cricket, James reveals himself to be one of the truly decisive Marxist cultural theorists of our century," comparing him to Lukács. Lazarus, "Cricket and National Culture in the Writings of C. L. R. James," 93.

111. McKibbin, *Classes and Cultures*, 332.

112. A. Smith, "'A Conception of the Beautiful,'" 52.

113. Trotsky, *On Britain*, 148.

114. While this needs more investigation, it seems that the CPGB paper the *Daily Worker* accordingly decided to stop reporting "capitalist" sport completely in 1930, but later it established a regular page devoted to sports coverage. For some discussion of the complicated relationship between the CPGB and sport during the 1930s, see Jones, *Sport, Politics and the Working Class*, 73–103.

115. C. L. R. James, *Beyond a Boundary*, 151, 205–6.

116. *Glasgow Herald*, July 28, 1937. McDonald had died in a car accident on July 26, 1937. In the article, James recalls playing a friendly match for Nelson in 1934 against McDonald, who had been an outstanding test cricketer in the 1920s before playing for Lancashire and then as a professional in the Lancashire League for Bacup. James remembered, "I played in a friendly match with him about three years ago, when he was long past his best. Standing at mid-on, I watched him closely, as well I might. Mere scribes do not often get the chance to watch such men in action at close quarters. . . . He was taking things easily that day, and his action had already dropped a little, but it was still the most perfect thing on the cricket field, and half his success was due to it."

117. Christopher Hitchens, "Mid Off, Not Right On," *Times Literary Supplement*, January 18, 2002.

118. *Glasgow Herald*, August 17, 1938. One other cricketer who might have had a chance of winning over a revolutionary workers' tribunal deciding on the fate of cricket was H. M. Hyndman, leader of the Social Democratic Federation, who Bernard Porter notes "may be the only Marxist leader in history who has played county cricket as a 'Gentleman,'" a right-hand middle-order batsman for Sussex from 1863–64 with an average of 16.26 runs. Porter, *The Absent-Minded Imperialists*, 217, 403.

5. "There Is No Drama Like the Drama of History"

1. *Times*, February 15, 1936.

2. See C. L. R. James, *Toussaint Louverture*. In 1846, George Dibdin Pitt's blackface minstrel play *Toussaint L'Ouverture, or the Black Spartacus,* had been performed at London's Britannia Theatre. See Waters, *Racism on the Victorian Stage*, 118, 122, 190, 214.

3. C. L. R. James, *The Black Jacobins*, 237.

4. For more on the 1936 production of *Toussaint Louverture*, see Chambers, *Black and Asian Theatre in Britain*.

5. C. L. R. James, *The Black Jacobins*, xiii.

6. Henry and Buhle, *C. L. R. James's Caribbean*, 22. Cyril Ransome—father of the more famous radical journalist and writer Arthur—had written a number of works on English history, including *A Short History of England* (1928).

7. Buhle, "The Making of a Literary Life," 58.

8. Besson, *Caribbean Reflections*, 49.

9. Samuel, "British Marxist Historians, 1880–1980."

10. S. Hall, "A Conversation with C. L. R. James," 22.

11. Small, "The Training of an Intellectual, the Making of a Marxist," 57.

12. Trotsky, *My Life*, 123. On Labriola's Marxist theory of history, see Rees, *The Algebra of Revolution*, 264–65.

13. C. L. R. James, "The Problem of Knowledge."

14. C. L. R. James, "Review of *Mahatma Gandhi.*"

15. Buhle, "The Making of a Literary Life," 58. It was not until 1939 that West Indian history was recognized formally as a subject for a certificate and part of the school curriculum. See E. Williams, *Inward Hunger*, 35; Rosengarten, *Urbane Revolutionary*, 11.

16. Ramchand, *Life on the Edge*, 59.

17. MARHO, *Visions of History*, 267; S. Hall, "A Conversation with C. L. R. James," 21. For James's thoughts on Beard and Waxman, see C. L. R. James, *The Black Jacobins*, xv, 336.

18. C. L. R. James, "The Intelligence of the Negro."

19. R. Hill, "C. L. R. James," 256–57.

20. Brereton, "Haiti and the Haitian Revolution in the Political Discourse of Nineteenth-Century Trinidad," 144.

21. On Froude at Oxford, see Symonds, *Oxford and Empire*, 49–51.

22. In 1896, Joseph Chamberlain, secretary of state for the colonies under Salisbury, declared that black West Indians were "totally unfit for representative institutions."

British colonial officials echoed such "respectable" sentiments subsequently. In 1906, Walsh Wrightson, director of public works in Trinidad, told the legislative council that "it would appear that in the tropics the great mass of the people have not that energy, self reliance and determination to be masters of their own destiny which characterise the people of Great Britain." See Gomes, *Through a Maze of Colour*, x.

23. E. Williams, *British Historians and the West Indies*, 138.

24. Froude, *The English in the West Indies*, 50, 56, 80–81. In a private journal Froude kept while in the Caribbean, he declared, "Niggerdom perfect happiness," and referred to seeing "swarms of niggers[,] . . . all of them perfectly happy, without a notion of morality." Quoted in Fryer, *Black People in the British Empire*, 149.

25. Thomas, *Froudacity*, 165, 175–76.

26. C. L. R. James, "The West Indian Intellectual," 39.

27. C. L. R. James, *The Black Jacobins*, xv.

28. Oldfield, "Chords of Freedom," 92–104. See also Pennybacker, *From Scottsboro to Munich*, 117–26.

29. See *Listener*, April 26, 1933; *Listener*, May 3, 1933; *Listener*, May 10, 1933; *Listener*, May 24, 1933.

30. Anstey, *The Atlantic Slave Trade and British Abolition*, xx. On the possible misquotation of Lecky, see Darity, "The Williams Abolition Thesis before Williams," 29.

31. Coupland, *Wilberforce*, 510.

32. Simon, *Slavery*, 206. On the British imperial doctrine of trusteeship, see K. Robinson, *The Dilemmas of Trusteeship*. See also Reginald Coupland, "The British Commonwealth and Colonial Empire: Trusteeship for Backward Peoples," *Port of Spain Gazette*, October 11, 1936.

33. C. L. R. James, "A Century of Freedom."

34. C. L. R. James, *Beyond a Boundary*, 121. James remembers Constantine was "very, very pleased" by the broadcast, while *Keys* also noted its satisfaction with James's intervention. See "The Second Mile-stone," *Keys* 1, no. 1 (July 1933): 17.

35. *Port of Spain Gazette*, June 17, 1933; *Port of Spain Gazette*, July 2, 1933; and *Port of Spain Gazette*, July 9, 1933.

36. C. L. R. James, "A Century of Freedom."

37. C. L. R. James, "Slavery Today."

38. C. L. R. James, *Toussaint Louverture*, 45.

39. Trotsky, *The History of the Russian Revolution*, 17, 508.

40. C. L. R. James, *Toussaint Louverture*. *Toussaint Louverture*'s subtitle, "the only successful slave revolt in history," perhaps deserves more discussion. Robin Blackburn notes that "resistance has been ubiquitous in slave systems but has usually been particularistic, seeking freedom for a given person or group, and frustrated. In fact the Haitian Revolution is the only successful large-scale and generalized slave revolt known in history." See Blackburn, "Haiti, Slavery, and the Age of the Democratic Revolution."

41. Miller, *Elusive Origins*, 78.

42. C. L. R. James, *The Black Jacobins*, 294.

43. "I had long intended to write a biography of Toussaint L'Ouverture as a study in colonial revolution," James once recalled. C. L. R. James, "Notes on the Life of George Padmore," 28.

44. C. L. R. James, *The Black Jacobins*, xviii–xix.

45. C. L. R. James, *The Black Jacobins*, 201–2.

46. Grimshaw, "C. L. R. James," 7.

47. C. L. R. James, *The Black Jacobins*, 348. On Tarlé, who was arrested, imprisoned, and briefly exiled by the Stalinist regime in the early 1930s, see Erickson, "E.V. Tarle."

48. Tarlé, *Bonaparte*, 9–11.

49. Trotsky, *The History of the Russian Revolution*, 343–44.

50. Deutscher, *The Prophet Outcast*, 241–47. For a defense of Trotsky here against Deutscher, see N. Davidson, "The Prophet, His Biographer and the Watchtower."

51. Maingot, "Politics and Populist Historiography in the Caribbean," 150–51; Engels, *The Peasant War in Germany*, 50, 77.

52. "Politics and Psychology," *Fight* 1, no. 7 (June 1937): 14–15. For more on the possible relevance of Engels on Müntzer for James's imagining of Toussaint, see Høgsbjerg, "C. L. R. James and the Black Jacobins," 112–13.

53. E. Williams, *Inward Hunger*, 39.

54. C. L. R. James, "Dr. Eric Williams," 332.

55. E. Williams, *Inward Hunger*, 40, 49. The closest thing to political activity Williams seems to have undertaken while an undergraduate was to attend "regular meetings of the Indian nationalist students in their club, the Majliss." Boodhoo, *The Elusive Eric Williams*, 157.

56. Munro and Sander, *Kas-Kas*, 36–37.

57. Grimshaw, *The C. L. R. James Archive*, 59.

58. E. Williams, *Inward Hunger*, 43, 45.

59. Ryan, *Eric Williams*, 24–25.

60. Munro and Sander, *Kas-Kas*, 36–37.

61. E. Williams, *Inward Hunger*, 49, 51. See also Ryan, *Eric Williams*, 26.

62. Munro and Sander, *Kas-Kas*, 36–37.

63. E. Williams, *Inward Hunger*, 49; E. Williams, *British Historians and the West Indies*, 182. There were some limited moves toward economic history with respect to abolition among English scholars before Williams. See Darity, "The Williams Abolition Thesis before Williams," 32; MacInnes, *England and Slavery*, 157–58; and Temperley, "Eric Williams and Abolition," 235.

64. For Williams's praise of Hochstetter's *Die wirtschaftlichen und politischen motive für die abschaffung des britischen sklavenhandels im jahre 1806–1807*, see E. Williams, "The Economic Aspect of the Abolition of the West Indian Slave Trade and Slavery," 30, 408; Anstey, *The Atlantic Slave Trade and British Abolition*, xxi.

65. S. Hall, "A Conversation with C. L. R. James," 22.

66. "The West Indian negro had all the characteristics of his race. He stole, he lied, he was simple, suspicious, inefficient, irresponsible, lazy, superstitious, and loose in his sex relations." Ragatz, *The Fall of the Planter Class in the British Caribbean*, 27.

67. Ragatz, *The Fall of the Planter Class in the British Caribbean*, vii, 50. Ragatz noted the time King George III and Prime Minister Pitt were visiting Weymouth and their encounter with a wealthy, white, Jamaican absentee planter who had an imposing array of servants and luxuries even greater than that of the king himself. "His Majesty, much displeased, is reputed to have exclaimed, 'sugar, sugar, eh! All *that* sugar! How are the duties, eh, Pitt, how are the duties?'"

68. Ragatz, *The Fall of the Planter Class in the British Caribbean*, vii.

69. C. L. R. James, *The Black Jacobins*, 334.

70. E. Williams, *Capitalism and Slavery*, iv. See also E. Williams, "The Economic Aspect of the Abolition of the West Indian Slave Trade and Slavery," 407. According to James, Ragatz himself, "the acknowledged master of this period," "encouraged Williams all the way for what he recognised was a highly significant revaluation of one of the most important historical events in world history." C. L. R. James, "Dr. Eric Williams," 336.

71. Quoted in E. Williams, *British Historians and the West Indies*, 157.

72. C. L. R. James, "Slavery Today."

73. C. L. R. James, *The Black Jacobins*, 18, 21.

74. C. L. R. James, *The Black Jacobins*, 42.

75. C. L. R. James, *The Black Jacobins* (1938), 311.

76. C. L. R. James, *The Black Jacobins*, 41–43; Anstey, *The Atlantic Slave Trade and British Abolition*, xxi. For more discussion of James's achievements, see D. Richardson, *Abolition and Its Aftermath*.

77. E. Williams, *Inward Hunger*, 50. James apparently also read two drafts of Williams's thesis. Worcester, *C. L. R. James*, 39.

78. Ryan, *Eric Williams*, 27; Madden, "The Commonwealth, Commonwealth History, and Oxford, 1905–1971," 12. On Williams and the IASB, see Boodhoo, *The Elusive Eric Williams*, 63; and Polsgrove, *Ending British Rule in Africa*, 67–68.

79. E. Williams, *Inward Hunger*, 52–53. *Capitalism and Slavery* would not be published in Britain until 1964.

80. E. Williams, *Capitalism and Slavery*, 268. Williams refers specifically to pages 38–41 of the 1938 edition of *The Black Jacobins*.

81. C. L. R. James, *The Black Jacobins*, 6, 38–40. For more on "slavery and accumulation," see part 2 of Blackburn, *The Making of New World Slavery*.

82. C. L. R. James, *The Black Jacobins*, 69, 71, 73.

83. C. L. R. James, *The Black Jacobins*, 224.

84. For more on the relationship between capitalism and slavery, see Blackburn, *The Making of New World Slavery*, 376–77; and Callinicos, *Imperialism and Global Political Economy*, 113.

85. C. L. R. James, *The Black Jacobins* (1938), 311.

86. C. L. R. James, *The Black Jacobins*, 41.

87. C. L. R. James, *A History of Negro Revolt*, 7.

88. C. L. R. James, *The Black Jacobins*, 113.

89. Benjamin, *Illuminations*, 254.

90. C. L. R. James, *The Black Jacobins*, 311.

91. Fortescue, *A History of the British Army*; C. L. R. James, *The Black Jacobins*, 174–75.

92. The words in quotation marks are those of James Walvin. C. L. R. James, *The Black Jacobins*, viii.

93. C. L. R. James, *The Black Jacobins*, 20.

94. Scott, *Conscripts of Modernity*, 58–59.

95. Rosengarten, *Urbane Revolutionary*, 17.

96. C. L. R. James, *Beyond a Boundary*, 26; Small, "The Training of an Intellectual, the Making of a Marxist," 51.

97. Lukács, *The Historical Novel*, 56–57, 70.

98. Lukács, *The Historical Novel*, 59.

99. In 1852, Marx, in his famous letter to Joseph Weydemeyer, written in 1852, noted, "It is not I who should receive credit for having discovered either the existence of classes in modern society or the struggle between them. Long before me, bourgeois historians had described the historical development of this class struggle." In 1854, in a letter to Engels, Marx praised Thierry as "this father of the class struggle in French historiography." See Soboul, *Understanding the French Revolution*, 229.

100. Rigney, *The Rhetoric of Historical Representation*, 1.

101. Gossman, *Between History and Literature*, 96.

102. Gossman, *Between History and Literature*, 95; and Gooch, *History and Historians in the Nineteenth Century*, 228.

103. Gossman, *Between History and Literature*, 155, 167, 203. For more on Michelet, see Scott, *Conscripts of Modernity*, 66–68.

104. C. L. R. James, *The Black Jacobins*, 331–32. In 1940, James would pay tribute to the "erratic passion" of Michelet, and his "fiery" *History of the French Revolution*, as well as mentioning Guizot. See C. L. R. James, "Trotsky's Place in History," 120–21. For more on Michelet's influence on James, see Foot, "C. L. R. James."

105. Michelet always identified more with the artisans and the historic "sans culottes" as opposed to the emerging industrial working class. For his reaction to the events of June 1848, see Gossman, *Between History and Literature*, 191, 195.

106. Engels, "Preface to the Third German Edition," 9. The classic account of what Marx owes to Michelet is Edmund Wilson's *To the Finland Station* (1940), which James himself reviewed. C. L. R. James, "To and from the Finland Station."

107. Deutscher, *The Prophet Outcast*, 219.

108. Scott, *Conscripts of Modernity*, 68.

109. C. L. R. James, "Trotsky's Place in History," 118, 123. For more discussion of the debates between Marxists about Trotsky's *History*, see Blackledge, "Leon Trotsky's Contribution to the Marxist Theory of History," and Blackledge, *Reflections on the Marxist Theory of History*.

110. Deutscher, *The Prophet Outcast*, 219–20, 230.

111. C. L. R. James, *The Black Jacobins*, 294; E. Hill, "Emergence of a National Drama in the West Indies," 20.

112. Rosengarten, *Urbane Revolutionary*, 157.

113. R. A. Hill, "C. L. R. James," 255. For an illuminating discussion of *War and Peace*, see White, "Against Historical Realism."

114. Trotsky, *How the Revolution Armed*, xviii.

115. C. L. R. James, *The Black Jacobins*, 11, 15.

116. This was essentially the thesis of the American academic T. Lothrop Stoddard's *The French Revolution in San Domingo* (1914), the most "serious" official account of the Haitian Revolution before James, and the one recommended, for example, by Ragatz. On Stoddard's "vendetta against the Negro race," see C. L. R. James, *The Black Jacobins*, 335.

117. C. L. R. James, *The Black Jacobins*, 104.

118. James of course did not ignore race, but throughout the work stressed the centrality of class. See C. L. R. James, *The Black Jacobins*, 230. "The race question is subsidiary to the class question in politics, and to think of imperialism in terms of race is disastrous. But to neglect the racial factor as merely incidental is an error only less grave than to make it fundamental."

119. C. L. R. James, *The Black Jacobins*, 9, 12, 69.

120. For one outstanding recent history of the slave trade, see Rediker, *The Slave Ship*.

121. Deutscher, *The Prophet Outcast*, 231.

122. C. L. R. James, "Lectures on *The Black Jacobins*," 94.

123. C. L. R. James, *The Black Jacobins*, 14.

124. Harman, "Haiti," 19. See also Renda, *Taking Haiti*.

125. Lamming, *Enterprise of the Indies*, 230.

126. C. L. R. James, *The Black Jacobins* (1938), 317. James notes his address in Haiti.

127. C. L. R. James, *The Black Jacobins*, 69.

128. C. L. R. James, *The Black Jacobins*, 332. See also Hobsbawm, "History from Below."

129. As Alfred Rosmer recalled in *Moscou sous Lenine* (1953), Lenin praised *The Great French Revolution*, as Kropotkin "well understood and demonstrated the role of the people in that bourgeois revolution." See Rosmer, *Lenin's Moscow*, 117. Trotsky is also said to have preferred Kropotkin's history to that of Jaurès. See Guérin, *Le feu du sang*, 133.

130. It might be noted in passing that Kropotkin's book was translated into Italian by one Benito Mussolini, then a young revolutionary socialist. Incidentally, Kropotkin thought Mussolini's translation "brilliant." Kropotkin, *The Great French Revolution*, xv, 15.

131. See C. L. R. James, *The Black Jacobins* (1938), 320. In 1963, in the revised edition of *The Black Jacobins*, James would continue to praise "Kropotkin's brief history of over fifty years ago" as "the best general book in English [on the French Revolution].

... Kropotkin thought the Revolution was a wonderful event and was neither afraid nor embarrassed to say so." C. L. R. James, *The Black Jacobins*, 332.

132. C. L. R. James, *The Black Jacobins*, 68.

133. Kropotkin, *The Great French Revolution*, 95.

134. C. L. R. James, *The Black Jacobins*, 69, 71.

135. C. L. R. James, *The Black Jacobins*, 291.

136. C. L. R. James, *The Black Jacobins*, 56.

137. C. L. R. James, *The Black Jacobins*, xviii.

138. C. L. R. James, *The Black Jacobins*, 197–98.

139. C. L. R. James, *The Black Jacobins*, xix.

140. Quoted in Callinicos, *Theories and Narratives*, 44.

141. C. L. R. James, *The Black Jacobins*, xix; Callinicos, *Theories and Narratives*, 44.

142. C. L. R. James, *The Black Jacobins*, xix.

143. Marx and Engels, *Selected Works*, 181–82.

144. C. L. R. James, *The Black Jacobins*, 36, 46.

145. C. L. R. James, *Nkrumah and the Ghana Revolution*, 66.

146. Trotsky, *History of the Russian Revolution*, 19–20, 33.

147. Trotsky, *The Struggle against Fascism in Germany*, 180.

148. Löwy, *The Politics of Combined and Uneven Development*, 86.

149. Trotsky, *The History of the Russian Revolution*, 27.

150. C. L. R. James, *The Black Jacobins*, 219.

151. C. L. R. James, *The Black Jacobins*, 112, 144; Kropotkin, *The Great French Revolution*, 484–92.

152. Benjamin, *Illuminations*, 247.

153. C. L. R. James, *The Black Jacobins* (1938), 314–15.

154. C. L. R. James, *The Black Jacobins*, xix–xx.

155. On Morocco and the Spanish Civil War, see Balfour, *Deadly Embrace*.

156. As James put it in 1960, "There is no question about it, the main opposition to imperialism must come from the proletariat of the advanced countries." C. L. R. James, *Modern Politics*, 64.

157. C. L. R. James, *A History of Negro Revolt*, 4.

158. Fryer, *Staying Power*, 207.

159. Grierson, "Man's Inhumanity to Man." Seventy years later, in 2009, the *New Statesman* would make amends, hailing *The Black Jacobins* as their first-choice "Red Read," heading up a list of their "top fifty books guaranteed to inspire" and "change your life." See "Red Reads," *New Statesman*, August 10, 2009.

160. James recalled that the translation of the Soviet novelist Anatoli Vinogradov's work on Toussaint, *The Black Consul* (1935), received an "enthusiastic welcome . . . in almost the whole British press." C. L. R. James, *The Black Jacobins*, 336. Pennybacker, *From Scottsboro to Munich*, 53.

161. Genovese, *In Red and Black*, 155.

162. See Hobsbawm, "The Historians' Group of the Communist Party," 23. Hobsbawm's *The Age of Revolution* (1962) recommended *The Black Jacobins*. Hobsbawm, *The Age of Revolution*, 389.

163. C. J. Robinson, *Black Marxism*, 375.

164. C. L. R. James, "Lectures on *The Black Jacobins*," 85, 91.

165. TNA, KV/2/1824/36A.

166. George Padmore, "Toussaint, the Black Liberator," *The People*, November 12 and 19, 1938. It seems the *African Standard* carried Padmore's review on January 1, 1939. See Denzer, "Wallace-Johnson and the Sierra Leone Labor Crisis of 1939."

167. C. L. R. James, *The Black Jacobins*, 236.

168. Georgakas and Surkin, *Detroit*, xi, 16, 262.

169. Trouillot, *Silencing the Past*, 73, 97.

170. Coupland, *Wilberforce*, 153, 188.

171. C. L. R. James, *The Black Jacobins* (1938), 311. James's use of the phrase "beyond the boundaries" in 1938 is perhaps noteworthy.

172. Paul Foot, "Black Jacobin," *New Statesman*, February 2, 1979. See also Nesbitt, *Universal Emancipation*.

173. C. L. R. James, "Revolution and the Negro," 77. For some of the context of this article, see Høgsbjerg, "The Prophet and Black Power."

Conclusion

1. C. L. R. James, "Twilight of the British Empire."

2. Glaberman, "C. L. R. James," 47.

3. "Goodwill Ambassador in America," *International African Opinion* 1, no. 6 (February–March 1939): 16.

4. See C. L. R. James, *Toussaint Louverture*, 217.

5. C. L. R. James, "The Passing of Colonialism."

6. C. L. R. James, *The Black Jacobins* (1938), 288.

7. J. M. MacKenzie, *Propaganda and Empire*, 10–11.

8. C. L. R. James, *The Black Jacobins*, 5.

9. Stalin is quoted in Brockway, *Inside the Left*, 262.

10. Barnes, *Skeleton of the Empire*, 8, 10, 87–88.

11. A. MacKenzie, "British Marxists and the Empire," 294–96; Owen, *The British Left and India*, 244.

12. Grierson, "Man's Inhumanity to Man."

13. Sivanandan, *A Different Hunger*, 3.

14. George Padmore, "A Negro Looks at British Imperialism," *Crisis* 45, no. 12 (December 1938): 396–97.

15. TNA, KV/2/1824/23A.

16. C. L. R. James, "Notes on the Life of George Padmore," 24, 33.

17. C. L. R. James, *The Black Jacobins*, 229.

18. Martin, *Amy Ashwood Garvey*, 145.

19. W. James, "The Black Experience in Twentieth-Century Britain," 363, 365–66. Estimates vary on the size of Britain's interwar black population, though by the 1930s it was around ten thousand strong. See Whittall, "Creolising London," 125. For 1935, James D. Young gives a figure of twenty thousand, while that year Hannen Swaffer gave a figure of 2,200 black people in London and 7,000 nationally. See Young, *The World of C. L. R. James*, 126; *Daily Herald*, August 24, 1935.

20. TNA, KV/2/1824/1Z. See also Bush, *Imperialism, Race and Resistance*, 187, 233, 319.

21. Laughlin, *Letters from London*, 28; C. L. R. James, "Africans and Afro-Caribbeans," 54.

22. Laughlin, *Letters from London*, 54.

23. Buhle, "The Making of a Literary Life," 60.

24. Orwell, *Inside the Whale and Other Essays*, 32.

25. C. L. R. James, "Marxism and the Intellectuals," 114; C. L. R. James, "Dr. Eric Williams," 332–33.

26. Cliff, *In the Thick of Workers' Struggle*, 106.

27. For James's report of the "stay-in" strike in autumn 1935 across South Wales, and his interview with William Mitchell and Bert Kear, two leading striking miners at the Nine Mile Point Colliery in Monmouthshire, see *New Leader*, November 1, 1935. For background on this struggle to stop the employment of nonmembers of the Miners' Federation, which was ultimately to be victorious with the help of local railwaymen who refused to run trains carrying blacklegs, see Francis and Smith, *The Fed*, 276–91.

28. C. L. R. James, "Africans and Afro-Caribbeans"; Young, *The World of C. L. R. James*, 129, 136, 140; Webb, *Not without Love*, 73.

29. C. L. R. James, "Abyssinia and the Imperialists," 66.

30. S. Hall, "A Conversation with C. L. R. James," 20.

31. Laughlin, *Letters from London*, 97, 117.

32. Reisner, *Documents of the Fourth International*, 300, 302.

33. C. L. R. James, "Trotsky's Place in History," 123.

34. C. J. Robinson, *Black Marxism*, 5.

35. Grimshaw, *Special Delivery*, 136.

36. Richardson, Chrysostom, and Grimshaw, *C. L. R. James and British Trotskyism*, 2.

37. Draper, *The Two Souls of Socialism*.

38. C. L. R. James, *World Revolution*, 123.

39. For more on some of this, see C. L. R. James, introduction to *Red Spanish Notebook*; and Høgsbjerg, "A 'Bohemian Freelancer'?"

40. C. L. R. James, "Dr. Eric Williams," 335.

41. Quoted in Thornton, *The Imperial Idea and Its Enemies*, 72.

42. C. L. R. James, "Notes on the Life of George Padmore," 21.

43. Helen Davies, "The Rise and Fall of Padmore," *Negro Worker*, August 1934; Wicks, *Keeping My Head*, 180.

44. C. L. R. James, "Notes on the Life of George Padmore," 29.

45. James also alleges that the radical Pan-Africanists in London were also under surveillance by German Nazi agents. The Gestapo "had agents who used to take photographs of all of us who spoke in Hyde Park: they were preparing to arrest us as soon as they had conquered England." C. L. R. James, "Notes on the Life of George Padmore," 12.

46. Sergeev, "The Communist International and a 'Trotskyite Menace' to the British Communist Movement on the Eve of World War II," 89.

47. C. L. R. James, "Notes on the Life of George Padmore," 29, 31a.

48. Serge, *From Lenin to Stalin*, 112. This work was reviewed in the pages of *Fight*, where James praised Serge, "a life-long revolutionary worker," for his "brilliant study of the degeneration of the Comintern." See "The Apothesis," *Fight* 1, no. 9 (August 1937): 8–9.

49. Serge, *From Lenin to Stalin*, 56, 110.

50. C. L. R. James, "The Struggle for the Fourth International," *Fight* 1, no. 11 (November 1937): 6–8; C. L. R. James, *World Revolution*, 16, 208.

51. Davison, *The Complete Works of George Orwell*, 38, 87. For more on Orwell and "literary Trotskyism," see Newsinger, *Orwell's Politics*.

52. Cripps, *C. L. R. James*, 21.

53. Orwell, "Why I Joined the Independent Labour Party," 384.

54. Serge, *From Lenin to Stalin*, 10, 104–5. In February 1939, Serge would develop this metaphor, noting in the *New International*, "It is often said that 'the germ of all Stalinism was in Bolshevism at its beginning.' Well, I have no objection. Only, Bolshevism also contained many other germs—a mass of other germs—and those who lived through the enthusiasm of the first years of the first victorious revolution ought not to forget it. To judge the living man by the death germs which the autopsy reveals in a corpse—and which he may have carried in him since his birth—is this very sensible?" Quoted in Sedgwick, introduction to *Memoirs of a Revolutionary*, xxx.

55. The "Zimmerwald mentality" equally gave (with hindsight, sadly unjustified) confidence to the Trotskyist movement. As James put it in slightly messianic fashion in 1937, "A few hundred of us can face the future with enormous confidence. Once we get a strong nucleus we shall grow automatically." C. L. R. James, "The Struggle for the Fourth International," *Fight* 1, no. 11 (November 1937): 6–8.

56. Richardson, Chrysostom, and Grimshaw, *C. L. R. James and British Trotskyism*, 7; McLemee and Le Blanc, *C. L. R. James and Revolutionary Marxism*, 98.

57. This difficulty did not stop at least one British Communist from trying to claim that by criticizing Stalin, James was not only objectively on the same side as "German and Italian Fascism, British imperialism and Japanese militarism" but somehow guilty of "Fascist activity" himself. See Crossey and Monaghan, "The Origins of Trotskyism in Ireland," 53.

58. Wicks, *Keeping My Head*, 182. Indeed, according to Logie Barrow, Wicks once even declared James "the greatest Marxist of the 1930s [in Britain]." Barrow, "Harry Wicks," 235.

59. Others included Marcus Garvey, W. Arthur Lewis, George Padmore, Eric Williams, Learie Constantine, Harold Moody, Ras T. Makonnen, Amy Ashwood Garvey, Sam Manning, Chris Braithwaite, Arnold Ward, and Una Marson.

60. Warburg, *An Occupation for Gentlemen*, 185; C. L. R. James, *Beyond a Boundary*, 124; and S. Hall, "A Conversation with C. L. R. James," 18. *Minty Alley* was reviewed in the *Times Literary Supplement* on October 31, 1936.

61. Brennan, *At Home in the World*, 222.

62. See Birchall, *Tony Cliff*, 400.

63. Buhle, *C. L. R. James*, 51.

64. C. L. R. James, "Trotskyism."

65. R. A. Hill, "In England, 1932–1938," 80.

66. Bornstein and Richardson, *War and the International*, 46.

67. Quoted in McLemee, *C. L. R. James on the "Negro Question*," xiv.

68. Buhle, "Marxism in the USA." For more on this, see McLemee, *The Dialectics of State Capitalism*.

69. Brennan, *At Home in the World*, 223, 225.

70. Quoted in McLemee, afterword to *C. L. R. James and Revolutionary Marxism*, 225–26. For my brief discussion of James's return to Britain in the 1950s and his attempt to build a new "Marxist Group," see Høgsbjerg, "Beyond the Boundary of Leninism?"

71. James and Grimshaw, *Cricket*, 117.

72. E. Williams, *Inward Hunger*, 77.

73. C. L. R. James, *Nkrumah and the Ghana Revolution*, 120.

BIBLIOGRAPHY

Unpublished Primary Sources

James, C. L. R. "Autobiography, 1932–38." Columbia University, Rare Books and Manuscript Library, C. L. R. James Papers: box 4, folder 7.

——. "Charlie Lahr." 1975. Unpublished manuscript in the possession of David Goodway.

——. "Harry Spencer." Unpublished manuscript. University of West Indies, St. Augustine, Trinidad and Tobago, the Alma Jordan Library, West Indiana and Special Collections, C. L. R. James collection.

——. "Notes on the Life of George Padmore." 1960. Unpublished manuscript. Institute of Commonwealth Studies, London.

——. "The Passing of Colonialism." Lecture, Grenada, October 6, 1958.

——. "Twilight of the British Empire." Summary of Speech at Irving Plaza, November 30, 1938. Issued by Educational Committee, Socialist Workers Party, New York Local, Fourth International. Wayne State University, Walter P. Reuther Library, Dwyer Collection: box 5, folder 18.

Published Primary Sources

Archer, John. "C. L. R. James in Britain, 1932–38." *Revolutionary History* 6, nos. 2–3 (1996): 58–73.

Barnes, Leonard. *Skeleton of the Empire*. London: FACT, 1937.

Baxandall, Lee, ed. *Karl Marx and Friedrich Engels on Literature and Art*. New York: International General, 1974.

Benjamin, Walter. *Illuminations*. London: Pimlico, 1999.

Besson, William W. *Caribbean Reflections: The Life and Times of a Trinidad Scholar, 1901–1986: An Oral History*. London: Karia, 1989.

Brockway, Fenner. *Inside the Left*. London: Allen and Unwin, 1942.

——. *Towards Tomorrow: The Autobiography of Fenner Brockway*. London: Hart-Davis, 1977.

Buhle, Paul, ed. *C.L.R. James: His Life and Work.* London: Allison and Busby, 1986.

———. "The Making of a Literary Life: C. L. R. James Interviewed." In *C. L. R. James's Caribbean,* edited by Henry Paget and Paul Buhle, 56–63. Durham, NC: Duke University Press, 1992.

Cardus, Neville. *English Cricket.* London: Collins, 1945.

———. *Good Days: A Book of Cricket.* London: Cape, 1934.

Césaire, Aimé. *Discourse on Colonialism.* New York: Monthly Review, 2000.

Comma, Olga. "Folklore in Trinidad." In *Negro: Anthology Made by Nancy Cunard, 1931–1933,* edited by Nancy Cunard, 486–88. London: Wishart, 1934.

Constantine, Learie. *Colour Bar.* London: Stanley Paul, 1954.

———. *Cricket and I.* London: Philip Allan, 1933.

Coupland, Reginald. *Wilberforce: A Narrative.* Oxford: Clarendon, 1923.

Cripps, Louise. *C. L. R. James: Memories and Commentaries.* London: Cornwall, 1997.

Cunard, Nancy, ed. *Negro: Anthology Made by Nancy Cunard, 1931–1933.* London: Wishart, 1934.

Dance, Daryl Cumber. "Conversation with C. L. R. James." 1980. In *New World Adams: Conversations with Contemporary West Indian Writers,* 109–19. Leeds, UK: Peepal Tree, 1992.

Davison, Peter, ed. *The Complete Works of George Orwell.* Vol. 11. London: Secker and Warburg, 1998.

Dutt, Rajani Palme. *World Politics, 1918–1936.* London: Victor Gollancz, 1936.

Engel, Matthew, ed. *The Guardian Book of Cricket: An Anthology of the Best from a Hundred Years of Cricket Reporting.* London: Pavilion, 1986.

Engels, Friedrich. *The Peasant War in Germany.* Moscow: Foreign Languages, 1956.

———. "Preface to the Third German Edition." *The Eighteenth Brumaire of Louis Bonaparte,* by Karl Marx, 8–9. London: Lawrence and Wishart, 1984.

Fingleton, Jack. *Cricket Crisis: Bodyline and Other Lives.* London: Pavilion, 1985.

Foner, Philip S., ed. *Paul Robeson Speaks: Writings, Speeches, Interviews, 1918–1974.* Secaucus, NJ: Citadel, 1978.

Foot, Michael. "C. L. R. James." In *C. L. R. James: His Intellectual Legacies,* edited by Selwyn R. Cudjoe and William E. Cain, 98–105. Amherst: University of Massachusetts Press, 1995.

Fortescue, J. W. *A History of the British Army.* Vol. 4, no. 1. London: Macmillan, 1906.

Froude, James Anthony. *The English in the West Indies, or the Bow of Ulysses.* London: Longmans, 1888.

Glaberman, Martin. "C. L. R. James: A Recollection." In *C. L. R. James and Revolutionary Marxism: Selected Writings of C. L. R. James, 1939–49,* edited by Scott McLemee and Paul Le Blanc, 45–52. New York: Humanity, 2000.

Gomes, Albert. *Through a Maze of Colour.* Port of Spain: Key Caribbean, 1974.

Grierson, Flora. "Man's Inhumanity to Man." *New Statesman,* October 8, 1938, 536.

Grimshaw, Anna. *The C. L. R. James Archive: A Reader's Guide.* New York: C. L. R. James Institute, 1991.

————, ed. *The C. L. R. James Reader*. Oxford: Blackwell, 1992.

————, ed. *Special Delivery: The Letters of C. L. R. James to Constance Webb, 1939–1948*. Oxford: Blackwell, 1990.

Guérin, Daniel. *Le feu du sang: Autobiographie politique et charnelle*. Paris: B. Grasset, 1977.

Guillaume, Paul, and Thomas Munro. *Primitive Negro Sculpture*. London: Cape, 1926.

Hall, Stuart. "A Conversation with C. L. R. James." In *Rethinking C. L. R. James*, edited by Grant Farred, 15–44. Oxford: Blackwell, 1996.

Hamilton, Alex. "Profile: An Interview with C. L. R. James." *Guardian*, June 25, 1980.

James, C. L. R. "Abyssinia and the Imperialists." 1936. In *The C. L. R. James Reader*, edited by Anna Grimshaw, 63–66. Oxford: Blackwell, 1992.

————. "Africans and Afro-Caribbeans: A Personal View." *TEN.8* 16 (1984): 54–55.

————. *American Civilization*. Oxford: Blackwell, 1993.

————. *At the Rendezvous of Victory: Selected Writings*. Vol. 3. London: Allison and Busby, 1984.

————. *Beyond a Boundary*. London: Hutchinson, 1963.

————. "Black Intellectuals in Britain." In *Colour, Culture and Consciousness: Immigrant Intellectuals in Britain*, edited by Bhikhu Parekh, 154–63. London: Allen and Unwin, 1974.

————. *The Black Jacobins: Toussaint Louverture and the San Domingo Revolution*. London: Secker and Warburg, 1938.

————. *The Black Jacobins: Toussaint L'Ouverture and the San Domingo Revolution*. London: Penguin, 2001.

————. "The British Vote for Socialism." 1945. In *The Future in the Present: Selected Writings*, vol. 1, 106–18. London: Allison and Busby, 1977.

————. *The Case for West Indian Self-Government*. London: Hogarth, 1933.

————. "A Century of Freedom." *Listener*, May 31, 1933.

————. "'Civilising' the 'Blacks': Why Britain Needs to Maintain Her African Possessions." *New Leader*, May 29, 1936, 5.

————. "Colour: Another View." *New Society*, December 10, 1964, 5.

————. "Discovering Literature in Trinidad: The 1930s." 1969. In *Spheres of Existence: Selected Writings*, vol. 2, 237–44. London: Allison and Busby, 1980.

————. "Dr. Eric Williams, First Premier of Trinidad and Tobago: A Biographical Sketch." 1960. In *Eric E. Williams Speaks: Essays on Colonialism and Independence*, edited by Selwyn R. Cudjoe, 327–51.Wellesley, MA: Calaloux, 1993.

————. *Eightieth Birthday Lectures*. London: Race Today, 1984.

————. *The Future in the Present: Selected Writings*. Vol. 1. London: Allison and Busby, 1977.

————. "George Padmore: Black Marxist Revolutionary—A Memoir." 1976. In *At the Rendezvous of Victory: Selected Writings*, vol. 3, 251–63. London: Allison and Busby, 1984.

————. *A History of Negro Revolt*. London: FACT, 1938.

————. *A History of Pan-African Revolt.* Chicago: Charles H. Kerr, 1995.

————. "The Intelligence of the Negro." *The Beacon* 1, no. 5 (August 1931): 6–10.

————. Introduction to *Red Spanish Notebook: The First Six Months of the Revolution and the Civil War,* by Mary Low and Juan Breá, v–vii. London: Secker and Warburg, 1937.

————. "Lectures on *The Black Jacobins.*" *Small Axe* 8 (2000): 65–112.

————. *The Life of Captain Cipriani: An Account of British Government in the West Indies.* Nelson, UK: Coulton, 1932.

————. *A Majestic Innings: Writings on Cricket.* London: Aurum, 2006.

————. *Mariners, Renegades, and Castaways: The Story of Herman Melville and the World We Live In.* Hanover, NH: University Press of New England, 2001.

————. "Marxism and the Intellectuals." 1962. In *Spheres of Existence: Selected Writings,* vol. 2, 113–30. London: Allison and Busby, 1980.

————. "Michel Maxwell Philip: 1829–1888." 1931. In *Michel Maxwell Philip: A Trinidad Patriot of the 19th Century,* edited by Selwyn R. Cudjoe, 87–103. Wellesley, MA: Calaloux, 1999.

————. *Modern Politics.* Port of Spain: PNM.

————. "My Knowledge of Damas Is Unique." In *Leon-Gontran Damas, 1912–1978: Father of Negritude: A Memorial Casebook,* edited by Daniel L. Racine, 131–34. Washington, DC: University Press of America, 1979.

————. *Nkrumah and the Ghana Revolution.* London: Allison and Busby, 1977.

————. *Notes on Dialectics: Hegel, Marx, Lenin.* London: Allison and Busby, 1980.

————. "The Old World and the New." 1971. In *At the Rendezvous of Victory: Selected Writings,* vol. 3, 202–17. London: Allison and Busby, 1984.

————. "Paul Robeson: Black Star." 1970. In *Spheres of Existence: Selected Writings,* vol. 2, 256–64. London: Allison and Busby, 1980.

————. "Presence of Blacks in the Caribbean and Its Impact on Culture." 1975. In *At the Rendezvous of Victory: Selected Writings,* vol. 3, 218–35. London: Allison and Busby, 1984.

————. "The Problem of Knowledge." *The Beacon* 1, no. 1 (March 1931): 22–24.

————. "Review of *Mahatma Gandhi: His Own Story.*" *The Beacon* 1, no. 5 (August 1931): 17–19.

————. "Revolution and the Negro." 1939. In *C. L. R. James and Revolutionary Marxism: Selected Writings of C. L. R. James, 1939–49,* edited by Scott McLemee and Paul Le Blanc, 77–87. New York: Humanity, 2000.

————. "Slavery Today: A Shocking Exposure." *Tit-Bits,* August 5, 1933, 16–17.

————. *Spheres of Existence: Selected Writings.* Vol. 2. London: Allison and Busby, 1980.

————. "To and from the Finland Station." 1941. In *C. L. R. James and Revolutionary Marxism: Selected Writings of C. L. R. James, 1939–49,* edited by Scott McLemee and Paul Le Blanc, 141–43. New York: Humanity, 2000.

———. *Toussaint Louverture: The Story of the Only Successful Slave Revolt in History: A Play in Three Acts*. Durham, NC: Duke University Press, 2013.

———. "Towards the Seventh: The Pan-African Congress—Past, Present and Future." 1976. In *At the Rendezvous of Victory: Selected Writings*, vol. 3, 236–50. London: Allison and Busby, 1984.

———. "Trotskyism." *Controversy* 1 (October 1937): 5–8.

———. "Trotsky's Place in History." 1940. In *C. L. R. James and Revolutionary Marxism: Selected Writings of C. L. R. James, 1939–49*, edited by Scott McLemee and Paul Le Blanc, 92–130. New York: Humanity, 2000.

———. "The West Indian Intellectual." In John Jacob Thomas, *Froudacity: West Indian Fables Explained*, 23–49. London: New Beacon, 1969.

———. *World Revolution, 1917–1936: The Rise and Fall of the Communist International*. Atlantic Heights, NJ: Humanities, 1994.

———. "Writings from *The Nation*." In *The C. L. R. James Reader*, edited by Anna Grimshaw, 281–95. Oxford: Blackwell, 1992.

James, C. L. R., Raya Dunayevskaya, and Grace Lee Boggs. *State Capitalism and World Revolution*. Chicago: Charles H. Kerr, 1986.

James, C. L. R., and Anna Grimshaw. *Cricket*. London: Allison and Busby, 1989.

Johnson, Linton Kwesi. *Mi Revalueshanary Fren: Selected Poems*. London: Penguin, 2002.

Keating, P. J., ed. *Matthew Arnold: Selected Prose*. Harmondsworth, UK: Penguin, 1970.

Kilburn, J. M. *In Search of Cricket*. London: Pavilion, 1990.

Kropotkin, Peter. *The Great French Revolution*. Quebec: Black Rose, 1989.

Lamming, George. *The Pleasures of Exile*. London: Pluto, 2005.

Laughlin, Nicholas, ed. *Letters from London: Seven Essays by C. L. R. James*. Oxford: Signal, 2003.

Lawrence, D. H. *Selected Poems*. Harmondsworth, UK: Penguin, 1960.

Lenin, Vladimir I. *Report of Commission on National and Colonial Questions*. 1920. In *On National Liberation and Social Emancipation*, 284–89. Moscow: Progress, 1986.

———. *The State and Revolution*. London: Penguin, 1992.

Levy, Michèle, ed. *The Autobiography of Alfred H. Mendes, 1897–1991*. Kingston, Jamaica: University of the West Indies Press, 2002.

Lukács, Georg. *The Historical Novel*. Harmondsworth, UK: Penguin, 1969.

———. *History and Class Consciousness: Studies in Marxist Dialectics*. London: Merlin, 1971.

Macdonald, Roderick J., ed. *The Keys: The Official Organ of the League of Coloured Peoples*. New York: Kraus, 1976.

MacInnes, C. M. *England and Slavery*. Bristol, UK: Arrowsmith, 1934.

Madden, Frederick, and John Darwin, eds. *Select Documents on the Constitutional His-*

tory of the British Empire and Commonwealth, Volume VII: The Dependent Empire, 1900–1948: Colonies, Protectorates, and Mandates. London: Greenwood, 1994.

Makonnen, Ras. Pan-Africanism from Within. London: Oxford University Press, 1973.

Mannin, Ethel. Comrade O Comrade: Or, Low-Down on the Left. London: Jarrolds, 1947.

MARHO, ed. Visions of History. Manchester, UK: Manchester University Press, 1984.

Marx, Karl, and Friedrich Engels. Selected Works. London: Lawrence and Wishart, 1973.

McLemee, Scott, ed. C. L. R. James on the "Negro Question." Jackson: University Press of Mississippi, 1996.

——, ed. The Dialectics of State Capitalism: Writings on Marxist Theory by C. L. R. James. Chicago: Haymarket, 2013.

McLemee, Scott, and Paul Le Blanc, eds. C. L. R. James and Revolutionary Marxism: Selected Writings of C. L. R. James, 1939–49. New York: Humanity, 2000.

Miller, Paul B. Elusive Origins: The Enlightenment in the Modern Caribbean Historical Imagination. Charlottesville: University of Virginia Press, 2010.

Moses, Knolly. "Thoughts of C.L.R. James." December 1986. Interview. Accessed July 4, 2013. http://panmedia.com.jm/blog/201307/thoughts-clr-james.

Munro, Ian, and Reinhard Sander, eds. Kas-Kas: Interviews with Three Caribbean Writers in Texas: George Lamming, C. L. R. James, Wilson Harris. Austin: University of Texas Press, 1972.

Naipaul, V. S. A House for Mr. Biswas. London: A. Deutsch, 1961.

Orwell, George. Inside the Whale and Other Essays. London: Penguin, 1991.

——. "Review of Union Now by Clarence K. Streit." In The Complete Works of George Orwell, vol. 11, edited by Peter Davison, 358–61. London: Secker and Warburg, 1998.

——. "Why I Joined the Independent Labour Party." In History in Our Hands: A Critical Anthology of Writings on Literature, Culture and Politics from the 1930s, edited by Patrick Deane, 383–85. London: Leicester University Press, 1998.

Padmore, George. Africa and World Peace. London: Frank Cass, 1972.

——. How Britain Rules Africa. London: Wishart, 1936.

——. The Life and Struggles of Negro Toilers. London: Red International of Labour Unions, 1931.

——. Pan-Africanism or Communism? The Coming Struggle for Africa. London: Dobson, 1956.

Ragatz, Lowell Joseph. The Fall of the Planter Class in the British Caribbean, 1763–1833: A Study in Social and Economic History. New York: Octagon, 1963.

Ramchand, Kenneth, ed. Life on the Edge: The Autobiography of Ralph de Boissière. Caroni, Jamaica: Lexicon Trinidad, 2010.

Reisner, Will, ed. Documents of the Fourth International (1933–40). New York: Pathfinder, 1973.

Report of the Commission Appointed to Enquire into the Disturbances in the Copperbelt, Northern Rhodesia. Cmd. 5009. London, 1935.

Reynolds, Reginald. *My Life and Crimes.* London: Jarrolds, 1956.

Richardson, Al, Clarence Chrysostom, and Anna Grimshaw. *C. L. R. James and British Trotskyism: An Interview.* London: Socialist Platform, 1987.

Rosmer, Alfred. *Lenin's Moscow.* London: Bookmarks, 1987.

Samaroo, Brinsley, ed. *The Beacon, Volumes I–IV, 1931–1939.* New York: Kraus, 1977.

Sander, Reinhard W., ed. *From Trinidad: An Anthology of Early West Indian Writing.* London: Hodder Arnold, 1978.

Schuyler, George S. *Black Empire.* Boston: Northeastern University Press, 1991.

———. *Ethiopian Stories.* Boston: Northeastern University Press, 1994.

Serge, Victor. *From Lenin to Stalin.* New York: Pioneer, 1937.

Simon, Lady. *Slavery.* London: Hodder and Stoughton, 1929.

Smith, Philip. *The Century Speaks: Recollections of Lancashire over the Last 100 Years.* Lancaster, UK: Carnegie, 1999.

Souvarine, Boris. *Stalin: A Critical Survey of Bolshevism.* London: Secker and Warburg, 1939.

Spengler, Oswald. *The Decline of the West.* Vol. 1. New York: Alfred A Knopf, 2003.

———. *The Decline of the West.* Vol. 2. London: Allen and Unwin, 2003.

Tarlé, Eugene. *Bonaparte.* London: Secker and Warburg, 1937.

Thomas, John Jacob. *Froudacity: West Indian Fables Explained.* London: New Beacon, 1969.

Topham, Tony, ed. *Report of the 5th National Conference on Workers' Control and Industrial Democracy Held at Transport House, Coventry on June 10th and 11th, 1967.* Hull, UK: Centre for Socialist Education, 1967.

Trotsky, Leon. *The History of the Russian Revolution.* London: Pluto, 1977.

———. *How the Revolution Armed: The Military Writings and Speeches of Leon Trotsky.* Vol. 1. London: New Park, 1979.

———. *My Life: An Attempt at an Autobiography.* Harmondsworth, UK: Penguin, 1979.

———. *On Britain.* New York: Monad, 1973.

———. *The Permanent Revolution and Results and Prospects.* New York: Pathfinder, 1972.

———. *The Revolution Betrayed.* New York: Pathfinder, 1989.

———. *The Struggle against Fascism in Germany.* Harmondsworth, UK: Penguin, 1975.

———. *Writings, 1935–6.* New York: Pathfinder, 1970.

Van Gelderen, Charles. "C. L. R. James—Thinker, Writer, Revolutionary." In *C. L. R. James and Revolutionary Marxism: Selected Writings of C. L. R. James, 1939–49,* edited by Scott McLemee and Paul Le Blanc, 41–44. New York: Humanity, 2000.

Warburg, Fredric. *An Occupation for Gentlemen.* London: Secker and Warburg, 1959.

Webb, Constance. *Not without Love: Memoirs*. Hanover, NH: Dartmouth College, 2003.

Wicks, Harry. *Keeping My Head: The Memoirs of a British Bolshevik*. London: Socialist Platform, 1992.

Williams, Eric. *British Historians and the West Indies*. New York: A and B, 1994.

———. *Capitalism and Slavery*. London: Andre Deutsch, 1981.

———. "The Economic Aspect of the Abolition of the West Indian Slave Trade and Slavery." PhD diss., Oxford University, 1938.

———. *Inward Hunger: The Education of a Prime Minister*. London: Deutsch, 1969.

Zilliacus, Konni. *Abyssinia*. London: New Statesman and Nation, 1935.

Newspapers and Periodicals

Africa and the World

African Sentinel

The Beacon

Colne Times

Controversy

The Crisis

Daily Herald (London)

Fight

Glasgow Herald

Guardian (London)

International African Opinion

The Keys

Left

The Listener

Manchester Guardian

The Nation

Negro Worker

Nelson Gazette

Nelson Leader

New International

New Leader

New Society

New Statesman

News Chronicle

The People

The Plebs

Port of Spain Gazette

Socialist Leader

Times (London)

Times Literary Supplement

Tit-Bits

Trinidad Guardian

West Africa

Workers' Fight

Secondary Sources

Adi, Hakim. *West Africans in Britain, 1900–1960: Nationalism, Pan-Africanism and Communism*. London: Lawrence and Wishart, 1998.

Alexander, Robert J. *International Trotskyism, 1929–1985*. Durham, NC: Duke University Press, 1991.

Allen, David Rayvern, ed. *Cricket's Silver Lining, 1864–1914*. London: Willow, 1987.

Anderson, Kevin B. *Marx at the Margins: On Nationalism, Ethnicity, and Non-Western Societies*. Chicago: University of Chicago Press, 2010.

Anstey, Roger. *The Atlantic Slave Trade and British Abolition, 1760–1810*. London: Macmillan, 1975.

Arato, Andrew, and Paul Breines. *The Young Lukács and the Origins of Western Marxism*. London: Pluto, 1979.

Arlott, John. "C. L. R. James: Behind the Marxist Crease." *Guardian*, June 1, 1989.

Asante, S. K. B. *Pan-African Protest: West Africa and the Italo-Ethiopian Crisis, 1934–1941*. London: Longman, 1977.

Balfour, Sebastian. *Deadly Embrace: Morocco and the Road to the Spanish Civil War*. Oxford: Oxford University Press, 2002.

Baptiste, Fitzroy, and Rupert Lewis. *George Padmore: Pan-African Revolutionary*. Kingston, Jamaica: Ian Randle, 2009.

Barkan, Elazar. *The Retreat of Scientific Racism: Changing Concepts of Race in Britain and the United States between the World Wars*. Cambridge: Cambridge University Press, 1996.

Barrow, Logie. "Harry Wicks, 1905–1989." *History Workshop* 31 (1991): 235–38.

Bateman, Anthony. "'More Mighty than the Bat, the Pen . . .': Culture, Hegemony and the Literaturisation of Cricket." *Sport in History* 23, no. 1 (2003): 27–44.

Beckles, Hilary McD. "The Political Ideology of West Indies Cricket Culture." In *Liberation Cricket: West Indies Cricket Culture*, edited by Hilary McD. Beckles and Brian Stoddart, 148–61. Manchester, UK: Manchester University Press, 1995.

Bellamy, Joyce, John Saville, and Diana Wylie. "Leys, Norman, Maclean (1875–1944)." In *Dictionary of Labour Biography*, vol. 8, edited by Joyce M. Bellamy and John Saville, 134–42. Basingstoke, UK: Macmillan, 1987.

Birchall, Ian. *Tony Cliff: A Marxist for His Time*. London: Bookmarks, 2011.

Blackburn, Robin. "Haiti, Slavery and the Age of the Democratic Revolution." *William and Mary Quarterly*, 63, no. 4 (2006): 643–74.

———. *The Making of New World Slavery: From the Baroque to the Modern, 1492–1800*. London: Verso, 1998.

———. *The Overthrow of Colonial Slavery, 1776–1848*. London: Verso, 1988.

Blackledge, Paul. "Leon Trotsky's Contribution to the Marxist Theory of History." *Studies in East European Thought* 58 (2006): 1–31.

———. *Reflections on the Marxist Theory of History*. Manchester, UK: Manchester University Press, 2006.

Bogues, Anthony. *Caliban's Freedom: The Early Political Thought of C. L. R. James*. London: Pluto, 1997.

Bolland, O. Nigel. *On the March: Labour Rebellions in the British Caribbean, 1934–39*. Kingston, Jamaica: Ian Randle, 1995.

Boodhoo, Ken. *The Elusive Eric Williams*. Kingston, Jamaica: Ian Randle, 2001.

Bornstein, Sam, and Al Richardson. *Against the Stream: A History of the Trotskyist Movement in Britain, 1924–1938*. London: Socialist Platform, 1986.

———. *War and the International: A History of the Trotskyist Movement in Britain, 1937–1949*. London: Socialist Platform, 1986.

Breines, Paul. "Karl Korsch's 'Road to Marx.'" *Telos* 26 (1975): 42–56.

Brendon, Piers. *The Dark Valley: A Panorama of the 1930s*. London: Cape, 2000.

Brennan, Timothy. *At Home in the World: Cosmopolitanism Now*. Cambridge, MA: Harvard University Press, 1997.

Brereton, Bridget. "Haiti and the Haitian Revolution in the Political Discourse of Nineteenth-Century Trinidad." In *Reinterpreting the Haitian Revolution and Its Cultural Aftershocks*, edited by Martin Munro and Elizabeth Walcott-Hackshaw, 123–49. Kingston, Jamaica: University of the West Indies Press, 2006.

Brereton, Bridget, and Melisse Thomas-Bailey. "Trinidad and Tobago." In *The Marcus Garvey and Universal Negro Improvement Association Papers: Volume XI: The Caribbean Diaspora 1910–1920*, edited by Robert A. Hill, cclxiii–cclxix. Durham, NC: Duke University Press, 2011.

Bright-Holmes, John, ed. *The Joy of Cricket*. London: Allen and Unwin, 1985.

Brotherstone, Terry, and Geoff Pilling, eds. *History, Economic History and the Future of Marxism: Essays in Memory of Tom Kemp*. London: Porcupine, 1996.

Bruley, Sue. "Women and Communism: A Case Study of the Lancashire Weavers in the Depression." In *Opening the Books: Essays on the Social and Cultural History of the British Communist Party*, edited by Geoff Andrews, Nine Fishman, and Kevin Morgan, 64–82. London: Pluto, 1995.

Buhle, Paul. *C. L. R. James: The Artist as Revolutionary*. London: Verso, 1989.

———. "From a Biographer's Notebook: The Field of C. L. R. James Scholarship." In *C. L. R. James: His Intellectual Legacies*, edited by Selwyn R. Cudjoe and William E. Cain, 435–51. Amherst: University of Massachusetts Press, 1995.

———. "Marxism in the USA." In *C. L. R James: His Life and Work*, edited by Paul Buhle, 81–104. London: Allison and Busby, 1986.

———. *Tim Hector: A Caribbean Radical's Story*. Kingston, Jamaica: Ian Randle, 2006.

Bush, Barbara. *Imperialism, Race and Resistance: Africa and Britain, 1919–1945*. London: Routledge, 1999.

Calder, Angus. "A Man for All Cultures: The Careers of Learie Constantine." *Culture, Sport, Society* 6, no. 1 (2003): 19–42.

Callinicos, Alex. *Imperialism and Global Political Economy*. Cambridge, UK: Polity, 2009.

———. *Theories and Narratives: Reflections on the Philosophy of History*. Oxford: Polity, 1995.

Campbell, Susan. "Carnival, Calypso and Class Struggle in Nineteenth Century Trinidad." *History Workshop* 26 (1988): 1–27.

Carr, E. H. *What Is History?* Basingstoke, UK: Macmillan, 2001.

Castoriadis, Cornelius. "C. L. R. James and the Fate of Marxism." In *C. L. R. James: His Intellectual Legacies*, edited by Selwyn R. Cudjoe and William E. Cain, 277–97. Amherst: University of Massachusetts Press, 1995.

Chambers, Colin. *Black and Asian Theatre in Britain: A History*. London: Routledge, 2011.

Chase, William J. *Enemies within the Gate? The Comintern and the Stalinist Repression, 1934–1939.* New Haven, CT: Yale University Press, 2001.

Chisholm, Anne. *Nancy Cunard.* Harmondsworth, UK: Penguin, 1981.

Clark, VèVè A. "Haiti's Tragic Overture: (Mis) Representations of the Haitian Revolution in World Drama (1796–1975)." In *Representing the French Revolution: Literature, Historiography, and Art,* edited by James Heffernan, 237–60. London: Dartmouth College, 1992.

Cliff, Tony. *In the Thick of Workers' Struggle: Selected Writings.* Vol. 2. London: Bookmarks, 2002.

Cliff, Tony, and Donny Gluckstein. *The Labour Party: A Marxist History.* London: Bookmarks, 1996.

Cohen, Gidon. *The Failure of a Dream: The Independent Labour Party from Disaffiliation to World War II.* London: I. B. Taurus, 2007.

Cole, Margaret. "Woolf, Leonard Sidney (1880–1969)." In *Dictionary of Labour Biography,* vol. 5, edited by Joyce M. Bellamy and John Saville, 240–47. London: Macmillan, 1979.

Collini, Stefan. *Arnold.* Oxford: Oxford University Press, 1988.

———. "Radical on the Boundary." *Times Literary Supplement,* September 25, 1987.

Coombes, Annie E. *Reinventing Africa: Museums, Material Culture and Popular Imagination.* New Haven, CT: Yale University Press, 1997.

Cooper, Frederick. *Decolonization and African Society: The Labor Question in French and British Africa.* Cambridge: Cambridge University Press, 1996.

Cornforth, Maurice, ed. *Rebels and Their Causes: Essays in Honour of A. L. Morton.* London: Lawrence and Wishart, 1978.

Craven, David. "C. L. R. James as a Critical Theorist of Modernist Art." In *Cosmopolitan Modernisms,* edited by Kobena Mercer, 146–67. London: Institute of International Visual Arts, 2005.

Croft, Andy. "Ethel Mannin: The Red Rose of Love and the Red Flower of Liberty." In *Rediscovering Forgotten Radicals: British Women Writers, 1889–1939,* edited by Angela Ingram and Daphne Patai, 205–25. Chapel Hill: University of North Carolina Press, 1993.

Cronin, Mike, and Richard Holt. "The Imperial Game in Crisis: English Cricket and Decolonisation." In *British Culture and the End of Empire,* edited by Stuart Ward, 111–27. Manchester, UK: Manchester University Press, 2001.

Crossey, Ciaran, and James Monaghan. "The Origins of Trotskyism in Ireland." *Revolutionary History* 6, nos. 2–3 (1996): 4–57.

Cudjoe, Selwyn R. *Beyond Boundaries: The Intellectual Tradition of Trinidad and Tobago in the Nineteenth Century.* Wellesley: University of Massachusetts Press, 2003.

———. "C. L. R. James and the Trinidad and Tobago Intellectual Tradition, Or, Not Learning Shakespeare Under a Mango Tree." *New Left Review* 223 (1997): 114–25.

Darity, William. "The Williams Abolition Thesis before Williams." *Slavery and Abolition* 9, no. 1 (1988): 29–41.

Davidson, Basil. *Africa in History*. London: Orien, 1992.

Davidson, Neil. "From Uneven to Combined Development." In *100 Years of Permanent Revolution: Results and Prospects*, edited by Bill Dunn and Hugo Radice, 10–26. London: Pluto, 2006.

———. "The Prophet, His Biographer and the Watchtower." *International Socialism* 104 (2004): 95–118.

Denzer, LaRay. "Wallace-Johnson and the Sierra Leone Labor Crisis of 1939." *African Studies Review* 25, nos. 2 and 3 (1982): 159–84.

Derrick, Jonathan. *Africa's "Agitators": Militant Anti-colonialism in Africa and the West, 1918–1939*. London: Hurst, 2008.

Deutscher, Isaac, *Heretics and Renegades*. London: Jonathan Cape, 1969.

———. *The Prophet Outcast: Trotsky: 1929–1940*. Oxford: Oxford University Press, 1979.

Dewar, Hugo. *Communist Politics in Britain: The CPGB from Its Origins to the Second World War*. London: Pluto, 1976.

Dhondy, Farrukh. *C. L. R. James: A Life*. New York: Pantheon, 2001.

Drake, St. Clair. "Mbiyu Koinange and the Pan-African Movement." In *Pan-African Biography*, edited by Robert Hill, 161–207. Los Angeles: African Studies Center, University of California, Los Angeles, 1987.

Draper, Hal. *The Two Souls of Socialism*. London: Bookmarks, 1996.

Drescher, Seymour. *From Slavery to Freedom: Comparative Studies in the Rise and Fall of Atlantic Slavery*. Basingstoke, UK: Macmillan, 1999.

Duberman, Martin B. *Paul Robeson*. New York: New Press, 1989.

Dubois, Laurent. *Avengers of the New World: The Story of the Haitian Revolution*. Cambridge, MA: Harvard University Press, 2004.

Dunn, Bill, and Hugo Radice, eds. *100 Years of Permanent Revolution: Results and Prospects*. London: Pluto, 2006.

Eburne, Jonathan P., and Jeremy Braddock. "Introduction: Paris, Capital of the Black Atlantic." *Modern Fiction Studies* 51, no. 4 (2005): 731–40.

Edwards, Brent Hayes. *The Practice of Diaspora: Literature, Translation, and the Rise of Black Internationalism*. Cambridge, MA: Harvard University Press, 2003.

Erickson, Ann K. "E.V. Tarle: The Career of a Historian under the Soviet Regime." *American Slavic and East European Review* 19, no. 2 (1960): 202–16.

Farred, Grant. "First Stop, Port-au-Prince: Mapping Postcolonial Africa through Toussaint L'Ouverture and His Black Jacobins." In *The Politics of Culture in the Shadow of Capital*, edited by Lisa Lowe and David Lloyd, 227–47. Durham, NC: Duke University Press, 1997.

———. "The Maple Man: How Cricket Made a Postcolonial Intellectual." In *Rethinking C. L. R. James*, edited by Grant Farred, 165–86. Oxford: Blackwell, 1996.

———, ed. *Rethinking C. L. R. James*. Oxford: Blackwell, 1995.

Flinn, Andrew, and Gidon Cohen. "The Abyssinia Crisis, British Labour and the Fracturing of the Anti-war Movement." *Socialist History* 28 (2006): 37–59.

Foot, Paul, "Black Jacobin." *New Statesman*, February 2, 1979, 155–56.

Forsdick, Charles. "The Black Jacobin in Paris." *Journal of Romance Studies* 5, no. 3 (2005): 9–24.

Foster, R. F. *W. B. Yeats: A Life, Vol. II: The Arch-Poet, 1915–1939*. Oxford: Oxford University Press, 2003.

Fowler, Alan. *Lancashire Cotton Operatives and Work, 1900–1950: A Social History of Lancashire Cotton Operatives in the Twentieth Century*. Aldershot, UK: Ashgate, 2003.

Francis, Hywel, and David Smith. *The Fed: A History of the South Wales Miners in the Twentieth Century*. London: Lawrence and Wishart, 1980.

Frassinelli, Pier Paolo. "Repositioning C. L. R. James." *Journal of Postcolonial Writing* 45, no. 1 (2009): 91–96.

Frederiksen, Bodil Folke. "Jomo Kenyatta, Marie Bonaparte and Bronislaw Malinowski on Clitoridectomy and Female Sexuality." *History Workshop Journal* 65 (2008): 23–48.

Fryer, Peter. *Black People in the British Empire: An Introduction*. London: Pluto, 1988.

———. *Staying Power: The History of Black People in Britain*. London: Pluto, 1987.

Gair, Christopher, ed. *Beyond Boundaries: C. L. R. James and Postnational Studies*. London: Pluto, 2006.

———. "Beyond Boundaries: Cricket, Herman Melville, and C. L. R. James's Cold War." In *Beyond Boundaries: C. L. R. James and Postnational Studies*, edited by Christopher Gair, 89–107. London: Pluto, 2006.

Geiss, Imanuel. *The Pan-African Movement*. London: Methuen, 1974.

Genders, Roy. *League Cricket in England*. London: Laurie, 1952.

Georgakas, Dan, and Marvin Surkin. *Detroit: I Do Mind Dying: A Study in Urban Revolution*. London: Redwords, 1998.

Genovese, Eugene D. *In Red and Black: Marxian Explorations in Southern and Afro-American History*. London: Allen Lane, 1971.

George, T. J. S. *Krishna Menon: A Biography*. London: Cape, 1964.

Giddings, Robert, ed. *Literature and Imperialism*. London: Macmillan, 1991.

Gikandi, Simon. "The Embarrassment of Victorianism: Colonial Subjects and the Lure of Englishness." In *Victorian Afterlife: Postmodern Culture Rewrites the Nineteenth Century*, edited by John Kucich and Dianne Sadoff, 157–85. Minneapolis: University of Minnesota Press, 2000.

———. "The Ghost of Matthew Arnold: Englishness and the Politics of Culture." *Nineteenth-Century Contexts* 29, nos. 2–3 (2007): 187–99.

———. "Pan-Africanism and Cosmopolitanism: The Case of Jomo Kenyatta." *English Studies in Africa: A Journal of the Humanities* 43, no. 1 (2000): 3–27.

Gilbert, Martin. *Winston S. Churchill, Vol. 5: 1922–1939*. London: Heinemann, 1976.

Gooch, G. P. *History and Historians in the Nineteenth Century*. London: Longmans, Green, 1913.

Goodway, David. *Anarchist Seeds beneath the Snow: Left-Libertarian Thought and British Writers from William Morris to Colin Ward*. Liverpool: Liverpool University Press, 2006.

———. "Charles Lahr." *London Magazine*, June–July 1977, 46–55.

Gossman, Lionel. *Between History and Literature*. Cambridge, MA: Harvard University Press, 1990.

Greig, J. Y. T. "The Social Critic." In *Thackeray: A Collection of Critical Essays*, edited by A. Welsh, 38–48. Englewood Cliffs, NJ: Prentice-Hall, 1968.

Grimshaw, Anna. "C. L. R. James: A Revolutionary Vision for the Twentieth Century." In *The C. L. R. James Reader*, edited by Anna Grimshaw, 1–22. Oxford: Blackwell, 1992.

Guha, Ramachandra, ed. *The Picador Book of Cricket*. London: Picador, 2006.

Hallas, Duncan. *Trotsky's Marxism and Other Essays*. Chicago: Haymarket, 2003.

Hall, Catherine. "What Is a West Indian?" In *West Indian Intellectuals in Britain*, edited by Bill Schwarz, 31–50. Manchester, UK: Manchester University Press, 2003.

Hall, Stuart. "Breaking Bread with History: C. L. R. James and *The Black Jacobins*: Stuart Hall Interviewed by Bill Schwarz." *History Workshop Journal* 46 (1998): 17–32.

———. "C.L.R. James: A Portrait." In *C. L. R. James's Caribbean*, edited by Paget Henry and Paul Buhle, 3–16. Durham, NC: Duke University Press, 1992.

———. "C.L.R. James, 1901–1989." *History Workshop* 29 (1990): 213–15.

Harman, Chris, "Haiti: Pawn in Their Game." *Socialist Worker Review* 85 (March 1986): 18–20.

———. *A People's History of the World*. London: Bookmarks, 1999.

Healey, Denis. *The Time of My Life*. London: Penguin, 1990.

Henry, Paget. "Africana Phenomenology: Its Philosophical Implications." *The C.L.R. James Journal* 11, no. 1 (2005): 79–112.

———. "Africana Political Philosophy and the Crisis of the Post-colony." *Socialism and Democracy* 45 (2007): 36–59.

———. "C.L.R. James and the Antiguan Left." In *C. L. R. James's Caribbean*, edited by Paget Henry and Paul Buhle, 225–62. Durham, NC: Duke University Press, 1992.

Henry, Paget, and Paul Buhle, eds. *C. L. R. James's Caribbean*. Durham, NC: Duke University Press, 1992.

Hill, Errol. "The Caribbean Connection." In *A History of African American Theatre*, edited by Errol G. Hill and James V. Hatch, 273–306. Cambridge: Cambridge University Press, 2005.

———. "Emergence of a National Drama in the West Indies." *Caribbean Quarterly* 18, no. 4 (1972): 9–40.

Hill, Jeffrey. *Nelson: Politics, Economy, Community.* Edinburgh: Keele University Press, 1997.

Hill, Robert A. "C. L. R. James: The Myth of Western Civilization." In *Enterprise of the Indies,* edited by George Lamming, 255–59. Port of Spain: Trinidad and Tobago Institute of the West Indies, 1999.

———. "In England, 1932–1938." In *C. L. R. James: His Life and Work,* edited by Paul Buhle, 61–80. London: Allison and Busby, 1986.

———. "Literary Executor's Afterword." In *American Civilization,* by C. L. R. James, 293–366. Oxford: Blackwell, 1993.

Hobsbawm, Eric, J. *The Age of Revolution, 1789–1848.* London: Abacus, 2002.

———. "The Historians' Group of the Communist Party." In *Rebels and Their Causes: Essays in Honour of A.L. Morton,* edited by Maurice Cornforth, 21–47. London: Lawrence and Wishart, 1978.

———. "History from Below: Some Reflections." In *History from Below: Studies in Popular Protest and Popular Identity,* edited by Frederick Krantz, 63–73. Montreal: Concordia University, 1985.

———. *Industry and Empire.* Harmondsworth, UK: Penguin, 1975.

Høgsbjerg, Christian, "Beyond the Boundary of Leninism? C.L.R. James and 1956." *Revolutionary History* 9, no. 3 (2006): 144–59.

———. "The Black International as Social Movement Wave: C. L. R. James's *History of Pan-African Revolt.*" In *Marxism and Social Movements,* edited by Colin Barker, Laurence Cox, John Krinsky, and Alf Nilsen, 317–35. Leiden, Netherlands: Brill, 2013.

———. "A 'Bohemian Freelancer'? C.L.R. James, His Early Relationship to Anarchism and the Intellectual Origins of Autonomism." In *Libertarian Socialism: Politics in Black and Red,* edited by Dave Berry, Ruth Kinna, Saku Pinta, and Alex Prichard, 143–66. Basingstoke, UK: Palgrave Macmillan, 2012.

———. "C.L.R. James: The Revolutionary as Artist." *International Socialism* 112 (2006): 163–82.

———. "C.L.R. James and Italy's Conquest of Abyssinia." *Socialist History* 28 (2006): 17–36.

———. "C.L.R. James and the Black Jacobins." *International Socialism* 126 (2010): 95–120.

———. "Facing Post-colonial Reality? C. L. R. James, the Black Atlantic and 1956." In *1956 and All That,* edited by Keith Flett, 181–201. Newcastle, UK: Cambridge Scholars, 2007.

———. "'A Kind of Bible of Trotskyism': Reflections on C.L.R. James's *World Revolution.*" *The C.L.R. James Journal* 19, no. 1 (2013).

———. "Mariner, Renegade, Castaway: Chris Braithwaite, Seamen's Organiser and Pan-Africanist." *Race and Class* 53, no. 2 (October 2011): 36–57.

———. "The Prophet and Black Power: Trotsky on Race in the US." *International Socialism* 121 (2008): 99–119.

———. "Remembering C. L. R. James, Forgetting C. L. R. James." *Historical Materialism* 17, no. 3 (2009): 221–34.

———. "'A Thorn in the Side of Great Britain': C.L.R. James and the Caribbean Labour Rebellions of the 1930s." *Small Axe* 35 (2011): 24–42.

———. "'We Lived According to the Tenets of Matthew Arnold': Reflections on the 'Colonial Victorianism' of the Young C. L. R. James." *Twentieth Century British History* 24, no. 2 (2013): 201–23.

Hooker, James R. *Black Revolutionary: George Padmore's Path from Communism to Pan-Africanism*. London: Pall Mall, 1967.

Howat, Gerald. *Learie Constantine*. Devon: Allen and Unwin, 1976.

Howe, Darcus. "Beyond a Boundary." BBC Radio 3, February 19, 2006.

———. "Great Lives: C.L.R. James." BBC Radio 4, November 1, 2002.

Howe, Stephen. *Anticolonialism in British Politics: The Left and the End of Empire, 1918–1964*. Oxford: Clarendon, 1993.

———. "C.L.R. James: Visions of History, Visions of Britain." In *West Indian Intellectuals in Britain*, edited by Bill Schwarz, 153–74. Manchester, UK: Manchester University Press 2003.

Howell, David. *British Social Democracy: A Study in Development and Decay*. London: Croom Helm, 1980.

Hughes, H. Stuart. *Consciousness and Society: The Reorientation of European Social Thought, 1890–1930*. Brighton, UK: Knopf, 1979.

Huxter, Robert. *Reg and Ethel: Reginald Reynolds (1905–1958), His Life and Work and His Marriage to Ethel Mannin (1900–1984)*. York, UK: Sessions, 1992.

Jacobs, Richard W. "The Politics of Protest in Trinidad: The Strikes and Disturbances of 1937." *Caribbean Studies* 17, nos. 1–2 (1974): 5–54.

James, Leslie. "'What We Put in Black and White': George Padmore and the Practice of Anti-imperial Politics." PhD diss., The London School of Economics and Political Science, 2012.

James, Winston. "The Black Experience in Twentieth-Century Britain." In *Black Experience and the Empire*, edited by Philip Morgan and Sean Hawkins, 347–86. Oxford: Oxford University Press, 2004.

Jarrett-Macauley, Delia. *The Life of Una Marson, 1905–1965*. Manchester, UK: Manchester University Press, 1998.

Jones, Stephen G. *Sport, Politics and the Working Class: Organised Labour and Sport in Inter-war Britain*. Manchester, UK: Manchester University Press, 1988.

Kelley, Robin D. G. "The World the Diaspora Made: C.L.R. James and the Politics of History." In *Rethinking C. L. R. James*, edited by Grant Farred, 103–30. Oxford: Blackwell, 1996.

Kendall, Walter. *The Revolutionary Movement in Britain, 1900–21: The Origins of British Communism*. London: Weidenfeld and Nicolson, 1969.

Lamming, George, ed. *Enterprise of the Indies*. Port of Spain: Trinidad and Tobago Institute of the West Indies, 1999.

Lazarus, Neil. "Cricket and National Culture in the Writings of C. L. R. James." In *C. L. R. James's Caribbean*, edited by Paget Henry and Paul Buhle, 92–110. Durham, NC: Duke University Press, 1992.

———. *The Postcolonial Unconscious*. Cambridge: Cambridge University Press, 2012.

Le Blanc, Paul. Introduction to *C. L. R. James and Revolutionary Marxism: Selected Writings of C.L.R. James, 1939–49*, edited by Scott McLemee and Paul Le Blanc, 1–37. New York: Humanity, 2000.

Lee, Francis. *Fabianism and Colonialism: The Life and Political Thought of Lord Sydney Olivier*. London: Defiant, 1988.

Leventhal, F. M. *Arthur Henderson*. Manchester, UK: Manchester University Press, 1989.

Lewis, Rupert. *Marcus Garvey: Anti-colonial Champion*. London: Karia, 1987.

Liddington, Jill. *The Life and Times of a Respectable Rebel: Selina Cooper, 1864–1946*. London: Virago, 1984.

Löwy, Michael. *The Politics of Combined and Uneven Development: The Theory of Permanent Revolution*. London: NLB, 1981.

Macdonald, Roderick J. "Dr. Harold Arundel Moody and the League of Coloured Peoples, 1931–1947: A Retrospective View." *Race* 14, no. 3 (1973): 291–310.

Macey, David. *Frantz Fanon: A Life*. London: Granta, 2000.

Macintyre, Stuart. *Little Moscows: Communism and Working-Class Militancy in Interwar Britain*. London: Croom Helm, 1980.

———. *A Proletarian Science: Marxism in Britain, 1917–1933*. Cambridge: Cambridge University Press, 1980.

MacKenzie, Alan John. "British Marxists and the Empire: Anti-imperialist Theory and Practice, 1920–1945." PhD diss., University of London, 1978.

MacKenzie, John M. *Propaganda and Empire: The Manipulation of British Public Opinion, 1880–1960*. Manchester, UK: Manchester University Press, 1985.

Madden, Frederick. "The Commonwealth, Commonwealth History, and Oxford, 1905–1971." In *Oxford and the Idea of Commonwealth*, edited by Frederick Madden and D. K. Fieldhouse, 7–29. London: Croom Helm, 1982.

Maingot, Anthony P. "Politics and Populist Historiography in the Caribbean: Juan Bosch and Eric Williams." In *Intellectuals in the Twentieth-Century Caribbean: Volume II, Unity in Variety: The Hispanic and Francophone Caribbean*, edited by Alistair Hennessy, 145–74. London: Macmillan Caribbean, 1992.

Makalani, Minkah. *In the Cause of Freedom: Radical Black Internationalism from Harlem to London, 1917–1939*. Chapel Hill: University of North Carolina Press, 2011.

Malmsten, Neal R. "The British Labour Party and the West Indies, 1918–39." *Journal of Imperial and Commonwealth History* 5, no. 2 (1977): 172–205.

Marable, Manning. *Black Leadership*. Harmondsworth, UK: Penguin, 1999.

Martin, Tony. *Amy Ashwood Garvey*. Dover, UK: Majority, 2007.

Mayall, David. "Rescued from the Shadow of Exile: Nellie Driver, Autobiography and the British Union of Fascists." In *The Politics of Marginality: Race, the Radical Right and Minorities in Twentieth Century Britain*, edited by Tony Kushner and Kenneth Lunn, 19–39. London: Cass, 1990.

McIlroy, John. "Sara, Henry Thomas William (1886–1953)." In *Dictionary of Labour Biography*, vol. 11, edited by Keith Gildart and David Howell, 238–50. Basingstoke, UK: Palgrave Macmillan, 2003.

McKibbin, Ross. *Classes and Cultures: England, 1918–1951*. Oxford: Oxford University Press, 1998.

McLemee, Scott. Afterword to *C. L. R. James and Revolutionary Marxism: Selected Writings of C. L. R. James, 1939–49*, edited by Scott McLemee and Paul Le Blanc, 209–38. New York: Humanity, 2000.

———. Introduction to *C. L. R. James on the "Negro Question,"* edited by Scott McLemee, xi–xxxvii. Jackson: University of Mississippi Press, 1996.

Miliband, Ralph. *Parliamentary Socialism: A Study in the Politics of Labour*. London: Merlin, 1973.

Miller, James A., Susan D. Pennybacker, and Eve Rosenhaft. "Mother Ada Wright and the International Campaign to Free the Scottsboro Boys, 1931–1934." *American Historical Review* 106, no. 2 (April 2001): 387–430.

Molyneux, John. *Leon Trotsky's Theory of Revolution*. Brighton, UK: Harvester, 1981.

Morrell, Robert. *The Gentle Revolutionary: The Life and Work of Frank Ridley, Socialist and Secularist*. London: Freethought History Research Group, 2003.

Naison, Mark. *Communists in Harlem during the Depression*. Urbana: University of Illinois Press, 2005.

Naylor, John F. *Labour's International Policy: The Labour Party in the 1930s*. London: Weidenfeld and Nicolson, 1969.

Neptune, Harvey R. *Caliban and the Yankees: Trinidad and the United States Occupation*. Chapel Hill: University of North Carolina Press, 2007.

Nesbitt, Nick. *Universal Emancipation: The Haitian Revolution and the Radical Enlightenment*. Charlottesville: University of Virginia Press, 2008.

Newman, Michael. "Democracy versus Dictatorship: Labour's Role in the Struggle against British Fascism, 1933–1936." *History Workshop Journal* 5 (1978): 67–88.

Newsinger, John. *The Blood Never Dried: A People's History of the British Empire*. London: Bookmarks, 2006.

———. *Orwell's Politics*. Basingstoke, UK: Macmillan, 1999.

Nielsen, Aldon Lynn. *C. L. R. James: A Critical Introduction*. Jackson: University Press of Mississippi, 1997.

Nimtz, August. "The Eurocentric Marx and Engels and Other Related Myths." In *Marxism, Modernity, and Postcolonial Studies*, edited by Crystal Bartolovich and Neil Lazarus, 65–80. Cambridge: Cambridge University Press, 2002.

Oldfield, J. R. *"Chords of Freedom": Commemoration, Ritual and British Transatlantic Slavery*. Manchester, UK: Manchester University Press, 2007.

Owen, Nicolas. *The British Left and India: Metropolitan Anti-imperialism, 1885–1947.* Oxford: Oxford University Press, 2007.

———. "Critics of Empire in Britain." In *Oxford History of the British Empire, Vol. IV: The Twentieth Century,* edited by Judith M. Brown and W. M. Roger Louis, 188–211. Oxford: Oxford University Press, 1999.

Pennybacker, Susan D. *From Scottsboro to Munich: Race and Political Culture in 1930s Britain.* Oxford: Princeton University Press, 2009.

Phillips, Caryl. "C. L. R. James: Mariner, Renegade and Castaway." In *A New World Order: Selected Essays,* 152–71. London: Secker and Warburg, 2001.

Pimlott, Ben. *Labour and the Left in the 1930s.* Cambridge: Cambridge University Press, 1977.

Polsgrove, Carol. *Ending British Rule in Africa: Writers in a Common Cause.* Manchester, UK: Manchester University Press, 2009.

Porter, Bernard. *The Absent-Minded Imperialists: Empire, Society, and Culture in Britain.* Oxford: Oxford University Press, 2007.

Postgate, John, and Mary Postgate. *A Stomach for Dissent: The Life of Raymond Postgate: Writer, Radical Socialist and Founder of The Good Food Guide.* Staffordshire, UK: Keele University Press, 1994.

Prawer, S. S. *Karl Marx and World Literature.* Oxford: Oxford University Press, 1978.

Quest, Matthew. "George Padmore's and C.L.R. James's *International African Opinion.*" In *George Padmore: Pan-African Revolutionary,* edited by Fitzroy Baptiste and Rupert Lewis, 105–32. Kingston: Ian Randle, 2009.

Ramchand, Kenneth. Introduction to *Minty Alley,* by C. L. R. James, 5–15. London: New Beacon, 1994.

Ramcharitar, Raymond. "The Beacon Short Story and the Colonial Imaginary in Trinidad." In *The Caribbean Short Story: Critical Perspectives,* edited by Lucy Evans, Mark McWatt, and Emma Smith, 59–76. Leeds, UK: Peepal Tree, 2011.

Rediker, Marcus. *The Slave Ship: A Human History.* London: John Murray, 2007.

Rees, John. *The Algebra of Revolution: The Dialectic and the Classical Marxist Tradition.* London: Routledge, 1998.

Renda, Mary A. *Taking Haiti: Military Occupation and the Culture of U.S. Imperialism, 1915–1940.* Chapel Hill: University of North Carolina Press, 2001.

Renton, Dave. *C. L. R. James: Cricket's Philosopher King.* London: Haus, 2007.

Rich, Paul B. *Race and Empire in British Politics.* Cambridge: Cambridge University Press, 1986.

Richardson, Al. Introduction to *World Revolution, 1917–1936: The Rise and Fall of the Communist International,* by C. L. R. James, xi–xxiii. Paperback ed. Atlantic Heights, NJ: Humanities, 1994.

Richardson, David, ed. *Abolition and Its Aftermath: The Historical Context, 1790–1916.* London: Frank Cass, 1985.

Rigney, Ann. *The Rhetoric of Historical Representation.* Cambridge: Cambridge University Press, 1990.

Robinson, Cedric J. "The African Diaspora and the Italo-Ethiopian Crisis." *Race and Class* 27, no. 2 (1995): 51–65.

———. *Black Marxism: The Making of the Black Radical Tradition*. London: Zed, 1991.

Robinson, Kenneth. *The Dilemmas of Trusteeship: Aspects of British Colonial Policy between the Wars*. Oxford: Oxford University Press, 1965.

Rohdie, Samuel. "The Gold Coast Aborigines Abroad." *Journal of African History* 6, no. 3 (1965): 389–411.

Romero, Patricia W. *E. Sylvia Pankhurst: Portrait of a Radical*. New Haven, CT: Yale University Press, 1987.

Rose, Jonathan. *The Intellectual Life of the British Working Classes*. New Haven, CT: Yale University Press, 2001.

Rosengarten, Frank. *Urbane Revolutionary: C. L. R. James and the Struggle for a New Society*. Jackson: University Press of Mississippi, 2008.

Rush, Anne Spry. *Bonds of Empire: West Indians and Britishness from Victoria to Decolonization*. Oxford: Oxford University Press, 2011.

Ryan, Selwyn. *Eric Williams: The Myth and the Man*. Mona, Jamaica: University of the West Indies Press, 2009.

———. *Race and Nationalism in Trinidad and Tobago*. Toronto: University of Toronto Press, 1972.

Samuel, Raphael. "British Marxist Historians, 1880–1980: Part One." *New Left Review* 120 (1980): 21–96.

Sander, Reinhard W. Introduction to *The Beacon, Volumes I–IV, 1931–1939*, edited by Brinsley Samaroo, xv–xxv. New York: Kraus, 1977.

———. *The Trinidad Awakening: West Indian Literature of the Nineteen-Thirties*. London: Greenwood, 1988.

Saunders, Frances Stoner. *Who Paid the Piper? The C.I.A. and the Cultural Cold War*. London: Granta, 1999.

Saville, John. "Barnes, Leonard John (1895–1977)." In *Dictionary of Labour Biography*, vol. 8, edited by Joyce M. Bellamy and John Saville, 4–9. Basingstoke, UK: Macmillan, 1987.

———. "The League against Imperialism, 1927–1937." In *Dictionary of Labour Biography*, vol. 7, edited by Joyce M. Bellamy and John Saville, 40–50. Basingstoke, UK: Macmillan, 1984.

———. "Olivier, Sydney Haldane (1st Baron Olivier of Ramsden) (1859–1943)." In *Dictionary of Labour Biography*, vol. 8, edited by Joyce M. Bellamy and John Saville, 181–87. Basingstoke, UK: Macmillan, 1987.

Sbacelli, Alberto. *Legacy of Bitterness: Ethiopia and Fascist Italy, 1935–1941*. Lawrenceville, NJ: Red Sea, 1997.

Schwarz, Bill. "C.L.R. James's *American Civilization*." In *Beyond Boundaries: C.L.R. James and Postnational Studies*, edited by Christopher Gair, 128–56. London: Pluto, 2006.

———. "Crossing the Seas." In *West Indian Intellectuals in Britain*, edited by Bill Schwarz, 1–30. Manchester, UK: Manchester University Press, 2003.

———. "George Padmore." In *West Indian Intellectuals in Britain*, edited by Bill Schwarz, 132–52. Manchester, UK: Manchester University Press, 2003.

———. "'Shivering in the Noonday Sun.' The British World and the Dynamics of 'Nativization.'" In *Britishness Abroad: Transnational Movements and Imperial Cultures*, edited by Kate Darian-Smith, Patricia Grimshaw, and Stuart Macintyre, 19–44. Melbourne: Melbourne University, 2007.

———, ed. *West Indian Intellectuals in Britain*. Manchester, UK: Manchester University Press, 2003.

Scott, David. *Conscripts of Modernity: The Tragedy of Colonial Enlightenment*. Durham, NC: Duke University Press, 2004.

Sedgwick, Peter. Introduction to *Memoirs of a Revolutionary*, by Victor Serge, xxiii–xxxix. New York: New York Review of Books, 2012.

Sergeev, Yevgeny. "The Communist International and a 'Trotskyite Menace' to the British Communist Movement on the Eve of World War II." In *International Communism and the Communist International*, edited by Tim Rees and Andrew Thorpe, 87–94. Manchester, UK: Manchester University Press, 1998.

Shawki, Ahmed. *Black Liberation and Socialism*. Chicago: Haymarket, 2006.

Sherwood, Marika. "Amy Ashwood Garvey," In Hakim Adi and Marika Sherwood, *Pan-African History: Political Figures from Africa and the Diaspora since 1787*, 69–75. London: Routledge, 2003.

———. "Broadhurst, Robert (1859/60–1948)." In *Oxford Dictionary of National Biography*, vol. 7, edited by H. C. G. Matthew and Brian Harrison, 734–35. Oxford: Oxford University Press, 2004.

———. "Ethiopia and Black Organizations in the UK 1935–36." *Black and Asian Studies Association Newsletter* 43 (September 2005): 18–23.

Sivanandan, A. *A Different Hunger: Writings on Black Resistance*. London: Pluto, 1991.

Small, Richard. "The Training of an Intellectual, the Making of a Marxist." In *C. L. R. James: His Life and Work*, edited by Paul Buhle, 49–60. London: Allison and Busby, 1986.

Smith, Andrew. "'Beyond a Boundary' (of a 'Field of Cultural Production'): Reading C. L. R. James with Bourdieu." *Theory, Culture and Society* 23, no. 4 (2006): 95–112.

———. *C. L. R. James and the Study of Culture*. Basingstoke, UK: Palgrave Macmillan, 2010.

———. "'A Conception of the Beautiful': C. L. R. James' *Glasgow Herald* Cricket Articles, 1937–1938." *International Journal of the History of Sport* 23, no. 1 (2006): 46–66.

Soboul, Albert. *Understanding the French Revolution*. London: Merlin, 1988.

Spitzer, Leo, and LaRay Denzer. "I.T.A. Wallace Johnson and the West African Youth League." *International Journal of African Historical Studies* 6, no. 3 (1973): 413–52.

Springfield, Consuelo López. "Through the People's Eyes: C. L. R. James's Rhetoric of History." *Caribbean Quarterly* 36, nos. 1–2 (1990): 85–97.

Stephens, Michelle Ann. *Black Empire: The Masculine Global Imaginary of Caribbean Intellectuals in the United States, 1914–1962*. Durham, NC: Duke University Press, 2005.

Stevenson, John, and Chris Cook. *Britain in the Depression: Society and Politics, 1929–39*. London: Longman, 1994.

St. Louis, Brett. *Rethinking Race, Politics, and Poetics: C. L. R. James' Critique of Modernity*. London: Routledge, 2007.

Stoddart, Brian, and Keith A. P. Sandiford, eds. *The Imperial Game: Cricket, Culture and Society*. Manchester, UK: Manchester University Press, 1998.

Symonds, Richard. *Oxford and Empire: The Last Lost Cause?* Oxford: Clarendon, 1991.

Taylor, Caldwell. "Patrick Alexander Jones ('Lord Protector'): Cynosure of Early Calypso." August 5, 2012. Accessed June 30, 2013. http://www.spiceislandertalkshop.com/talkshop/messages/834499.html.

Temperley, Howard. "Eric Williams and Abolition: The Birth of a New Orthodoxy." In *British Capitalism and Caribbean Slavery: The Legacy of Eric Williams*, edited by Barbara L. Solow and Stanley L. Engerman, 229–57. Cambridge: Cambridge University Press, 1987.

Thompson, E. P. "C. L. R. James at 80." In *C. L. R. James: His Life and Work*, edited by Paul Buhle, 249. London: Allison and Busby, 1986.

———. *The Making of the English Working Class*. Harmondsworth, UK: Penguin, 1986.

———. *William Morris: Romantic to Revolutionary*. London: Merlin, 1976.

Thornton, A. P. *The Imperial Idea and Its Enemies: A Study in British Power*. London: Macmillan, 1959.

Thorpe, Andrew. *Britain in the 1930s*. Oxford: Blackwell, 1992.

Trilling, Lionel. *Matthew Arnold*. London: Unwin University Books, 1963.

Trouillot, Michel-Rolph. *Silencing the Past: Power and the Production of History*. Boston: Beacon, 1995.

Upham, Martin. "The Marxist Group in the ILP (1933–1936)." 1980. Accessed June 30, 2013. http://www.marxists.org/history/etol/revhist/upham/04upham.html.

Wald, Alan, M. *The New York Intellectuals: The Rise and Decline of the Anti-Stalinist Left from the 1930s to the 1980s*. Chapel Hill: University of North Carolina Press, 1987.

Waley, Daniel. *British Public Opinion and the Abyssinian War, 1935–6*. London: Temple Smith, 1975.

Walmsley, Anna. *The Caribbean Artists Movement, 1966–1972: A Literary and Cultural History*. London: New Beacon, 1992.

Waters, Hazel. *Racism on the Victorian Stage: Representation of Slavery and the Black Character*. Cambridge: Cambridge University Press, 2007.

Weisbord, Robert G. "British West Indian Reaction to the Italian-Ethiopian War: An Episode in Pan-Africanism." *Caribbean Studies* 10, no. 1 (1970): 34–41.

———. *Ebony Kinship: Africa, Africans, and the Afro-American.* London: Greenwood, 1973.

West, Michael O., William G. Martin, and Fanon Che Wilkins, eds. *From Toussaint to Tupac: The Black International since the Age of Revolution.* Chapel Hill: University of North Carolina Press, 2009.

———. "Haiti, I'm Sorry: The Haitian Revolution and the Forging of the Black International." In *From Toussaint to Tupac: The Black International since the Age of Revolution,* edited by Michael O. West, William G. Martin, and Fanon Che Wilkins, 72–104. Chapel Hill: University of North Carolina Press, 2009.

White, Hayden. "Against Historical Realism: A Reading of 'War and Peace.'" *New Left Review* 46 (2007): 89–110.

Whittall, Daniel. "Creating Black Places in Imperial London: The League of Coloured Peoples and Aggrey House, 1931–1943." *London Journal* 36, no. 3 (November 2011): 225–46.

———. "Creolising London: Black West Indian Activism and the Politics of Race and Empire in Britain, 1931–1948." PhD diss., Royal Holloway, University of London, 2012.

Widgery, David. "C.L.R. James." In *Preserving Disorder: Selected Essays 1968–88,* 122–27. London: Pluto, 1989.

Wilder, Gary. *The French Imperial Nation-State: Negritude and Colonial Humanism between the Two World Wars.* Chicago: University of Chicago Press, 2005.

Williams, Jack. *Cricket and Race.* Oxford: Berg, 2001.

Williams, Raymond. *Culture and Society, 1780–1950.* Harmondsworth, UK: Penguin, 1976.

Wilson, Edward T. *Russia and Black Africa before World War II.* New York: Holmes and Meier, 1974.

Worcester, Kent. *C. L. R. James: A Political Biography.* Albany: State University of New York Press, 1996.

Wynter, Sylvia. "In Quest of Matthew Bondman: Some Cultural Notes on the Jamesian Journey." In *C. L. R. James: His Life and Work,* edited by Paul Buhle, 131–45. London: Allison and Busby, 1986.

Yelvington, Kevin A. "The War in Ethiopia and Trinidad, 1935–1936." In *The Colonial Caribbean in Transition: Essays on Postemancipation Social and Cultural History,* edited by Bridget Brereton and Kevin A. Yelvington, 189–225. Kingston, Jamaica: University of West Indies Press, 1999.

Young, James, D. *The World of C. L. R. James: His Unfragmented Vision.* Glasgow: Clydeside, 1999.

INDEX

Aborigines' Rights Protection Society
(ARPS), 90, 93, 237n94
Abyssinia. *See* Ethiopia
Aeschylus, 135
Africa and the World, 6, 111–12, 140,
242n204
Africa House Defence Committee, 88
African art, 71–74
African Sentinel, 111–12, 120, 242n204
Afro-Victorianism, 21, 220n31
Aggrey House, 88, 173, 236n81
America, 8–9, 76, 80, 100, 105, 110, 118,
121, 177, 200, 204; American Civil
War, 58, 185; American Revolu-
tion, 198; race and racism, 21, 24–25,
67–68; scholarship in, 174–75; Trot-
skyist movement in, 75, 198–99, 205,
214. *See also American Civilization*
(James); Association for the Study
of Negro Life and History; National
Association for the Advancement
of Colored People; National Negro
Congress; Scottsboro campaign
American Civilization (James), 126–27
anthropology, 72–74
Aristotle, 173
Arlott, John, 125
Arnold, Matthew, 14, 17–18, 28–29, 34,
38, 206, 214, 222n70, 222nn74–75,

223n101; ideas of, 17, 26–27, 30–31, 33,
35–36, 223n88, 223n96. *See also indi-
vidual works*
Arnold, Thomas, 125, 141
Association for the Study of Negro Life
and History, 200
Attlee, Clement, 122
Austen, Jane, 173
Austin, H. B. G., 132
Azikiwe, Nnamdi, 241n191

Bach, J. S., 44, 82
Bagot, Geoffrey, 82
Baldwin, Stanley, 93
Barnes, Leonard, 105, 201, 239n153
Barnes, Sydney, 50–51, 228n73
Beacon, The, 25–26, 28, 34, 162, 221n62
Beard, J. R., 164, 248n17
Beckles, Hilary, 132–33
Beethoven, Ludwig van, 44, 82
Belloc, Hilaire, 161
Benjamin, Walter, 85–86, 178, 192
Bennett, Arnold, 7, 144
Bergson, Henri, 84–85
Besson, William, 160
Beyond a Boundary (James), 4, 17,
20–21, 30–31, 36, 125–28, 137, 147,
153–54, 215, 234n43, 245n56
Black Jacobins, The (James), 4, 7, 14–15,

General Confederation of Labour
  (CGT), 83
Genovese, Eugene, 196
George, David Lloyd, 144
Germany, 59, 79–80, 82, 103, 107, 174;
  German Revolution, 106–7
Gibbon, Edward, 155, 162–63, 182
Gillies, William, 50, 55–56, 59–62, 79,
  231n120
Gikandi, Simon, 18–19
Glaberman, Martin, 2–3, 199
Glasgow Herald, 6, 127–28, 135, 137–38,
  140, 143, 147, 214
Gold Coast (Ghana), 67, 94, 116,
  242n204. *See also* Aborigines' Rights
  Protection Society
Goldenweiser, Alexander, 73–74
Gollancz, Victor, 112
Gomes, Albert, 28
Grace, W. G., 133, 141, 157
Gramsci, Antonio, 153, 213
Grant, Jack, 132–34, 244n29, 244n32
Great War, 22, 40, 51, 65, 78, 168, 210,
  212; anti-militarism, 58, 229n106;
  colonial troops, 193; cricket and,
  147; propaganda, 176. *See also* British
  West Indies Regiment
Green, John Richard, 160–61, 186
Greenwood, Arthur, 47, 51
Grenada, 56
Grierson, Flora, 196, 202
Guizot, François, 180, 252n104
Gunn, William, 141–42
Guyana, 23

Haitian Revolution, 16, 71, 82, 84, 86,
  106, 115, 118, 121–24, 133, 159–160,
  169–71, 177–79, 190–93, 198, 204, 213,
  249n40; collective memory of, 164;
  historiography, 183–87, 197, 253n116;
  Italo-Ethiopian war, 97–98, 104; racist
  representations of, 165, 183, 253n116.

See also *Black Jacobins, The* (James);
  Christophe, Henri; Dessalines, Jean-
  Jacques; Louverture, Toussaint; *Tous-
  saint Louverture* (James)
Hall, Stuart, 21, 25, 51, 161, 174, 206
Harber, Denzil Dean, 13
Harber, Paul, 13
Harland, Sidney, 26, 164, 221n62
Harlow, Vincent, 174
Harman, Chris, 185
Harris, John, 167
Harrison, William, 242n201, 242n218
Hazlitt, William, 7, 21, 179
Headley, George, 133–34, 148, 156,
  244n37
Hegel, G. W. F., 82
Henderson, Arthur, 47, 53, 55
Henry, Paget, 18–19, 219n9
Henry, Vivian, 61–63, 231n119, 231n125
Hill, Errol, 183
Hill, Jeffrey, 39
Hill, Robert, 6–7, 13–14, 90, 164, 183,
  213–14
History of Negro Revolt, A (James), 7,
  114–20, 178, 192, 213
History of the Russian Revolution, The
  (Trotsky), 47–49, 66, 74, 77, 169–70,
  172, 182–83, 185, 207, 227n56, 252n109
Hitchens, Christopher, 155
Hitler, Adolf, 59, 64–66, 75, 79, 82–83,
  101, 107, 212
Hoare, Samuel, 97
Hobbs, Jack, 141, 147
Hobsbawm, Eric, 63, 196, 254n162
Hochstetter, Franz, 174, 250n64
Hollis, Claud, 29
How Britain Rules Africa (Padmore),
  102–4, 116, 118, 239n148
Howe, Darcus, 40, 49
Hughes, H. Stuart, 48
Hutton, Len, 146
Hyndman, H. M., 247n118

Laski, Harold, 65

Lawrence, D. H., 42–43, 46, 206, 225n32

League against Imperialism (LAI), 88, 102, 111, 236n82

League of Coloured Peoples (LCP), 6, 67–70, 74, 88, 90, 100, 104, 169, 203–4, 245n39. *See also* Aggrey House; Britishness; *Keys, The*; Moody, Harold

League of Nations, 71, 93–94, 99, 107–8, 116, 119, 150, 167, 173, 203

League of Revolutionary Black Workers, 197

Lecky, W. E. H., 167, 249n30

Lefebvre, Georges, 186

Left Book Club, 106, 204

Lenin, Vladimir, 1, 7, 75, 103, 120, 144–45, 172, 193, 206, 208, 210, 213; on Kropotkin, 186, 253n129; on League of Nations, 93; on peasant soviets, 109, 118, 213. *See also* Russian Revolution

Letters from London (James), 15

Lewis, W. Arthur, 205, 257n59

Leys, Norman, 105, 239n153

Liberia, 89, 105

Liddington, Jill, 39–40

Life and Struggles of Negro Toilers, The (Padmore), 79, 110, 114, 231n121

Life of Captain Cipriani, The (James), 6, 30–33, 35, 49–50, 52–53, 56, 61, 67, 218n25, 231n116

Listener, The, 71–72, 167–68

London Federation of Peace Councils, 122

London Group on African Affairs, 203

Louverture, Toussaint, 15–16, 106, 120, 159, 169–72, 183, 187, 192, 194–98, 204, 213, 250n43; biographies of, 164; memory of, 97. *See also* Christophe, Henri; Dessalines, Jean-Jacques; Haitian Revolution

Luddites, 178

Lukács, Georg, 85, 153, 179–80, 247n110

Macaulay, T. B., 162, 182, 188

MacDonald, Ramsay, 46, 48, 53

Macey, David, 3, 217n10

Macintyre, Stuart, 65

Maclean, John, 208

Makonnen, Ras, 96–97, 110–11, 113–14, 120, 257n59

Manchester Guardian, 6, 51, 60, 81, 92, 127–30, 134

Mann, Tom, 63

Mannin, Ethel, 11–12, 111

Manning, Sam, 10–11, 91, 257n59

Marable, Manning, 114, 197

Mariners, Renegades, and Castaways (James), 5, 38, 63

Marryshow, T. A., 56, 91, 229n97, 237n96

Marson, Una, 257n59

Martin, Kingsley, 56, 59, 94

Martindale, Emmanuel, 131–34, 244n29

Marx, Karl, 1, 11, 65, 75, 120, 126, 173, 220n27, 234n38, 252n106; on Thackeray, 220n30; theory of history, 181–82, 185, 188–90, 252n99. *See also* individual works

Marxist Group, 6, 108, 208, 211, 238n137, 258n70. See also *Fight*; Trotskyism

Maverick Club, 24

Maxton, James, 99

McCabe, Stan, 143, 145, 152, 246n78

McDonald, E. A., 155, 247n116

McKibbin, Ross, 137, 154

Mellor, William, 110

Melville, Herman, 38. *See also individual works*

Mendes, Alfred, 25

Menon, Krishna, 110, 241n180

Methodism, 39–40, 224n16

Michelet, Jules, 180–82, 186, 252nn103–6

Mignet, François, 180
Mill, John Stuart, 139
Milliard, Peter, 91, 156
Milton, Nan, 208
Minty Alley (James), 33–34, 36, 212–13, 218n25, 258n60
missionaries, 68, 104–5, 119, 239nn154–55
Moby Dick (Melville), 5, 38
Monolulu, Ras, 96, 237n113
Moody, Harold, 67–69, 88, 203, 230n112, 257n59. *See also* League of Coloured Peoples
Moody, Ronald, 233n122
Moore, George, 90, 93, 237n103
Moscow Trials, 107–8, 212, 240n167
Mosley, Oswald, 83. *See also* British Union of Fascists
Mozart, W. A., 44, 82
Müntzer, Thomas, 172, 250n52
Mussolini, Benito, 30, 83, 236n90, 253n130; Italo-Ethiopian war, 89–90, 94, 97–100, 102, 109, 173, 204, 212, 236n88
My Life (Trotsky), 161–62, 234n43

Naipaul, V. S., 19–21, 34, 215
Napoleon III, 182
National Association for the Advancement of Colored People (NAACP), 67, 102. See also *Crisis, The*
National Council for Civil Liberties, 88
National Council of Labour Colleges, 210
national government, 46–47, 52–53, 93, 202, 205, 228n79
National Negro Congress, 110
Negritude, 86, 235n75
Negro (Cunard), 89, 236n86
Negro Welfare Association (NWA), 88, 102, 236n82
Negro Worker, 30, 55, 74, 79, 121, 209, 222n73, 231n125

Negro World, The, 24, 221n53
Nehru, Jawaharlal, 13, 122, 209
Nelson, xi, 14, 38–43, 47, 49, 57–58, 63, 86, 204–5, 207, 215; "Little Moscow," 44, 52, 63; Nelson Cricket Club, 39–43, 49–51, 225n30, 228n75, 232n129; Nelson Weavers' Association, 40, 44, 226n40; "Red Nelson," 44–46, 51–53, 58, 229n106. See also *Nelson Gazette; Nelson Leader*
Nelson, Lord, 63, 96, 144–45, 232n129
Nelson Gazette, 59
Nelson Leader, 42, 51–52, 57–59, 86, 227n54
Nemours, Auguste, 86, 236n76
Neptune, Harvey, 17, 26
New International, 198, 257n54
New Leader, 97–99, 211, 238n129
New Statesman and Nation, 57, 59, 94, 108, 196, 202, 230n113, 254n159
Nigeria, 111, 117
Noel-Baker, Philip, 112
Northern Rhodesia (Zambia), 117–18
Nurse, Malcolm. *See* Padmore, George

Olivier, Sydney, 35, 54, 60, 223n94, 231n121
Olympic Games, 135, 150
opera, 135
O'Reilly, W. J., 145, 152
Orwell, George, 122, 155, 204, 211, 243n227, 257n51
Oxford University, 71, 84, 146, 164, 167, 173–76, 200, 248n21

Padmore, George: on *The Black Jacobins*, 196–97; on C. L. R. James, 200; Communist activism, 79–81, 83, 87, 101, 204, 206, 209–10, 231n121, 239n143, 239n145; early life in Trinidad, 22, 25; International African Friends of Abyssinia, 90–91,

102; International African Service Bureau, 110–16, 120–22, 140, 208, 238n131, 240nn175–76, 257n59; on Marcus Garvey, 203; on racism, 202. *See also individual works*

Palestine, 199

Pan-African Federation, 110

Pan-Africanism: "class struggle Pan-Africanism," 67, 115, 118, 121; cultural, 102, 119–20; political, 9, 12, 14, 66, 86–90, 95–97, 101–5, 110–14, 123–24, 169, 176, 202–4, 209, 229n97, 240n176, 256n45

Pankhurst, Sylvia, 112, 208

people's history, 161

permanent revolution, theory of, 75–77, 109, 190–91, 194, 234n35. *See also* Trotsky, Leon; uneven and combined development, law of

Philip, M. M., 28–29, 33, 222n70

Phillips, Caryl, 34

Pitt, William, 176, 251n67

Pizer, Dorothy, 209

Plato, 173

Plekhanov, Georgi, 172

Port of Spain Gazette, 15, 23, 38, 45, 130, 168, 225n26

postcolonial studies, 2–4, 217n10, 217n11

Postgate, Raymond, 108, 114, 119. See also *Fact*

Price-Mars, Jean, 185, 253n126

Pritt, D. N., 112

Profintern. *See* Red International of Labour Unions

Proust, Marcel, 169

Queen's Royal College (QRC), 19–22, 36, 160, 162, 173, 219n13

race and racism: anti-racism, 58, 85–88, 91–92, 165–66, 187–88, 253n118; colonial Trinidad, 21–22, 25–26, 28, 31–32, 37, 54, 126, 154, 164–66, 221n62, 248n22, 249n24; "empire-increasing racial hatred," 89, 103, 159, 199, 202; imperial Britain, 38, 41, 68–69, 72, 86, 91–92, 202, 206, 220n34; nationalist historiography, 162, 183–84, 198, 250n66, 253n116. *See also* America; Colour Bar

Ragatz, L. J., 174–75, 188, 250n66, 251n67, 251n70, 253n116

Ramchand, Kenneth, 15, 33

Ramcharitar, Raymond, 26, 34

Ranjitsinhji, K. S., 129, 146, 157

Ransome, Cyril, 160, 248n6

rationalism, 84–85

Rawick, George, 220n24

Raynal, Abbé, 193

Red International of Labour Unions (RILU), 79–80. *See also* Communist (Third) International

Revolution Betrayed, The (Trotsky), 108, 212

Reynolds, Reginald, 11–13, 15, 79, 91–92, 111

Rhodes, Cecil, 48, 178

Ridley, F. A., 111–12, 241n196

Rivet, Paul, 72, 233n20

Robeson, Paul, 6, 12, 123, 159–60, 196

Robinson, Cedric, 46, 52, 207

Robinson, E. E., 224n16, 225n22, 226n40, 226n45, 229n106, 230n112

Romanticism, 142, 162, 179–83

Rosengarten, Frank, 20–21, 183

Rothermere, Lord, 83

Rousseau, Jean-Jacques, 173

Roux, Jacques, 191

Rush, Anne Spry, 17–18, 68

Russian Revolution, 65, 74–76, 172, 178, 190, 193, 206, 208, 210, 212, 257n54; impact in Trinidad, 23; Russian Civil War, 58. See also *History of the Russian Revolution, The* (Trotsky); Lenin,